DREAMS NEVER DIE

*Surviving Road Rash*
*& Living To Tell About It*

# RIDING THE
# AMERICAN
# DREAM

## The Official Story of
## Excelsior-Henderson Motorcycles
### DAN HANLON

Union Hill Press

RIDING THE AMERICAN DREAM
*www.RidingTheAmericanDream.com*

Copyright © 2003 Daniel L. Hanlon

All Rights Reserved

Published By:

*www.UnionHillPress.com*

Manufactured in the United States of America

Limited First Edition
First Printing

07  06  05  04  03    5  4  3  2  1


ISBN: 0-9742302-6-X

LCCN: 2003093910

*Dedicated to those who dream . . .*
*and pursue them.*

AUTHOR'S NOTE

The most challenging part of writing this book was doing so in the first person. There is an old saying, "There is no 'I' in team," and I believe this. I desire to only play on teams. However, even on a team, we are all individuals—independent, yet interdependent. Therefore, this story is of *my* experiences as a member of *our* team, as we bravely ventured onto the business battlefield.

CONTENTS

# INTRODUCTION

This book is written for those who believe in the American Dream. Whether you have lived it, witnessed it, or desire to live it. It is also a story of Excelsior-Henderson Motorcycles, which for me, was a chance to experience the American Dream. And I still do. The real story of Excelsior-Henderson Motorcycles is not just a motorcycle story, but much more. It is the true, modern-day story of heroes. Not the glamour seeking type, but the grassroots, hardworking, team building type of heroes. The kind you never hear about. Well, this is a story about them, and for them.

By the reckoning of some, since the business entity of Excelsior-Henderson has ceased, they would critically acclaim the business didn't succeed. But did it? The telling of the Excelsior-Henderson story would not be complete if it were merely about an entrepreneurial start-up company raising capital and executing on business plans. This would be an injustice to the hard-working people who were taking on the industry giants. For those who were involved in this great struggle, we will never forget, and we have forever left our mark in history— there are those who will carry this torch for generations to come. This is the story of the life learning episodes of ordinary people who united together, separate and independent, yet equal. I relate this story in the hope that it will help you live your American Dream, as it has me.

Recently, I had someone say to me that what saddened him the most was it meant the dream was over. That perplexed me, and so I related to him my philosophy, that no matter what happened, we can still dream, and the dream is not over.

*Dreams never die.*

# PART ONE

PREPARE TO GET OFF

# 1

## *Running Out Of Gas*

The morning of December 21, 1999. A typical cold blustery Minnesota winter morning, after another night's restless sleep. You would think I'd be used to it by now. I was up, showered, and out of the house before my children were even up. Yet another day of not seeing them. I fired up my Chevrolet Tahoe, warmed it up, and shifted it into four-wheel drive for the long, cold, and solemn drive from the city to the countryside, where we had built our new motorcycle factory. Usually I enjoyed the drive, but today was different. For a moment, it felt as if I was driving to my own funeral. Today was going to be a tough day, as though yesterday wasn't. We had just laid off almost the entire Road Crew Team at Excelsior-Henderson Motorcycles—right before the holidays. That didn't feel good. Last evening, I had signed the documents for the Court Petition, and in a few short hours these documents would be filed with the U.S. Bankruptcy Court to officially put the company into Chapter 11 Reorganization. A company I had started, and now had to lay to rest, hopefully only temporarily.

Over the past seven years of my life I had launched and led a new independent American motorcycle manufacturing company—the only one in over 75 years. With more than 225 employees (the Road Crew) and revenue of over $30 million, we had raised nearly $100 million on our way toward building the company. That seemed like a lot of money, but it was never projected to be enough, and it wasn't. We had started the race knowing we didn't have enough fuel to win, but we'd hoped to find a way to add enough fuel to get to the finish line. We almost made it, too—we ran a darn good race while we had the fuel. But the forces of the market weren't with us.

We had developed the business further than what the critics and our competitors had ever thought we would, and as an independent start-up proprietary original equipment motorcycle manufacturer (OEM), we had progressed farther than anyone else in over a half-century. But obviously, it wasn't far enough.

Just a year earlier my net worth in company stock was nearly $20 million. In a few short moments, since my net-worth was harnessed to the company, I would witness it dissolve, and the company and I would become a poster child for a few hypercritical writers. As if we were the only start-up manufacturing company that wasn't able to raise enough money to fund our business plan. I wondered, what ever happened to that inexhaustible American spirit that persevered even if the likelihood of success is negligible? Well, that spirit was still alive and well in the people who had strived to undertake great odds in building the company of Excelsior-Henderson, but I knew that message may never be heard.

No wonder so many people are afraid of failure. As though it is permanent. Early stage, product development driven companies are a real challenge to launch, and most don't make it for varying reasons, and yet they are the backbone of this great mighty nation. The company had just plain run out of fuel. Just like internal combustion engines, whether two-, four-, six-, or eight-cylinder, turbo-charged or not, or even a rocket ship, without fuel they are all the same. Stopped. Put in the fuel, and then hold on because it's going to go as fast as you are capable of driving—until the fuel runs out. That is what it is like in an early stage company; only cash is the fuel. Without it, you go nowhere, and with it, the race is on. As I pulled into the nearly empty factory parking lot, I was glad my children were not old enough to read the newspaper.

As I was stepping into my office I greeted Kathy, the company administrative assistant. We were all trying our best to smile, and it was easy to smile back and say, "good morning." Maybe, just maybe, it would be.

The message light on my telephone was flashing, so I immediately checked it. It was our lawyer, or one of several of them, informing me that our company was considered a high-profile case by the U.S. Bankruptcy District Court and we were being utilized as a test case on the Internet, making it easier for people to follow the case. Great. Just great (read as: not great). I managed a wry smile—yes—the price of a high-profile company in trouble. And now anyone, at anytime, around the world, could watch. And as I found out later, they would watch, tracking us faster than our own corporate bankruptcy lawyer could.

The price of leadership. Leadership: a simple word, yet difficult and complex to implement. I looked out my window, past the flags flying gently in the breeze near the large, bold Excelsior-Henderson sign that was solidly embedded in concrete outside the headquarters' entrance, gazing off into the distance, toward the town of Belle Plaine and the steeples of its local churches. Belle Plaine, Minnesota—my hometown. My brothers and sisters, my parents, grandparents, great and great-great grandparents had tilled the soil here since the mid 1800s. This was our birthplace. A lot had happened here over the years.

*Yes, I was going to make it be another good morning.*

# 2

## Creating A Road Map

Seven years earlier, on December 25th, 1992, the family was all gathered for Christmas dinner at the Hanlon Farm six miles south of Belle Plaine, in Derrynane Township. My dad and mom, Jerry and Mary, and the five Hanlon brothers, three sisters, and spouses and grandchildren were all there. That must be why old farmhouses are so big, so they can hold large families and multiple generations at the holiday gatherings. After dinner, it didn't take too long for the conversation to drift around to the events of our lives, including family, careers, and hobbies.

It was another tough business year for my wife Carol and I, and now for our first newborn child, Hannah, who was fortunately too young to know the battles we faced. I had launched a start-up manufacturing company in 1989, which, like most start-up companies manufacturing a newly developed proprietary product, was short on fuel, but long on opportunity. We were in production, nearing cash flow positive and gaining market share, but nevertheless, the tank of fuel had been only half full when we started, and it was now getting real low. We had just entered into an agreement to sell the company, and already my mind was turning to new opportunities.

As always with the brothers, we drifted off to our own section of the farmhouse and began our normal jostling of one another. As a reward for recently selling my company, I had just placed an order for a new Harley. Yes, back then you had to put in an order, or call all over the country to find one, and then practically pay whatever it was the dealer said you had to. At the time, Harley buyers always had to pay over manufacturer's suggested retail price (MSRP). Imagine that—having to put in an order and wait, and then pay over MSRP to buy a product! Unless you're in the market to buy an American heavyweight cruiser motorcycle, you might not know that there is only one independent manufacturer here in America. There is no one else. (This certainly peaked my interest in a potential business opportunity—where was the competition? Find a problem, and then go solve it.)

But my brother Tom had the best story. He was about to buy an Indian. There was a lot of laughter and raised eyebrows over that one, because there was no such thing as a modern day Indian motorcycle. But he assured us skeptical brothers that yes indeed, in Albuquerque, New Mexico, there was a new Indian motorcycle company claiming they would be producing new Indian motorcycles within a year, and he was going to put money down on one to reserve it.

He claimed to even have the paperwork to prove it. This kindled my interest, and sensing a chance to help a brother, and learn a little bit more about what was going on in the motorcycle industry, I asked him to hold off on putting money down and letting me check them out a little. After all, I was thirty-six years old with a lot of energy, and with my company now sold I was searching for a new business opportunity to launch.

I quickly found out that it wasn't going to be a difficult matter to do the initial research on the Indian motorcycle project. Because the motorcycle industry press had not chronicled a new OEM start-up since early in the 20th century, there were dozens of articles all over the trade press about the resurgence of the Indian name, and of several false starts throughout the years. The press was excited, and most articles were generally favorable about the project, but more importantly, it appeared they believed there was a market opportunity for another American brand.

However, based upon my experience developing products for significant ventures, it appeared that the timelines and investments being quoted in the magazines by the current management of Indian were fairly unrealistic, and not being challenged by the media at that time, so I proceeded to investigate the Indian company for myself.

My research yielded a different picture of the Indian motorcycle company than what the articles, and the Indian company itself, were projecting, yet the fact still remained there appeared to be a viable market for an alternate American motorcycle brand. That was the interesting part that continued to stir up my inquisitiveness.

It began to appear that the motorcycle market *would* have interest in another traditional American brand alongside Harley-Davidson. I redirected my focus from trying to determine if the Indian project was on track and instead shifted it to researching whether there was indeed an economically feasible business plan that would support a new proprietary motorcycle entrant.

During one of its biggest marketing and sales pushes, Indian was promoting the official unveiling of its new Indian motorcycle at the Sturgis,

South Dakota motorcycle rally coming up in August 1993. If you don't know what the Sturgis Motorcycle Rally is, you will need to experience it. Everyone who goes there for the first time leaves with an impression that will last a lifetime. It is a life-altering experience—for some.

The annual motorcycle event, which started out small and local, has taken place since 1938, three years before the United States' entry into World War II. Today, it is like motorcycle heaven, where well over a quarter million motorcyclists make the annual sojourn and converge on a small town in western South Dakota for a week of—well, just getting away and doing their own thing.

It's hard to explain, and needs to be experienced. There is an old, but true saying in the motorcycle industry, "*If I have to explain, you wouldn't understand.*" You can even buy T-shirts with that slogan. Bikers from all walks of life and from all corners of the world come to Sturgis. I began early to make my plans. This would be a good opportunity to not only learn firsthand about the Indian company, but also to review the progress of their prototype, meet their management staff, and do some field research on market acceptance of another brand in order to validate my own business plan.

I conferred with my brother Tom, who indicated that he'd decided to hold-off on putting money down on an Indian and would wait and see what happened with the company. But he was ready for a motorcycle road trip with some of the brothers.

As the end of July approached we began to make plans to ride together to the Sturgis Rally. This would be the first time that four of the five Hanlon brothers would ride there together. We were pretty excited about it. We all had our own different careers and interests, but our farm upbringing instilled in us the love of adventure—your face in the wind, and the feeling of freedom and independence once you swung your leg over the seat of your bike and fired it up. As a boy growing up on the farm, I always enjoyed the harvest time—driving field equipment with the wind in my face and the abundant smells and sounds all around, especially on an autumn moonlit night—motorcycling would bring back these sensory memories. It's hard to explain.

By that time period, I'd earnestly been working on the business plan and had completed several drafts. In the early learning phase, it seemed as if every day I would discover a new roadblock, and believe I would need to abandon the plan. But, somehow through further research and analysis, and creative thinking, a solution to the problem would develop. It was time to head to the Sturgis Rally for some field research and confirmation of some of the business plan assumptions.

We made our riding plans, and the day finally arrived. Brothers Terry, Tom, and myself would leave Minneapolis and meet up with Dave and his wife in southern Minnesota, and then we would all ride together to Sturgis. It was a great ride. It always is. Riding across South Dakota on a motorcycle you can just feel the openness, along with the dry heat. It's always windy and hot on that ride. When we finally pulled into Sturgis it was a welcome relief, and we were all grins through sun-cracked lips with wind-burned faces. We looked so bad we looked good. We made our way to Deadwood to stay at the First Gold Hotel. With rooms at a premium, we shacked up with a few friends, and got a reminder of what it was like to have too many people in one room, and all there to have fun. Motorcycle style.

Indian was the buzz of the Rally. But maybe not the buzz they were looking for. The Sturgis crowd can be real tough. Yes, everyone might look rough and tough, but most of that is a reflection of riding hard with your face in the wind, for days on end, along with limited rest, and a few drinks. The tough I am talking about is the tough-minded part. This is where you separate the men-from-the-boys, so to speak. Where you either walk the talk, or you don't. So many people say one thing, and do another, and act as though no one notices.

With a true American motorcyclist, especially at an American rally, one had better be prepared to walk the talk. Well, Indian wasn't, and Wayne Baughman, the Chief Executive Officer (CEO), was on a heightened defensive alert. The prototype motorcycle he showed, claiming it would run, was simply not so. No one could get close to it, unless of course you jumped over the fence surrounding it. Word got out that the engine was made of wood, and that it was a wooden Indian. The company denied it, but there was no denying it. The riders couldn't and wouldn't be fooled.

So I had to jump the fence. Yes, it was a wooden engine. But it was the best woodcarving I've ever seen. It did almost look real. I had to take pictures.

One interesting observation though was the passion it created. The riders weren't critical because another brand was attempting to be resurrected to compete against the almighty Harley, but in my opinion, they were critical because of the false attempt. In my experience in business, usually the customer of a current brand is somewhat critical of a new brand, as it justifies the purchase and loyalty to their brand.

What I witnessed here though was that even though the majority of motorcyclists were riding Harleys, and Sturgis is an *American* motorcycle rally, the riders were not critical of the resurrected brand. Only the perception of being misled about the company and the product. A good business lesson here. Not surprising. No one likes to be misled; yet it happens all the time in marketing. Say one thing, do another. Who will notice? The customer.

When I got back to Minneapolis I was excited. I knew there was a better way to launch a new motorcycle business—a much better way. I had never observed a market opportunity like this before. There was a large and growing market segment of motorcycle riders preferring an authentic American brand, and only one brand in the marketplace: Harley-Davidson, which had a two-year waiting list, with bikes selling for over MSRP, and hitting record stock highs.

I didn't need to be too bright of a financial or marketing analyst, or gearhead, to recognize the opportunity here. But the barriers to entry were significant. Who had ever successfully accomplished this in our lifetime? Nobody.

All of my life I had been preparing to launch a motorcycle or automobile company, and now in my heart I felt it was time. The planets were starting to line up. Call it entrepreneur's intuition, or "instinct." I already had one patent and a manufacturing start-up under my belt, and had worked with several other early-stage ventures. I began to "feel" like the market timing was good for a new entrant to an old established, capital intensive industry.

• • •

I grew up on a dairy farm in Derrynane Township in Le Sueur County, which is located just outside the small town of Belle Plaine, Minnesota. I was the fourth child in the family, and grew up with four brothers and three sisters. There was a set of twin brothers just eleven months younger than me, so we were somewhat like the three musketeers growing up.

The farm had been in the Hanlon family line of descendants since the Civil War, when it was deeded over by-then President Lincoln. My parents still have the original deed signed by him.

We grew up fully understanding heritage and roots—we were living it. The original house that was built on the farm in the 1870s was still there, but it had been converted into use as a granary for storing soybeans from the annual autumn harvest.

The original windmill still stands over the water well, along with one severely bent leg support. In the early 1900s a team of workhorses were tethered to the windmill, and when they somehow got spooked, they nearly pulled the windmill down before the leather harnesses gave way.

In the early 1960s, as a young boy of about six years old, I remember my grandfather taking my hand and walking me around the farm and explaining the history of the buildings. Only years later after he had passed away, did I learn that I was named after his father, Dan Hanlon, who was killed on the farm in the 1880s when a bolt of lightening hit him, leaving his youngest of five—my grandfather—at eight months old to be eventually raised as an orphan.

Derrynane Township is an Irish Township, and most of our immediate neighbors had names that reflected the original settlers: Callahan, Mahoney, Fogarty, Moriarty, Sullivan, McCue, O'Brien, and Murphy. This wasn't unique, as within just a few miles in all directions, there were also original settlements of Polish, German, and Czechoslovakian immigrants. My generation was the first of the "mixed nationalities," with my father being all Irish, and my mother all Czechoslovakian. My mother spoke fluent Czech and English—obviously I only heard her speak Czech when she was saying something she didn't want us kids to understand.

It was a great way to start out life. We pumped all our water from the windmill and stored it in a tank for when the wind ceased. That got a little challenging sometimes.

The rules and people were fairly straightforward. Work hard, and have some fun. Honor your family and your word. Everybody knew you, and you knew everybody.

All of our neighbors had also been on their land for generations. Anyone who hadn't been there for over thirty years was still considered new to the area.

Well, that's how I thought life was, and how I thought it would continue. But when I grew up and left the farm, I found my new world was quite different, and by the perceptions of some, I was different. Certain things get rooted in a person.

During my senior year in high school in Belle Plaine, I attended a regional vocational school and received a certificate as an automobile mechanic. This worked out great because it gave me a chance to get my own car.

My dad had given me a "new" car, a jet-black 1961 Chevrolet Impala that had a blown-up engine, thanks to one of my siblings. Never mind that the former family car was already thirteen years old. It was now a cool, but non-operating car. My dad said if I would rebuild the engine, I could have the car. So I set about learning how to rebuild my first of many engines. I remember my dad and brothers letting me skip milking the cows the first night I put the rebuilt engine back in the '61 Chevy and was ready to "fire-it-up."

In order to put myself through a private college, I worked as a mechanic, and painted motorized vehicles, as a side business. Two of my younger brothers, Tom and Bob, helped me convert our old chicken coop into a workshop. We blew out an end wall and installed large doors, insulated it, installed a paint booth with huge fans, welders, and a furnace for the cold winters. It was a great shop. My sister Eileen painted a sign for the front that said "Cruis-In Auto Roost." We were in business.

We restored and painted some cool stuff in there. Cars, motorcycles, boats, tractors, trucks and vans—you name it. It was the time period of flame paintjobs and metalflake paint. I even painted a car metalflake-flame paint. But then we all grew up and left.

In college I was a bit of a rebel, and on the last day of school, my Irish buddy from Saint Paul, Kevin Reilly (also a rebel) and I drove his maroon-colored Pontiac Firebird to the Highland Bridge that crosses the Mississippi River between the cities of Minneapolis and Saint Paul. We threw our books over the bridge and into the river, figuring we wouldn't get much for them anyway.

Accounting came easy to me since it was fairly logical, so I earned a B.A. degree in accounting from Saint Thomas University in Saint Paul. I didn't even yet know an accountant, but now degree-wise, I was one. I would have preferred to study something in the engineering area due to my mechanical aptitude and interest, but at the time there were no engineering-related courses available. I also never knew any engineers then either—I thought they worked on trains.

College was somewhat peculiar for me. I wasn't so sure I wanted to be there. My parents dropped me off with my new set of luggage from

Pedros in Saint Paul, and a new plaid suit on my back from Foreman & Clarke. At the time it was an all-male, private Catholic college. Which I had to pay for. Fortunately for me, my parents had enrolled me; otherwise I probably never would have. After my enrollment, while still at the farm, I was perusing some literature about the school that said *"Four Years Of Hard Work"* in bold letters. Privately I thought, *If I wanted hard work, I should just stay on the farm.*

Previously I'd heard about all the fun that college would be, but for me it was simply hard work. Being a bit of a gearhead, and actually enjoying the freedom of farm life, I had made a private pact to myself. I would give college a go if I didn't have to study on weekends.

I accomplished this by making sure I went to every class—and not skipping any—hoping to pick up what the instructor thought was important, then working at my job in the afternoons, and finally going to study at the library in the evening. I must have been a little bit of a workaholic, or possibly simply financially broke, because I didn't think about partying. Until the weekend, that is. Then it was time to look at college in the rearview mirror, engaging in my hobbies of restoring cars and motorcycles, working on the farm, and going to some local parties. I guess to some degree, I'm a gas and oil guy. Not too exciting, but it worked for me.

My wife, Carol, says I never learned how to play. She might be right. I always thought city kids played, and the only reason they did was because they were bored and didn't have any work to do. Maybe I was wrong there too.

The college summers were the time to make big money. I worked for the Green Giant Canning Company as a mechanic in the field, fixing combines and related field equipment. Back then, they allowed you to work as many hours as you could humanly stand, and oftentimes I worked 30 to 40 hours straight, which resulted in 100-plus hour weeks. It reminded me of dairy farming, only now I was getting paid time and a half, or double time. There was also the added benefit of not having time to spend the income, until college started in the fall.

In addition to my school loans, the first loan I took out was for $350 from the State Bank of Belle Plaine to buy a new suit for interviews, so I could replace my old plaid suit. This also gave me enough money for some pocket change for food and gas while I looked for a job in my new career field. Plus I wanted to buy a new Holley four-barrel carburetor for one of my cars, but I didn't mention that to Bob Zvanovec, the banker.

My life game plan then was to get a background in mechanical and manufacturing combined with finance and marketing, which I hoped would someday help me when I was ready to launch a manufacturing company. I didn't know what the word entrepreneur meant when I graduated in 1978, and maybe the word wasn't even yet coined. But I did know that I wanted to work for myself someday, and that I needed more skillful tools in my toolbox.

Similar to my dad, I was, and still am an avid reader. As a small child on the farm, after evening chores, I remember my mother lining up the kids in the kitchen and having us read, out loud, all at the same time. I guess you needed to do that after having eight kids, plus it helped us learn to focus and concentrate in spite of distractions.

Even though I liked the farm life, reading books took my mind to places and things that I had never heard of before. For some reason, I really liked mechanical things, and read book after book about products and the people who built them. I admired those who faced great odds and overcame them. I read about people like George Washington, Abe Lincoln, the Wright Brothers, Henry Ford and Charles Lindbergh. All of them born with next to nothing but who nonetheless created a lot. It certainly was inspiring, and seemed far-fetched.

After college, I was employed in two Fortune 500 companies headquartered in Minnesota. This was a bit of a cultural shock for me, and I observed and learned a lot of things. Some good and some not so good.

During this time companies promoted training and development of employees, and I participated in everything I could. I remember replacing one accountant who was overworked, and I was able to get the job done in half the time, which allowed me a lot of time to volunteer for other company special projects. It was very good learning, at least from a business perspective.

While at Honeywell, I worked for a while in the design engineering area for Military Aviation, and Commercial Aviation, and I gained a great appreciation for long and complicated product development cycles. I also became experienced with writing business plans and computer models. At the same time, I attended night school to get my MBA, also from Saint Thomas University. Even though I was labeled a finance guy by my undergraduate studies, during my MBA studies, I took all the marketing and international courses the school offered. I was on a mission.

Another thing I learned from these large corporations was corporate politics. I found out I didn't like it, and wouldn't be a party to it. I worked at the home office of two Fortune 500 companies where all the various leaders of the disciplines of engineering, manufacturing, marketing, sales, finance, administration, human resources, etc., had to work together. Even though we all worked together and had the semblance of a team, oftentimes there was a different current just below the surface—an undercurrent. I came to learn a new word and concept—corporate politics. I vowed that someday I would have my own company and treat people with real respect and honor. This was also where I first learned about lip service. Say one thing, and do another. And do it without remorse. No conscience. I witnessed it, and had it happen to me. But I still don't believe in it.

Early in the 1980s after just starting with Honeywell, I had a boss named Dave. He was a great guy, and would always challenge me to work harder on my leadership, as *he was smoking and swearing in his office!* I wasn't so sure he was exhibiting good leadership, but I knew enough to keep my opinions to myself. I actually liked him.

I liked to keep my boss apprised of what was going on in the engineering area I handled, and as time went on, I kept filling him in on some things I believed he should carry forward to upper management. Weeks later, however, we were both in a meeting with upper management, who had just learned of a surprise problem, and things were hot. All fingers were pointing at me for not identifying the problem earlier. I looked at my boss Dave, and he denied ever knowing. I persisted once more, and with a look at me that I will never forget, he sternly denied it again. I was dumbfounded.

When we left the meeting, again I naively asked my boss why he couldn't remember. He told me to leave it alone. But I couldn't. I pride myself on being honest and accepting responsibility, and I needed answers so I could learn. After showing him my notes from our much earlier meeting, he blurted out, "Well, I knew that, but between your ass and my ass, whose ass do you think I'm going to save?" I guess that was where it all hit home for me on some of the things I had been witnessing in some corporate leadership. It wasn't about truth, or honesty, or responsibility—although the words were there. The actions were about covering one's behind if there were problems, or if seeking to get ahead. That is where I rooted the motto I believe in today, *"Walk the Talk."* Be real careful about believing one's words until you can see if their actions follow through.

This new stuff I was observing, in particular the lack of honesty, respect and integrity, was very different than what I had grown up with and believed in, and I wasn't so sure I liked it. Sure, they were all smart enough to use these words in their conversations, but the actions weren't consistent with the words. I had to think about this for awhile.

That day I told myself that I would leave Honeywell on the anniversary of my fifth year. I was convinced I would become a product of the environment if I stayed too long, but I needed to stay long enough to not be a job hopper. Back then it was not good to be a job hopper.

So I had to learn to "play the game" until I got out. But I played it my way, under my life rules. It must have worked reasonably okay since I averaged a promotion every year. Or maybe they were just trying to move me to new divisions to get rid of me. In retrospect, I learned a lot and it was a good, rewarding, productive experience. I left on November 1, 1984, five years to the day after I had started.

At the time, I was quite naïve to the ways of some of the interactions between some business executives. Even today, although I am no longer naïve to it, privately I am not tolerant of it. I thought I would make a great employee: ethical, hard working, high expectations of myself and others, and using a forthright straight-shooting style. The only game I like to play is for the team to win, with integrity and honesty—that way even if the team doesn't win, you can still hold your head up with pride since you handled the situation with dignity. A word and concept that has gone out of style.

It was hard to maintain a positive attitude during my years at the corporate home office of publicly held companies, and in a cultural environment that I personally didn't completely believe in. As a self-imposed diversion I immersed myself in going to night school and reading books.

Among the many books I read during this time period, there were four that changed my life and my outlook forever. The first one was *Think and Grow Rich*, by Napoleon Hill; the second was *Success Through A Positive Mental Attitude*, by Napoleon Hill and W. Clement Stone; the third was *You Can Negotiate Everything*, by Herb Cohen; and the fourth was *How To Win Friends And Influence People*, by Dale Carnegie. By happenstance, I read these books in succession, and even though the first two books were over twenty years old and the fourth book was originally published in the 1930s, for some reason they influenced me. I really don't know why. I still keep extra copies of these on my bookshelf and offer them for others to read.

During the mid 1980s personal computers were just on the horizon, and they brought the creation of business plans and forecasting models into a forever changed world. What formerly took me all night to recalculate could now be done in minutes, once the computer model was built.

In one of our departments at Honeywell, the first personal computer we had was a RadioShack TRS 80, loaded with VisiCalc. The first month the machine just sat there on an empty desk, and did nothing. By the second month, we all wanted one on our desks.

Today, computers do everything for us, even replacing human interaction—when they are working. Talk about reliability and compatibility, or sometimes lack thereof. Years later I would remind our Road Crew Team Members at Excelsior-Henderson; human beings design and manufacture computers, not the other way around. Computers are to be a tool that we as humans can use or not use.

Okay, now you know a little about me. You might have guessed I have an attitude. That I am educated. That I have worked for large public and small private companies. And that I am a gearhead. It was within this framework that I created the business plan and officially launched Hanlon Manufacturing, which later became Excelsior-Henderson Motorcycles.

*This was going to be a ride.*

# 3

## Building And Paving The Roads

Business plans to an early stage company are like the architect's drawings for a building. You need to have them in order to know what you are going to build. Also, it is a good way to educate others on what you are building. We've all heard the clichés about failing to plan is planning to fail. Well, maybe it doesn't always happen, but if your entire life is on the line, and if you plan on possibly taking a few with you, like employees, family, friends, shareholders, etc., then you might want a plan. A good one. One that will hold up under intense scrutiny.

The term business plan is a slight misnomer to my concept of a business plan for an early stage company. It really is also a strategic plan. While I worked at the larger Fortune 500 companies, at the home office we had separate business plans and strategic plans, since they do serve slightly different functions in a large mature organization. However, a start-up isn't quite there yet, and no need to overly complicate the process. My business plans also included the strategy, which to me with an early stage company is truly the first and most important step.

The strategy is what gets inside your head, and is more closely related to the mission, principles, and lifetime goals of the company—almost like what I would consider the soul of a company. The word strategy is derived from the Greek language, and means "office of the general." After the strategy is determined, I view the business plan as the implementation plan of the strategy. Not everyone in business may agree with me on my philosophy of this, but it is how I look at the planning phases of an early stage company. With this mindset I developed the Business Plan for Hanlon Manufacturing Company, which years later was renamed the Excelsior-Henderson Motorcycle Manufacturing Company.

The business plan is one of the most critical elements to an early stage company. It is like your road map. It may not be perfect, as it is extremely difficult to forecast the future, especially with a new company, product, people, and layering in the financing at the appropriate times. But nevertheless, it is a vital document.

Not only does the outside world that you will bring into the venture need to review the plan to understand it and accordingly offer help, but you also need to have a clear picture of your plan, and have given thought to all the variables and addressed them. This will make or break the business.

Today I often get asked, "How did you raise over $95 million?" All of it in negative cash flow. And not an Internet story. Nor a high technology or medical story either! We raised an average of over a million dollars a month, for seven years, and all in negative cash flow, and for a new manufacturing company in America entering a one-hundred-year-old industry.

Well, it wasn't easy. But we had a good plan, hired great people, and the plan had clearly laid out milestones. And we hit them. Building credibility. That is part of the magic and the secret of our plan. Take the time to do the homework and carefully lay out the plan, and then execute like crazy.

If you haven't figured it out by now, I like mottoes. They help me keep it simple, are easy to memorize, and give me something to focus on when the pressure is on. For me, the most important ways to execute the business plan are encapsulated in the following three simple statements:

1) Do What You Said You Would Do,

2) When You Said You Would Do It, and

3) For How Much You Said It Would Cost

People who know me well in business have heard this so often they must feel it's stamped on my forehead. This is what achieving milestones is all about.

These three simple statements were the foundation to the magic in executing the Excelsior-Henderson plan, to my personal beliefs, and to the corporate culture of Excelsior. Think about these statements real hard. The execution, or lack thereof, of these three statements led to our success, and periodically to our lack of it.

For any of our successes, it was due to our completing all three of those statements, and when we didn't, we didn't meet with success. Oftentimes, the accomplishment of an organization's goals depends on many individuals or companies agreeing to the goals, and if they miss, it can create a domino effect.

The next secret to our plan was to "always work with the A-Team." No matter how good a plan is, without the proper skilled team on the field, there is no successful execution. I always believed since we were the new players in the equation executing our plan, we needed to work with experienced pros in the execution of it. *"If you did it before, you can do it again."* This held true to our Road Crew Team Members, and to the organizations we recruited to work with us.

A well-constructed business plan has all the facets to the business covered and should leave no stone untouched or unchallenged.

• • •

During 1993 I worked on the Hanlon Manufacturing business plan almost exclusively for the entire year. While I was working on developing the plan, I believed I needed to operate quietly so as not to trigger any person or company that could thwart the plans while they were so young and fragile. Yet at the same time I needed access to people and companies to learn more about the industry and what opportunity there might be. Besides that, some people I did confide in seemed to think I was crazy and seemed bent on derailing my plans. Negative thinking that I had to stay away from, so I had to pick my resources carefully. I was on a mission.

Early in 1993 I set up the business entity as Hanlon Manufacturing, a sole proprietorship, and when I handed out my business card, invariably the question came up, "What do you manufacture?" and I would have to say, "Nothing for now, but looking…" I'm sure some people were scratching their heads about this, but I knew what the game plan was, and part of it was that "loose lips sink ships." Those that I wanted to know, knew very well.

When you start a company, there is no such thing as an incoming phone call. All calls are outgoing—and if you don't reach the intended party and have to leave a message, don't expect it to be returned. Why would someone return the call from a company they never heard of that didn't have any business yet?

I had set up an office in a spare bedroom in the lower level of our house and put up a small barricade to minimize the diversions created by one-year-old daughter Hannah. That doesn't sound too nice, but it seemed right at the time.

It's great working at a home office, at least in the formative stages of a company, and from a time convenience perspective. I would get up at 6, be in the office by 6:30, work for 12 hours or more, and still have time to spend with the family, then go back to work after they had gone to bed. Years later, I would learn the hard way that this type of work schedule outside the home did not permit a family life, nor any other kind of life for that matter, but at the time, it was working just great.

This was even before the Internet was developed to its current status, so research had to be conducted the old fashioned way of reading, calling, faxing and mailing, and visiting businesses—but the plus side was that it led to a lot of human interaction and the early building of relationships that would last for years to come.

• • •

It didn't take very long to figure out that developing a proprietary motorcycle company was going to be difficult. When was the last time it had been successfully done? Well, not in my lifetime. The sole remaining American motorcycle manufacturing company was Harley-Davidson, which was launched in 1903. Well, not a lot of current information to learn from them for a new start-up, but I did read every book on them, that I could.

Next, I began looking at the automotive industry for possible parallels since the industries were related. Both industries manufactured federally regulated transportation vehicles to Environmental Protection Association (EPA) and Department of Transportation (DOT) laws, and also had State and Federally regulated distribution of product through franchised dealers.

The auto industry also had great barriers to entry and did not have any recent successful new entrants. The most notable were the Tucker Automobile Company of the late 1940s, and the Delorean Automobile Company of the early 1980s. Both of them had significant challenges in taking on a capital intensive, highly regulated, mature industry. So that was not good. A concern, but not totally alarming.

A key concept to recognize here is that the plan was to design and build a *proprietary* motorcycle as an independent company. Proprietary. That meant it had to have its own styling design and engineering characteristics, and subsequently our own manufacturing tooling—not just some cosmetic makeover of a product. That is why there were no current examples in the automotive or motorcycle marketplace. Too many barriers to entry for a proprietary product.

We weren't going to use someone else's engine, frame, fuel tank, handlebars, etc., and then slap our name on it and call it our bike. First off, the OEMs wouldn't sell us their proprietary components, and secondly, even if they did, components from one OEM are not compatible with components from another. So it simply would not work.

Industry estimates at the time were that to design, tool, manufacture, and build out distribution for a new automobile was about a billion dollars, and for a motorcycle, about a quarter of that. Either way, those are big numbers. How do you raise that kind of money for a manufacturing venture in the United States, that will take years (five to seven) before a revenue stream is derived? It is so difficult it had not been successful in more than 75 years, and everyone who had tried it since then had failed. The industries were simply too mature and the barriers of entry too significant.

But how about the customer? Were customers of the industries pleased, and would they welcome a new entrant? No, they weren't pleased, and yes, they would welcome someone new. Especially a product that didn't look like a clone of everything else. But who was going to be that adventuresome? Most large established bureaucratic organizations build homogenized products. Maybe okay for the shareholders, but not for the customers.

So what was the probability of a customer having a chance to even consider a new product from a new company? Very unlikely. So the industries continued to chug along, and in particular, compared to themselves, they were doing a good job.

Well none of this dismayed me. It only furthered my conviction that the time was right. I knew a motorcycle could be designed, built and sold. I had just bought one and rode it that morning, so someone was doing it. No one could tell me it was impossible. It was in the realm of possibility. Risky and improbable, but possible if one could get through the barriers to entry.

The buying experience also left me frustrated. If I tried to contact the parent OEM company, I could never get through the complicated phone system to talk to a live person. And then the recordings began speaking so many languages that I wasn't sure what country I had called. I know the OEMs employ thousands of people, but who were they all talking to? Generally not to the customer, but to their own internal community.

Next, I would try the dealer. Now in defense of the dealer, they are the middle person and to some degree, do get it from both barrels. They have to be "nice" to the OEMs, and to the customers. But in the motorcycle industry, for some of the dealers that were selling Harley-Davidsons, you had to set an appointment with the salesman and convince him why you should be able to buy the bike, and at more than MSRP. Or just put your name on a waiting list and wait for two years, and then pay over MSRP.

So part of the reason I desired to launch the company came from being a frustrated consumer of the motorcycle industry. If I had these problems as a customer of the industry, and presuming others did too, then if a solution to the problem was offered, therein would be the market opportunity. I also believed that if the company started from the perspective of a customer, and developed the company culture with the focus on the customer, we shouldn't stray too far from success. Simply put, *start with the focus on the customer and keep it there*.

There were six chief barriers to entry that were of grave concern to me regarding the realism of the Plan:

1. A *long incubation* period of five to seven years to revenue,
2. *Aggressive competitors* that were household names,
3. A *manufactured* product here in America,
4. *Proprietary*, meaning we were going to spend a lot of time and money developing our own motorcycle,
5. *Capital intensive* to the tune of over $150 million, and
6. *No one had been successful* in our lifetime.

The execution of the Business Plan was going to be tough. The Plan showed that for over seven years we had to hit the bullseye every time we drew the bow. So I laid out milestones for each year we had to hit in the plan for a seven-year time period. This way we would know right upfront that if we missed a milestone, it was going to impact us down the road unless we found a way to bring it back on schedule.

These milestones also had a beneficial secondary purpose that would work in perfect harmony with the primary purpose. No one would logically write a check for $150 million right upfront, and then wait seven years to see what developed—instead we would focus on milestone driven financing, commonly known as "bootstrapping." Yes, we would bootstrap a start-up proprietary motorcycle company.

• • •

Almost everyone will tell you that a business needs a mission, whether you are a start-up or a mature business. And it's true—you do need a mission. I like to take it one step further though, and that is *"What are the principles that will be followed in carrying out the mission?"*

Another key factor is to develop a mission and principles that are timeless. This way they don't need to be redrafted as the winds of "correctness" dictate, but rather to use terminology and actions that have already stood the test of time. Also what I have found is that the more simple, logical, and honest the mission and principles are, the more simply they can be understood, believed, and followed. And as the founder of the company, my job was to create the vision and the strategy for the company, and properly set the tone and culture right from the start.

In my head I had been mulling this over for nearly fifteen years. Now I would have my chance to put an imprint on my beliefs and actions. The Mission for Hanlon Manufacturing was simply:

TO DESIGN, MANUFACTURE AND SELL PROFITABLY THROUGHOUT THE WORLD PREMIUM QUALITY AMERICAN MADE MOTORCYCLES THAT ARE REMINISCENT OF THE LEGENDARY UNEQUALED LIFESTYLE EXPERIENCES OF THE EARLIER YEARS OF MOTORCYCLING.

Now, for just starting, the Mission stated fairly clearly what the company was setting out to do. I have to admit though, in presentations on Wall Street and in classrooms, the Mission would be too lengthy for a slideshow and not yield the desired impact, so I sometimes abbreviated it to: *To Re-establish A Proprietary, Authentic, American Motorcycle Brand.*

So if this was the Mission for a company that would need to raise well over one hundred million dollars, under what culture would that Mission be executed? That's where the Principles came in, and in my opinion, a mission without principles is asking for future chaos in culture. This is where the belief and values, also known as corporate culture, gets established. Rather than leave it to chance for future employees to guess what that culture would be, it needed to be laid out right up front. And it was expected that we all abide by it.

By articulating the Principles early on in the business it would help set the tone for the tough decisions that were sure to be forthcoming. Also, the Mission and Principles would be reviewed by all prospective employees for them to evaluate as part of the process of determining whether or not they wanted to join a tough start-up venture. If they didn't agree with the Mission and Principles, then so be it—we would wish each other well, and go on our separate journeys. But if they agreed with the Mission and Principles, then we would march forward earnestly together.

There are nine Principles that I believed were important to carry out the Mission of the company, and they are all about people and use the word "our" or "we." I will mention three of them here as they especially stand out; without these three Principles, the other six could not be successfully accomplished. The Appendix lists the entire nine Principles.

The first principle is "People Are Our Greatest Asset." Easy to say, but again *"walk the talk, and prove it."* Look for the actions.

The second principle is "We Will Maximize Our Enterprise Value By Working As A Team." This Principle goes along with number one. If you focus on getting the highest quality talent, sometimes those individuals play for themselves and don't do well on a team. In our company, it was the leader's job to ensure that we all played together on the team. If you weren't a team player, then you were off the team.

The last principle I want to mention is Principle number eight: "Integrity, Honesty, Persistence, And Knowledge Will Be Expected, Fostered, And Rewarded." No explanation needed here. Look for the actions, not the words. From everyone, including the leaders.

• • •

Being the founder of Hanlon Manufacturing, I initially thought that, as is common to the automobile and motorcycle industry, the company and product is named after the founder. Obviously the motorcycle could simply be named Hanlon Motorcycle. But frankly, that didn't feel right. I wasn't in it for me. I'm too much of a team player, and one of my goals was to create a company that had a culture of equality and respect. It just didn't feel right having my name on the future product, when in fact the product would be the result of a team—a hard-charging team of equals.

Furthermore, after riding and being a Harley owner, and witnessing the biker and media excitement regarding the launch of the Indian motorcycle company, I believed that in order to compete we would also need to have a brand with a rich authentic American heritage.

After scouring every resource I could locate on the history of the motorcycle industry in America, I became fascinated with a lore that today is almost forgotten, except among the die-hard collectors of old motorcycles and literature. Earlier in the twentieth century when the country was becoming more modernized, and guys like Henry Ford, James Packard, and thousands of others were building the automobile industry, the motorcycle industry was also born. It was truly a respected family sport, and the only means of transportation for some families.

There were over 300 independent motorcycle manufacturers in the United States from 1900 to 1935. Today, there is only one that survived, Harley-Davidson in Milwaukee, Wisconsin, where they have been since they started in 1903. Like many new industries that get started, there was a rush of enterprising individuals who sought to build their companies in this new burgeoning industry. A modern day comparison would be the personal computer rush of the 1980s when it seemed everyone was building or trying to build a personal computer. Now that the industry has matured, the large dominant manufacturers control the market, creating significant barriers to entry for a new entrant.

Well, sixty years earlier, the motorcycle industry was no different, and it soon became dominated by what was then known as the "Big Three" of motorcycle manufacturers—Harley-Davidson, Excelsior-Henderson, and Indian. These three motorcycle manufacturers controlled over 90% of the market, while the remaining manufacturers struggled with low volumes and poor distribution, and would have short company lives.

Being a marketing driven finance and technical guy, I was seeking an old motorcycle brand name from the past that could be "resurrected." I was searching for a brand that had American heritage, something we called "soul" in the motorcycle industry. And either you have it, or you don't. You can't create it, but if you have it, you can nurture it.

A rich authentic American motorcycle history, if properly and respectfully nurtured, might allow the customers to feel the soul of the company—to feel the roots of the heritage. I strongly believed we could build on this theme, and have a neat "resurrected" story that would not only compete with Harley, but also quite possibly move beyond their brand in certain areas. After all, they had about 70% market share in their market segment, and certainly some bikers had to be looking for more. It's hard for one brand to solve all consumers' interests.

Knowing that this could be tricky, but also successful, the old brands had to be scrutinized for availability, and also, even though dormant, for what they represented when they weren't dormant, since we were going to breathe renewed life into one of them.

Well, of the big three former manufacturers, Harley and Indian were already taken, but Excelsior-Henderson, what about them? Because so much of the future marketing and soul of the company was at stake, I simply couldn't take the easy obvious approach without conducting full research on additional old brand names. Besides, if we were successful in resurrecting an old brand, I thought other entrepreneurs might follow suit, and I wanted to know the history of the other brands in the event we would ever be questioned about or needed to compete with them. The research included about two hundred different brand names, but I would eventually discard them for one reason or another. However, the Excelsior-Henderson name would continue to withstand the test of time as the research continued.

What I have found for me is that sometimes good things take time, and also that time itself can solve many issues. The more I researched, the more the lore of the original Excelsior-Henderson motorcycle started to appeal to me.

The company and motorcycles were known for quality, styling and durability. They were one of the big three motorcycle manufacturers. Good. First motorcycle to crack the 100-mph barrier in 1912. Even better. First motorcycle to go around the world in 1913. Hmm, who was the second? Who knows, and who cares in the record books?

Former motorcycle owners included the likes of Henry Ford and Charles Lindbergh. Now this was getting real good. Almost everybody who knows of America has heard of these guys. Owned by police departments throughout the entire United States; the largest motorcycle factory in the world in 1914; the first poured concrete building…It kept getting better. Modern day collectors of Excelsior-Henderson motorcycles included Jay Leno and the late Steve McQueen.

The original Excelsior-Henderson Company had been dormant since 1931 when its owner shut it down during the Depression. The owner? Ignatz Schwinn. Yes, Ignatz shut down his motorcycle business in Chicago in order to concentrate on bicycle production because he thought bicycles would sell better than motorcycles during the Depression.

According to an old magazine article on the subject, the motorcycle industry shuddered and would never recover when Ignatz shut it down unexpectedly on March 31, 1931, but his company went out the same way it went in—BOLDLY. Now, this story was starting to have some excitement, and I found myself believing that the flame of the old company had not been extinguished, but was quietly waiting to be rekindled.

It didn't matter to me that very few people in the current motorcycle industry had ever heard of the old Excelsior-Henderson brand. In fact that was good. We could sneak up on the competition through their tailpipes. That's what was going to make the marketing fun: creating brand awareness. Only now, we had the power of a former brand, with rich American heritage.

It was time for brand resurrection. From the bottom up. Grassroots style.

# 4

## *Finding The Throttle*

*E*xecution time. The Business Plan was complete and it was time to start the transition from strategy to implementation. I knew what I was going to do. I started marching forward and kept marching and never looked back.

There was a lot of work ahead, and this is probably where the sleepless nights started.

My wife, Carol, and I had just built a new house in Burnsville, Minnesota, on a lot that we had bought about five years earlier when the real estate market was soft and interest rates were high. We thought it looked like a good time to buy since the prices were depressed. It turned out it was.

Overlooking a small lake on a quiet cul-de-sac, it was the perfect place for working on the business plan, but now it was time to move the business forward and begin to look for a commercial building in which to locate the business. Carol also worked out of our house as a freelance court reporter in the converted office next to mine, and it was probably time to give her some space. Oftentimes she would over-hear my constant phone conversations, and I'm sure it had to be distracting. We already had three phone lines running into the house, and this was before the Internet!

There was really no big bang to kicking off the execution of the Plan. After working on it for so long, it was a logical extension to just keep on implementing it to see how far it would go. If you have ever started a company, at least for most companies, you know what I mean.

Looking back, the company actually started when the planning for it started, which was in January 1993. For example, when a new store opens, the public sees it as starting the day they can go into it, but for the owner, we all know that the start was actually several months and possibly years before.

For most entrepreneurs the start becomes anticlimactic because to some degree it evolves over time. When I first started working on the Business Plan, I was also working on other prospective ventures—I wasn't sure which would look the best until after the research and due diligence was finished and developed into a business plan. At least for the companies I have launched, this is how it is to me. An evolutionary process, exhilarating on the one hand, and darn frightening on the other.

I believe the first day you start a business is the first day you are going out of business. It's like jumping off a cliff and not only having to build your wings on the way down, you also need to then learn how to fly. If you can build them and learn to fly, then you can soar forward. Otherwise you're just going to crash. It's inevitable.

My goal was to save the big bang for the future, when several years down the road we would be in motorcycle production. And we would have customers. I knew that's when I would feel it all comes home— when I saw someone riding our motorcycles that they had bought from one of our dealers. Until then, there was too much work to focus on.

In order to get the legal side of the business going, and to open a corporate checking account, I executed the documents to incorporate the company on December 20th, 1993, as the sole shareholder. It was hard to say if this was a good feeling or not, knowing I held 100% of the stock, but also knowing that unless millions of dollars were raised and a motorcycle company was built, the stock was worth nothing.

Because the company was still in the basement of my house, the official corporate mailing address was my home in Burnsville. Years later I continued receiving numerous documents at my house, including notices from the United States Trademark Office, even though the company had moved several times. So many different aspects of the Plan were being kicked off by filing government documents, that only later did I realize the extra effort it would take to keep up with addresses.

It was also time to start raising money for this big venture. I had already worked on it for about a year and had been financing it from my savings. That is never fun to do, but I didn't know any other way. In reviewing the projected costs for the next six months of the Plan it looked like I could fund the business out of my savings, if I was lucky.

Frankly, that was also quite discomforting. If we weren't able to raise funds after that to keep the business going, my wife and I would be out of savings, and the company would have no money. No savings, no job, no company. Not good.

I contacted my banker, Dan Ringstad, at New Market Bank and set up a meeting to come in and talk to him and explain what I was about to do. Fortunately I knew him from my days in Rotary, and I had been a customer of the bank for some time. Little did either of us realize that over the next several years, tens of millions of dollars were going to be flowing in and out of the account I was opening. And we would be receiving and wiring funds throughout the world.

If you have ever heard of small town country banks, then New Market Bank is one of them. The main bank started in the early 1900s in a small farm community and was still owned by the same family. Generation after generation. Next to the bank was the local pub, and across the street up the hill, the local church. At the bottom of the hill was a ball field. To some degree, that really says it all. It is still run with the same level of trust and community service that it was founded on. I like this kind of bank. No lip service here.

My plan was to set aside twenty thousand dollars from my savings, and then take out a loan for fifty thousand dollars collateralized by my remaining savings and assets, including my Harley-Davidson motorcycle, and I sold some of my Harley-Davidson stock. That would give me about seventy thousand dollars to work with while the initial milestones to the Plan were reached. Hopefully then, we would close on additional financing to keep the company going.

That first year though we did have a Christmas party. My wife, Carol, invited me out to dinner. Carol had assisted the company and me a lot during the formative stages of the business, and we had a lot to celebrate. The sale of my former company, our new house, our young daughter, and now our new company. So, on behalf of the company we did have an official Christmas party—a small one. And Carol was pregnant with our second child.

• • •

There were several milestones on the seven-year timeline that needed immediate attention to start the momentum—and they had to be accomplished right, since they would impact the company for years to come. Also, they had to be accomplished simultaneously, not sequentially.

First, I had decided on the Excelsior-Henderson brand names, and now I needed to lock them up by filing trademark applications.

Second, the outside investor financing had to get kicked off, and fast since each round takes so long.

Third, it was time to start making contacts in the motorcycle industry for a future announcement of the company.

Fourth, the initial drawings of the bike would have to be started; and Fifth, the engine. The engine design needed to be started, as that was the longest lead-time milestone in the Business Plan—and the riskiest. Engines take several years to develop.

Plus, the company needed to move out of my basement and into a commercial building. My wife was due with our second child and it was time to kick the business out of the house.

All of these milestones were going to set the stage for the future. They were part of a building block and even though they were independent of each other, they were interdependent. If one of these milestones got established wrong or set into the wrong direction, it could be terminal to the company in the future. These milestones already represented different functions of the company that would someday grow into different departments with many people.

As the founder, you have to wear many hats, and a person had better get used to that fairly quickly. When I started my former company, it was frustrating at first having to do so many different functions. But my years of education and various business experiences had paid off. This time, I immediately kicked it into high gear and, within reason, knew just what to do—or more importantly, I knew "who" and "how" to recruit in order to do it.

After my research on the brand names of Excelsior and Henderson, and any related former marks, I was ready to file trademark applications with the United States Patent and Trademark Office. But before I did, I wanted to have some independent qualified opinions—i.e., a trademark lawyer.

I met with two separate trademark lawyers from two different firms in downtown Minneapolis. These types of lawyers are familiar with working with entrepreneurs and inventors who have creative and out-of-the-box thinking. So, these are the fun lawyers. Also, they know how to help you avoid the minefields.

In each meeting with the lawyers I had asked them what their opinions were regarding our ability to get the trademark rights to the former Excelsior and Henderson brand names. Since they had been long ago abandoned, and there was no residual use, the answer was fairly simple and confirmed my research. Yes, you should be able to establish rights by filing an ITU—an "intent-to-use" application.

I distinctly remember one lawyer looking at me and asking with a perplexed look on his face: "What would you want to do with a sixty-year-old motorcycle name?" I smiled to myself. Most people at this point in time just wouldn't believe the answer. I just asked him to work on getting the name for me, and I'll figure out something to do with it.

So, in December 1993, under the name of Hanlon Manufacturing, I executed the ITU trademark applications for the names of Excelsior, Henderson, Super X, and American X. Five and a half years and $80 million dollars later these names would find themselves on an OEM manufactured proprietary motorcycle that a customer was riding, and they had bought from a dealer. But I didn't know this at the time. I just had to prepare for it as though I did know.

• • •

Raising money for a start-up company is always difficult, and there is no surefire way of accomplishing it, or of guaranteeing its success. With some parts of the business there is logical progression with fairly predictable results, such as making a mechanical part. However in raising capital, there is no predictable blueprint. Also, if you are raising money based upon accomplishing set milestones, there still is no guarantee you'll get funded for each accomplishment. It is an inherent risk to the business.

Financing the business was going to be the biggest challenge, but for a different reason than most start-ups. Our primary issue was we were going to need a lot of money for a long time before revenue was possible. And if we didn't get the money at the right time according to our milestones, it would be all over. Just like that. That is the price for admission to the proprietary OEM motorcycle or automotive industry. You've got to pay to play.

To a great degree, everything in our Business Plan could be accomplished; assuming we had a rich parent corporation, or the money to do it. That was a key ingredient to the Plan. We weren't reinventing any wheels. There was no "new invention" that had to be created; therefore the skills and the technology were already available. We were simply going to employ this current technology and the skills to enter a mature but growing industry with an additional product.

In some new ventures you have to invent a new way or product, or create an industry for the need of your product. Actually, a lot of com-

panies and industries get started this way—take for example the automotive and motorcycle industries ninety years earlier. Those pioneer-
ing companies then had to invent product and an industry. Or look at
modern times to the computer and Internet industry. We all witnessed
firsthand the costs of inventing those products and creating an industry. Many companies, and millions of dollars, come and go when you
are inventing or creating new industries. That was too risky for me.

We weren't going to need to do any of that though. That was
indeed the beauty of the Plan. There were already customers in a
proven market that weren't having their needs entirely met. I knew
motorcycles could be built; I was riding one. Now we just had to convince others.

One of the key ingredients to raising capital is to have a solid
Business Plan, and then start contacting family, friends, angel investors
and venture capitalists with the goal of setting up a meeting with them.
Initially I started with some members of the family, and friends, and
they appeared willing to invest some, but we all knew that we would
need a bigger game plan than that. This was a big venture and we
would need to immediately start bringing in outside investors.

So I felt fairly confident with a few family and friends on board,
which would help lead to the next step of private investors or venture
capitalists. Granted, I'm sure some of the family and friends thought it
was crazy to start a motorcycle company, but they were polite enough
to indicate they would be *"in the first deal"* if we were able to get additional investors. It was a start.

• • •

Now it was time to figure out a way to attract outside investors. A
logical place to start was with industry financial angels, or venture capitalists who fund within the industry. Unfortunately, there weren't any
angels or venture capitalists that specialized in the motorcycle industry. Frankly, it was impossible to locate *anyone* from this group who had
invested in a start-up motorcycle company. Now, that was a problem
on the one hand since there was no clear path, but on the other hand,
there was also an opportunity to create one.

Since there are never any incoming phone calls to a start-up company it was time to continue working the outgoing phone calls.
Through a broker contact of mine in Minneapolis who took early

interest in the venture (Brad Amundson, a friend from my Green Giant farming days), a phone conference was set up with a seasoned venture capitalist, John Siegler, located in Seattle, who worked for Piper Jaffray.

After placing several phone calls and not having them returned, I was able to catch John in Seattle late on a Friday afternoon, and I could tell he was real short of interest and was pushing to end the call. But I appealed for his viewpoints, and persisted on with my vision for the company. For some reason, he relaxed a bit, and we were able to converse for over an hour.

As we spoke I continued to outline the Business Plan and milestones to him, and he continued to give me feedback and suggestions. He indicated that he and his firm were not candidates to assist in the raising of the money, but we proceeded to dialog back and forth about various financing scenarios and under what structure they might work.

This was good news. Finally someone within the venture capital industry took enough time to hear the story and suggest a roadmap. Over the weekend I fine tuned a potential capital-raising scenario for the next several years and overlaid it onto the Business Plan and the milestones.

Now, for the first time, there was an outline of how the financing would integrate into the Plan. It was probable that the financing plan would change over time as it was executed, but at least now there was a plan to use as a guideline.

Years later I bumped into this Seattle guy (John) in the elevator at a financing conference in New York, and had the chance to thank him personally. He remembered the phone conversation and said even he was surprised he took the time to talk, especially since he didn't know anything about motorcycles, other than he would like to have one someday. I knew he was right about taking the time to talk since I had tried to call him several times before and since, and never had the chance to reach him again.

• • •

Contacting venture capitalists can be a frustrating experience. They represent money and talent, and depending upon the current economic climate, they may or may not have a lot of each. In our case, it was somewhat unique. We were not high technology, nor medical or computer related. A real negative here in America.

It is important to create a Non-Disclosure Agreement, known as an NDA in financing parlance. All successful larger companies use these routinely, and an early stage company should also. It is a legal document that basically states confidential information—which includes the Business Plan—that you provide to a party will be kept confidential. Most investors to an early stage company will not be offended if asked to review and execute an NDA, and if they are, beware.

Since our Business Plan was the only one known to exist for a new motorcycle company, and I took a lot of pride in its authorship, I wasn't about to let anyone improperly use it. Since the first day of business, I adopted the policy of having an NDA executed, and *never wavered* from the policy. Some companies and individuals routinely said they never executed one, yet we held firm in not providing anything until they did.

Over the next several months I made hundreds of phone calls and sent an equal number of letters and information packages to potential sources of venture capital. Since the vast majority of them never took my phone call nor responded by mail, it would be safe to conclude they had no interest—I think.

There were a few venture capitalists and angel investors who took the time to learn a very little more about the story, but the reality was the venture was too large and we were too much in the early stages to be a viable financing opportunity. Most of them had zero interest in the motorcycle industry. But they oftentimes did wish us good luck. Well, luck is okay.

As a consumer, however, I knew there was market opportunity. I knew it when visiting the local motorcycle dealership where the lines for buying motorcycles were long, and when I looked at the stock market, my investment in Harley-Davidson's stock continued to outperform the market. The lack of interest by the venture capital market was not a deterrent, but instead maybe even a motivator.

I could say the time invested of several months of contacting venture capitalists was wasted, but from the lack of success came an idea for an alternative method. We didn't need them. It was that simple. Really, they believed they didn't need us, so I just adopted a reciprocal attitude. I like the concept of reciprocity. Relationships cut both ways and it was obvious there was no interest, at least that we knew of.

The solution was too plain to see until all the traditional options had been explored. This is the point when many early stage companies cease to exist. It was very obvious after trying the traditional route to financing—there would be no financing. Hence the company would have had to shut down at that point, if not for the inspiration of a new financing plan.

Being a true entrepreneur, I discovered a new unexpected solution that developed from this problem. The big question was: Who are the funding sources for the venture capitalists? Where do they get their money? Well, sometimes from wealthy individuals. Hmm, maybe I could bypass the venture capitalists and go directly to wealthy individual investors. Only I didn't know enough of them.

So, that's what we did for the most part of the next several years. Contact individual investors. One on one—grassroots style.

These types of decisions come from the gut, from instinct. Not research.

• • •

Deciding on this new focus of going directly to the investor was a real coup. There are only so many hours in each day and the company needed to move forward faster. Now rather than focus on locating an investment banking firm or venture capitalist, we would act in their place. Except we had not done that before: it was now time to learn.

In following the rules of the Securities Exchange Commission (SEC), there are some genuine opportunities for early stage companies to legitimately raise capital. For one, your company does not need to have an investment banker represent you in the sale of your company stock. Instead, as an officer of your own company you can locate and work directly with prospective investors, as long as you follow the rules of the SEC. This is where you will want to make sure you have good lawyers, and we did.

Basically, if you are a privately held company, the SEC allows you to have a certain number of *non-accredited* investors, and *accredited* investors—before the requirement to become an SEC reporting company. Those terms are generally specific to the SEC, and to be an accredited investor, you need to have greater than a million dollar net worth, or over a $200 thousand annual income. Some of the logic behind that thinking is that if you have a million dollar net worth, presumably you have the financial ability to invest in early stage companies, and can afford the legal and financial advisors to assist you on your decision.

It was time to do homework on how to locate and contact these types of investors. Being a believer in keeping it simple, I asked myself the question: *"What type of investors would have interest in our story?"* The answer was simple, and it is the same for all business plans. Look within the Plan for the answer.

The product in our Plan was a consumer durable item. Who are the potential customers, service providers, dealers, suppliers, enthusiasts, etc.? Our Business Plan was primarily a newly designed manufactured product (motorcycle) that would need good marketing and sales. So basically, we'd need to seek wealthy individuals who had backgrounds in these areas.

Accordingly, we focused primarily on two strategic skill areas: 1) look for accredited investors with a manufacturing background, and/or 2) look for accredited investors with a sales or marketing driven background.

This concept also fit within the logical framework of what I was learning when explaining the company story to someone. If they had a background in marketing and sales, we would quickly get all the different ways our company could be positioned in the marketplace against, or alongside, the industry leader of Harley—yet invariably the investor would have grave concerns about how a product like that could be manufactured.

If they had a manufacturing background, we would get great ideas on how the motorcycle could be manufactured—yet invariably they would have similar grave concerns, but about the marketing and sales part of our plan. These manufacturing companies are great when you go visit them. For a reason, the sales office is usually tucked in a small office behind manufacturing.

Each type didn't view their own area of expertise as a problem because they knew how to solve it, and had built their business and their wealth around their skill set. But they saw the areas in which they didn't have expertise to be a potential problem. Now if we could harness as advisors these two differently skilled areas, then it might be a strong team.

The lesson of all this is the manufacturing leaders saw the manufacturing opportunity, and the marketing leaders saw the market opportunity. We didn't need to do too much educating in those areas. Here again the motto applied to some degree, *"If I have to explain, you won't understand."* Well they understood, and we could now more quickly communicate.

• • •

As I continued doing the homework on this new investor-financing plan, another concept struck me. For years I had sought out the advice of more experienced people who had already accomplished what I was setting out to do. I felt that if they had already done something, I could learn from the way they did it, and they might also have some ideas on how it could be done again.

What I had learned from meeting wealthy individuals like this was that most were genuinely nice people and would allocate some time and free advice, while some were not nearly as helpful or nice. Right or wrong, I came to the conclusion that most of the people who took interest in giving genuine advice had created their own wealth, as contrasted with inheriting it.

Also, for the most part, those who had created their own wealth had gone through the learning experience of an underfunded start-up themselves and could probably identify with where the company was at. To some degree I was hoping they would adopt the company, and be a private investor and advisor. This is getting a bit more toward the psychological level—the psychographic profile—and less to the financial.

These types of individuals had been there before, and it did not deter them. In fact I think privately the risk motivated them too. Nothing ventured, nothing gained.

This type of investor can also quickly spot certain holes in your plan that you might not otherwise catch right away until it is too late—so they might have some candid advice on some issues. And it is usually free. All they want to do is see your venture succeed, and get some satisfaction knowing they helped you.

And they want to get a return on their investment.

The goal is to do both. Let them give advice and hopefully your company will succeed in part due to their advice, and give them a return on their investment.

One final thought regarding asking for advice. Most of the time those giving you the advice don't expect you to take all of it and implement it. Instead, I have found that advice is like a toolbox provided to you: you utilize the tools that make sense for your situation. Since you are the closest to it, you need to be responsible for your own decisions. Of course, some people do get offended if you don't take their advice, but don't let that be your problem.

Now putting this all together let's summarize. *We will focus on wealthy accredited investors who have created their own wealth from their expertise in launching or building a company that is either a manufacturing or marketing driven company, and who have the time and inclination to give advice.* And guess what? These types of individuals are risk takers, and many ride motorcycles!

This now added a new dimension. What if one of their hobbies was motorcycle riding? All of a sudden we had a potentially winning combination. We now had the added ingredient of passion.

From that point forward, we used this profile to some degree that would vary in intensity from time to time, to search for the right type of investors for Excelsior-Henderson Motorcycles.

And it worked. When we varied from it, the results were disastrous.

# 5

## *Learning How To Tell The Story*

For the first time we were starting to get some return phone calls. It made sense. We were now contacting people who had a manufacturing or marketing background, liked motorcycles, and invariably had an interest in learning more about our company.

They wanted to hear the story.

This is where the story comes in. A founder to a start-up company had better learn to give a compelling story about the company. Tell it well. Tell it fast. Tell it clearly. And keep it factual. Most people can spot a phony a mile away, and now is not the time to over dramatize, although some do.

If you are not a natural born salesperson, then you are going to need to have a little learning here. It is time to be more sales driven or your story may not get heard correctly. When you truly believe in yourself, your company, and your plan, your natural intensity and determination should show through, and others will recognize it.

Also, if you need to raise a lot of money, and need to tell your story often, create a video. It doesn't need to be movie quality, but it will help you get your message out.

We created a thirteen-minute video that did cost the company a little more than I expected, but it turned out to be a better tool in explaining the company than what was anticipated. Motorcycling and the building of the company was all about people, and it was difficult to explain the passion and desires over the phone. Now a video could be sent overnight, and within 13 minutes I could have an interested party well informed about the company. It was another tool in the toolbox that worked.

And it allowed others to pass on the story by passing on the video.

• • •

The lower level of my house was beginning to get a little hectic, and the business was progressing far enough along that it didn't appear very professional to still be operating out of the home. Setting meetings and not having a place to meet except in a restaurant, a coffee shop, or in the other person's office was getting difficult. Anyone who wanted to meet at my "business" would have to come to my house, and it just wasn't working out anymore.

In some business meetings, giving out a business address that was a residential home was uncomfortable. I was concerned that the business would not be perceived as being serious about its goals. There was no turning back—it was time to move forward.

Also, on February 5th, my wife Carol had given birth to our second child, our son Hunter, and we were all adjusting to his new young life. With our daughter Hannah two years old, and Hunter as our newborn, the house was taking on a new meaning. Even though my office was in the lower level, it was no longer a good place to focus on the business. So the timing seemed right on many fronts.

It wasn't easy locating a commercial building owner who was interested in providing a lease to an underfunded start-up motorcycle company. Invariably the question of the Business Plan and financing would come up, and it clearly showed there was only enough financing to pay rent for the next three to five months. I thought that was pretty good, but most landlords didn't. The company was in product development; hence it was in negative cash flow, and planned to be for at least the next six years. Unless money was raised promptly, the landlords all knew there would be no future rent paid. In other words, we did not look like a good viable tenant.

This was another time to start telling the story and the dream— that a lot of good things started from nothing, but I believed that with their help, we would be one step closer to making the dream a reality. It never ceased to amaze me. This is a great country where if you truly and sincerely ask those with means to help, they just might. As long as they believe in you and your plan.

Close to my home in Burnsville, Minnesota was a business campus owned by Kraus Anderson, one of the largest commercial/industrial developers in the Minneapolis/Saint Paul region. It was called Gateway Business Park and it was perfectly located on a hill that overlooked busy Interstate 35W. Off into the distance you could see downtown Minneapolis. The interstate also served as the gateway into and out of Minnesota and the Minneapolis area, and was only a fifteen-minute drive to the airport. This location would be very convenient and also give great exposure to the business. We had to get this location.

Well, the property manager said the landlord wasn't biting. They weren't interested in us as a tenant. Being a large commercial developer, they generally had the ability to attract solid well-established companies. It was time to overcome another hurdle. Their first answer back was "no." My personal opinion: *"no"* just means *not today, but maybe tomorrow.*

There were other commercial property owners who were willing to rent to us, but none of the available buildings within a reasonable commute were just right. Either the location had poor visibility, or was an older non-updated property, or just didn't feel right. Maybe that was why these managers were more willing to sign a lease—they didn't have many prospects better than us.

But I had an instinct that the location in Burnsville was the best for now and for the future. By overlooking a major freeway, the location appeared busy and alive. It just looked successful. I felt successful just standing there.

There had to be a way to convince the developer, so I asked the property manager if we could meet directly with the top decision-maker for the property. It turned out to be a guy in the home office in downtown Minneapolis who was the Chief Financial Officer (CFO).

Well, fortunately for us, the CFO was more than just a numbers man. He was not only interested in the plan, but also how it was going to be executed. He seemed genuine in trying to find a way for our company to meet their criteria, and a primary one was they wanted to have limited financial exposure. In other words, they didn't want to lose any money. The building we were looking at had some vacant space that did need some form of buildout, and the CFO was concerned about incurring those costs.

This was a matter where family could help. I knew my brother Terry was experienced in the commercial construction trades, and did a lot of commercial space buildout. I proposed a deal to the CFO of a two-year lease, with three months paid upfront, and we would pay for all the buildout costs upfront if they would allow us to do the work ourselves.

After conferring on it for a day, the developer got back to me and said it was a go. Now I could finally get out of my home, and commute to work. Fortunately for me, it was going to be about a seven-minute commute on the side streets—whether in sun or snow.

The space, a combination of office and warehouse, was only 2750 square feet, but it was all the company needed for now. In the years to come, by a strange twist of fate, as the company grew and needed more space, the tenants next door would be moving out—on each side of us! I often wondered why. As motorcyclists we did tend to be a little louder and certainly did add some spice to the complex, but we had great neighbors. We were able to expand five times to twenty thousand square feet and never had to move the front door or my office. I even liked the address: 607 West Travelers Trail.

Without any of us knowing it at the time, we would be in that location for nearly four years, until we moved into the new motorcycle factory we built in 1997.

Another interesting sidebar is the office furniture. You can get some great deals on used stuff and you can get it fast with minimal lead-times. When I had sold my previous company in 1993, the new owners consolidated the two locations into one, and had sold my office furniture to a used furniture broker. When I was out scouring for used furniture I was pleasantly shocked to see my old furniture available for sale. So I bought it again and outfitted the new company.

# 6

## *Cloning Is For Sheep—Make Mine Proprietary*

Next to financing the business, product development was a big hurdle. Just how do you go about developing a new motorcycle? To be more precise: a proprietary motorcycle.

A quick note on the proprietary concept here. Proprietary in my concept means the engineering design of the product is uniquely your own—meaning it's not a copy of someone else's product, nor does it consist of common components to another manufacturer of OEM products. Realistically, there might be some off-the-shelf components, such as tires, batteries, oil, spark plugs, bolts, etc., but otherwise, the engine, pistons, transmissions, fuel tank, fenders, etc. would be our own engineering design, and would not mate up to a product made by a competing OEM. For example, Harley engines don't fit in Hondas.

Keep in mind that all motorcycles and cars today do not represent an entirely new product, even though there are new models each year. OEMs don't need to have entirely new product offerings, since each can benefit from being in continuing business and using parts and designs from each previous year. Each year they freshen up the design, add some new parts, and take off some old, fix any known warranty issues, and voila! You have a new model for the marketing department and the customer.

This does not minimize the task any; it just makes it more predictable and less costly. Why reinvent the wheel every year, when you can just make continuous improvement? It is a great proven concept in manufacturing—practically a requirement—and one that we hoped to emulate someday when we had our first motorcycle in the market.

In our case, we didn't have any current product to make improvements to. We had to start with a new product. Just like Henry Ford and Harley-Davidson did in 1903. From that point forward they never had to design a completely new automobile or motorcycle. For each new model they were able to utilize some designs and components of the former model, leading more to a typical evolutionary process rather than revolutionary. That is a key ingredient to designing products that serve as a platform for future models. I knew this well from my manufacturing days.

•••

Getting back to how to design a new proprietary motorcycle: first, you need to decide what type of motorcycle you're going to design— which means a decision has to be made on what market segment to enter, and then design for that market. For us at Excelsior, the market research and the Business Plan had already resolved the market segment. It was also determined by instinct. If you study an industry long enough and hard enough, and creatively, soon opportunities will be apparent. It was a no-brainer that the cruiser and touring motorcycle segments were the ones to be in.

Within the motorcycle industry there are certain distinct market segments that are quite different from each other. To an outsider, some people think all motorcycles and motorcyclists are alike. Well, they're not.

In the United States, there are primarily two categories of motorcycles: heavyweight and non-heavyweight. What this really means is the heavyweight bikes are the bigger road bikes that are ridden on the street, and the non-heavyweight motorcycles are the smaller road bikes, dirt bikes, and other off-road bikes.

Within the heavyweight category there are three primary classes of motorcycles: 1) cruisers, 2) touring, and 3) sport bikes. To keep it simple here, cruisers are the largest class of motorcycles with about 60% of sales, while the touring and sport bikes each have about 20%. The cruising and touring class is about 80% of the market, and is dominated strongly by mature men and women. Most riders are married, or formerly married, and with children. You get the idea of the market segment.

Contrast this to the sport bike class, which is about 20% market share, and dominated by young male riders. These motorcycles have the ability to reach tremendous speeds, upwards of 140 mph, unlike a cruiser and tourer. The riders who have these bikes generally go fast, like I used to. Upon maturing a bit over the years, if a rider stays in the motorcycle industry, they oftentimes move on to the cruising/touring classes.

Generally, a cruiser/touring rider is not a sport bike rider, and vice versa. There is some crossover, but generally each OEM will make distinctly different bikes for each class.

Looking at Harley-Davidson, they primarily make motorcycles for the cruiser and touring class, and traditionally have over 50% market share in the cruiser class and clearly dominate. In essence, they were in the largest most profitable market segments, and they were the 800-pound gorilla.

If you can picture a new Harley in your mind, you know what a cruiser is.

When I was younger—in my twenties—I remember looking at the Harley riders and wondering why all these old fat guys and women rode those overly expensive bikes that didn't go very fast. Well, fifteen years later, they weren't all so fat or old, and I was riding one too!

Within the cruiser class, Harley is so dominant the foreign OEM manufacturers really don't design their own unique look. The engineering design is generally proprietary, but the styling design is more or less an imitation of the American cruiser motorcycle look. The foreign OEMs primarily design bikes that look like Harleys, but at a lower price. It's a strange phenomenon in the industry. Even though it is a passionate and emotional consumer purchase, the foreign OEM manufacturers felt it was best to just follow the look of the leader. So you wind up having products in the marketplace that are the real McCoys (a diamond), and the imitations (a cubic zirconia). To an untrained motorcycle eye, it is sometimes hard to tell the bikes apart.

In a way, that is good. It forces genuineness and proprietary price points. What sells for more? An original or a copy? You guessed it, an original.

And we all know the market is large enough for both originals and copies. Both have their appropriate places in the market and rightfully so.

Anytime Harley took a right turn, others followed to the right. If Harley turned left, others turned left. Well, if everyone in the industry was turning left, maybe it was time to turn right.

So we at Excelsior-Henderson decided to turn right. I would later find out some in the industry didn't like this. I was surprised to find out we were on their radar screen.

• • •

Our Super X motorcycle was not going to be a copy of anyone, except ourselves. That's what made it proprietary, and that's why it cost a lot of money and time to design and build. The Excelsior-Henderson brand already had uniqueness. It's just that most riders of today didn't know about it. Well, we were going to change that. Over time. With marketing. And branding.

Our first motorcycle design was for a cruiser motorcycle that within the Business Plan was already named the Super X, a motorcycle brand name we were resurrecting from the former Excelsior-Henderson Company that had shut down during the Depression. Hopefully the U.S. Trademark Office would approve the trademark application in time for product launch.

The design of the Super X was in keeping with the consumer's expectations of a motorcycle in that class, of being fairly large, yet low, powerful, and with muscular curves. Also, nice paint jobs, flashy chrome, and the ability to accessorize. To some degree, a statement motorcycle that almost roared—I've arrived.

The concept for designing the motorcycle was already in my head and in the Business Plan, but we now needed to translate that to trained product designers.

The inspiration for the look of the new Super X was essentially a transformation of the Super X of 1929. According to industry historians and articles from that time period, the 1929 Super X took the industry by storm with its new unique designs. It was long and low, with gracefully curved fenders and a round muscular fuel tank, and, in an industry first, you actually sat well into the motorcycle, rather than on top of it. And it had the traditional V-twin engine.

This sort of sounds like the cruiser motorcycles of today. Well, the 1929 Super X is credited by industry historians with being the first to usher in the new look that other manufacturers would soon follow. Today it is known as a cruiser motorcycle; back in 1929 it was just known as a bold new look, which the competitors did later quietly adopt. Everyone. Even through today.

And importantly, Excelsior retained its signature styling icon: *the front fork tubes would pierce the front fender*. This was the only motorcycle from over hundreds of manufacturers and over several decades that had this distinct styling. It was so distinctive, and bold, that some liked it and some did not.

The key design goal was to now instill in the minds of our designers how to bridge the gap from 1929 to 1999—in other words, how it would have evolved over time. In essence, it would be like closing your eyes and imagining what a 1929 Super X would be like today if it had carried on the tradition and product refinements to 1999. That was our new proprietary bike. At least in my head. Now my vision had to be translated to paper in drawings.

It would almost be like there were a few generations missing, but there would be family resemblance. This was paying proper homage to the brand, and again it just felt right. I didn't read about this stuff in a marketing class while getting my MBA. Instead, this was instinct.

The Plan for the company was to initially outsource the talent for translating the vision of the motorcycle to paper, and later bring the talent in-house several years down the road when the company was more stable and more adequately funded. The good thing about outsourcing, it is more of a variable cost and would give our business more flexibility. The downside though, was that it is more difficult to manage expectations and completion schedules. But we had limited choices. We had to go for financial flexibility, which meant outsourcing.

The good news, fortunately in the product development area there are excellent firms that specialize in assisting companies with product design. The bad news, try to find one that has motorcycle experience, of an entire motorcycle. Scarce to nonexistent. Most motorcycle and automotive OEMs do the vast majority of their styling and design in-house, and so the outsourcing marketplace for those product lines is more limited.

Also, we wanted to stay with talent in America as much as we could. There were several potential product design firms outside the country, but it didn't feel right designing an American nostalgic motorcycle overseas.

After a lot of homework, which included a lot of research and phone calls and meetings, and advice from various advisors, we had narrowed down the search to a firm that we thought would do the best job.

Next World Design, located in Columbus, Ohio, was a rather young company, but it did seem to have good experience and an energetic can-do attitude. Although they hadn't designed a complete motorcycle, they had designed significant components, and as riders themselves, they seemed to have a good grasp of the industry and the product.

After executing a Non-Disclosure Agreement and hammering out an initial Design Agreement that we all thought made sense, we engaged them to go forward with some styling drawings.

In engaging and working with designers or design companies, it is important to stay in frequent contact, otherwise the task and the product can get inadvertently derailed. By nature, most styling designers need to have a creative flair, and do, and that creativity needs to be allowed freedom. As a businessperson operating on a financial and time budget though, that creativity needed some management. It was important for our company to stay in constant communication with our designers, and we did.

We set up various milestones to reach over a period of several months with the design team that primarily consisted of stages of one-dimensional hand drawings. Initially the drawings would be scaled about 1/5th actual size. After numerous versions and revisions, and meetings, and red-faces, the next phase was moving onto full-size drawings, and more revisions, etc., until we got a full-size drawing of what we wanted the bike to look like.

If you are not familiar with styling design, basically it is comprised of hand- or computer-generated drawings, and eventually actual-size hand-built models. These models aren't engineered out yet, and basically nothing—or practically nothing—works on them, as it is for viewing only to determine if the look is right. If it is, then the next logical step is to bring in the engineering department to try to make everything work. This is oversimplification and some steps get prolonged or short-circuited, but it is the essence of what the process is. Sometimes this happens concurrently, sometimes purely sequentially, and sometimes engineers get mad at stylers, and vice versa. It's a beautiful process, and I remember it well from my Honeywell days, and from my first patent a few years earlier.

It's also a frustrating process for many reasons. One, which is egos, can get in the way. But if you know that in advance and try to put the blame for any problems on yourself, then you manage through it with others.

I remember about a month after we had engaged the firm, they called us to come and view a multitude of initial drawings that represented their interpretation of what the Super X motorcycle could look like, based upon the very detailed and specific input they had been given by our company.

This was going to be exciting. It's always fun visiting a design facility, as it is so creative, with secret designs, and some half-started and completed designs scattered about. And always secrecy. This is where ideas germinate into substance, and the models get built that someday well into the future the final product will be used in the hands of a consumer. Competitors would love to have access to this area, and some try in creative ways.

Upon arriving at the design offices in Columbus, we were given the usual tour and ushered into a private viewing area to view the first drawings. There were about a dozen of them, and one by one they were unveiled and explained by the excited design staff.

It wasn't good. To a great degree the bike drawings looked too futuristic and unrealistic. There was apparently a bit of a disconnect between what our company wanted and what the design firm thought we wanted. The first of many typical business issues that unexpectedly crop up, particularly with design. We knew we didn't want the Super X to look like a Harley, but right now it wasn't looking the way I had envisioned. We packed up the drawings and left, and they never saw the light of day.

This is all part of a normal process though, and part of the natural evolution of designing a product from a clean sheet to a finished manufactured product. We needed to know the styling design limits.

Fortunately, after providing feedback and additional variations of drawings, we were able to make significant progress. We were working with some good guys, and we continued marching toward the milestones. If we could keep on schedule, in a few months we would have full-size drawings, and then on to full-size mockups.

• • •

In the execution of a fairly complicated business plan, particularly the Excelsior-Henderson Business Plan, I believed the company ought to dual-track some tasks. What I mean by this is to not have only one alternative method planned to accomplish a milestone, but to develop several alternatives that could be immediately deployed in order to achieve the milestone—similar to the concept of dual navigation systems in an airplane cockpit. This was a key strategic success factor. In our case, the milestones could not be missed, or the credibility of the company would be severely questioned, and inevitably cause the financing to dry up.

If we didn't *"do what we said we would do, when we said we would do it, for how much we said it would cost,"* our credibility would be ruined.

Many times over the seven years we would have alternative plans, and sometimes kick them off early just in the event the first plan got derailed. This is what I call dual-tracking. Have another train ready to go down the next track, and if necessary, use your judgment and be ready to send it out.

Rule number one here: Never have just one plan. Always plan an option. In our case, several times the first method wouldn't work, or something would go haywire, and we would already be kicking off the execution of the second method and literally not miss a beat.

Rule number two here: Work with experienced people and organizations. There is no substitute for experience. If they did it before, they might just do it again. There is credibility. By choice, everyone we worked with in key areas had more experience than we did. This is not a time to have an inelastic ego, but rather have hat in hand and ask for help.

The third rule at this point was to maximize the opportunity of outsourcing, and keep the overhead extremely low within our company. We didn't only preach being lean, we were. For example, by mid 1997 the company had been in existence for four and a half years, had built engines and prototype motorcycles, was building the factory, had raised nearly $60 million, and had 27 Team Members. Only 27 people! We were lean and mean. But this is getting ahead of the story.

• • •

It was with the mindset of dual-tracking Next World Design's efforts that I first met Frank and Larry. They were quite a pair. One of my favorite photos is of standing with them in England, with each one flanked on my side, all of us smiling and looking professional. They tried to take us for a ride, but at least it was fun for a while.

Larry is the famous Larry Shinoda. Famous at least in the automotive styling designer circuits; sadly, he is now deceased.

Larry was based in Detroit. He stood about five and a half feet tall and when I met him, he was like a bull in a china closet. He had an attitude. He had a lot of energy. He was a lot of fun. And he had his heart in the right place—he exuded passion. And stories. He had a lot of stories. If half of them were at least half-true, he had lived a full intense life. Frankly, I think the stories were true. He claimed to have punched so many people in his life, I just hoped I wouldn't be one of them.

One of his stories was about the recently redesigned Ford Mustang. He grabbed a magazine in his office that had a picture of the Mustang and he pointed at it, laughing. Still laughing, he jammed his thick, stubby fingers into the magazine and said, "I called the designer and told him that it looked liked he had put lipstick on a pig, but that it was still a pig." I still laugh at that. Lipstick on a pig. But I thought the car looked good.

One of his claims to fame was being a designer on the original split window 1963 Corvette back in the early 1960s when he worked for General Motors. He had also worked for Ford, Packard, Studebaker, and had been involved in the design of almost everything, and was well known and respected.

Larry liked anything with wheels and an internal combustion engine, and he'd worked on the design of a lot of them. But he didn't have much experience with motorcycles, even though he said he liked them. He also thought he could assist in the styling design of a better bike than Harley-Davidson. Now we were getting somewhere.

He mentioned he had a friend in Florida named Frank, and together they could design and build a complete running prototype of our bike. He said they had all types of people lined up who could do this for us. We were to pay him two hundred thousand dollars a month for five months, and at the end he would deliver a running bike, with blueprints. For a million dollars. Not bad. This sounded almost too good to be true. It was time to meet Frank.

Frank and Larry had a few new connections in England so we decided to meet there. England still has a great cottage industry of product styling, design and prototyping, and the plan was to meet up with Frank and Larry and some prospective contacts.

So I first met Frank in England, just outside of London. I think that was the last time I met Frank face-to-face too. The first thing I remember was him complaining about a washcloth—the place he was staying didn't furnish a washcloth, and he was perturbed about this. I kind of believe you can measure a person by the size of the things that upset them—I didn't take that as a good sign.

After a few quirky meetings that were reasonably unproductive, it was quickly obvious these guys didn't have a solid plan, other than to develop one as we went along, but with our money!

While in England, however, they did introduce us to the engine development company, Weslake. There we met Michael Daniels, son-in-law of the late great Harry Weslake. These guys knew engines, and I had heard of them thirty years earlier when I was still on the farm in Belle Plaine. I was truly honored to meet them.

Back in the United States it appeared best to take things a little slowly with Frank and Larry as there were a few red flags that showed up in England. To initiate a relationship, Larry said he would do some preliminary drawings of the Super X for a reasonable price. After thinking it over, the price looked fair, and so he was given the green light.

After numerous design conversations, the drawings arrived a month later. They looked exactly like a Harley, except with a Weslake type motor in it. We were dumbfounded. It was simply a Harley with a different motor. Not good. These drawings also never saw daylight.

About this time, Frank and Larry were itching to get a contract signed and collect their first check for two hundred grand—the pressure tactics were starting. I was thinking Larry might start punching someone. Things didn't look too good for the start of a relationship. Time to change direction. That was the last I ever saw or heard from either of them.

I honestly don't think they were really planning to take us for a ride, but it seemed that way at the time. It just didn't work out the way we each expected, and I think they were just trying to have fun, at our expense.

# 7

## Get Your Motor Running—
## Creating The High-Octane Heart

*This next section is about the engine and is oriented a little toward the gearhead—it may be tougher reading for the non-gearheads, but I will keep it simple—and it is important to the company, the motorcycle, and the story.*

While the company was moving forward on the initial styling of the motorcycle, it was also time to figure out the engine situation. We had to have an engine, and we had to have our own. Also, I knew this would be the single most expensive part of the plan, with the longest lead time. A lot of money. A lot of time. And few engine design firms in the world to choose from.

Some would question: Why have your own engine? Well, for many reasons. First, every OEM in the motorcycle industry had their own engines, and everyone knew it. It wasn't accepted in the marketplace at all to not have your own. The engine is the heart of the bike and gives it its soul. It is the genuine start of brand building. No faking allowed here.

Second, with a motorcycle, the engine sits in the frame exposed for the world to see—unlike a car—and is right between the rider's legs. This makes it very visible, and if you had someone else's engine in your bike, the customers and the industry would know that. The market would just say, well there's that "X" bike with a Honda engine. In other words, not proprietary, and not good if you are trying to build your own brand.

Third, no OEM has sold complete engines to another company to use in their bikes, and they sure weren't lining up to sell them to us. There were no available twin cylinder engines in the marketplace for us to use at the time. Many reasons for this, some make sense and some don't, but that is the industry.

Plus, engines aren't universal. An engine from one OEM motorcycle manufacturer won't fit in the frame of another. If they were all universal and fit each other, we would all have homogenized product. As humans, that would be the same thing if we were all clones of one another—a generic commodity—and no unique characteristics.

Keep in mind the motorcycle industry has been around for over one hundred years (and in three centuries) so there are certain things that take time to change. In fact the word change has a unique meaning in the industry. Not changing much—or changing in increments—is part of the culture of motorcycling. There is history, nostalgia, tradition, and the reverence of time working here. Time to slow down and check out from when the world is moving too fast.

On the one hand we *had* to have our own engine, and on the other we *wanted* to have our own engine. The company was launched as a future OEM, and no reason to abandon the Plan.

It was time to do more homework. Initial research indicated there were a few engine development companies in the world who just might be able to help out. Primarily, one in Texas, several in Detroit, and several in Europe. Plus there were some firms we contacted that said they could design an engine for us, but they had never designed a complete one before, just components—too much risk for us to consider.

Most of the engine quotes were coming in at several million dollars with a two- to four-year development period. This cost and time frame were similar to those projected in the Plan, but this was a big decision and all avenues had to be explored, and possibly dual-tracked to ensure success.

It was during this same time period, when all the homework was going on regarding the engine, that we met Frank and Larry and had our England fact-finding trip.

We now knew the Weslake engine guys in England. Weslake had been founded in England during the mid 1930s by Harry Weslake, who had built quite a reputation for himself and his company by designing engines for automobiles, motorcycles and aircraft. Like most passionately driven technical people, Harry and his company had tremendous highs and lows over the years, depending upon the receipt of engineering contracts, and of their engines winning races. Suffice it to say that Harry was probably better suited for his technical prowess with engines than for focusing on the art of the business.

Throughout the years, Harry and his firm worked with many OEM manufacturers, both in the United States and in Europe, notably Jaguar Motors, Ford Motor Corporation, Triumph and Norton Motorcycles, and with Chrysler Corporation on the design of their new "426 Hemi" engine in the mid 1960s. The "Hemi" engine took the world by storm and is still legendary today. Many an American racer in the mid 1960s remembers the famous Gurney/Weslake racecars, driven by the racer Dan Gurney.

There is a book published about Harry titled *Lucky All My Life*. Although he passed away in his early-80s, a few weeks after watching one of his new motorcycle engines win a race, some say he left this world with a smile on his face.

I never had the chance to meet Harry, but I felt like I knew him through my awe for his accomplishments, and the lore that was passed on from those who had firsthand experience. I was told that Harry's passion was for motorcycles, and in particular motorcycle engines.

It was during a lull in Weslake's business contracts during the late 1970s and into the early 1980s that the firm took it upon themselves to design a motorcycle engine in order to keep themselves busy. There were several variations of their newly designed engine, including single cylinder and V-twins, and with pushrods or dual overhead camshafts. They aptly named their new motorcycle engines Weslake.

This engine series quickly became the force to reckon with in European motorcycle races. The engine's glory was summarized in a book titled, *Winning Motorcycle Engines*, in which 14 of the world's most significant motorcycle engines were profiled. Quite an accomplishment. All other engines listed in the book were built by established, well-known OEM motorcycle manufacturers, except for the engine designed and built by this little company in the southern part of England.

The Weslake company had been designing air-cooled fuel injected dual overhead camshaft engines for so long that it was routine to them, although still relatively new for the rest of the OEM motorcycle industry. The Weslake motorcycle engine, after proving itself on the racetrack, was offered for sale, but was never sold to an OEM. It was put on the shelf as other new contracts came and went.

Harry passed on the business to his capable apprentice and son-in-law, Michael Daniels. It was Michael that I was introduced to and had the occasion to get to know well.

Michael is an easy guy to get to know, as long as you have gas and oil in your veins. He is fairly intense on his tasks. On the surface he is a friendly and amiable English chap, but do not underestimate his competitiveness and resolve. He doesn't mind being underestimated.

In initiating a dialogue with Michael and the Weslake company, we found they were now in a lull in their contracts and possibly in a downsized mode from their earlier, more prosperous years. But the good can-do attitude and optimism were still there—along with several of their employees and equipment that had to have been there for the last 30 to 40 years. Their history was evident.

Weslake gave us a quote on designing a new engine and it was in line with the other estimates we had received from other firms. But, in this case, they had a new suggestion—why not dust off the engine they had designed ten years earlier, and freshen up the design to our current needs. Now this was an interesting proposal and needed closer scrutiny and thought. Several positives and negatives to consider.

Handled correctly, this would be a great boon, since we would have a proven engine design, a shorter lead time, with less cost and a more predictable result, i.e., a higher probability of getting a working engine on time and on budget.

Mishandled though, it could be a marketing and timeline disaster. The core of my vision for Excelsior-Henderson was to have our own proprietary American motorcycle, including the engine. Even though all OEM motorcycle manufacturers utilized components from international suppliers, since we were the new OEM kid on the block, I believed we—and/or the origin of the engine—might be more closely scrutinized, or possibly over scrutinized in the marketplace.

Also, Weslake was in a financial bind and a fragile company existence in their own right. Not unusual for engineering design companies, but if their financial challenges impacted their ability to complete our agreements, then we could be doomed in the middle of a task, and have lost a ton of money and time. It could be terminal to the business. This was where some otherwise simple solutions might not be so simple, because there might have been some undesirable consequences down the road that would be hard to predict.

Weslake was at a point in their company life where the larger and more established OEM manufacturers were choosing to work with larger design firms, and probably felt that Weslake was too much of a business risk, as opposed to a skill risk. At Excelsior, I already knew we were a great risk, and had to strongly think through adding more risk to the equation. But maybe, just maybe, the two underdog organizations could work together and become stronger. The arrogance of working with the larger organizations was difficult to handle, but with Weslake they were just modestly confident. That spoke volumes.

My philosophy of *"Live to Fight Another Day"* was too overwhelming. We were too young of a company and had to make some of our decisions on what was right for today, and then try to manage any future consequences, if any. It was a roll of the dice, and the odds were in favor of Michael Daniels and his team at Weslake Motors.

We engaged Weslake during 1994 to work with us on the development of our first engines and they also had access to a transmission we could initially use. The agreement our company had with Weslake was for an upfront payment for all of the rights and tooling to their former Weslake motorcycle engine(s), and for contracting their engineering services to modify the design and create new tooling to fit the specifications for our engine. With a bit of luck and skill along the way, we hoped to have our new engines running within the next eighteen months—in 1996.

This was a great way to jump-start our engine design and gave us confidence that we would have our own engine that no one else was using or could use. Plus, the engine did have a reputable past, although now forgotten except in the racing history books.

The engine design with some modifications was just as I'd hoped. The basic platform of the Weslake engine was a 50 degree V-twin cylinder, air cooled, dual overhead cam, four valve and either carbureted or fuel injected. The original designs were also of a short stroke and were high revving engines, capable of over 10,000 rpm and over 150 horsepower—to some degree a great air-cooled sport bike engine, but we were entering the cruiser and touring class of motorcycles where the engines were more low revving and high torque driven. By most standards, these are good strong specifications, but in our case, we were looking for a motor with a longer stroke, and so we basically had Michael and Weslake redesign the motor to a longer stroke, which resulted in more torque, but less horsepower. This also gave our engines the desirable deeper sounding exhaust. The rumble. The one you feel before you hear it.

Keep in mind here that Weslake was an engine design company, not an engine manufacturing company. On several occasions Michael reminded us of that fact—they only preferred to work on the creative side of building something, and after making about 20 prototypes of something, they were done. The next step was manufacturing, and they considered that boring, and certainly not in their area of interest. After the final designs were prototyped, tested and approved, we still had to manufacture them, or find someone to do it for us, or a combination of both.

The engine design we were embarking on with Weslake was significantly different than what was available from any of the other OEM motorcycle manufacturers, and most significantly, it was worlds apart from the current Harley engines. I liked that. We had our own differentiating characteristics—unique—and arguably better.

I was convinced that Harley and others in a few short years would also be redesigning their motors more in our configuration. I am not saying here that I thought they and others would follow our direction, but rather I believed the consumers were on the cusp of demanding more modern technology in their motorcycles, and we were poised to meet it, and other OEMs were probably contemplating it. Since the competitors were larger, more mature firms, they were researching what we had already set out to do. And I knew that once the new direction was set in the industry, they could all quickly react, which they did. None of them wanted the underdog to surpass them.

The decision to go with the Weslake design was not a popular decision within Excelsior initially. Some wanted it to be more like the traditional Harley engine. I didn't. I liked how it was different and—in my opinion—better, since I am a bit of a performance driven guy, and always looking for ways to legitimately differentiate ourselves from the competition—not only the Japanese manufacturers, but Harley as well. Early on, these others thought we should not stray too far from the Harley design, but most of them were more steeped in the history of Harley than I was. I was more open-minded on the issue, but the jury was still out on whether we were headed down the right track. Fortunately, we all later determined we were on the right track, and the further we progressed in the business, the more we realized the company had to build its own identity and brand, and not follow the leader. Instead, be the new leader, in new directions. We may not lead by volume, but we could lead by innovation and creativity. The marketplace was large enough to support new directions. In hindsight, it was a good move.

When we launched the redesign of the former Weslake engine in 1994, it was going to be the largest, most powerful OEM manufactured cruiser motorcycle engine in the world. Five years later in 1999 when we hit production, it no longer was. The competition had found out what we were up to, and had decided to do something about it. While they were criticizing our efforts and designs, some of them were also privately adopting them and seeking to one-up-it—no surprise here.

# 8

## *Writing Our Own Rulebook*

*F*iguring out a way to properly reintroduce the brand of Excelsior-Henderson was an interesting challenge. I thought at the time that our brand marketing plan was well crafted from the start, but in reality, it evolved over time. And maybe that's what made it more genuine.

The Excelsior-Henderson of old was known as an innovator in the industry and dared to be uniquely itself. There was no reason to change that position for the new. It was a great concept in the *early* 1900s, and it certainly was a concept that stood the test of time to be adopted for use in the *late* 1900s. So we adopted it.

The new Excelsior-Henderson was founded as a company with an attitude—probably reflecting my attitude as the founder—and I believed it important that we enter the motorcycle industry as a change agent. We weren't planning on quietly entering the motorcycle industry and then waiting for a reaction from them on what they thought. Nor did we plan on asking for their permission. It wouldn't be too hard to figure out their reaction.

By a change agent, I mean we weren't entering the industry to play by industry rules and be just another "me-too" OEM manufacturer of motorcycles. I didn't want us to be just another box of cereal on the grocery shelf—kind of ho hum news. The industry had been too mature and product stable for some time; it needed a little shaking up, along with a little more intensity and passion re-introduced to it. My goal would be that the industry would never be the same after our entry into it—at least that was my opinion on the matter.

The motorcycle industry is a mature industry, and as with many industries, there are industry rules that to a great degree everyone follows, in part because over a period of time they've written the rulebook. By objectively studying the industry, my primary goal was to have our company rewrite the rulebook. I knew if we tried to follow their rulebook, they would win since they wrote and could rewrite the rules at anytime. Instead, we needed to write our own rulebook, and be damned with anyone else's. In other words, let's cut our own path in the industry, and for those who were up to the challenge, let them join our pilgrimage.

So we had no problem with setting out to be different in the industry. Later, that was sometimes misunderstood, but all it really meant was that we were comfortable being our own company and didn't need to imitate anyone else. We didn't mind learning from them, though. Besides, it would have to be that way in some respect. It was unrealistic to expect the industry to embrace us, particularly the OEMs. They were all fierce competitors and didn't seek to help one another, and they certainly weren't going to offer us any help. Nor did they ever. The only time I witnessed them working together was when they all ganged up on a possible new entrant, like us. Then they had something they could all rally around, and they would and did. Privately, I wished they had stuck a little more to their own knitting.

Excelsior-Henderson was founded with humble beginnings in the basement of my home, and espousing the values that I believe in—like the company mission and principles—it was only natural that we would gravitate towards being a grassroots company. For some reason, that is where it felt right to be. Therefore, it was important that we endeavor to recruit people who also believed in a grassroots driven organization, and especially important to recruit marketing and communications firms who had this as their expertise.

There was a guy who I thought could help us early on whom I'd met as a result of the previous company I had launched. His name was Jack Klobucar and he was a founding partner in the Added Value marketing firm in Edina, Minnesota.

A few years earlier Jack had been hired by a competitor of mine to analyze my previous business and what we were doing since we were taking market share away from our competitors, and at a higher price. I just love that—adding enough value to a manufactured product that you can actually sell it at a higher price than the competition. You know then that your customers are recognizing the value of the service and brand that goes along with the product. So I met Jack in a roundabout way since he worked for a competitor, but I liked his levelheaded practical knowledge and his personal style.

Anyway, Jack and his firm had experience in the motorsports industry—they'd worked with Bombardier of Canada and Ford Motors in Detroit, and they seemed to actually understand our business objective.

Our firm initially engaged Jack for two primary tasks: first, to conduct formal market research on the industry as it related to a new entrant, and second, to break out the marketing section of the Business

Plan and create a more detailed marketing strategy and implementation timeline.

Working with his firm, we put together what we called a "Pre-Production Integrated Marketing Plan." Our reason for doing this was that we had not yet designed a motorcycle, nor had we raised outside capital, and production was still five years away. I wanted to use those five years effectively by educating the market on the company. I knew this would be difficult because technically we would have no product to show anyone for several years.

But we did have something that only one other motorcycle manufacturer in the world had. Our brand had a rich American heritage—genuine—and other than Harley-Davidson, no one else had it, nor could they create it. American heritage in the motorcycle industry is important, especially if you make it so. Some bikers will buy based *only* on this distinguishing characteristic.

The motorcycle manufacturers that didn't have any American heritage—i.e. foreign brands—would obviously downplay the importance of it since they didn't have any, and sought to build their brands by focusing on their bike and pricing. My viewpoint: there is opportunity in the industry for many types of brands and marketing, but why give up an advantage if you have it? We were a small company and needed every advantage we could create. We were part of the diamond mines, not the cubic zirconias.

The "Pre-Production Integrated Marketing Plan" that we put together with Jack was the baseline strategy and implementation plan for brand marketing of the company that we would use as a reference for years to come. I remember years later and millions of dollars later, as our marketing department grew and implementation got more complicated, I would still pull out the original plan we had with Jack and refer to it as a reference guide.

The other item we needed immediately from Jack was some formal market research. Now I'm not always a proponent of formal market research as it relates to product development and new ideas, because sometimes those in the industry, and consumers, aren't initially receptive to new ideas, and then the research report oftentimes gets sanitized before it reaches the product development area. I generally believe in more hands-on type research, and ongoing daily research with customers and new prospects, so that instinct can be developed and then acted upon.

I'll give you an example here. Could you imagine if one hundred years ago Henry Ford had interviewed horse riders in a livery stable and asked them what they thought about a new creation he was working on that would be called a *"horseless carriage, and had tiller rods to steer with rather than reins, and you would put petrol from a filling station into the gas tank, rather than oats from a bin in a livery stable...?"* Maybe you get my drift here. The horse riders would think he was nuts and he would be run out of town. It was just too much change for a person to comprehend verbally. Until they saw it, and saw it in use, and saw others using it, over a period of time—*then* they might be convinced.

What I mean here is that you should research, but be very careful in who and how you are interviewing, and what is going to be done with the information. And be careful about where you are in the development cycle when conducting the different types of research. Try a balance between research and instinct. If competing companies only relied on research, then everybody's product would be the same. Which today, in some industries, they are, since they rely too much on formal research.

Also, in theory and practicality, the research should substantiate the underlying Business Plan; it was important for prospective investors to know that formal research was conducted. Even though I had researched the industry myself, and repeatedly interviewed industry-related parties and consumers, some would think the research had little value because I didn't pay myself. So for many reasons, it was an appropriate time to hire an outside firm for research.

It was with this frame of mind that we conducted some formal market research with some dealers in the industry. We anonymously observed from behind a one-way glass screen as the interviewer asked questions of dealers. This was interesting, but nothing alarming. Most had never heard of the old Excelsior-Henderson brand, and they also unilaterally believed that we should build bikes that looked just like a Harley, and then sell it for less. Now that would be a hard thing to do.

Fortunately, we did have enough substantive information that supported the premises in the Business Plan, and the formal research validated that just fine. We could now check that part off and keep moving forward.

Another thing we learned from this was seeing some dealers in action. From this initial research group we ultimately recruited one dealer to be on our Advisory Board, and he remained active in the company for the next six years. Although we didn't know or plan that at the time.

Just before leaving for the Sturgis Motorcycle Rally in 1994, Jack had a graphics and apparel buddy of his make up some Excelsior-Henderson T-shirts. They were nothing wild, but they were our first T-shirts, and he surprised me by doing that—I'll never forget it. And I don't think he billed us for it either.

I proudly wore that T-shirt all over Sturgis—and didn't get one comment. In seven days, over two hundred thousand bikers, and not one comment. Hmm…I knew we had our brand work cut out for us. Little did I know, that just two years later, in 1996, if you wore an Excelsior-Henderson T-shirt at the Sturgis Rally, you would not get a moment's rest. You would always be the center of attention and be asked questions. I would have to don a Harley shirt just to blend in and be ignored. How fast things can change, or just maybe we were executing some good grassroots brand marketing.

Part of our marketing plan was to use the next few years of product development time to market the historic aspect of our brand. Witnessing the difference in reaction from motorcyclists at the Sturgis Rally in just two years told me we were on the right track, grassroots style.

I am not sure what ever happened to our business relationship with Jack and his firm, but over a period of time, some people in our company apparently recommended that we quit working with his firm. What I have noticed is that sometimes as companies grow and new personalities develop, change happens. All I know is that during the important formative very early stages of the company, he and his firm did a great job. But we did test each other.

Another thing I learned early on in marketing, particularly motorcycles, is that *everyone is an expert!* Later, marketing firms and individuals who claimed they would make us the next Harley-Davidson were constantly contacting us. I would ask them if they rode a motorcycle or had ever brand marketed in the motorcycle industry. Their answer was the same—no—but they could still do it for us, and with our money to train them! That didn't sound like the type of assistance I was looking for.

But we did get a call from someone who answered yes to those questions, and we'll learn more about him later.

# 9

## Fuel-Injecting A Start-Up With Cash

The company, Hanlon Manufacturing, was privately financed by myself in 1993. The next year, 1994, was the first year we received outside private investment. During the subsequent six-year period, from 1994 thru 1999, the company raised about $95 million. If you divide that out, it is about $1.3 million per month, for seventy-two months, each and every month. And every dollar raised, was raised while the company was in negative cash flow. Try raising money for a new manufacturing company that will manufacture its products here in America—a double negative: manufacturing, and American manufacturing. This is not exciting stuff to the venture capitalists and the Wall Street crowd—at least it wasn't during the 1990s.

During this same six-year time period, the capital was raised in various rounds, or closings, that corresponded to the company achieving certain milestones, and if we were fortunate enough, we would use the accomplishment of the milestone as a precursor to seek another round of financing in order to then accomplish the next milestone, and so on. Simply put, after the accomplishment of set milestones, we would raise enough money that we projected would get us to the next milestone. It wasn't that we desired to raise money in this fashion, but rather we were unable to raise enough capital at one time to do it any other way.

We had sixteen significant rounds of financing in this time period: ten equity transactions, and six debt transactions. Dividing this out, we averaged a $6 million closing every 4.5 months. Just stop to think about this, as I often did and do. Closing on $6 million every 4.5 months for six years, while in negative cash flow. It was stressful, and not fun. I think for every day, I aged two.

We basically never had more capital than looking out into the future for 4.5 months. What that meant to me was every 4.5 months the company was going to be out of business. After the close of each financing round, invariably someone would say to me that I must feel good now that we had some financial breathing room. I didn't know how to answer that, since the company had just gone from being nearly dead, to now given 4.5 months to live. To me it meant I had about 4 months to figure out the next form of lifeblood for the company.

Arranging financing for a venture like this is complicated. Each round of financing is independent of each other, yet they are interdependent on one another. If you set some crazy terms in one transaction, it may impact the next, or severely cripple a transaction several years down the road. Each financing transaction had to take into account the previous investments, and also any subsequent transactions, which we all knew would be occurring, but none of us knew what it would look like until we got there, if we did. So strategically, we had to spend a lot of time agonizing over the structure of each deal, that would make it appropriate for the current and past investors, and not jeopardize the interest of future investors.

Probably the most overbearing issue regarding each of the sixteen financing transactions was the fact that after each and every one, if there was not another one, it meant the *"party was over."* Finished. Done. At any time over these sixteen rounds of financing, if the next round did not come in, the company was gone. I knew this, the Road Crew Team Members in our company knew this, and the investors in each transaction knew this. They were putting their money in knowing it would not get us to cash flow positive. In other words, their money would be spent, with no guarantee of a future round. Talk about faith and support of willing this to happen.

Early in 1993 I knew the company would be forced into financing on a milestone basis. I didn't know how many or when, but that it would be learned as the execution of the Business Plan unfolded, one day at a time. I never said it at the time, but I thought if the company was going to fail to raise money, it would happen long before we hit production. There were too many bumps in the road ahead during the next six years. But I tried not to focus on that, and instead focused on accomplishing each task that we set out to do. Privately, I thought if—God willing—we could reach production, we would be able to raise the money to stay in production.

The fundraising started out slow in 1994. The United States was just coming out of a dip in the economy. After some early advice, we put together a Private Placement Memorandum (PPM) for a $1 million investment at $2.50 per share. We had no investment bankers, no venture capitalists, and no private angel financiers at this point.

After months of slogging through phone calls and meetings with prospective investors, it was time to give up. The Memorandum was put together while the company was still in the basement of my house and now that the company had progressed further; the timing of the document was getting stale. We never had any momentum on it—it was time to put it to rest and relaunch with a new one.

We had about $65,000 of outside investment funding and that was it. And all of it from family, friends, or referrals. Not a good start. With this first outside round of financing, the company now totaled ten investors, including myself, my four brothers, two distant relatives, one friend from my Rotary Club, and two referrals. Not a glorious start, but one step better than when I was the sole shareholder. Feeling somewhat embarrassed by the lack of investment interest, I decided to lower the price per share from $2.50 to $0.50, and closed on the $65,000. In just five years, this investment would be worth nearly ten times as much, but none of us knew that at the time. So, our million dollar offering grossed us $65,000, and after legal and accounting fees, we might have netted about half that. Already a good lesson about legal and accounting fees. Necessary, but comparatively costly on small transactions.

Immediately after closing on this round and issuing the new stock, it was time to commence another offering since the company was making some milestone progress, and we were now smarter. This next round was not planned for a million dollars, but rather the Private Placement Memorandum was drafted for a more modest total of $240,000 at $0.60 per share. Based on some things we had learned from the previous transaction, this amount and price seemed to be in line with investor interest.

This time it worked better. In less than two months, we were able to close out this second round for a total of $540,000—about $300,000 more than we had projected! This was great news and a real boost to our confidence. We gained about 40 additional investors to the company.

These new investors included most of my family, and my wife Carol's family, including her parents. We were all committed now. None of them were large investors as we all had modest backgrounds and careers, but the significance of having them involved meant something. It also meant we had better give this a good run, otherwise it wasn't going to be very pleasant around the holiday times—but I don't think it was really about the money anyway. They were all just trying to help, and they did. Within the next five years, the investment would grow exponentially by a factor of nine, but we never talked about whether any of them sold their stock. I still don't know, nor do I need to.

We also brought in this investor named John T. My cousin Milo, who was my barber and also an early investor, networked me to him. From his barbershop chair in Minneapolis, Milo was a good source of referrals, and our families had known each other since our days of growing up together on the farm. He had this guy John call us who wanted to come out and hear the story of the company, and then have lunch. Everything went well and he subsequently invested a sizable amount for that stage of our company.

Several years later I remember John telling me that he couldn't believe how frugal we were. Our offices were low budget, and when we went to lunch, I picked him up in my ten-year-old car, my 1984 Pontiac 6000LE—nicknamed "ole" since the 600 had fallen off—with nearly 200,000 thousand miles on it—but it was in great shape. After seeing this, he offered to buy lunch, so I thought we should splurge, and we went to the closest Subway sandwich shop. It was quick, and low cost, and close enough to get back to the office fast. I don't know whether he ever sold his stock either.

During that same time period, a high school acquaintance of mine, Dave Pomije, also invested, becoming the largest outside investor at that point. He was also my first customer at the previous business I had launched. I remember calling on him for my then-new business, and he asked me if I had any references from customers. I sheepishly had to tell him I didn't have any customers yet, and he said, "Well, I'll be your first customer and now you have a reference." I guess a person never forgets that, do they.

• • •

The last financing transaction during 1994 closed on November 22, and despite the holidays, in just two months a new private equity offering was drafted and *"on the street,"* dated January 30, 1995. If you are familiar with the regulations for complying with the SEC on private placements, you know that drafting and publishing an Offering Memorandum takes at least two months; so you can see from this time-line, the next offering was being kicked off simultaneously with the previous one's closing. I never had a chance to enjoy the closing, as my mind and actions were already strategizing for the next one.

This next financing was going to be a little more fun. We were going to try and raise $4 million privately. It was time to try and attract a few of the heavier hitters, and we needed a larger investment this time. Defying the cries of the critics, the company continued gaining momentum. By frugal attention to the budget, and the effective use of contracting for outside services, we were continuing to knock off milestones. One at a time. And on schedule and on budget. We were doing what we said we would do. When we said we would do it. For how much we said it would cost.

This next offering was a little bit different than our last ones. The execution of the plan was continuing, and per plan, the capital needs were starting to grow exponentially. The offering was drafted for a maximum of $4 million, priced at $1.25 per share. One of the new twists on this document was there was now a new minimum total investment of $500,000 that had to be raised before escrows could be released. What this means is that if you raise up to $499,999 and not a dollar more, the company cannot retain any of the new equity and must return every dollar to the prospective investors. So it was real important that we exceeded raising the minimum, otherwise we would have to contemplate shutting down the company, once again.

Up to and including this time period, we as a company had managed the company's private equity offerings. What this means is we had no investment banker managing or leading the transaction for us. We had to act as our own investment banker, and as both the CEO and CFO, I was becoming well indoctrinated into the world of investment banking. It wasn't that we didn't want an investment banking firm, we just weren't able to attract one. A good one that is.

Once you put out notice that you are looking to raise money, you would be surprised at the people and firms that come out of the woodwork and claim they can help. And I am not talking about the seasoned mature Wall Street companies here, but rather the opposite. Whereas some of them in all sincerity may be successful and ethical, just as many are not. And it is sometimes hard to tell the difference until further due diligence and homework are conducted.

The primary method I learned at the time to differentiate between the real players and those who were out to take our money was that the real players weren't calling us. If someone called making claims to help us raise money in ways that sounded too good to be true, they usually were. Almost always, these types of players required money up front, and I just wasn't buying. I kept thinking, *"Why would I pay you to do something we are already doing, and the reason we are doing it ourselves is because we can't find anyone else credible to do it?"* But we did check out a few, just hoping for some help in raising money.

On one occasion, while looking for investment bankers, we came across a firm in Denver, Colorado. Actually, I think they came across us and were aggressively pursuing "inking" a deal with us—in investment banking it is okay to call a transaction a deal. Denver is sometimes known for its active "penny stock" market and swashbuckling mentality when it comes to investment banking.

The firm, Paramount Investments, was managed by a guy named Terry. He and a few partners were the owners, but as we later learned, Terry couldn't be listed as an owner due to some complications with the SEC, so he was and he wasn't an owner, depending upon whom he was talking to. After the customary mutual visits in which he and a small delegation visited our offices in Burnsville and we in turn visited his business in Denver, it was time to start drafting documents.

During this process, we—our legal and accounting staff and myself—started seeing some red flags, both in the backgrounds of the individuals at Paramount and in their expertise. Even if we completed this deal, there would be too much risk to future transactions because of the way they were attempting to structure it. It was at this same time I had a chance to meet two of the top producers for their company, both brothers from a farm in Nebraska.

I liked these two guys right away, but again, red flags cropped up all over the place. It seems that these two brothers, who were both in their twenties, had left Nebraska for Denver to seek their fortunes in the world of finance. One of them, Bob, seemed to take a liking to our company, and privately told us he was leaving the firm to strike out on his own. I distinctly remember meeting him later in Denver where, as he was driving down the interstate with one hand on the wheel and the other propped outside the open window, he kept telling me how he was going to raise millions for us, and all we had to do was pay him an upfront $50,000 fee to get started.

After a few brief conversations, I asked both Paramount and Bob for some references so I could verify their statements. I never heard from Bob again, and we unhooked from Paramount. Paramount was mad and sent us a nasty letter, with several obvious typos in it. Bad form when you are angry. Later, I read about some troubles with the SEC that Paramount had and their subsequent shutdown.

So, in a way we were anxious to have an investment banking firm lead and manage our offerings, but in a way we were not. We had to have the right one for our company's current status. Generally, if you hooked up with an investment banking firm, it was on an exclusive basis, and if the transaction didn't succeed, you were out of luck and time. In our case, we were in negative cash flow, and if we didn't successfully complete a financing we weren't only out of luck and time, but we were also out of business!

It was in this framework in early 1995 that we engaged a small, somewhat obscure investment banking firm, Capital Management Securities in Minneapolis, to help manage our new $4 million offering. It was a rather unique structure because it was non-exclusive; our company could continue raising capital on its own while engaging other investment bankers, and Capital Management would receive a 1% fee to manage all the paperwork. As a hybrid structure, it seemed to be the best of all worlds, but some investment bankers didn't like it. The structure required them to work together equally, large or small, new or mature. But in the end, through repeated appeals for mutual respect, the respective firms did manage to work well together.

The process, although working great, was off to a slow start. The first several hundred thousand dollars was coming in fast, but unless we hit a half-million dollars, we could not break escrows. The offering began to stall right around $450,000 when a phone call came in that I will never forget. It was from Gale Mellum, our lead attorney, inquiring about how the deal was going. I told him the honest truth: it was going good, but it looked as if it would stall before the half-million dollar mark. He quietly stated that he and a few of his partners were investing. This would now put us over the minimum, and we could break escrows. It was like a call from up above.

I never forgot that call.

Here were lawyers from our legal firm investing money in our venture. Talk about a pleasant surprise. Gale and his law firm, who had worked with us since very early in 1994, would be with the company through good times and bad for the next six years. A lot of these events marked the beginning of long relationships that would be tested through the many struggles ahead. The team was growing and I never knew when I would next be surprised by the willingness of someone to step out and help in tough times. We needed it, and not just lip service.

By August of 1995, it looked as if the offering was about as far along as it could be pushed. The total offering had been ambitiously projected at $4 million, and we had raised just over $3 million, but after six months, momentum was waning. It was time to close it out and keep moving forward. During this same timeframe I brought in an interim person, Jerry Doran, to help bird-dog the financing, and we added another 125 accredited private investors, which brought the total to about 165 people.

Closing out the offering just before the start of the annual Sturgis Motorcycle Rally was perfect timing, and we all headed out with the wind at our backs. It was a great feeling knowing we had just completed a round of financing, and we now took the time to mentally and physically unwind, while still conducting industry research at the Rally. Just before we left, we announced the successful closing by placing a tombstone advertisement in the Wall Street Journal. I didn't expect it at the time, but for the week we were at Sturgis, almost two thousand phone calls came in to the office from the ad. We were finally getting incoming phone calls, and lots of them. This was the start of a new challenge.

We added some great investors in this round: a Nascar driver, an Indy race team owner, Board members and executives from Arctic Cat, a professional All-Star wrestler, a couple of pro football players, OEM motorcycle dealers, motorcycle industry people, a Chicago radio personality, several owners of manufacturing companies, several entrepreneurs, and even one gentleman, a banker, who was in his eighties. The momentum was building again.

Some fun stories came from meeting all these prospective investors. After an introductory phone conversation, we would schedule private meetings at the office to go through the company story with them. Sometimes these were one-on-one meetings, and sometimes they were in small groups. We even had several doctors who invested, even though they didn't ride motorcycles. I remember one doctor explaining to me that he was concerned because he thought the motorcycle industry was dangerous and that it killed people. Being a bit bold by nature, I just smiled and looked him in the eye, and politely told him that his industry did too.

During this financing round, a successful motorsports dealer from Chicago became interested in the venture, and between himself, his brother, and many of their friends, they put in about a million dollars of the $3 million total. The dealer who led this investment network, Ted Nielsen, remained involved with the company throughout the anticipated tough times ahead, and ultimately became one of our earliest and best dealers. Ted was the kind of guy with whom you could have a reasonably strong conversation on opposed issues and still remain friends. He never wavered like some others did on the tough road that followed.

It was through Ted that I had a chance to meet Bernie Weber. Bernie was a stockbroker in Minneapolis who had a lot of contacts, and between his contacts and Ted's contacts, they contributed a lot to this round of financing. Bernie was a unique individual—always smiling or laughing—who stood about six feet tall and wore ill-fitting suits with his tennis shoes. When we closed our deal, I tried to get those shoes off of him so I could have them bronzed, but he wouldn't give them up.

There were also two guys who came in on this round who, between them, invested three quarters of a million dollars. Just two guys: Ralph B. and Richard N. They were in their mid to late sixties, had built prosperous businesses from humble beginnings, and had been friends since high school. What I remember most about meeting these guys is that they had great can-do attitudes.

Before he invested, Ralph was busy doing his homework on our venture, and called a meeting at his office. He kicked off the meeting, and indicated he had done some homework on the Hanlons from Belle Plaine, and found out our large farm family was a little wild growing up in the rural countryside—motorcycles and fast cars with flame paint jobs, doing burnouts on the state highway. We even had our own quarter-mile track marked off. After we discussed this briefly and seriously, he looked me in the eye, and asked a little sternly, "Well, what do you have to say about this?" I'm not afraid of the truth, and I responded, "Damn proud of every minute of it, and I would do it again if I could!" He just chuckled, and told me about his days growing up when he was also a bit untamed.

I later found out his source of information was one of his employees, a former neighbor of mine who grew up on an adjoining farm. What a small world.

By this time I had already told the Excelsior-Henderson story over five hundred times, and had heard many objections and questions about the venture. The ones from non-motorcyclists were the best, like "Why would someone ride a motorcycle?" That's a hard one to explain to someone who doesn't ride a motorcycle—remember the old saying, *"If I have to explain, you won't understand."* I would suggest to them, the next time you're driving home from work, roll down your window and stick your head out into the wind. Your car won't feel the same and neither will you—you'll look and feel different, and people will look at you funny. Good. If that doesn't do something for you, then I can't explain it any better than that. Try it sometime.

We've already talked about how some, if not most, motorcyclists have an attitude. Not a bad attitude, just an attitude. And yes, motorcycling is inherently dangerous. Motorcyclists and motorcycling are a bit of a study in contrasts, and I've often been quoted as saying: "Motorcycling is the safest most dangerous thing you can do, or, the most dangerous safest thing you can do." It is a bit on the edge, and that's okay.

• • •

Let me tell you a little story about our company stock certificates that I don't think ever got fully explained. We had some pretty neat stock certificates. Ignatz Schwinn owned the former Chicago-based Excelsior-Henderson Company until the Great Depression in 1931. I was able to buy from an antique collector an original stock certificate signed by Ignatz himself. Late one night I was working in my office and having a beer; it had to be around midnight. I needed a diversion, and I was looking at the original stock certificate when my mind started wandering back in time. On the very bottom of the stock certificate, in small print, was the name GOES Printing. I hit the speaker button on my telephone and dialed information for Chicago, thinking that just maybe Schwinn used a printing company in Chicago, and just maybe seventy years later they might still be in business. A long shot, but I play long shots.

After dialing several times, I got an information operator who was helpful, and when she finally located a company named GOES, she gave me the number. I put the number aside and headed home, thinking that if I had a few minutes the next day I would ring them up.

The next day I called the number and a live person answered the phone. Rare. After introducing myself I proceeded to inform the receptionist about my quest for these stock certificates. She wasn't biting, and tried to get me off the phone. "Good grief," she finally said in exasperation, "they are over sixty years old!" But I persisted, and finally, in a bit of desperation since I thought she was going to hang up on me, I asked if she had anyone working there who was in their sixties, seventies or eighties. I know how printers are; once they get ink in their veins, they are into printing forever, and I was hopeful to stumble into someone who might have the time and the inclination to step back in time.

Luck was with me. The receptionist's voice perked up as she realized she could get rid of me and she exclaimed, "Yes, we have a guy here who is in his late seventies and just won't retire. I'll transfer you to him." Well, to make a long story short, over a several week period of time, he was able to recall and found the original plates and stock certificates from the old Schwinn company.

With some very minor modifications to fit the current legal rules and our corporate legal name, we were able to use the original style of certificate. We began using that stock certificate in 1994, and it was the only certificate we had for common stock from that point forward. When we went public in 1997, the stock transfer agent indicated that the certificate was not in a format they could use on their computers. I love that, when someone says they can't do something because the computer won't let them: Who is in control here? After a little coaxing, and a reminder of who is the more dominant species—a computer or a human—they were able to get their systems to accept the certificates.

• • •

Since inception through the end of 1995, we raised over $3.5 million in total equity capital, and it was enough to continue executing milestones to the Plan. There was more fuel in the fuel tank, and we had to race to the next milestone.

We now had 165 sales people in the field—private investors—telling our story. Most of these investors we'd met personally before they invested and had encouraged them to join the dream of building a new American motorcycle company. And they did, and told others about it.

# 10

## The Right Riders—Our Advisors

We also began to see the emergence of an outside advisory group that was starting to naturally develop, and it felt like the right time to formally set up an outside/inside team to help advise the venture. This was something that I had given a lot of thought to, long before the company was even officially launched. There is nothing like the reality of experience as a teacher, and I had learned some things from starting my last company. I don't know whether I would classify what I had learned as bad or good, but I certainly had an enlightened perspective.

My previous company, EverGreen Solutions, was launched to manufacture a newly invented packaging product that was designed to compete against an old mature product line. Accordingly, we had to struggle to raise capital, get into production, and then slowly build our sales—which we did. I also learned that things don't always get executed to the anticipated timelines and budgets, especially when you are an independent company inventing things. We simply lacked the financial and staffing resources and oftentimes needed a heck of a lot of luck to improvise a solution to a problem that just came up. This is very different than a mature company with momentum. We had no momentum and had to create it.

Early on at EverGreen, I was advised to create a solid Board of Directors, as that would help me raise money and help give advice to the company. So I set out to do that, and for a young underfunded company, we actually attracted some well-respected local business people. I was pretty pleased with that.

I quickly learned there were some unique dynamics occurring also. All of the Directors were investors in the company and had been chosen from the small pool of shareholders. One of them was a partner in a venture capital firm. The venture capitalist wanted to have monthly Board meetings, so we did. That meant every 22 business days I would have to prepare for a Board meeting. If you have ever been the Chairman of the Board, and the CEO, and running a small start-up company, there is no one who can practically assist you in preparing for the meetings. I had to do it mostly myself, and it took a lot of time and energy, and wound up being distracting to the company. I spent almost as much time preparing for the meeting as I did running the company.

Not only that, we had more members on our Board of Directors than we had employees in the company. Think about that. We had more people sitting in the makeshift boardroom telling us what to do, than there were people doing it. A few of our employees and I would privately chuckle a little bit about that. There is no substitute for the old saying, *"many hands make light work."*

Well we didn't have many hands. Our company by plan was too small. All of our Board members were either retired or current executives of a large corporation. The retired ones seemed to have a lot of time on their hands and would have wonderful stories, whereas the executives from the larger companies seemed to expect our small army to accomplish what their big army did. It just all seemed not too productive for me, and I take the responsibility for that. After all, I was the CEO and founder, and I set up the Board. I had just set it up wrong.

I might not have been paying enough attention to some of the nuances of the different personalities and styles and life status. I liked all these guys and they were trying to help. But I found successful people sometimes have a fairly well-developed ego, and I needed to do a better job of picking styles and experiences that would work well together. Oftentimes relationships can be developed over time, but in a small company there is no time. You start from nothing, and then go. There is no continuity or momentum unless you create it, so I learned the hard way to do more homework on the people side of things. What I learned was that even though it is awfully lonely starting a company, you have to be very selective in recruiting the talent you want to work with.

At one of the last Board meetings I chaired at EverGreen, this older, wiser, more wealthy gentleman named Dick C. was again berating me. He knew everything, or so it seemed, and he was being dogmatic on how most everything we did was wrong, smugly pointing out problem after problem, but worse yet, not offering up any solutions that could be implemented. Any solution I suggested, he cast aside. With the approving nods of the fellow outside Board members, he looked me sternly in the eye and said, "We'll have another Board meeting next week, and you had better come up with some good solutions."

Well, I came up with a good solution. I sold the company. In spite of the strong overpowering Board, I was majority stockholder. I made some quick phone calls, and in a few short days struck a deal for the sale. At the next Board meeting I had a solution that no one liked. Yet they should have liked it; they all averaged a 40% return on their investment in just a year.

They say you sometimes have seller's remorse. If I did, it didn't last long. There was a little legal tussle with some Board members, but my position prevailed. Afterward, Dick the Board member called me up and asked if I would pay his legal bills, which amounted to over $15,000. I smiled inwardly—I had been deprived of my company, I had no job, a new family to raise, and was living in an apartment. I was glad to let him know, "I'll think about it," as I hung up the phone and headed to the countryside to celebrate Saint Patrick's Day in my hometown of Belle Plaine.

• • •

Based upon these and other experiences, I believed it was very important to be selective when setting up a Board of Directors for Excelsior-Henderson. Legally, the company was Hanlon Manufacturing Company, and I was the CEO and CFO, and Chairman of the Board, and the largest shareholder. Excelsior-Henderson had been set up as a division of the parent company. With a large Board of Directors comes a lot of formality and liability, which I thought the company didn't need yet. I kept the Board small, but I still wanted to have the advice and accountability that outsiders could bring. In that context, the concept of formally establishing a Board of Advisors was created.

In setting up an advisory board, there was little experience to draw from in the marketplace, so I primarily patterned the Board of Advisors to be quite similar to a Board of Directors. We operated it about the same. Routine, formal meetings with agendas and meeting minutes, and a formal review of the budgets and progress reports on the company. Most of us wore suits or business casual. I was serious about getting good, practical, usable advice, along with the power of a true debate that only a synergistic group can provide, without the legal liability and posturing that sometimes occurs with a Board of Directors. A secondary and equally important benefit: the Advisory Board may provide appropriate candidates for the future expanded Board of Directors.

The Advisory Board, set up in 1995, consisted of six outside individuals with whom we had been networked or we had worked with on company projects. Since I had laid the plan several years earlier, I was always on the lookout for prospective members for when the time was right to set it up. I was seeking talented team players for all the various disciplines that I thought our company would need as it grew, from financing to manufacturing to sales, etc. This way a person wouldn't have to start from ground zero, but rather since the homework was done, we could just start pushing buttons when the time was right.

I always believed that in order for the company to be successful, we had to have the "A-Team." Even though we were a young struggling company, and most of the firms we worked with were larger and profitable, I always requested to work with their A-Team. Oftentimes the response was their entire company was the A-Team. But I knew better, and so did they. We proceeded getting the A-Team. I was convinced we had to be working with the best, the brightest, and the toughest in order for our venture to succeed—and more importantly, they had to be good people and have a good teamwork style. These qualities had to hold true for our Advisory Board as well.

The Board of Advisors consisted of the following people: Butch Donahue, Wayne Fortun, Carl Haas, Gale Mellum, Jim Morrell, and Ron Sackett. I also invited Earl Klein to attend, even though he was not an official member.

If you had to describe Butch Donahue in one word, it would have to be "Rebel." His record speaks for itself, since he is so modest he won't tell you about it. He's been a motorcycle dealer since the mid 1950s, and has been elected to the Dealer Advisory Council for Arctic Cat, Kawasaki, and was recently the President of the Harley-Davidson Dealer Council. He's a street-smart grassroots guy, and can cut through the bullshit in an effective manner.

Wayne Fortun was a bull-rider turned CEO. His $500 million publicly held company manufactured precision suspension assemblies for disk drives in computers. And they had the largest market share. He worked his way up the company, and was acutely knowledgeable about all facets of a manufacturing driven company. He had intensity, and an equally team driven tactful style—and he rode motorcycles.

Carl Haas, who lived in the Chicago area, flew fast in his personal jets. As the namesake partner to the famous Newman/Haas racing teams with Paul Newman, Carl was known as one of the most influential people in racing and motorsports. He'd come up through the ranks the hard way, by coming from behind and winning races. Even though he wasn't large in stature, he just seemed tough, in a quiet Chicago style. He no longer smoked, but he always brandished a huge, unlit, expensive cigar. (After one of our meetings, as I was cleaning up the room, I was tempted to cut off the tip and light one up; they looked pretty good.)

Gale Mellum was our key legal man—a partner in the top tiered Minneapolis law firm of Faegre & Benson. Gale was the type of person who did everything twice. Not because it wasn't right the first time, but just to be exactly sure it was done right and legally proper. From a legal perspective he is detailed and thorough, yet he can rise above and look at the big picture. He had been with us since the very early days of the company, and had a soft-spoken style—he kept our nose clean. He was a real team player, and not afraid to voice his opinion, diplomatically.

I was looking for the inside scoop on the investment banking industry, and while at a financing conference in New York, I was given the name of Jim Morrell, who had recently retired from Dain Bosworth in Minneapolis. When I first met Jim, he looked my age, and said he was retired. I knew he did something right. Like the rest of our developing Team, Jim had a quiet but intense style, and quickly shed the mystery of investment banking. Sometime later we were in San Francisco for a round of financing meetings, and at breakfast I asked Jim how he was. He said great, but that he had just called home and his house had burned down. The only clothes he had were on his back—and none of this dissuaded him.

Filling out the Advisory Team, we brought in Ron Sackett, who had his own marketing firm. For 11 years Ron was the creative director on the Harley-Davidson account at Carmichael Lynch, the marketing agency of record for Harley-Davidson. When Ron looked you in the eye, he was looking clear into your soul. Being an ingratiating guy, he seldom talked of his accomplishments, but others did. Ron was one of the few people who called us early on and said he could help us, and had the credentials to prove it. And he did. He knew how to help build a brand.

I also invited a person on the Advisory Board who declined to be a formal member since he didn't want to potentially compromise his integrity or the integrity of his firm. His name was Earl Klein, a senior partner in the Minneapolis office of the Arthur Andersen accounting firm. Earl was our senior advisor on financing and managed the auditing of our account, and he knew a lot of people in the business community. He was a great quiet networker, and he rode motorcycles and drove fast cars. On several occasions I called Earl to request that he tap his network for a certain skilled person, meeting our tough criteria. After a few weeks would pass, he would call me up and give me a name. In the past, he had introduced me to several people, two of whom ultimately became Advisory Board members: Gale Mellum and Wayne Fortun.

There were two additional advisors to the company who were real helpful over many years, particularly in the manufacturing area, although they were not on the Advisory Board.

I met one advisor, Fred Zimmerman, in the early 1980s while getting my MBA at the University of Saint Thomas. He was an instructor in several of my classes, and I liked his straightforward practical approach (and he gave me good grades). After class one evening I was asking Fred some questions and we got talking about collector cars, in which we both had interest. Fred knew I was a financial analyst at Honeywell, and he called me *"the accountant with a toolbox."* While I was building my first manufacturing company in the early 1990s, I had frequently consulted with Fred, and at Excelsior I continued to frequently contact him since the early launch of the venture. Fred was the Director of Manufacturing Systems Engineering at the University, and was also on the Board of Directors of Winnebago Industries, along with being an accomplished writer on business subjects.

Another helpful advisor, Seiji Yamada, based in Japan, was the former President of Kawasaki Motorcycles USA before his retirement. Seiji was actually on our payroll as a consultant, and we provided him with Excelsior-Henderson business cards that read Honorary Advisor. Seiji was our go-to man in Japan for working with our OEM motorcycle parts suppliers, and without his help I am confident we would have had problems overseas. Seiji was a quiet, respected man in Japan, particularly in the motorcycle industry. He was referred to me by one of our investors, Bill Ness, the Chairman of the Board of Arctic Cat Industries.

• • •

None of our Advisory Board members received cash compensation. They were granted stock options in a private company. It was quite obvious they weren't here for the money or prestige. There was little to none of either.

Even though I am not fond of frequent Board meetings, we wound up having frequent Board of Advisors meetings since they were productive, and also helped forge our camaraderie.

One common trait our Advisors shared, besides being focused and gearheads, was a good attitude and a great sense of humor. Even under stressful situations, we found humor with each other, and ourselves, while we conducted intense business. Even after tough moments, we could generally laugh at ourselves later.

In hindsight, I thought the Advisory Board worked very well, and I would do it again in a New York second.

# 11

## Road Warriors: How Guerillas Meet Gorillas

The further along in life I progressed, the more I understood and believed in the power of networking and getting to know people. Whether it was on a personal or business side, the entire world revolved around people. Or so I believe.

It was time to broaden our venture's horizon and get to know some of the leading industry executives. The list of OEM motorcycle manufacturers is rather small. There is only one domestic independent American motorcycle manufacturer, and just a few European and Japanese manufacturers, so there weren't a whole lot of phone calls to be made. But nevertheless they were important phone calls.

I am a firm believer in getting to know the senior executives of the competing firms in an industry. There are many reasons for this, one of which is maybe they can help in some manner. Even though they are looking to put you out of business, they are also looking to expand their businesses. With Excelsior-Henderson being an independent start-up motorcycle company, we needed to be prepared to partner with others in the industry in the event we needed to. And I was convinced we needed to.

In placing calls to the CEOs of all of the motorcycle OEM manufacturers in the world, I was surprised to discover that they either all took the phone call, or returned the call. Now that was an impressive response.

I was about to get a lesson that would become a constant lesson for the future. People were just darned curious what we were about, and wanted to hear the story, whether they were the CEO of the company, or the man on the line. And rightly so. It wasn't every day that someone launched a new independent, proprietary American motorcycle venture. In fact it was quite unheard of since the task was too monumental, and certain to be doomed. I was convinced the CEOs took the meeting to see who was behind this crazy venture.

Dressed in the best business suit I owned, I attended one of my first CEO meetings with Rich Teerlink, the CEO of Harley-Davidson, now retired. Rich was part of the leveraged buyout group that several years ago had purchased Harley from AMF when it was teetering. And they had a remarkable turnaround story—he was certainly an insider to it all, and achieved great wealth and status because of it.

But he was still an approachable guy. His background was in finance, but it seemed more to me like a sales background. He knew how to make you feel immediately at ease, and would look you comfortably in the eye when he spoke. We met in his conference room that adjoined the CEO's office at the corporate offices on Juneau Avenue in Milwaukee. It was near the same general location they had been since 1903.

Rich was a progressive thinker who kept his sights set on new developments in the industry and knew the Excelsior-Henderson story remarkably well. Excelsior-Henderson was once a competitor to Harley-Davidson, and was positioning to be once again. And he knew it. We were utilizing some of the same effective marketing and branding tools that they were, and we both knew how to use them. They just had more ammunition and guns. His company was the gorilla, and we had to be the guerillas.

Even though in his heart of hearts he had to believe our venture was doomed from the start, he never told me so or intimated it. He would sincerely wish us good luck, and I think he meant it since he knew we would need it. He had firsthand experience at knowing just how immensely difficult it was.

I'll never forget that meeting. Shortly before it wrapped up he leaned across the table, and in a lowered voice stated, "We're not the real enemies, and we both know who the real enemies are." I loved that statement. Harley, and now once again Excelsior, weren't marketing the American heritage simply because it was considered good marketing in the motorcycle industry, but rather because we believed in it. It cut through the core of the marketing slogans and into the soul. It couldn't be faked.

Throughout several meetings and phone conversations we had with Rich and Harley-Davidson, the concept of buying us out arose in 1995, for a value right around $4 million, or to invest in one of our current offerings. Now, there was some enticement here to seriously consider this, but when Rich brought in the rest of his deal team, they seemed less than enamored in working with Excelsior. After all, to them, we were the competition, and they didn't like it. We were like a burr under their saddle and they wanted little to do with us. For me, I wasn't offended—I just kept thinking about the David and Goliath story and who won.

• • •

During one of the many travels to Europe to meet with our engine developer and other potential suppliers, it was time to meet John Bloor. John is the CEO and founder of Triumph motorcycles, located in Hinckley, Leicestershire, England, and was the only person in modern times to resurrect a former motorcycle brand and start building new proprietary OEM motorcycles. Prior to launching Triumph, John had built a small fortune in England and was regarded as one of the ten wealthiest people in England. He was also known to be a private person, rarely granting interviews.

From America, I rang John up in England, introduced my venture to him, and asked if he would be willing to meet. He had heard of our company, and was agreeable to meet, so we set a time for my next visit to England.

The Triumph factory is located just north of Birmingham, England, and a bit in the countryside. It is a beautiful area. Arriving in Birmingham the night before, I found it difficult in the dark to find lodging. After pulling off the roadway, I spied across the street a quaint old pub named the Plow & Harrow, located in the small village of Shenstone. At the Plow & Harrow—as a farm kid from the midwest— I felt like I was in heaven. The proprietor of the pub, named Mick, poured pints all night for his weary American guest, and arranged lodging across the street at a local B & B. The next morning I awoke to the clamor of kegs being rolled up and down from the cellar. It was a great life, but I knew I was moving on.

John Bloor was very accommodating in our meeting, and we exchanged numerous pleasantries about the industry and business in general. I was impressed. Here I was sitting with the man who had accomplished in England what we were trying to accomplish in America. Granted, he was previously wealthy and had his own money to breathe life into his project, but nevertheless, he did do it. He was willing to answer questions, and my mind raced with questions that only he might be able to shed some light on the answers.

Just before the meeting adjourned, I had one last question. I asked, "John, if you had to do this over again, would you?" He was silent, and in thought, but not for long. He looked me in the eye, and quietly said, "No." He didn't elaborate, and something in my gut and his serious tone told me not to go there. I let it be, but I knew he knew something

I didn't. He knew the sacrifice. He also knew, that once you're in it, you can't get out—it's a one-way trip. You either make it, or you don't.

John extended an open invitation to visit him again, and in the future I took him up on it. On one visit about a year later, I stopped at his office early in the morning for our scheduled visit, and his secretary said he was out of the country. Jeez, I thought, I traveled all the way here for a scheduled meeting and he is not here? Apparently he was called away for an emergency matter that he had to attend to in Germany. In his stead, his secretary arranged a meeting with one of his direct reports, Allan Hurd. Almost a year later we would hire Allan, and John disapproved of this—he even faxed me an unusual letter about it. I heard he is still mad.

●●●

Meeting with the Japanese OEM motorcycle manufacturers was a whole new ballgame, and I wasn't perfectly sure I wanted to play their game. Don't get me wrong here, but I sometimes question their motives and the concept of teamwork and openness. Maybe it is more of a cultural thing than reality, but I knew I had a lot to learn and was looking forward to meeting with them.

There is a certain structure and lingo that I learned goes with the American management of a Japanese-based company. What I mean here is the parent company is based in Japan where it is managed by the Japanese. No problem. In the motorcycle industry, they customarily establish a North American corporation to handle the North American markets, and generally locate the administrative offices in sunny California. Now all of this is pretty darn good business logic.

But, I quickly learned the power base was in Japan, and the American company they established was a bit of a façade and didn't have the normal operating authority. Privately, I was told many times that I would have to call a meeting with the top "round-eye." That is part of the lingo I am talking about, along with the culture of the organization. The top "round-eye" is the key person go-between with the American company and the Japanese company. I really don't know what this means, but it must work for them.

One of the first meetings was with Honda of America located in Torrance, California. They didn't manufacture any motorcycles there, as it was the U.S.A. administrative offices. Ray Blank was the top executive, with a traditional American title of National Sales and Marketing Manager.

Upon arriving at their business campus I found it impressive, but eerily sterile. The day was December 7th, Pearl Harbor Day. It wasn't a coincidence, as I had purposely planned for that day. Even though it is California, and I'm from the Midwest, they all seemed so serious. Maybe that was good, as they are tough competition.

After waiting an enormous amount of time for the scheduled meeting, Ray finally came out into the lobby and introduced himself, and we stepped into a small conference room just off the lobby. It had no windows. Generally, I never felt claustrophobic, but I did there.

Ray Blank was the consummate professional: well groomed, articulate, and obviously intelligent. In our meeting he displayed a professional sense of humor, but it became painfully obvious as the meeting wore on that he, or his company of Honda, had a bit of an issue with us at Excelsior-Henderson. Several times he intimated how big and powerful and financially strong Honda was—privately I was thinking the big gorilla—and how little we had of any of it. But I didn't mind. We were the underdogs. We were the guerillas of the motorcycle industry.

To some degree I was flattered that he even knew as much as he did about our venture, but on the other hand, I was slightly uncomfortable that he did. He knew a lot, and I don't think he was planning on using it to help us. It was obvious there was no help here. I don't think Ray meant to be judgmental, but I found myself getting slightly uncomfortable with his line of questioning. It was clear he thought our venture could never be successful, and I am confident he privately told others this. It was all over his face and demeanor; but still he was one of the more nice ones to confront me directly. After all, we were both professionals.

Like some of these ego driven meetings, there is a bit of a climax before the meeting adjourns. It's like the clash of two titans—only this isn't physical, but intellectual. I never quite understood this in business, but I learned to be on top of my game. I didn't know what someone was going to throw at me to try and derail my confidence, but I always felt I could rely on my wit to handle anything that was hurtled toward me. Even though I was always sweating about how our venture was going to make it, I didn't want them to know it.

Ray was ready and had prepared beforehand. He laid his cards on the table and leaned forward, looked me seriously in the eye, and said,

"How do you ever plan on selling over 1,000 cruiser motorcycles a year in America when we have a hard time doing it?"

I looked at Ray—and I leaned forward too—and didn't hesitate in my soft-spoken answer, "Because we have something you want but that you will never have, Ray."

I thought he would leave it at that since I perceived he knew what I meant, but he fell for it and asked, "What's that?"

"American heritage," I answered and repeated, "American heritage, Ray."

# 12

## Where Slide Rules And Sketch Boards Intersect

Product development was continuing to move along, and it was a challenge keeping the projects on schedule and on budget. Just when it looked like the train was going to jump the track, a minor miracle would happen and we would get it righted. So far, things were looking good: fairly well on budget and on our time schedule. Our styling models were progressing, and engine development was continuing.

The company primarily relied upon outside contracted services for practically all facets of our business, and internal staffing was kept to a bare minimum. This certainly cut our fixed overhead, which was practically nonexistent, and allowed great flexibility to the business as the financing would layer in. It seemed the financing never came at the exact time it was needed, so quite frequently we had to put the company into a momentary stall position until the company got funded. It was not unusual for me to call the landlord or a contract supplier and let them know we were short on cash until the next round came in, if it did. Almost without question, they were willing to work with us, and would carry us for a short time.

The plan was to have real prototype motorcycles to unveil to the public in 1996, so most of the year of 1995 was involved in managing the contracts we had with our outside suppliers, and ensuring that schedules and product development stayed on schedule.

Our styling firm, Next World Design, was continuing the natural progression of product design development. After numerous revisions, we finally got a set of scaled-down artistic drawings that looked somewhat like I had envisioned, and with what we thought the marketplace might like to see. Even though everything was still only on paper, it was starting to get exciting because progress was being made.

There's a real art to product design and the scalability of design. Even though some designs looked good when scaled down, when we were satisfied with the scaled-down drawings, we moved to full-sized drawings. This is usually the first indication that some elements of design just aren't working out. But it is the process, and you may as well have fun doing it. And we did.

After we were satisfied with the full-sized drawings it was time to move to actual three-dimensional models. Here is where the tire starts to meet the road. Costs escalate, timelines expand, and there is less opportunity to retrace steps. This is where Next World's strengths were starting to pay off. They had experience with full-size models and were motorcyclists themselves. But they still were designers, which meant they had to be reasonably tightly managed or next thing you knew, they were designing their bike with our money. I would always reiterate, *"Our money, our way. Your money, your way."* I didn't want to be mean about it, but I had a company to run and I had to keep the venture on schedule.

With our money and interactive guidance, Next World produced for us several sequences of full-size models made out of styling foam, metal and plastic. The old method of building models was by using clay, but the current trend was to use this special foam and carve things out. It actually worked well. Keep in mind, these types of models are for styling only, and nothing works. You have to fool your imagination and pretend that it is a real motorcycle. If you sat on it, it would most likely break. It was a mockup with no engineering applied. By the third and fourth generation of models, the new Super X motorcycle was starting to look pretty cool, and it certainly had our own look. There would be no mistaking it for someone else's brand. It had its own distinctive style.

The last non-working foam model built I distinctly remember. When I see pictures of it today, I still think if that exact bike could be built, it would sell real well. It had the ancestral lines of an American cruiser motorcycle on steroids. There was something about the look, the lines, everything, that spoke of individuality. It had the classic combined ruggedness and elegance of a pre-war Packard—I still get goose bumps when I think about it. I knew that exact bike could never be made, since no matter how hard you tried, when you moved from styling to engineering, and then engineering to production, a lot changes. Everything works on paper and in the styling studio. Now we had to move to the real world.

• • •

Our engine company in England, Weslake Motors, was continuing to make progress, but it was a bit of a start–stop process. Again, on paper the modifications we were making to the engines may not have appeared significant, but in reality they were and required a lot of time. And all of the engineering blueprints were being hand-drawn. Weslake was the perfect blend of Old World and New World. They would design New World stuff using Old World techniques.

Not that they didn't have computers. They did and used them a lot. Just not for the initial design. I especially liked that. Practical. Our entire engine was drawn and re-drawn by hand by Michael Daniels and one of his designers named Chris. Being designers, and more specifically, technical designers, they had an analytical and creative mindset. They worked hard on our project, but I wasn't always so sure which hours of the day. Also, their surroundings were quite humble. I still have a picture of our Weslake designer Chris, sitting in his makeshift design area, drawing by the glow of a dimly lit light fixture crookedly hanging on the wall. I didn't know whether to show that picture to our shareholders and Advisors or not. It showed both intensity and fragility. But again, we had to play long shots.

It would be nearly two years since the launch of the contract with Weslake until we actually had a running prototype engine delivered to us. That was a bit scary. What if something bad happened, like the new design didn't work, or we didn't like it, or whatever? There would be no turning back, as too much time and money would be lost. The venture depended on the success with Weslake. But our entire venture was also like this. There were so many potentially catastrophic issues; it was a question of which bullet do you try to dodge. We had to dodge them all.

We did get a few scares with Weslake. On one occasion when Michael called he indicated things were looking real bad for his business as a whole. He was wondering if we could advance more money ahead of schedule on our contract. We were sympathetic, but we were in negative cash flow ourselves and it didn't make good business sense, nor was it a good use of our shareholders' money. Unfortunately, for many reasons, Weslake had to file bankruptcy in England, while we were midway in our contract. Not good.

Except Michael and his crew were men of honor and integrity, liked designing, and were underdogs themselves. Michael shut down, or lost, his old company and started a new one. This new company was based out of his homestead in the countryside, and he converted an old, but large garage into a workshop. He even put an engine dyno and machining centers in there. None of that would have passed any regulations here in the States, and I don't know if it would in England. I never asked since I didn't want to know. I wasn't ready for the answer. He had everything externally well concealed.

Several months later when I visited him, I was mildly impressed. It was a bit of a makeshift operation, and reminded me of a movie I would watch with my kids: Willie Wonka and the Chocolate Factory. But heck, Michael and his crew didn't mind, they were just glad to be doing what they loved to do. So I didn't mind.

I really don't know how Michael was able to pull together our contract and parts from his old company and location and get them to his new site, but knowing what he thought of banks, he figured out a way to get things done. He was enterprising, and our venture needed to continue working with enterprising individuals and companies that would overcome obstacles to stay the course. We were all on a mission, sometimes together and sometimes not.

• • •

With the styling and the engine development continuing to move along, it was now time to introduce the "artists of reality," the engineers. We finally had enough styling substance and models, and engine parameters, that we could now start putting together some of the bike on paper, to see if we could get things to work from an engineering perspective. Finally a chance to start seeing what was real and what was not.

For those not familiar, I'll give a brief explanation on the product development cycle of a new proprietary motorcycle, especially as it related to our venture. First you start with the concept that is in your head or from the specifications and concepts that you have put on paper, and then either you draw it out, or hire a designer or artist to sketch a scaled-down model for you. Next, from the approved scaled-down sketches, you move into full-sized sketches, and from there into three-dimension nonfunctioning styling models. For all of these previous items we had been working alongside Next World Design for assistance in developing the concept of the Super X motorcycle into some nonfunctioning three-dimensional styling prototypes. They may look good, but you can't use them.

Once you get to the full-sized nonfunctioning styling models, the next step is to bring in the engineering perspective of taking the nonfunctioning model and breathing life into it to make it work. In a perfect world, engineering and styling work sometimes concurrently. But, since we don't live or function in a perfect world, most times some of the styling and engineering occur independently of each other.

While you are in the styling phase, it is important to not be encumbered with too strong a concept of what will work or not work from an engineering perspective, as this may limit creativity in the styling. You don't want to be bothering the artists, who have a flair for creativity, versus the engineering mindset, which is more technical and structured around getting things to work right. In many companies, there is a strong debate between the engineering and the styling departments. When you view the final product, you can usually see which department was most successful.

As tough as it is to get a well-styled three-dimensional motorcycle styling model, introducing the engineering into it is really the tough, long, and expensive next step. Obviously, as engineering progressed, the engineers would need to make changes to the styling in order to accommodate making it work, and that is where the interaction—friction—of styling and engineering gets created. Again, in a perfect method, you would like to do both simultaneously, but most of it is a step-at-a-time process, which is why it is difficult to speed up the process.

For those who are still struggling a bit with the concept, while at Honeywell I once heard it explained in terms of having a baby—that to have a baby takes nine months—period. It can't be accelerated. It will still take nine months. So in styling and engineering, certain things are going to take some time, and will happen in sequence. The only way to speed it up is to work more hours, like nights and weekends, which we often did.

Once the design engineering department is introduced, they are soon joined by the next department, which is the manufacturing engineers, who have a keen aptitude for ensuring that engineering models can be readily adapted to production. To some degree, the design engineers are receiving input from both sides of the spectrum—the stylist giving input on how to keep the styling look, and the manufacturing engineers giving input on ensuring it can be consistently manufactured at a high quality. No doubt this process requires a lot of communication, and sometimes in the heat of the battle, things can get a little intense, which they did and do. In our case, the ones who seemed to understand this process seemed more able to work within it, and we sought to recruit talent accordingly.

What does all this mean? Well, it means that even though we may have been working on styling models, we had to be looking at the early styling model from the perspective as it could be engineered and manufactured years down the road. That is another way to help speed up the process and ensure its accuracy. If you have an appreciation for the entire process, and the ability to communicate with the various departments, then you seek to ensure that the steps along the way get completed in a fashion that will ultimately ensure cost competitive, high-quality, consistent manufacturing. I've always loved the process of creating from concept to manufacturing. For all its worth, it is usually underrated, but it really is an art. And a lot of fun.

And the entire process revolves around people. Regardless if they work with their hands in manual sketches or drawings, or use computers, it nevertheless involves a significant amount of human interaction, and the better one is at it, possibly the better the outcome will be. That was part of my job—to ensure we recruited and developed people who not only had the technical skill, but more importantly, I believed, had the ability to communicate.

Another point to elaborate on quickly is the use of computers versus manual drawings. Both have their place, yet some seem to not think so. Oftentimes the early phases of product design start with a manual approach, as concepts and thoughts and designs are quickly put on paper in the freedom of allowing the mind to think in an unstructured fashion. Then, as the process moves further along and ultimately toward manufacturing, invariably the appropriate use of computers is introduced.

I hesitate to call the use of computers as high technology or sophisticated—others may say that but I reserve my judgment on that matter—because sometimes knowing when to use or not use one can make you sophisticated. Computers and technology cannot be creative on their own, and without the encumbrances of high technology, the human mind can think and be creative. That is something computers and technology cannot do, thankfully so. Some of the best engineers and designers I ever worked with made limited use of a computer, but made great use of their hands and minds—a bit of a lost art. Probably neither extreme is good long-term, and at Excelsior we had both. I think we had a better company for it.

Regarding the entire process of going from styling drawings to production, most companies need to complete the full process just once, and that is when the product is launched. Thereafter, most new products use some elements of the styling, engineering, or manufacturing from the previous product development cycle, or from similar products the company may be manufacturing. This is good, and this is where economies of being in an existing business come into play. Almost all motorcycle companies of today do not need to go through the entire process like we were doing. They were already in production, and would mostly have common elements of style or engineering or parts in all of their models.

But we at Excelsior didn't have that luxury, or encumbrance, as the case may be. We were a new company, designing a new motorcycle from a clean sheet of paper. Everything was new. This is both good and bad. Good, meaning a chance to be creative. Bad, being a higher cost and a longer time. But once we got through the phase of our first manufactured model, then our next models could be produced faster and at less cost. This factor is a key element in the barrier to entry for a new manufacturer. Also, this is where manufacturing and the continuity of being in business really become important. All of our competitors had this going for them, and I was hopeful that someday we would too.

So hopefully you now have a better appreciation of the product development process we were using.

• • •

For a long period of time, we had been interviewing prospective engineering candidates and firms in order to ascertain whom to engage for our engineering design. It would be difficult to recruit, hire and manage an entire engineering department overnight, and it would tax our limited resources and create fixed overhead, none of which we were looking for yet. There are certain benefits and detriments to working with outside contractors versus employees, and we needed the flexibility of outside contractors *if* we could find the right fit. That's a big if.

There are also certain specialties to engineering an entire motorcycle. These specialties are unique to their engineering area, and again are independent, yet interdependent on each other. It would be most effective to have an outside engineering firm that had all the different technical engineering skill sets and experience within their company, and they could then apply these skills and hours on an as-needed basis for each project.

After meeting with several national and international firms I still wasn't quite satisfied. The larger, most reputable firms had huge price tags and long lead times. No surprise, because they were probably most assured of successfully completing a project. If I was CEO of a publicly held mature company in positive cash flow and wanted marginal risk to the business, I would choose these firms since they were the safest, but the tradeoff was time and money and flexibility. I was no longer at Honeywell. We were in the trenches and bullets were flying.

It was time to once again call our trusted advisor Earl Klein of Arthur Andersen. I told Earl about our dilemma and he indicated he would go to work on it. Several days later he rang back with a recommendation: there was a company right in our backyard named KIT Corporation who might be able to help us out. I liked Earl's style. He just made it as a suggestion and left it up to us to check out.

It was an interesting first meeting with Al Benz, the President of KIT Corporation, at their office in the Saint Paul suburb of Mendota Heights. KIT was a high technology engineering firm that focused on the optimization of product design and had been in business since the early 1980s. They had a distinguished list of clients, including Harley-Davidson, John Deere, General Motors, Ford, Chrysler, and Mercury Marine. In other words, they had a good pedigree.

In the meeting I explained our venture to Al, who just sat and stared and remained quiet. I think he had heard every story under the sun, and my impression was that he had just heard the granddaddy of them all. He was the most quiet yet piercing person I had met, and he just kept looking at me, or rather through me. Either he was lost in thought, or was judging character, or possibly both. Later, I would learn that was his style, and I learned to appreciate it. I don't think he got fooled or intimidated very often.

Many times in this venture I could just feel the planets lining up, and it seemed to be happening again. KIT indicated they were in a flexible time in their contracts, and as our talks continued over several weeks, they genuinely became interested in more than just a contract for services. What happened was better than I could have imagined. We were able to put together a contract with KIT for a reasonable fee to engineer the complete motorcycle except for the driveline, and most impressive was Al agreed to lead from KIT and work with us and manage the engineering aspect.

We engaged KIT Corporation, and Al was on full-time assignment to the company. He would shortly move his office to our offices in Burnsville. Even though he was an outside contractor, I never really knew it as he fit in the company just like one of our Road Crew. Eventually, Excelsior would buy certain assets of KIT, and he would become the first nonfamily executive officer, but none of us knew that at the time. Again, relationships take time to develop, and early on all we could measure was technical talent and the ability to get along and get things done.

Because Al was able to capitalize on his own experiences and bring in the expertise from his company, the engineering project jumped ahead at a fast pace. He and his team of engineers started with our drawings and full-sized styling models and began earnestly working. We primarily started with the motorcycle frame since everything else attaches to it, including the engine and transmission.

We decided to engineer our own frame, and since our own engine wasn't going to be ready until mid 1996, for the short-term we were going to put a different motorcycle engine into our frame while we proved out our frame engineering concepts. This would not be a perfect match since each engine exhibits different characteristics and accordingly can impact frame design, but nevertheless we did feel it would still be helpful knowledge and allow us to get some generations of engineering models while we were waiting for our engines from Weslake.

Engineers are nearly opposite to styling designers. Engineers don't need the finished product to look stylistically good; they are almost exclusively concerned with the engineering principles at work. One of the first engineering models we put together to prove out our frame and suspension design was powered by a Harley Sportster engine. The entire prototype, called a "mule" in engineering parlance, was ugly from a styling perspective. Externally it was so unrefined looking it developed its own distinct character and invariably brought a smile to my face every time I looked at it. Even today. The entire mule was nearly bare metal with limited paint, for several reasons. We wanted to save money and needed to save time, along with having the ability to locate any stress cracks if they developed from testing. This first mule was put together with ability for adjustments, so we could fine-tune the suspension systems, giving the bike a real mechanical and functional look—but not a look for the marketplace.

Things were starting to get real exciting in the company, and momentum was building. On frequent occasions, I would ask Al to assist us in communicating our venture to prospective investors, and he confidently joined in telling his part of the story. The Team was continuing to grow.

# PART TWO

## YOU CAN'T FAKE SOUL

# 13

## Recruiting The Rough Riders— Management Team

*E*ven before the next year started, I knew 1996 was going to be a big year, as though the last one wasn't. Each year I would think it was going to be the most important year, and it was—until the next year rolled around. Our venture had to be executed out in minutes and days, and long-term milestones had to be reached, so only the passing of a year could significantly measure our progress.

According to the Business Plan, there were a lot of interim milestones to reach on our way to production. We were so far away that I sometimes wonder today how we kept it in focus. The venture was already three years established, and another three years before production would be launched, and we had yet to have real prototypes and running engines. But we were on the cusp of it, and with successful implementation, we would mark actual visible progress to the outside world. We had announced to the motorcycle world that we would be unveiling our prototype Super X motorcycles in August at the annual Sturgis Motorcycle Rally, and we would also need to raise about $10 million in the current year as we further developed. There was a lot of work to be done—it was time to bring in an executive management team.

At this point in the company's development, we were recruiting for primarily four different functions and skill sets: engineering, manufacturing, marketing and sales, and finance. Recruiting successful experienced talent to an underfunded, start-up manufacturing venture is always a challenge. For most people it is not on their career path. It is a lot of work with a lot of risk, but at the same time there is a lot of intrinsic reward that you don't get from established companies.

A certain type of mindset goes with working with early stage companies. You get a chance to really make your mark on something and the opportunity to contribute. Oftentimes the budget and resources are nearly nonexistent and a person has to utilize a lot of timely resourcefulness to get something done on time and on budget. There is also no previously set way to do things, and most times you are fording new streams. It is not a time for excuses, or trying to hide a problem. Many executives need an army around them to carry out the mission, but in a developing company there is no army, unless it is an army of one, and you continue to recruit as you march forward. Also, you must be willing to admit mistakes and problems, so we could all work together to get it solved. Otherwise, the impending results could be fatal to the venture.

In my mind and actions I had been privately recruiting talent since the start of the concept of Excelsior-Henderson. The formula was fairly simple—without the right talent the plan could not be executed, and I could not implement it myself. I was always on the search for talent.

• • •

We had now been working with KIT Corporation on the engineering of our motorcycle for nearly a year and had developed a good working relationship. In fact, they had moved their offices to a building right next to ours in Burnsville. From our back door we could see their front door, and we had worn a path in the grass hill between the two companies. We had also gotten the chance to know their staff and leadership. Since there was a lot of harmony in the interaction of the two companies, and with us looking to bring engineering in-house, it was only natural to explore this with KIT and their ownership structure.

We consummated a structure with KIT wherein Excelsior essentially bought certain assets consisting of engineering test equipment and software, and brought aboard several employees, two of whom were owners of KIT.

This was pretty exciting. On January 1, 1996, we officially hired Al Benz as our Vice President of Engineering, and John LaVoie as our Vice President of Sales and Marketing. This would now allow us to start bringing our engineering in-house, and from a sales and marketing perspective, we could also more effectively build our grassroots brand campaigns with consumers and dealers.

I was real glad to have both of these guys join our Team. Oftentimes executive talent comes with an ego, and the concern about the ability to get along with each other. Fortunately, both men had worked together in the past, and we had worked with them during the previous year, so we were all acquainted with each other personally and professionally and had probably already formed opinions of each other, yet we were still willing to work together.

This was a coup. Al, our VP of Engineering, cut an imposing stance. He was smart and had a quiet, confident solid stature. He was a North Dakota farm kid and several of his engineers had farm or small town backgrounds. That gets to be a great product development skill combination. A farm kid with an engineering degree. You take all that energy and practicality, and combine it with a technical degree and a can-do attitude. I just knew it was going to work out, and it did. But we did have our bumps in the road too.

Our VP of Sales and Marketing, John LaVoie, was probably one of the most enthusiastic people I had ever met, and was a great addition to the company. Just prior to his ownership structure with KIT Corporation, John had either owned or worked with several start-up companies and knew how to work with limited resources. He was a bundle of energy, and brought a new dimension to the venture. Handsomely tanned, well groomed, and well attired—an image he changed somewhat after joining us—John had such a way with words that he could talk himself into and out of trouble in short time. He was fun to observe in action.

Even today I still think of some of the unique "John" colloquialisms—when something exciting or passionately intense would happen, he would mention that it *"passed the goose bumps test;"* or when describing, in humor, what he perceived as his or the company's value compared to something else, he would often use the phrase of desiring *"our unfair share."* His unique way of saying things kept the humor alive in difficult circumstances. He was intense with a good sense of humor, like a lot of the people we engaged to work with.

John was one of the first that I witnessed go through a sort of transformation after he joined us. I don't mean this disparagingly in any manner, since I had gone through a bit of this myself. One of the first executive Team-building outings we had was scheduled during the Bike Week Rally in Daytona Beach, Florida, held in early March, just as the cold and snow is breaking for us northerners. Bike Week is billed as the largest motorcycle rally in the world. Say no more.

By this time John's slightly grayed hair was getting longer—eventually growing into a ponytail—and his face was not clean-shaven. While at Daytona Beach Bike Week, John got into the spirit of things and we indoctrinated him into the lifestyle world of a motorcycle rally. Before the rally was over, he had met thousands of bikers, from all walks of life and from all over the world, and most of them his age or older. John also had the chance to buy a flashy leather-fringed jacket, the kind that sales and marketing type guys who ride motorcycles would wear. Shortly thereafter, John bought a used motorcycle, a unique Harley-Davidson model that he aptly nicknamed *"Bub,"* for *"butt-ugly-bike."* Bikers like to name their own bikes, and usually you don't want to say anything bad about somebody else's bike. But since John called his bike *"Bub,"* we could too. It was ugly, but he got a good deal on it.

I often wondered what some of the spouses and kids thought of all this.

I like executives who can maintain a grassroots style and poke fun at themselves, even though they obviously take success and challenges quite seriously. That was the kind of guy John was. And frankly, he was the type of person we were building our company on. We never knew how long we would all work together, or how far we would get, but we were bound and determined to work hard together—do whatever it takes to hit our milestones, on time and on budget—and to have fun.

• • •

Recruiting for our next position, finance, was going to be a bit more of a challenge. Traditionally, finance guys, or Chief Financial Officers (CFOs), are a little more cerebral regarding risk, and rightly so. Their job is to minimize risk for their company, and most often also in their career—for the two go together. A CFO that mismanages risk will have a hard time finding another job. And, some traditional-type CFOs don't have the experience of raising capital for a start-up venture and transitioning to an operating company. Again, there is nothing like experience.

This position was going to require a change for me since I had been not only the CEO, but also the CFO since the launch of the venture. One of the first things I did three years earlier was to recruit Bob Dye, the CFO from my former company, to work on an interim part-time basis closing our books. For years, since Bob was a full-time CFO with another company, he worked with us nights and weekends to close out and reconcile our financial statements, and never required payment in cash. Being a true professional, all he wanted was stock options. Bob was one of the first outsiders that I had confided to about my plans many years earlier, and I'll never forget the incredulous look he gave me when over lunch I told him about my new venture. He chuckled, and said, "you're not really starting a motorcycle company, are you?"

By this time I had already led the company through several rounds of financing, and had planted the seeds for our future financing. This would require me to relinquish my CFO title, and yet I would still have to work closely together with the new CFO since I had already established relationships in the financing sector for our venture, and had developed a well-constructed Business Plan and presentation format. We needed to work well as a team, and not duplicate, but complement each other. This was a tall task for an early-stage company, especially when there generally are not talented people knocking on your door. You have to go get them personally.

I like to work through referrals, and was in the process of interviewing several well-qualified individuals, but mutually with the prospective CFOs, we just weren't intuitively strongly connecting. If our venture wasn't so fierce and capital intensive, the candidates would have been a good fit, but my gut still wasn't satisfied. I turned once again to our trusted advisor, Earl Klein from Arthur Andersen, and asked him if he had anyone in his network who would meet our tough guidelines, both technically and personally.

True to form, a short time later I got a call from Earl. Coincidentally, Earl had just recently been contacted by a former colleague, Tom Rootness, who was looking for a new opportunity, and his experience and demeanor seemed well suited for our venture. After Earl had a preliminary conversation with him, he faxed Tom's resume to me and I immediately contacted Tom directly.

Even on the telephone I liked Tom right away. He came across as experienced and intelligent, but was not using big words or concepts to prove it. He seemed at ease with who he was and what he was about. I just sensed chemistry with him, although we were not always in harmony. Maybe that was also what I liked about him, he didn't seem intimidated by my confronting him on certain issues, and vice-versa. There was an immediate mutual respect.

After several meetings, I learned Tom was a quick study and a strong negotiator. Fortunately, he was also a motorcyclist—he owned several Harleys and older Hondas—otherwise I am convinced that he would not have been as interested in our project. It was risky and he knew it. And if problems developed, oftentimes fingers get pointed in the direction of the CEO and CFO, and he knew it. He had to be cautious. Tom had also worked with several notable high profile entrepreneurs in Minnesota, and he was experienced in working with the transitions and personalities of entrepreneurs. I didn't take this lightly.

Trying to be objective, even though I may not have felt it, I knew that entrepreneurs like myself had a certain style or demeanor that could be challenging to work with at times. I didn't know what *"no"* meant, and I knew we were going to be successful, or else.

We put together a package for Tom and he joined us on March 31, 1996, as our CFO. I was glad to have him aboard; we had a lot of work to do on our financing in the years ahead. We were already in the early phases of our next round of financing, a $10 million private equity round, and Tom joined us mid-field and started carrying the ball. Two days prior to Tom officially joining the company, he joined us for the formal organizational meeting in downtown Minneapolis with our investment banking firm, John G. Kinnard and Company, who was leading the $10 million round.

Moving forward, Tom and I became the inside *"Deal Team"* for Excelsior, and I thought we worked very well together. During the next three and one-half years, we would raise nearly $90 million for the venture, and almost all of it from contacts that had been established prior to Tom joining us—did I ever learn the power of establishing and maintaining relationships! We got to know each other well, and respected each other's talents. Respectfully so, I was usually the visionary leader plowing new ground and pushing hard, and Tom was there alongside making sure the legal and financial structure was right. If it wasn't, he had no problem in telling me, and I would quickly look for some new ground to start plowing. We worked well together, and privately we had several "vigorous" conversations—as we called them—that were the true test of character. We both got pretty good at apologizing to each other afterward, and we knew the right thing to do was to earnestly debate issues for the benefit of the company.

• • •

While all this was happening, an interesting phone call came in from Allan Hurd, of Triumph Motorcycles in England. We had met Allan the previous year while visiting the Triumph Motorcycle headquarters. Allan contacted us and indicated he was interested in learning more about our venture, and possibly joining if we passed his due diligence. To coin an English phrase that Allan used, *"brilliant,"* I thought.

Allan had never been to Minnesota so we arranged a chance for him and his wife to meet us. It was January. January in Minnesota is the coldest month of the year. And it is cold. When Allan arrived on Friday, January 26th, it was brutally cold. Temperatures were well below zero, with a strong wind creating a dangerous wind chill factor. And we had a lot of snow. Privately, I thought when Allan would land and feel the climate, he would turn around at the airport gate and go back to England. But he didn't.

Allan showed up at our offices—driving an American car on the right side of the road—with a confident big smile on his face. I thought I had better get the negatives out of the way right away, so I conversed with him about the weather. Shockingly, he said in what I would later learn is his optimistic English style, the weather was not bad and he could easily get used to it—and he later proved himself right. He said he didn't feel the cold, and he was dressed lightly! The way he said it I could read he was sincere, and I knew I would like him. Adversity and change were no strangers to him.

Over the course of several months, several visits, and a lot of conversations, we were getting close to putting something together with Allan. We had another first of many in our venture: bringing someone in from outside the country. We would quickly become minor experts in the area of immigration and employing people from overseas. We had to meet the various requirements imposed by the Immigration and Naturalization Service (INS), and some of these take time to get processed. At this same time, there was a short-term under-allotment of work visas combined with the INS behind schedule, and we had to dutifully wait. Finally, the paperwork was approved, and Allan officially joined us on June 10th as the Vice President of Manufacturing. It would be two and one-half years before we hit production, and Allan had a lot of work to do. He was starting with a clean-sheet and had to make it happen.

Allan was a great hire. For the ten years just prior he had worked with Triumph Motorcycles in England and was part of the early management team that designed their motorcycles and launched them into production. In his last year with them, they had produced about fifteen thousand motorcycles. Prior to that he had extensive experience in engineering and manufacturing for Unipart Industries, Eaton Corporation, and Cosworth Engineering. All of these companies were well regarded in their respective industries.

It was a pleasure getting to know Allan and helping him integrate into America, and our company and management Team. Even though he was technically driven, he had a fun, dry sense of English styled humor. He was also passionate about motorcycles. This seemed to be a continually developing trend within our company. I knew I had it, but I wasn't quite ready to expect others to, but they did. Allan, like several before him, and like many after him, would make the decision to uproot his family and career, and strike out and join the laboring motorcycle company in Minnesota. It was a real adventure. I witnessed intelligent, rational, experienced, conservative business people make a decision mid-career to join us. I believed that the passion of the industry would help lure top adventure-seeking talent to us, but I couldn't plan on making that happen. When it did happen, it was humbling, to say the least.

Again, I often wondered what the spouses and families thought of this. Being a small intense company, we did have a chance to get to meet the families, and I found most of them enthusiastic about their spouse's new adventure. They were in it together. They also generally thought it was a bit crazy and out of character, but they witnessed a rejuvenated intensity for life from their spouse.

When moving his family from England to the United States, Allan desired to bring his dog and his gun along. He wasn't able to get his dog into the country, but was given approval on his gun. He would chuckle about that. Crazy Americans!

Later, when others asked Allan how we all joined up he would repeat the story of how we had met at Triumph Motorcycles: As I was departing England and shaking Allan's hand, I mentioned to him if he was ever interested in contemplating joining a new motorcycle company in America, that his call would be welcomed—even though at the time we were just barely out of the basement of my house. He said he went home that day and mentioned it to his wife, and it remained on his mind. Until one day when he decided to act upon it and call. I had always believed our venture had a sort of destiny to it, and it was happening again.

• • •

With the addition of Allan, we completed filling the initial management Team. We had our first executive management Team, three years into the venture. We had a VP of Engineering, a VP of Manufacturing, a VP of Marketing and Sales, and a VP of Finance (CFO). They were all experienced Generals marching confidently into war. Together, we believed we had the talent, and if appropriately funded at the right times, and with a bit of luck, we just might be able to give this venture a good run.

This new Team was also quite a change for the company. We had experienced talent leading all the key areas of the business. This was both good and bad, but most certainly the good far outweighed any bad. With a young developing company, I was always thinking hard on making sure the company was fair to people. This was hard. Some people might think being fair is being easygoing with them, but that is not how I mean it. We were in a war and a constant battle for the company to survive. That was a fact. Bullets were flying and the enemies of a start-up were constantly at our door. So many times we had to set aside our differences and any personality issues or egos to just get things done—*"do what we said we would do, when we said we would do it, for how much we said it would cost."*

With this concept in mind, we tried to structure everyone's compensation equally. All Vice Presidents received the same stock options and except for some minor variances, the same cash compensation, for better or worse. What was great to see was that they were all supportive of it, even though in other business experiences it had not been this way. There was a fixed base salary, set lower than what they had been making in the past, and a reasonable allotment of stock options, that could be worth a sizable amount if we accomplished our goals together. We all had skin in the game. Not too much, and not too little. And no perks, other than they had a motorcycle allowance. We didn't have car allowances, only motorcycle allowances.

And to prove to them my seriousness on their worth to the company and keeping my own ego in check, their salaries were set higher than mine.

I was the founder, the largest shareholder, the CEO, and the Chairman of the Board; and I was not privately wealthy. I still drove the same old car and lived in the same house. And I paid the Vice Presidents all more money than what I was making. This never really got reported or picked up by news sources, although it was clearly written out in our investment prospectus. But this wasn't intended for the optics of the public; this is how I believed. I didn't launch the venture for the money. My payday would be more internal, and come from the satisfaction of the success of the venture that I had launched, and seeing others succeed together as a team. Although sometimes when I was trying to pay my bills and raise my family, after seeing the sacrifices my wife and children were making by my absence from home, I could have been not so principled. Maybe I could have balanced it a little better. Another life lesson here.

# 14

## Bringing In The Hired Guns

The advantage of laying out a detailed business plan, and continually revising and updating it, is you get the chance to anticipate future events and the appropriate timeline and tasks to implement them. According to our current projections—again with a lot of luck and money—we projected to hit production in two to three years, or ideally in about thirty months. Working the schedule backwards, that meant we already needed to be zeroing in on our manufacturing processes and scouting for a building or location to commence production.

The first order of business was to determine the size of the building, which needed to be consistent with our Business Plan, which in turn was consistent with our Offering Memorandums that were being circulated during our many rounds of financing. Simply put, all facets of our planning and company operations needed to be in harmony with one another, not only to meet the tests of due diligence by outside parties, but it was simply a good way to run a business. The operations of the business were interlinked, and even though independent of each other, they were interdependent on each other. I know I have mentioned this several times, and I reiterate it here due to its importance and the reality of business life for a start-up.

Long before we were to commence production, and long before the money could be raised for a building and the subsequent start of production, we had to develop the parameters for our production process. This is where the strategy for manufacturing would be key. The *processes* we were going to use in manufacturing would dictate the type and size of building we would need, and not vice-versa. The building would simply be a shell put around the manufacturing operations, like clothes are to a person. So in order for us to determine the building, we first needed to strategize on the manufacturing processes we would employ, and then put a shell around it. Also, the costs of preparing the building inside for motorcycle assembly would most probably exceed the cost of the building itself, so it was the processes that were most important.

This is a bit of an educated shot in the dark when you don't have the money and you don't have a product, and you are an independent start-up company. The key here was to design a facility layout and time schedule that was flexible. Flexibility was important since we could then act accordingly as the business evolved in the short term, but eventually we needed to lock into definitive action in order to get things done.

By studying our national and international competitors, combined with our own knowledge of manufacturing, we knew there were some reasonably basic rules to follow. We weren't going into the casting or machining business, nor would we be a manufacturer of parts. Modern day OEM suppliers and the industry OEMs already had that competently in place. That was the good part. There were already established OEM suppliers for castings, machining, chroming, and parts. Granted, we would need to establish relationships and endeavor to have them make or supply our proprietary products for us, but nevertheless that segment should be possible to do, provided one has the time, skill, and money.

This last provision was always the most important. Money. Money. And Money. In that order. Money creates time, and you use the time to effectively implement and accomplish what you said you would do with the money. This cannot be stressed enough. This is a key differentiating concept—of being an independent start-up that never knew if and when it could raise money to stay alive, contrasted to a "start-up" within the arms of a publicly held parent company that is profitable and self-funding. Generally the only way to really learn this is: You need to experience the difference. Those who have, know the difference firsthand.

There were certain things we were required to do on our own, and internally, as it related to being a prospective OEM manufacturer. The term "manufacturer" here is a bit of a misnomer. Even though other OEMs of the world, including ourselves, were called OEM "manufacturers," we were really planning to be more of an assembly plant, and leave the traditional manufacturing to our suppliers. Not only is this prudent, it is also the method most of the industry has adopted to streamline their operations and effectively outsource to OEM suppliers. This was a key strategy of ours as a new entrant to the industry, and it would allow us to be highly efficient and significantly reduce our upfront investment. Existing OEM manufacturers in the motorcycle industry and automotive industry, including the likes of Ford, Chrysler, and General Motors, were adopting and implementing the concept as fast as their current constraints would allow them. Also, this concept is commonplace in the computer manufacturing industry. Just ask Michael Dell, the pioneer of this concept in his industry.

We desired to do our own final assembly on the motorcycle for several reasons. The final assembly is as it states: final assembly. This would allow us to control the finished quality of the product, without the added cost and burden of being the manufacturer of the parts that went into the final assembly. This factor was a hard point in our Business Plan, but we did have flexibility in which method we would use to complete it. Some favored an assembly line process where the motorcycle moves from station to station in a sequence to different people on the assembly line, while others—like me—favored a cellular process where the motorcycle was completely assembled in one place by a small team of people. Eventually, we did opt for the assembly line approach.

There were some key manufacturing processes and parts that we desired to do, but were still being studied, and again were reliant upon funding. Inherent to a motorcycle is the aforementioned engine. The word *"motor"* is in the word *"motorcycle"* and it is very visible to the rider and key to a motorcycle—it is the heart. We were hopeful to also do the final assembly and "cold test" on our engines, but this was not yet determined.

Another process under study and not yet determined was the motorcycle frame. Everything on the motorcycle, including the engine, bolted to it. That means if the frame is not consistently manufactured exactly to tolerance, everything else that bolts to it could potentially be incorrect. Besides all the potential problems this would cause in assembly, there could exist some potential liability in the field if the product didn't perform appropriately.

The last area we were studying was in regard to the final finishing of the motorcycle and the parts. In simple terms we called it painting, but it was much more than that. In order to meet established OEM criteria and the expectations of consumers, it was a high-technology step-by-step automated finishing process that included cleansing, e-coating (anti-rust), powder coating, painting, and baking of all metal components, including the frames, engines, fuel tanks, fenders, etc. Keeping it simple in concept here, if you ever have a chance to visit an OEM finishing facility, you can contrast that with your local body shop. Big difference.

With all these things in mind, we had to have some flexibility in the building design. Our initial building designs incorporated the hard point of doing our own final assembly, and we left flexibility in the design to later bring in-house the other processes as money and the studies dictated.

Once we locked in on that, it didn't take long to get the ball rolling on sourcing a building and location. But I also knew there was some real skill in knowing how to properly do this, and we didn't really have the expertise in-house. This is where I would bring in what I would call *"a hired gun."* By now you're probably getting to know me and my style fairly well. There are complicated things we needed to do, but I like to keep the application of them in simple terms so we could all understand them. Maybe I had watched too many western movies as a kid, but to me *"a hired gun"* was someone we could bring in who had precise skills and who we would ask to accomplish a specific or special task, basically walking shoulder to shoulder with them on that task. Some would call this a consultant, but to me it is much more than that—not only was I accountable for the final result, they were too, and generally most of their compensation was based on that. My *"hired gun"* would primarily be my right-arm person to work closely with me on a minute-by-minute basis, if necessary. This freed me up to continue the leadership of the company, and also brought in the necessary—very specific—expertise to get a specific project done (*on time and on budget—Do what you said you would do, when you said you would do it, for how much you said it would cost*). Furthermore, the hired gun was not there to only make recommendations, but to also work closely with us in managing the implementation, and would have hell to pay if they didn't get it done right and on time. And it was usually for a *"do or die"* milestone in the company. The factory was one of them.

Even though raising capital and developing a proprietary motorcycle was a formidable task, some start-up ventures in the past had completed various phases of that, but none of them could get through the tunnel and actually into production as a stand-alone company. The few that did—like Tucker and DeLorean—immediately had difficulties on all fronts, and shut down amidst a torrent of lawsuits and angry people. I knew that, and it bothered the hell out of me. Even though our management Team and Advisory Board were outspoken people, no one questioned the concept of the hired gun. We all knew we needed one, but where were we going to get one?

Long before, I had been planning for this and had kept my eyes and ears open. At my desk I turned to my phone and hit the speaker button, immediately dialing the phone number for the Public Resource Group in Minneapolis. Pat Pelstring was my target, and he was the perfect hired gun. He had a calm, relaxing style, and would appear at times to be a bit disorganized—almost like Columbo on TV—but you knew his mind was moving based on his effectiveness and consistency. Even though he would frequently wear a tie, it just never seemed to be straight.

Earlier I had met Pat through several venues. I like to work through a referral network along with my own due diligence in uncovering someone to work with. At the time we had over 150 private accredited investors, and all with significant net worth that they had each created the old fashioned way. They earned it through the school of hard work, and most of them had the years of experience and battle scars to prove it. By getting to know these investors, and sharing their business stories along with the ambitions of our company, periodically I would get a lot of good advice. One of our investors, Don S., had given me Pat's name, and suggested I use his name to follow-up.

Coincidentally, and possibly by destiny, Pat had just been recently featured in a local monthly business magazine, and after reading the article I had circled his name. He was on my watch and follow-up list— and now I had a direct referral from a shareholder. So over a period of several months, I had the chance to get to know Pat and his company well, and when the time came in our Business Plan to engage someone, I simply reached to the phone and started pushing buttons for a launch.

I quickly found out that others in the business community also knew him well, especially those that worked in the area of company relocation. Pat was the owner of his firm and they specialized in assisting companies find a new location for their business. Whether you were looking for a new location within your community, a new community, or a new state. And whether your needs could be met by an existing building or a new building. Pat also knew how to handle a calculated roll-of-the-dice, and agreed to work on a reduced fee, with the bulk of his fees due in cash and stock options upon successful completion of our project. So we engaged Pat and his firm.

Pat was a specialist in his field, and we quickly reviewed the various states and communities for existing buildings that would be suitable for motorcycle manufacturing. Naturally, there was nothing that would closely fit our specifications, as there were no idle motorcycle assembly facilities anywhere in the world. The industry was growing at double digit increases. Also, there were few existing buildings that could be converted at reasonable cost. Remember, by this time the economy had grown rather robust and companies and the stock market were continually hitting peaks with no valleys in sight. Available real estate was at a premium, if indeed you could find any. To some degree we already knew this, but the field research confirmed this, and it could be a real dilemma to our company. We were not positioned to be the type of tenant most building owners were looking for, especially owners of large buildings. They wanted established companies, whom they could usually attract, and not unprofitable early stage dreams, as we were often viewed. That's a fact and we just had to keep marching forward, fast.

We set about laying the groundwork for constructing a building in a new location where a community was desirous of having us. Some key elements here. We knew we had to move since our existing building location and lack of available real estate in our current community could not accommodate the needs of a motorcycle assembly plant. Also, not every building owner or community wanted to have a motorcycle plant. There isn't a whole lot of open-minded thinking when it comes to motorcycles. Those in the industry tend to have a certain attitude, and those outside the industry tend to have a certain attitude about those in the industry. I may not have liked it, but I had to deal with reality. No time here to grandstand and question why it was this way, and in a way, I kind of liked the attitudes anyway. It showed emotion, and usually I could easily detect where a person stood on the issue.

Without trying to oversimplify the strategy of location, to some degree it would be based on locating where we were wanted, and could financially afford. In some businesses and industries it would not matter, but in our case it did. We needed to work in mutual harmony with the community since motorcycles are a high visibility and potentially controversial product line, and we didn't need any problems on the home front. In fact we wanted to have the opposite. Somewhat like looking for a friend or a spouse. We wanted a community where we fit in well: All for one, and one for all. If both sides desire to work together, they can generally get things done, especially when tough things come up, as they usually do.

We put together a strategy and sent proposals out to the state economic development offices in nine different states, all of them primarily located in the mid part of the United States, where there is still a good solid bed of manufacturing, skilled labor, and available suppliers. The way the process works is that the state economic development offices forwarded the information to various communities in their state whom they felt met the criteria we established. Believe me, most states and community leaders have a fairly well orchestrated process of methods to grow their states and communities prosperously, including the attraction and retention of businesses, for obvious reasons.

Just before we sent out the proposals, Pat and I were meeting in our conference room going through the various proposed states and communities. When we were done, he looked at me, and gave me his—I hope this does not offend him—"Columbo" look. He said, *"You didn't include your hometown of Belle Plaine on your list, and they meet all of your criteria, and they might be offended if you don't at least include them on the list!"*

I don't know why, but I had to think about that, and restrain a chuckle. I liked growing up on our family farm just outside of Belle Plaine, but in a certain respect when I left Belle Plaine, it was in my rearview mirror. Not only that, most of the city leaders I think were pleased the eight Hanlon brothers and sisters had grown up and moved out of town. Most of us weren't high on their respected list. Being farmers, and periodically wild kids, that was already two strikes against us, or so I thought. I would later find out perceptions can change or be wrong, and that time itself can also change things. So, with a smile and a nod to Pat, we added Belle Plaine to the list, and adjourned the meeting.

In general, the response from the states and communities was overwhelming, and soul-searching. I was promptly called by the Governors' offices of several states, and would quickly acknowledge they knew Pat and his firm well—it looked like our homework was paying off. We toured several states and communities, primarily in Ohio, Wisconsin, and Minnesota. The local, regional, and some national media, both print and television, also made quite a story of this.

We were a bold company, with some bold people, seeking to accomplish some bold objectives, but in a down-to-earth straightforward manner.

# 15

## Not Even Lawyers, Guns, & Money Could Save Us

My mind was always preoccupied with the financing. As we discussed earlier, it was our fuel, and the longer we held the pedal to the floor and the more milestones we accomplished, the more fuel was consumed and needed to be replenished. As difficult as it was to keep everything straight and focused, a new trend was developing; we were gaining momentum. It was during this time that I first felt this in the company—momentum.

Despite the stressful uncertainty about the outcome of our venture, we periodically gained momentum, and climbing the mountain seemed possible. There was a certain amount of passion to building this business, and I planned on Excelsior being the last company I would need to build. It was an intense venture, but I was passionately convinced that we could make it happen. I planned to retire from it someday. Privately I would think, *"that's my mountain, and I'm going to climb it. Either you will find me waving from the top, or dead on the side, but I'm not going back."*

The company was becoming more visible, and we had frequent visitors at all hours of the day. Even though we weren't initially set up for any retail business and were exclusively the business office, we continued to get visitors just stopping in. I've never been in a business where people just show up unannounced. They were mostly curious and supportive of what were trying to do, and wanted to just hang out. Well, when you're trying to get things done, and in a business setting, that can be distracting, but it was also good and told us something.

We set up a museum of historical Excelsior-Henderson motorcycles and artifacts, and sold apparel in our museum. We had a company video, and motorcycle videos, and continually had them playing in the museum. It didn't take long for us to actually start generating some revenue from this area, along with increasing the market awareness of our venture. It was neat. Friday afternoons were usually the most busy with visitors, as our enthusiasts would take a half-day off to start the weekend early, and stop in just to visit and hang out in the museum area.

One nice summer night I decided to head home a little early, and was locking up the office about 7:00 p.m. I had just locked the inside

door to the vestibule, and was locking the outside door when I was star-
tled by a voice behind me. I hadn't heard any vehicles drive up, and as
I turned around I noticed it was a young boy on his bicycle. Since I had
my family waiting for me at home, I did want to get going—early for
once—but not wanting to be rude I proceeded to converse with him.
He was about nine years old, and had ridden his bike several blocks to
get to our museum after having supper. His dad was telling him about
our business and museum, and he decided to see if it was open.

I didn't want to break the young man's heart, and so I said sure, I'd
open up the museum and let him in. We went in and I explained the
history of the Excelsior-Henderson brand, and he just hung out for a
while and looked around. As he was ready to leave, I grabbed a youth
T-shirt off the rack and gave it to him. He said *"thank you"* and was on
his way, pedaling hard up the hill. I grabbed my two briefcases and
jumped into my car and thought again, *What a wonderful business.*

• • •

We would soon be publicly unveiling our running prototype
motorcycles in Sturgis, and announcing our new factory location, in
the midst of the next round of financing. Only this one was going to
be a little different.

We actually had an investment banking firm. *Another*—lucky—
*coup.* For three years we had been courting investment banking firms
and as a company we had finally progressed far enough that someone
credible was willing to join us and exclusively lead the process. Now,
we weren't at the level of the Wall Street crowd, but we were on the
first rung of the ladder that might lead us there. This may again be
redundant, but there is simply no replacement for persistence in developing relationships early on. I maintained frequent communication
with well over two hundred investment banking firms and individuals
for over three years. I didn't know any other way and didn't see any
other choice.

The firm we engaged was John G. Kinnard, headquartered in
downtown Minneapolis. Or really, they engaged us. Firms like that get
the opportunity to pick which negative cash flow start-up company
they are going to take a risk on. We had met their head of corporate
finance, Mike Norton, more than two years earlier via a referral and
introduction by our lawyer and Advisory Board member Gale Mellum.

I had really learned to respect investment bankers, especially ones like Mike. In his position, he had seen nearly every business plan ever drafted, and had heard every story, from every type of entrepreneur. On most occasions, he could be as bold and as callous as those presenting to him could be. Earlier in this venture Mike had let me know that he and his firm would never work with us, for a variety of reasons. He wasn't mean about it; he didn't have to be. It was just a fact, at the time. But for me, I always look at a *"no"* as meaning *"not today,"* but maybe *"some-day."* And now, several years later, that someday had come.

In kicking off rounds of financing like this, once the engagement letter is executed—which in itself is no small feat—you usually start with an organizational meeting. After high school if you ever won-dered where all the intelligent people ended up in their careers, you will find them in these organizational meetings. There are some pretty fast minds in these meetings, and people who pride themselves on being a bit intellectual, and periodically in a flash of ego, can over demonstrate their intellect. So you need to keep your wits about you. It's also wise to dress smart, as most of them do.

There is also some high-powered talent and high-priced talent at these meetings if you want things done right. Attending our kickoff meeting were two investment bankers, two lawyers, our outside audi-tor, an Advisory Board member, and representing the company, our new CFO, Tom Rootness, and myself. As I looked around the room, I made a mental note of the hourly cost, and realized we were investing well over $1,000 per hour. I thought that was a lot, but in years to come the hourly investment would multiply significantly. We had to make effective use of our time.

These guys were all pros and we worked diligently together. This offering round was going to be our largest to date: $10 million priced at $2.50 per share. For some, drafting the Offering Memorandum can be a tedious exercise, but it was one I had learned to appreciate. It is the closest I have ever been to where everything is carefully scrutinized with the intent of doing everything exactly right. No stone is left unturned because there are no sacred cows, so to speak. If things aren't done correctly and there is a problem later on, there could be signifi-cant legal ramifications, and potential crimes. So you had better be real focused on doing things right, with well-qualified people, and take the time to get the document legally correct. If there are any problems in your business or yourself, now is not the time to hide them, but instead be the opposite and forthcoming.

In our venture we had nothing to hide. I had learned long ago that doesn't work anyway, especially in a difficult venture like ours. In fact, I believed it was better to be upfront with as much bad news and risks that you could think of and directly communicate it to anyone who contemplated getting involved. If they could handle the bad truth, then there was something to really start discussing. It would immediately separate the chafe from the wheat. And if the truth either frightened them or discouraged them I didn't mind, at least we knew this upfront. If they couldn't be a player on the field taking the hits, maybe they could be a cheerleader on the sidelines; we needed both.

Therefore, in our Offering Memorandums, I had no problem with identifying any actual or perceived risks to our business. Hell, I knew it was a risk and likely one that would consume us all—and I desired that to be clearly communicated, not only verbally by our staff and me, but in our written legal documents that all the world could see and read as well. Since these documents sometimes fell into the hands of unintended parties—primarily vocal critics—they would use this as ammunition against us. But nevertheless, we didn't waver. It was the right thing to do and I believed then as I do now: do the rightful thing and be darned with the critics—usually they have a private agenda anyway.

Let me give you some specific examples of the wording from our Offering Memorandums. The following statement is extrapolated exactly from the cover, first paragraph, first line, of one of our Offering Memorandums.

**THE SECURITIES OFFERED HEREBY ARE HIGHLY SPECULATIVE AND INVOLVE A HIGH DEGREE OF RISK AND MAY NOT BE AN APPROPRIATE INVESTMENT FOR PERSONS WHO CANNOT AFFORD TO LOSE THEIR ENTIRE INVESTMENT.**

I have been told that some people don't read those things. Well, I know I do, and lawyers do, especially if they plan to sue you or your company. Another important element in the Offering Memorandums is to disclose the various risks to the business. Here is another direct sentence from the risk section, which is the first section of our Memorandums: "*in order for the company ever to commence assembly line manufacturing of the Super X motorcycle, significant financing in addition to the proceeds of this offering will be required...If additional financing is not obtained, the Company is expected to fail.*"

To some, this is some pretty brusque stuff. But I took it all in stride since it was the right thing to do, and it was true. I believed we would fail if we ran out of money, and it didn't matter where we were in the implementation of the Plan. No money. No fuel. No go. Therefore, why not just print the word fail for the entire world to see. Failure is not permanent.

Another part of the business and very important to the Offering Memorandums is the auditing and auditor statement. As a former accountant, I knew this well, and again didn't shy away from it. We weren't trying to capitalize things when we should be expensing. In product development I knew we were losing money, to the Plan, and we were expensing it all. No need to try and inflate earnings, we didn't have any.

One of the big things in auditing the books of a company is the final auditors' report, which should give concern to most CEOs and Boards since it can impact the perception, and sometimes reality, of the company to the public. Here again, the letter to the Board of Directors from Arthur Andersen said the same thing every year, and I quote: *"The factors discussed to the financial statements raise a substantial doubt about the ability of the Company to continue as a going concern."* These letters, and financial statements, verbatim, were also always included in our Offering Memorandums. What the letter from Arthur Andersen was saying, in accounting terms, is they had substantial inclination to believe the company was going to fail. And they started writing this to us in 1993, and continued doing so every year.

Maybe by now you believe me when I mention I believe in full disclosure. In good times it is the right thing to do, and in bad times it will save your integrity. Maybe that was why we never got sued. Fortunately, our lawyers, management Team, and Board members were also of the same mindset, and they should have been. I picked them.

Sometimes though, this full disclosure gave unneeded ammunition to our critics and competitors, and they seized upon it as though they had discovered something, singing our swan song for years. That was the penalty paid for full disclosure, and on occasion it did seem to harm the ability of the company to implement the Plan.

● ● ●

Drafting sessions for Offering Memorandums last hours at a time, and for over a period of weeks, and may include several months and numerous drafts of documents until all parties to the transaction are satisfied. No small feat. It is not unusual to strongly discuss the inclusion or exclusion of just one word for hours, and just when you think you have agreement, the next day you might be right back at it again with the same word. Every detail is reviewed several times by different people over a period of time. I have heard that many entrepreneurs get frustrated with this process, but I never did. It was too important to the business and my credibility, plus I enjoyed the intellectual debates.

Finally after several months of drafting we were ready to launch the Offering Memorandum. We scheduled a kick-off presentation at the downtown offices of our lead investment banker, John G. Kinnard & Company. About seventy-five people were in attendance, and we were having some serious fun presenting our company and story. But while we were presenting, there was an undercurrent happening that I didn't know about.

Early the next morning, one of our lawyers called me and delivered some news. While we were presenting the day before, Kinnard had a new or substitute receptionist who was coaxed into giving out one of our Offering Memorandums to a reporter from one of the major Twin City (Minneapolis and Saint Paul) daily newspapers. For legal, and morality reasons, everyone knew not to do that. Potentially, not good.

I don't really know why, but we were a frequent story to this newspaper, and depending upon the writer, the story could be good or bad. I never dwelt on it much—I didn't know if our issue was with the writer or the newspaper—and just tried to grin and bear it and keep moving forward. Anyway, this time it could be fatal to the business, again. The newspaper planned on running a big article on the offering we had just kicked off. It was time to send in the *lawyers, guns, and money*. This was real bad. On all of our offerings we had relied on exemptions from registrations to the SEC under rules 504 or 505 that governed the sale of private stock, and we had always met those and any other conditions. Bad things happen if you don't, and get caught. You could go to jail.

The SEC rule here that was impacting us was the one regarding solicitation. A company was not allowed—nor be a direct or indirect contributor—to advertise or publicly solicit its financing or offerings, and if the newspaper ran a story about the offering, potentially later a disgruntled shareholder could sue and claim we violated securities law, and maybe be right. Our lawyers and Kinnard's lawyers were well known in the area, and they knew some executives at the newspaper. An appeal was made to them to hold off on printing anything until our offering concluded in just a few days, and we would even give them an exclusive, something we had never done before. In summary, they weren't interested in hearing any of it. Even though they were told we would have to pull our offering and harm our company, they said as long as it didn't kill people, then they were going to run the story. So they did. That was too bad. They purposely did this knowing it would harm the company—they knew the rules on solicitation, and they didn't play by them. The other media did.

It wasn't the first time, nor the last time an article like this severely impacted our business. That was the only part I missed in putting together the Business Plan. I usually don't mind the heat, but this was affecting the livelihood of the company and myself. Even though I may not have fully understood the impact at the time, this one event set the destiny of all future company financing, and would forever haunt us—through a series of events—to the end. We didn't know this at the time. But I felt it in my gut.

So there went $10 million. Just before our public unveiling of our new Super X prototypes, and while we were negotiating factory sites. Nothing new. Another major obstacle.

I think that fazed me for about ten minutes. It wasn't a first round knockout, just a lucky punch. Time now for the second round. We needed the funding and without it we had to put the company into a stall pattern, and potentially shut it down. It wasn't the first time, but you still never get used to it since you don't know if you can pull out of it. This was just another example of how and why we built flexibility into the company. But damn.

We regrouped with our Deal Team and started reviewing options. Do we go forward anyway? Some companies would, some lawyers would, and some accounting firms would. We discussed it. It was only perceived risk; maybe it wouldn't be real. We had to predict the future. We could build a legal argument to go forward. If it was the last round of financing we would ever need to do, the risk might be less, but we all knew we had a long road of many financing transactions ahead, and we just couldn't jeopardize any future financing rounds. The offering was dead.

Timing is everything. Without getting too detailed regarding the complexities of raising money under the rules of the SEC, a few months earlier we had just completed a self-imposed quiet period. Simply put, our company had been raising numerous rounds of financing throughout the previous three years and in multiple offerings. If there wasn't a "seasoning" of six months between the offerings, in the event of an issue, the offerings could all be integrated together. In essence, the SEC could do a look-back, in our case for nearly three years, and declare all our offerings were not in compliance. Well, if you ever do have an issue with the SEC on an offering, you just want it on the one, and not be forced by a technicality to declare all the other previous offerings to be in noncompliance.

Therefore, not only are there challenges in properly raising equity, there are some interrelated issues to be cognizant of. Two things we knew: we needed to raise money for the company, and we had to stop our offering. Two opposing problems.

There weren't many options. Our lawyers called their contacts at the SEC in Washington D.C., and also contacted experienced securities lawyers in New York, Chicago, Los Angeles, and San Francisco. A game plan was starting to emerge. What we were about to embark on had seldom been done before in the manner we were going to do it. We would do a registered public offering—like an Initial Public Offering (IPO)—but to private accredited investors whom we restricted from being able to sell their shares. Basically, it was a combination of a public-private offering.

This would get us over the current hurdle of this financing round, but would require us to complete an SEC registration and subsequent IPO much earlier than we had planned. I didn't like this at all—it could restrict us in the future. It is not good to be a publicly held development stage company with negative cash flow, and that was what we were about to do—our hand was forced. It is better to be private, and go public later.

Over the course of several months, we re-drafted the Offering Memorandum to meet the requirements of a public offering and submitted it for approval to the SEC as a registered offering. Upon registration approval, which we received, the offering kicked off again. The people at the firm of Kinnard were doing a great job. What a team. By the end of September when we finally wrapped up the offering (nine months from when it originally started), it was oversubscribed and we raised $11.5 million. We now had about 400 shareholders who were our advocates in the field.

We *lived to fight another day.*

# 16

## *Resurrection Day In Sturgis*

*E*ngines. Don't let anyone ever tell you they are all alike. Our first engine from Weslake arrived late. But it was a euphoric late. In jump-start projects like this you never know if you will ever get an engine, so late was okay. We had a real live running engine that was our own. We could see, touch, hear, feel, and smell it. Not only that, there were several more coming right behind it, and just in time.

As a company we had announced to the industry that we would do a public unveiling of our prototype Super X motorcycles on the first official day of the annual Sturgis Motorcycle Rally, which was Monday, August 5, 1996. In order to generate the appropriate media coverage and consumer interest, we had to announce the event six months in advance. Well the big problem with all this was that we were making projections in advance, not knowing for sure if the milestone could be accomplished due to factors beyond our control.

Making predictions about delivery dates for working prototypes is always a problem, especially when they are announced publicly, and the company was a development stage company that had never done this before and needed to raise money. Our entire credibility relied on this. If we started missing milestones, especially one as important as this, momentum would wane and it would be all over. But this was nothing new; it was just another daily experience at Excelsior-Henderson.

*The pressure was on.*

• • •

Weslake had done a remarkable job on a fairly constrained budget. They had been running our engines on their dynamometer in England. The initial tests were real good. The engine was producing great power and showing great reliability. They couldn't get it to blow up, so that was real good. They finally shipped us one, and we had a chance to fire it up.

Just a little side bar here on our engine design. It was one of the most innovative designs in the motorcycle industry—an air-cooled twin cylinder, dual overhead cam, four-valve, fuel injected motor. Just writing that gives me goose bumps, and if you are any part of a gear-head it will move you also. It just boasts of future performance. And with a long stroke, for that stump pulling torque. A bit of an engine of contrast, by design. A great platform from which to build. If you are familiar with new car engines, their new designs incorporate these features. But in the motorcycle industry on a cruiser motorcycle, no one does. In the motorcycle industry the cruiser motorcycle is generally a nostalgic series and the engine designs reflect that, and some modern day consumers are looking for a little more. At Excelsior, we were the first and only within the motorcycle industry to offer these features. Would others copy it? Probably.

Getting our engine to run in our office complex in Burnsville was going to be another matter. Even though we had an adjoining small warehouse that housed our test engineering area, the neighboring businesses were significantly different than ours and real quiet and unobtrusive. Not like us. We had motorcycles coming in and out, along with hot-rod cars, and an assortment of people with very "unique" styles. All in one day we might have a group of investment bankers and wealthy investors dressed to the hilt, and at the same time a group of bikers with beards, long hair, and wearing riding gear would show up. We had to be flexible, and I know it had to be challenging for our business neighbors and our landlord.

We tried to be quiet about it, but motorcycle engines can be loud. In order to start doing some vibration and engine testing, we built a small engine test stand. And that is being kind. It was a couple of pieces of angle iron welded together, with the engine and transmission bolted to it, along with a fuel tank. We put some mufflers on the engine, and set a battery next to it, and fired it up. Many times I remember working in my office, and all of a sudden I'd hear this roar coming out of the back area. In testing, you want to work things hard, and soon enough the engineers had the thing bellowing. It sounded good. We would all leave our workstations and go running back to see what was going on. The engineers would look at us like they had sounded a dinner bell. I'd usually walk around a bit and ask a few questions, and we would all go back to work.

Oftentimes when I got back to the front area, either my phone was ringing, or our next-door neighbor was standing in the lobby waiting for me. He wasn't smiling. His employees were mad, and he had one lady who claimed she was continually getting nauseated and sick from our antics of doing our engine testing. He was usually pretty good about it, and seldom would I mention it to the engineers. Mechanical and design engineers like noise. If they would have known it was bothering the neighbors, they would have dialed it up to more decibels just for fun, and gotten us all kicked out.

Our small but busy engineering group had been making a lot of progress. The Team of engineers included both internal staff and outside contract engineers and designers. It was working pretty well and they were practically working around the clock. We had evolved the motorcycle frame several generations, and the styling was continuing to evolve. There were a few things we were trying out that were innovative; some that we would later find didn't work well and had to be scrapped, and other parts we were engineering that worked out very well and would become competitive advantages.

One of the innovative engineering designs we tried was on the rear suspension. Harking back to nostalgia, for the rear suspension style, we sought to hide the shock and springs from view, thereby creating a clean classic look. Other companies had tried this, but with unsatisfactory riding results. Well, we designed a suspension system that operated on a torsion bar principle that was hidden within the center bolts of the rear swing cage. This had never been done before on a motorcycle that we knew of. It looked pretty cool and the darn thing worked very well.

Only one problem: well, two big problems. First, it wasn't holding up to reliability testing unless we used some exotic metals to reduce the wear, along with an issue of what's called the stacking of tolerances in machining. Basically, this means if you have a lot of sequential pieces that interface with tolerances, you may wind up with potentially too much tolerance in mass production. Second, the cost to manufacture the suspension was prohibitive.

We had to scrap that idea. I really don't know how much time, energy, and money we put into that. It wasn't the first, and it wasn't the last. But this led us to another design, which we ultimately stepped into production and was better. The process of the evolution of design.

Another innovative engineering design we were working on was the front suspension. Our first model, the Super X, was styled to have what we refer to in the motorcycle world as a leading link front suspension. Unlike the rear suspension, which was hidden, the object of the front suspension was to be visible and functional looking, again harking back to earlier motorcycle styling designs. Our goal was to capture the look and functionality of the past, but with modern engineering that would allow us to design a better functioning suspension.

Since the engineering of the front suspension was unique, there were several trial and error attempts. In spite of all the best engineering minds and the use of the computer in creating models that work in the computer, nothing replaces building the actual part. That is where the tire meets the road and you find out if it works. Our early front suspensions had infinite adjustments built into them as we tested to find out what worked well. Ultimately, we came up with a pretty cool working front suspension that is among one of the best front suspension systems ever designed for a cruiser motorcycle. And it is unique and we patented it.

An unexpected side benefit to this new suspension was that for no added cost we were able to engineer into the front end an anti-dive characteristic when braking. It doesn't matter how hard or soft one brakes, the front end just won't dive; yet it still retains its needed suspension characteristics. The motorcycle simply stops. It is much safer than conventional front ends that dive and bounce around. Try braking in a corner and you get some interesting results, whereas with our bike it is predictable. There is no dive while breaking, which brings predictability and safety to the rider. Again, no other cruiser motorcycle in the world has this feature.

Product development on our motorcycle was taking primarily two parallel paths. We had Weslake, our engineering company in England developing our power train; and in Minnesota our group was leading the engineering on the frame and the rest of the components. With the arrival of the engines, it was now time to start integrating the two different paths, and put the engines into our frames for the next generation of prototypes. Only these were going to be slightly different. Engineering didn't need styled prototypes; they just wanted them for engineering and testing purposes. However, marketing needed styled prototypes for the public unveiling and to continue developing consumer and dealer interest. After three long years, the marketplace was getting a little impatient. Therefore these next generations of prototypes had to serve dual purposes. It would be too difficult with the limited time and resources to build separate engineering and marketing prototypes. Under ideal circumstances you wouldn't do it the way we did, but we weren't in ideal circumstances.

These generations of prototypes were known internally as the "Weslake powered" prototypes, and would become the series of prototypes we would show publicly, and were also used by engineering as test mules. Let me define the word prototype here. Even though these were engineering as well as marketing prototypes, they were primarily engineering since that was the most important phase of the project at that time. What this means is the final look and fit and finish were not consumer ready, yet we had to show the marketplace something. Before production would commence, the styling and engineering would continue to evolve and be better integrated, enough so that in several years when we hit production these prototypes would look like distant relatives of each other. Basically, these generations of prototypes weren't yet heavily styled. I have a hard time explaining this, but I have heard it said that if you saw some Hollywood stars without the makeup, airbrushing, fancy clothes and styling you wouldn't even recognize them. Our prototypes were somewhat on that order. Rough, but for a reason. Internally, we all knew they would look better some day.

Even though internally the styling was advanced beyond these Weslake powered prototypes, we hadn't yet fully integrated the styling into the engineering. That's just the way it was as development happens in sequential steps.

On occasion, I would get calls from investors who wanted to view the progress of the company. This was usually a bit of a judgment call. We wanted loyal disciples backing the company, but we also had to consider disclosure and confidentiality issues. We were always concerned about our competitors getting inside information, either purposefully or inadvertently. Most of the time I would allow investors to view the company progress, but only after getting to know them fairly well and discussing with them the strict confidentiality. I have to believe when some of them saw these rough engineering mules they must have wondered what in the heck they had invested in, but seldom did I ever hear an unkind word. They would usually ask a lot of questions, offer some advice, and then just encourage us to continue making progress, and to make a good quality product. And as they were leaving our offices, they would usually buy one of our branded shirts and hats from our museum and store.

• • •

Completing these next generations of Weslake powered prototypes was a major milestone, both internally, and externally to our shareholders, the industry, and prospective consumers. This would be the first time we would fully integrate our chassis, power train, and components into complete working prototypes. We knew everything might not work right, but we didn't know how far off things would be until the first few were built. So there was a lot of anxiety on all fronts.

For the public unveiling in Sturgis we had communicated to the marketplace that we would unveil a working prototype. We used the singular concept here, although we were planning to unveil several prototypes if things went okay. We were hoping to unveil four. The plan here was to under commit to the market, and then over deliver. This was another concept we continually sought to develop in all key facets of our business, and it certainly kept our investors content.

To put together this next generation of prototypes we engaged a firm in a small town in Wisconsin that was a highly skilled restoration shop, primarily for older expensive cars. We had several reasons for this. First off, this shop had craftsmen. In the product development cycle we were transitioning from nonfunctioning styling models to engineered functioning models. If you understand the making of a product, you need tooling to make the final product. Well, tooling is used in production, and you can generally make thousands of parts off of the tooling, but you don't want to make any tooling until you can verify that all the engineering works as you designed it to do. This is the often-misunderstood middle step between engineering and production.

So the big question is: How do you make parts before you have the tooling to make thousands of them? Well, you hand fabricate the parts from scratch and jury-rig some tooling to help you. There is a real art to this, and has been around as long as manufacturing has existed. The specialty making of one-off prototype parts is a big industry, albeit a rather quiet one operated by private owners, and sometimes passed on from generation to generation.

Now the hand fabrication of parts is time consuming and expensive, but it is significantly less expensive and time consuming than cutting the final production tooling for a part. For example, let's consider a rear fender to a motorcycle. The production tooling may cost about $120,000 and take five months to develop, and will then produce thousands of parts that cost about $50 each—high tooling cost but yields low per-piece cost. Contrast this with a hand fabricated fender, where the temporary wood tooling may cost $2500 and one month of lead time, and produce a few fenders that cost $500 each—low tooling cost but high per-piece price. If you understand the basics of what I have just outlined here, you understand the concept of product development and the sequential phases you go through as you ultimately step toward production. The implementation of all this is a lot more complicated than outlined here, but the concept, in principle, remains the same. And has for centuries.

The restoration shop we hired in Wisconsin had the skill sets we were looking for in this intermediary step toward production. In a skilled restoration shop oftentimes the craftsmen have to hand fit and hand fabricate parts out of steel for automobiles that are decades old, and no new parts exist. They develop keen hand-to-eye coordination in the shaping of metal to fit a particular pattern from blueprints or from the old broken part. In the end, they are also skilled in the final assembly and finishing of the components, and several months later and thousands of dollars later you have a beautifully restored car. I knew this well, as I had done enough of this myself, only these people were real skilled craftsmen.

Granted, we could have hired people with this talent and rented out a different facility to do this ourselves, but why reinvent the wheel when there were already skilled shops to work with? In addition, we wouldn't be requiring this volume of work long term in the company since once we hit production it becomes incremental changes. Therefore, for a lot of reasons, it didn't make sense to seek to do this ourselves. It would be better to manage an outside contractor. And these guys were great about it. A few of our staff people were constantly onsite around the clock with the shop, and they were making tremendous progress.

But the sand was running out of the hourglass. We almost didn't make it. We were unveiling in Sturgis on Monday morning at 9:00 a.m. At 5:00 p.m. the Friday before, we still didn't have any running prototypes. None. Seven hundred miles away, no running prototypes. Needless to say, there were no weekends at Excelsior. This was not unusual; this was just another daily Excelsior experience.

It was time to get down on my knees and pray again. Now, I'm not going to get real religious here, but in my biased opinion, when I give advice to those seeking to start a company, I encourage them to have two things—one, a family; and two, faith. If you don't have either one of them, I suggest just go get them because on the unknown journey that awaits, you will need both. On many a late night when I left the office, I had gotten into the habit of stopping at a church, often around midnight. Kneeling down at the base of the cross outside, I would pray my heart out, and leave a cash donation tucked in a crack. Each time I went back, the money was always gone. I figured someone needed it worse than me. To the drivers of the cars that would pass by, they must have wondered what was going on with that poor lost soul. I didn't care; my pride was elsewhere. It seemed to work.

With no time to lose, our Team was en route from Wisconsin with the prototypes. With a lot of luck, they believed they could finish them in time for the unveiling, but there was not enough time for travel. The solution was to put the bikes, people, and a makeshift shop into an enclosed trailer, and while en route to the Sturgis Rally, finish the bikes. That's what they did. It was a minor miracle, and it worked. We never even had a chance to test the engines before they were fired up on the prototypes. I remember Al, our VP of Engineering, telling me he hoped that Michael at Weslake had done a good job on the engines, since nobody had a chance to fire them up.

Well, destiny was with us.

This next part is a little hard for me to write since it touches me so much, and for those who were there, I believe it was also life altering, either for themselves, or they were witnessing it in others. This next paragraph is quoted directly from a Shareholder letter I wrote describing the unveiling:

"*Presented to our fellow bikers at Sturgis: four of our Super X prototypes. We were nervous. Being judged by our own kind. What if they don't all start? Nine o'clock August fifth, the sun is already hot, sweat breaks out...the police ask us to hurry up since the crowd is out of control...we move our schedule ahead...bike number one fires up...bike number two fires up...bike number three fires up...bike number four—nothing. The crowd doesn't notice over the roar of engines and cheers. Not perfect, like life, but we made it. Our biking brothers welcomed us back into the family—but now a larger and forever different family.*"

That's still probably the best way for me to describe the unveiling. This is also probably where the soul of the company arose. There was a transformation, and we could all feel it.

We received a tremendous amount of press coverage for the unveiling event, whether print, radio, television, and local, national and international. I'll quote a paragraph from a two-page article that one of the leading industry magazines published that gives a perspective: *"The Super X prototypes unveiled at Sturgis were something else; they were real and running. Rolled out before the most critical crowd possible, the bikers gathered in the Black Hills, it was like dropping four aces onto the table. Excelsior-Henderson had been doing more than just selling shirts, raising money, and negotiating a factory location; they'd designed and built a motorcycle, the 85-cubic-inch Super X. The 5,000 motorcyclists who almost tore down the tent for that first look on Monday, and those who saw the bike during the rest of Sturgis, all had the same question: When will these things be up and ready for sale?"*

Now let me give you some of the corporate logic that was going on regarding this event. We wanted to unveil more than one prototype since it would display more substance, replication, and multiple paint schemes. Also, I always wanted to be prepared for disaster. What if we had one prototype and by a stroke of bad luck it didn't fire in front of the media and five thousand intense witnesses? Real bad. But if we had more than one prototype, at least one of them should start.

As a farm kid, the one thing I had learned about mechanical things is that they can fool you at the wrong time. And I didn't want this to damage the company. We had four prototypes and at the unveiling the fourth didn't fire up. It was mine. I was at the controls. I hit start and nothing happened. Luckily, the other three were roaring, and the crowd was cheering. I was sweating. Much later when the crowd cleared, we found the problem. A fuse under the seat blew just as I hit the start button. Why? Never know. But it never blew again.

At the unveiling we had crowds of over five thousand people, and during the week it was estimated we had about twenty-five thousand bikers go through our display. Our marketing theme for the unveiling was *"Witness A Resurrection,"* and we had posters and flyers promoting the unveiling, claiming *"Today Is Resurrection Day."* If I were to look back on my nine years with Excelsior, this is the one single event that marked the company. It would never be the same, and if the unveiling had failed, the company would have failed.

If the marketplace had shown lackluster interest in our company and motorcycles, the show would be over. It really was judgment day. Fortunately, our Business Plan and marketing strategy was validated that day. Not only was it an emotional win, but also it was a formal validation of the market interest.

We now showed physical substance. The critics had said we would never design a proprietary bike. They now had to find something different.

Our Team of people had done a great job. We had a lot of volunteers helping us—friends and family, and future dealers and suppliers. Most working for free. I was glad to be just one small part of it.

Just two years earlier when I wore my first Excelsior-Henderson shirt in Sturgis, not one person noticed. Now, everywhere I went I was answering questions and signing autographs. One night I wore a Harley shirt just to blend in with the crowd, but even that didn't work. My life was beginning to change.

When I got back to my Burnsville office, I turned to the milestone chart on my wall, and checked one off.

*We did it.*

# 17

## The Governor, The Farm Kid, And The Golden Horses

In just a few days we were set to announce our new factory location, and there was a lot of work to do. The next milestone.

Along with everything else, over the last several months we had been zeroing in on a site location. By now we had toured sites in Minnesota, Ohio, and Wisconsin. It was becoming harder to focus on locations out of state. We just didn't have the momentum in the other states that we were building locally and regionally. Also, it was disconcerting to our employees and independent contractors not knowing if we were moving or not, as they would have to relocate or quit. Plus, it was hard recruiting people while we were based in Minnesota and then moving in two years. For these and a lot of interrelated reasons, the state of Minnesota was looking better.

Even though the state tax rate was among the highest in the nation, most of our future sales were going to come from outside the state—therefore reducing our taxes, and we did have a sizable tax loss-carry forward that would offset any profits. I remember calculating it out one day, and for the first ten years it was about a wash. Analytically, it was making sense.

Also, in my gut it was starting to feel right about staying in Minnesota. It was a good state, and it made a good story to stay there. It felt right. But we needed to make it work financially. States like North Dakota and South Dakota had some very attractive financing packages, and to a company like ours that was in negative cash flow, financing was always the driver. I would move to Alaska and make motorcycles there if that was our only choice.

Within our own little world, our venture was starting to get noticed: regionally, nationally, and internationally. We were rather bold, but in a quiet way. I guess the simplest way I have found to describe it is—"*our actions were bold but our mouths were not.*"

Months earlier I had mentioned to Pat Pelstring, our site location hired gun, that when we announced our location we would do it on the steps of the selected State Capitol. By then he was starting to get to know me well enough that he didn't question it. Neither he nor I knew it could be true. Let's give it a run and see. Also, when I met with representatives of the various states, I would mention this to them, quietly. Well, I can't take the full credit here, but I found out when you mention something like this to people who are people of action, they start working on it, and the next thing you know, one thing leads to another. I've done this a lot, and it is part of what I call my farm logic— sow some seeds, and see what grows. What hits fertile soil will produce. In working with good people, they usually only need a hint on the direction, and then they figure it out.

When all the research, state and community tours, and analysis were done, we decided to locate in Belle Plaine, Minnesota, the Hanlon family's hometown. I would never have predicted that, and six months earlier would have placed a bet against it. Shows how wrong a person can be, and I am open-minded to admit when I am wrong.

That darn town had changed, or I had, or both of us had. And they tried harder—to me they were like the little horse who started last in the race, but didn't know it was supposed to lose—they just kept on trying until they accomplished it. During our earlier site location tours, Belle Plaine didn't play by the rules. That was right up my marketing-alley. They did some unfair things, like invite my parents from their farm just a few miles down the road. And they invited the community to join in, from parents and grandparents, to children. They even brought in the high school band, and had the elementary kids write us letters. A lot of them. Some were written in crayon. This was unfair. They had everything including the apple pie and ice cream at Emma Krumbee's. It certainly wasn't all about the money, but rather a good fit in the community for our business. A community that would welcome and be proud to be the home of Excelsior-Henderson Motorcycles. Because it was such a good fit, I knew we could get things done and together overcome any future hurdles.

It was the best place to locate our world headquarters and new factory; only it took me some time to be convinced of it. Analytically, they met all of our established criteria perfectly—no more than an hour drive from an international airport, a four-lane freeway into the city, a blend of a rural and city skilled workforce, and an industrial park with land right on the freeway where our factory would be visible to everyone on the road. Location. Location. Location.

And it was important to locate in a community where we could establish deep roots...real fast. I didn't want us to be viewed as newcomers to a small, growing community. We wanted to be part of the fabric of the community, and welcome the community to join our business, and our business to join their community. This location would be our world headquarters, and we wanted to immediately establish good community relations. Not only is it a good business strategy, it is also simply the right thing to do. Belle Plaine was that type of community. They were already making us feel welcome and a part of the community. It felt like the right decision.

Plus there was a trump card that Pat had uncovered. Belle Plaine was just barely located far enough out in the country that under the right structure our factory might qualify for special low interest loans from the United States Department of Agriculture. Our hired gun was earning his keep.

And for a small, but evolving community, they had a progressive mayor—Mayor Gerry Meyer—and a progressive city council and skilled city staff. They are bright people and not afraid of hard work, and hiring skilled outside talent. Over about a year's time frame, I had attended dozens of City Council meetings; not only in Belle Plaine, but also in several cities where we'd contemplated locating the company. I was confident the Belle Plaine City Council would be fair-minded to work with, and they were.

The State Department of Economic Development, led by a guy named Jay Novak, was also very active and progressive. On several occasions, our staff met with his staff, and with him personally. He was a man of action, knew how to get things done, had a good staff around him, and was a good communicator. And most importantly, he was willing to be open-minded on our venture.

Combined with the City of Belle Plaine, and the State of Minnesota, we put together a financing package for about $12 million. On paper, and at the time, it all looked pretty good. Later, in the next year and a half, as the details got sorted out and the financing changed—lower—by several million, we would have to put several more million into the deal, but I didn't know that at the time, and it didn't matter. Things like that are to be expected, and we did. Even in the end, it was still the best financing terms we could get while in negative cash flow.

On August 21, 1996, on the steps of the Minnesota State Capitol, just under the golden horses displayed majestically above, Governor Arne Carlson announced in an official news conference that Excelsior-Henderson Motorcycles would locate its new headquarters and factory in Belle Plaine, Minnesota. More than that, he signed a proclamation, and declared the date in history as Excelsior-Henderson Day In Minnesota, presenting me personally with the plaque. In addition, he also issued an Official Press Release from the Office of the

Governor of the State of Minnesota. As I read the Official Press Release later in my office, I had to chuckle. At the bottom of the press release was listed the Deputy Chief of Staff, Cyndy Brucato, a former news anchor. I had met her about fifteen years earlier, when she was the Celebrity Grand Marshall for a parade in Saint Paul, and we led the parade as she rode in my 1968 Pontiac Firebird convertible. A black convertible, with a 428 cubic inch engine with three-two-barrel carburetors. I smoked the tires at that parade.

At the State Capitol there were over a thousand people in attendance, including employees, families, bikers, shareholders, politicians—and a busload of people from Belle Plaine. We also brought our large semi-trailer painted boldly with Excelsior-Henderson on the sides and parked it right on the front steps. It was grassroots. This was the real McCoy. Our company was starting to take on a life of its own, and we had thousands of grassroots people not only pulling for us, but also stepping in to help.

If we didn't have so much work to get done, this would be some pretty heady stuff.

Governor Arne Carlson said something in his presentation I will never forget. He was expressing his support for our decision to locate in an area outside of the main metropolitan region in a more rural setting that would help develop the state. He commented on the workforce, and I quote: *"When you hire a kid from the farm and ask them to be to work at eight o'clock in the morning, they wonder what they're going to do with those two extra hours."* Growing up on a dairy farm, I knew in my heart what he meant. We were milking cows before six in the morning.

I drove back to the office to get to work. I turned to the milestone chart on my wall, and checked another one off.

We did it.

• • •

We still had to close the financing on our Offering Memorandum, and find a developer willing to lend us money to build the factory we just announced. But this was all part of a well-orchestrated strategic business plan, and everything needed to be done in its sequential steps. One step at a time.

*Details.*

# 18

## *Reborn To Be Wild—Burnout Style*

The new year of 1997 was off to a fast start already. This was going to be another big year, with significant milestones to reach, and if we didn't reach them it would all be over. In general, the mood at the company was upbeat; we had just finished a tough year but we did make it through, and now we even had running engineered prototypes. We were starting to feel like a motorcycle company. We had bikes to ride, but they weren't very good yet.

There were many facets to the business that had to keep moving forward simultaneously with one another. The Bike Week Rally in Daytona Beach was looming on the immediate horizon, and we had a lot of work to do. As a company we had decided that the motorcycle event rallies were a good place for us to market. Each industry has some unique characteristics, and motorcycle rallies are one of the unique things about the motorcycle industry. Where else do you get grown men and women taking vacation time to go attend a rally, and usually year after year? And the rallies were continuing to grow. Daytona Beach Bike Week is billed as the largest motorcycle rally in the world—it started in 1937—and it is not uncommon to attract about a half-million motorcyclists from around the world during the one-week March event, which now stretches into about twice that length.

If you have never attended an American motorcycle rally, I would certainly encourage you to give it a try. It is a life-altering experience. What makes these rallies unique is that they are primarily created by grassroots consumers, not by the industry or manufacturer.

Most industries, including the computer and motorcycle industries, have consumer shows that are put on by the industry manufacturers to promote their product or service and introduce new products or services. Typical of most of these shows, they are fairly dry to attend, yet it is still one of the most effective ways to reach consumers directly and receive input, unless you have a better way. Which in the motorcycle industry, there is.

When I talk about the motorcycle rallies, such as at Sturgis, South Dakota; Daytona Beach, Florida; and Laconia, New Hampshire, these aren't the factory-type shows, but rather are created by the consumers.

In fact they are the opposite of factory-sponsored shows. I am not aware of any industry that has larger consumer-created grassroots rallies, compared to shows created by the industry. These rallies sprouted up on their own, by grassroots motorcyclists during more than a half-century time period.

For decades, the motorcycle industry and OEMs shunned these motorcycle rallies, and in some cases, rightly so, because these rallies sometimes had an intense reputation. But over the years as word of the rallies grew, they became populated more by mainstream motorcyclists, most of whom ride primarily American motorcycles. And with Harley-Davidson being the most dominant or exclusive manufacturer in America for decades, most of the riders at the rallies were riding primarily Harleys.

Well, an interesting development was taking place. As word of the rallies grew, by the late 1980s and headed into the 1990s, these rallies were receiving a larger attendance than the consumer trade shows, and most importantly, there was a huge target market of specific motorcyclists at these rallies. They really became the core, or the soul, of the motorcyclists in America who chose to ride American bikes, mainly Harleys. During this similar time frame the OEMs began to realize that just maybe it was a good venue for them to promote their company. This is a real interesting paradox—rather than have the consumers going to the factory-sponsored shows, here were the OEMs being attracted to the grassroots motorcycle events. So the OEMs decided to start going to the rallies to promote. Obviously, this in turn helped to give the rallies more industry support and structure, and the growth at the rallies magnified. It was a great example of a good thing getting bigger and better.

By attending the three largest rallies in the country, we would have access to over one million motorcyclists, and nearly all of them within our psychographic and demographic profile. This is some good marketing stuff, particularly for companies like us who were looking for a specific type of motorcyclist, and didn't have enough funds or clout to market in all the traditional ways of advertising, consumer shows, direct mail, etc.

Therefore, we came to the logical conclusion of utilizing the motorcycle events around the country as a significant part of our key early market strategic positioning. We would take our company directly to the consumer, and grassroots style. As a company, we were grassroots also, so it was a great blend. We didn't need to be too bright to figure this out. Usually anyone with a marketing degree who would challenge us on this business decision had never attended a rally. Once they did, they understood and became believers.

This did cause a few crossed wires for some in the industry though. They saw us as boycotting the traditional methods of media advertising and the consumer shows, and we were continually questioned on this, and criticized.

To some degree, we were a bit of a rebel of a company anyway, and chose our own path, so I didn't mind; but also, as a developing company we didn't have the budget or the time to do everything. We had to be the most effective, and as a consumer myself, believed it was best to get as close to the grassroots customer as we could—away from their place of work and away from home. Also, I thought we could really do a better and more effective job than our competition since we were more nimble at the grassroots level. Some of the things we did at the rallies came spontaneously, and not from planned meetings in the boardroom. We were in our element at the rallies, and we knew it. It didn't take long for the competition to figure this out also. It was one of our competitive edges.

We knew that those who took vacation time to travel to a motorcycle rally were serious—serious about their fun anyway. Therefore, for several reasons it was the best and the right thing to do, and it worked very well. As the company progressed, we naturally started to blend the motorcycle events with consumer shows, and advertising, since they do help integrate the marketing message.

Our marketing strategy was to not try and do everything, but rather pick a few things, and then do them exceedingly well. That was how we looked at the unveiling of our motorcycles in Sturgis the summer before, and now headed into spring, that was how we were approaching Daytona Beach. It was now time to move our marketing message south.

Our strategy with the events was to then integrate major development milestones within the company, and utilize the rallies as one effective method to communicate directly with the grassroots consumer about the progress of our company. For the Daytona Beach rally, we decided to move the company up a notch, and kick off the Inaugural Excelsior-Henderson Motorcycle Parade with our prototypes. It was a great idea. Harley-Davidson traditionally closes down the Daytona rally with a parade, but no one kicked it off. Hmm, maybe someone needed to kick off the rally, and we decided it would be us. Provided we could get the City of Daytona Beach to agree. Which we did.

In order to generate consumer and industry interest for the parade, we had to communicate it to the marketplace long before we really knew if we could achieve it. If we didn't, it would be a great public embarrassment.

In early 1997, we were preparing earnestly to get the company progressed far enough that we could "*do what we said we would do, when we said we would do it.*"

The bikes needed a little work. At the unveiling in Sturgis, even though those prototypes were our first engineered prototypes, they were also our first engineered—*untested*—prototypes. Not everything was as we had hoped. Some things turned out better than planned, and a few items needed work.

For one thing, the bikes were nearly unrideable but for one simple fix. Our engineering department was seeking a way to prevent premature bearing failure in the steering head that occurs on some bikes. The decision was made to go away from the traditional roller or ball bearing, and instead use a spherical bearing. I was very leery of this, but sometimes you just have to let people do their own exploring, even though I disagreed. There is a fine line between giving encouragement to be creative, and reigning a person in when you think they have gone too far.

The spherical bearing was supposed to wear less, therefore giving increased reliability to the steering. The offsetting factor though was what is called "break away torque," meaning simply how much pressure or resistance will it take to turn the bearing. According to the specifications provided by the factory supplier, it should be nearly identical to the various bearings—ball or roller—we were contemplating using. But I knew from my mechanic days, that at least in the applications I had experienced, it didn't work the way it was supposed to. In regard to our steering, what conceivably could happen is that it would create an ever so slight initial resistance for the motorcycle rider to turn the handlebars, thereby creating a sort of choppy turn back and forth. And unfortunately, that was happening with our engineered prototypes.

When we first went to ride them it was a whole new experience. And not a safe one. We went from jubilation to terror faster than I can write this. For most riders, and myself, after riding a motorcycle for so many years, the nuances of the slight leaning and slight adjusting of the handlebars as one rides are so ingrained they become instinctive, at least until something significant changes. I never knew that such a slight change in the smooth adjustment of a handlebar could impact so much on the stability. After trying to ride the bikes, and losing a few months "discussing" with the design Team an alternate plan, we finally had to scrap the spherical bearing concept until later (interpret as never). We called our machinist man, Dan Olberg, and he retrofitted all our existing prototypes with roller bearings, in just a few days and for a few thousand dollars.

So this steering head bearing area was one of the examples we learned that it was best to use more conventional and time-tested materials.

After the retrofit on the head bearings, the bikes took on a whole new meaning on the road. They felt like real motorcycles. Granted they needed some tweaking, a lot of testing, and continual styling to improve the fit and finish, but on the surface they worked pretty good. They had great power and handled pretty well.

These prototypes were being used for engineering, marketing, and styling purposes. What we did was split up some of the early prototypes between these three departments, with priority given to engineering and styling.

Styling was continuing to advance, and for the Daytona Beach Inaugural Parade we wanted to have our most current prototypes, since the engineering ones were really no longer viewable by the public as they were going through constant testing. The generation of prototypes we built for Daytona was similar to the first generation, but did have a few updated styling pieces and engineering updates. Like the first prototypes, these were also powered by the Weslake engines.

• • •

Daytona Beach is a great place to be in March if you are a motorcyclist from the north. It is unbelievable how many people show up riding their motorcycles, or have them brought by trailer. It is like motorcycle heaven of the south, and a lot of East Coast, West Coast, and northern people travel to Daytona Beach for the rally. It is a great break from the winter, and to relive memories with friends.

The rally officially started on Monday, March 3rd. For each rally we developed a theme, and our marketing theme for Bike Week was "Reborn To Be Wild." During our scouting trips the previous years we had uncovered a downtown location for our display. It was the Peabody Auditorium, situated on Wild Olive Boulevard. I've always liked that address: *"Wild Olive."* It somewhat spoke of our company, the wild part anyway. We were now located just across the street from the Harley-Davidson rally headquarters, and just off the main street. Sometimes I can't help but think the folks at Harley must have been a little peeved at us, as we would force ourselves upon them as neighbors. But we all know the logic of why it was good for us to do that, and it certainly didn't harm them either. We were in the same camp, only they had a much larger one.

The parade was to start at the racetrack about five miles away from our display downtown, and the parade route would take us through all the busy parts of the rally, through downtown, and then to our display. We had seven prototypes ready for the parade, and since they were in our display in the morning, we decided to ride them out to the parade location. All over town we had posted flyers and billboards about the parade, billing it as *"There Hasn't Been A Parade Around Here Like This In 65 Years,"* to mark the return of the Excelsior-Henderson brand in the marketplace.

On the way out we took some of the back streets to avoid attention and traffic, and as we were cruising down the road I smelled gasoline. I always liked the smell of gas, and didn't immediately think much of it. After a few more blocks though, I felt moisture hitting my face—sometimes a lot—and it smelled heavily of gasoline. I looked up just in front of me and there was Al Benz on one of the prototypes; it was shooting gas out the side of the engine, and the gas was hitting me in the face. He was oblivious to it, but I soon wasn't. I was starting to smell bad. I pulled up alongside of him, and we had to pull over to check it out.

On these types of maiden runs we generally had one of our test mechanics—this time my brother Terry—following in an unmarked truck and trailer, in the event we needed to do some roadside repairs. As a bold marketing company, we had a lot of well-marked trucks and trailers, but when it came to testing, we had unmarked vehicles—best that nobody else knew what was going on. The problem was quickly diagnosed as a ruptured fuel line, and with the fuel injection system under pressure, it was squirting out fuel. We quickly replaced the line and continued on our journey to the parade, arriving just in time. It seemed as if there was always something going wrong just to test us, but it was never enough to stop the show. But it did test the nerves.

Our marketing Team had done a good job of preparing for the parade. That was our style. Be thorough. Be bold. Be grassroots. And get our unfair share. It looked like we were just about to do that.

When our crew from Excelsior arrived at the Daytona Speedway Racetrack riding our seven Super X prototypes, we were greeted by a large enthusiastic crowd. Since it was a parade, it was only appropriate to affix flags to each of the bikes. We had the Excelsior-Henderson Company flag on one side of the bikes, and on the other was the U.S. flag. After a short introductory speech by the Daytona Beach Mayor, and ourselves, we fired up the bikes and kicked off the Inaugural Parade under motorcycle police escort.

We created quite a stir along the parade route. We had our special Daytona Drag Pipes on most of the bikes, including mine, and we were frequently gunning the engines. It was a time to be loud and proud, and we were. The police were all good about it too. We did lose one of the prototypes along the route as it developed mechanical problems, and again our Team of unmarked Road Crew helpers quietly got the bike attended to in one of our trailers.

We also had another first, and invited members of the Antique Motorcycle Club of America (AMCA) to ride along near the front of the parade. The AMCA is an eclectic group of people who all share a love of old American motorcycles, and it is impressive seeing the collections the various members have. Being a lover of old American motorcycles, I always encouraged our company to support the AMCA and its members. This group of people is the core of what makes motorcycling great here in America. Many of the people are about as old as their bikes, and most bikes range in age from 70 to 90 years old. If old bikes could talk, there would be quite a story. Instead, their owners tell the story for them.

Anyway, I was impressed that many members of the AMCA took up our offer to ride in the parade, and they brought out many different models of old motorcycles, primarily old Excelsiors, Hendersons, Harley-Davidsons, and Indian motorcycles. In all there must have been nearly three dozen antique motorcycles and riders. There is something pretty neat about watching a seventy-year-old man ride an eighty-year-old motorcycle, and add to that riding in a parade at high noon through Main Street during Daytona Beach Bike Week. I had a smile on my face that I couldn't wipe off.

During the parade I remember looking back at the old bikes and there was Dick Winger navigating one of his teens era Excelsiors, and Ernie Hartman cruising on our 1931 Excelsior Super X, and Joe Gardella riding and pedaling a 1909 Excelsior. There was some great iron in the parade. It was quite a show.

Later I had heard the old bikes stole the show from the new prototypes. But I didn't mind, as I think they meant it as a half-tease. The old and new bikes together felt like the right thing to do, and it also bridged any generation gaps that might have existed between riders.

We were always bold marketers at the rallies, and at this one we didn't disappoint. We had a plane flying overhead with the Excelsior-Henderson banner streaming behind it, and plenty of billboard and placard advertising. Our field crew of salespeople was pretty good about getting the bartenders and waitresses attired in Excelsior apparel. It was not at all unusual to visit nearly any bar within fifty miles of Daytona Beach, and either a bartender or waitress was in Excelsior apparel. I was not always sure how they arranged to get that done, but they did a great job. They were pretty good at it, and judging by the stories I heard, they had quite an art of making this happen. Being salespeople, of course they had to compete on who had the best story.

The one thing I remember most about this rally though was the burnouts. This was the rally in which the company initiated doing burnouts on our bikes. It was also the first rally we had Super X bikes to ride, so it was only natural to do something flashy and memorable. It didn't take long for it to become tradition, and over the next several years we went through a lot of rear tires. For some reason these Weslake engine prototype Super X motorcycles were just prone to doing massive burnouts—almost like they were begging to be pushed to the limit. There was something primeval about them. Over all the years of doing this, we never once blew a motor.

Usually a cruiser motorcycle is not well suited to doing a burnout, but these bikes were different. The front brake worked so well, and with the anti-dive characteristic designed into the front-end, by just lightly grabbing the front braking, and blipping the throttle and dropping the clutch, the rear tire would be spinning. Frequently I would do this, and wind it up through to fifth gear and the tire would be spinning at over one hundred miles per hour. Smoke from the tire would fill the air, until the bike could no longer be seen—only heard along with the smell of burnt rubber. We would frequently stage unexpected burnouts all over town, and the Super X with its bellowing drag pipes and its aggressive riders quickly got a reputation. It was great company promotion, but not the type of stuff that would get approved in the boardroom. But at the rally, it just seemed a matter of course as we would get caught up in the events.

Undoubtedly, we got to know some of the police a little better too.

• • •

When I got back to my office from the Daytona Beach Rally, I turned to the chart on my wall and checked off another successfully accomplished milestone.

# 19

## A Shaking Fist At The Groundbreaking

Things were starting to heat up on the factory front. We planned to be in production in late 1998; that meant we had to be in the factory about a year before that, which means we had to break ground at the factory site in the spring, and spring was nearly here. We didn't have the building and layout completely designed yet, nor had we solidified the financing.

One of the important items helping us on this project was the utilization of the skills of a hired gun once again. This assignment would require someone to shepherd the process through the city of Belle Plaine, Scott County, and the State of Minnesota, along with working closely with our inside production engineers, our external factory design engineers, our architectural firm, and our developer. We basically needed someone who would act as my right-arm person through this process, and we had engaged the services of a firm named Corporate Real Estate, which was owned by Bruce Maus, and his partner Jim Stoker. These two individuals were our external hired guns— my internal hired gun was Paul Van Brunt—on this project and they were all well versed in factory construction along with the nuances of working with the various governmental sectors. These external hired guns must have had about seventy years of experience between them, and Jim had just retired from 3M, where he was the head of corporate real estate. In the interviewing process these people really impressed me with their plain-spoken, get-things-done mentality, and as I would find our later, they didn't disappoint.

One of the first things I needed them to do after we had engaged them was to finalize a developer we would work with. Even though we had announced the previous August that we would be building our factory in Belle Plaine, at the time we didn't have the financing or the developer committed. Within thirty days of the announcement, we had engaged Bruce and his firm, and we went about pursuing the right developer for us.

Over the years many developers in the region had contacted us and now it was time to analyze which one to work with. Personally, I knew I wasn't an expert in this area, and because my expertise was in finding the experts to work with, I thought the investment of a hired gun would keep us on schedule, and on budget. That is why we needed a good hired gun, not lip service, and why we needed to get along well. I remember in the interviewing process when I interviewed Bruce Maus, I asked him about the frequency of written reports he would provide to me. In short, he explained he had never needed to do that formally, as he would have so much direct communication that it wouldn't be needed. It was hard to believe that statement, but his references verified this also. After working with him, I quickly learned that he was in such frequent and effective communication, we didn't need formal written progress reports, except as needed on unusual issues.

Bruce knew the executives of nearly all the large regional and national developers that would be a candidate for our factory project, and he wasted no time in setting up meetings for us. With his guidance, and our pretty well refined presentation, the meetings went very well. Like in most early relationships, there was one developer with whom we seemed to strike a chord almost immediately, and in the gut it felt right.

Bruce had arranged a meeting with Pat Ryan, President of Ryan Companies of Minneapolis. Ryan Companies was a well-known commercial developer, and had been a family held Minnesota company since 1938. They had completed commercial projects for the likes of Ford Motor Company, 3M, John Deere, Toro, AT&T, Target, and Honeywell. There seemed to be instant harmony between the two companies and the respective management, along with the attitude of getting things done. I had learned that Pat Ryan was a lawyer by education, so I was thinking his written agreement would be lengthy and verbose. Instead, it was the opposite. Written shortly and in plain English. I liked these guys. Even my mother could read this contract.

Pat told me they had launched deals on a handshake, and that if they shook hands on a deal, they got it done. As we were progressing in the various meetings in getting to know them, he mentioned that when they commit to a groundbreaking date, and a completion date, they hit it. Also, their references proved his statements. I like companies and people like this. My butt was on the line. If we worked with people and firms who couldn't commit to getting things done on time and on budget, I knew our story was history. We were constantly relying on the ability of our Team, and we needed the A-Team to continually produce results.

Also, Ryan Companies agreed to finance up to $5 million of the anticipated $10 million construction cost—these guys knew how to close a deal. We struck a deal, and when it came time to sign the contract, Pat Ryan stopped out and signed the Construction Agreement. He signed it with green ink. I'll never forget that. I usually use green ink also. I asked him about that, and he said it is part of his company's heritage. They sign all their contracts in green ink.

•••

Running parallel to the developer contract was the architectural design phase. Prior to engaging Ryan as our developer for the factory, we had engaged the services of an architectural firm. For most established businesses looking to construct additional facilities, they may use a different process than what we used, but we needed to accelerate everything and keep flexibility at the same time. One of the ways we did this on the early design phase was to engage a separate architectural firm, in conjunction with reviewing proposals from developers. My goal was that ultimately when a final developer was selected, we would either hook up with the developer's architect, or in the best-case scenario, retain our architectural firm to work together with our developer. If we kept true to our strategy of working with the A-Team type companies, and with the A-Team staff of these companies, ultimately when we engaged the firms we should be able to have the different companies work effectively together. Plus, if they were truly of A-Team caliber, the probability was high that they had already worked together on previous projects.

Excelsior-Henderson was getting to be pretty well known in the regional area, and most architectural firms knew we would be soon constructing a facility, and accordingly we were receiving brochures from firms around the country. For logistics purposes, we primarily preferred someone local, as it should lower our costs and streamline communications. More importantly though, was finding someone, or a firm with someone who had a penchant for our type of building design, and doing so at moderate cost. The ultimate goal was to design a building and factory that would look more expensive than what it really was. With the right architect and firm, I knew this could be done.

We also desired a timeless design in our facility. By timeless design I mean a design that won't go out of style, and from a passersby perspective might lead to some confusion as to whether the building was a new building designed to look old, or an old building renovated to modern standards—a study in contrasts. Similar to our company of being both new and with old heritage. It just seemed logical to the authenticity of the brand.

One of the best ways I found to locate an architect was to drive around and look for buildings that I liked, and then find out who designed them, along with using referrals from others who previously had buildings designed. After interviewing several firms, we finally selected a firm in Saint Paul named Pope Architects, lead by Jon Pope.

Jon Pope and his crew were prudent architects, and they had previously worked with Ryan Companies in designing and constructing buildings. Therefore, they had already established a working relationship, and we could immediately start working together and not lose time on relationship building.

One of the main reasons I wanted to hire Pope Architects was because of Mark Mednikov, an architect of their firm who we thought would be the right candidate to design our building. In the interviewing process we had a chance to meet Mark, and he impressed me early on with his approach to our building design. He was one of the few who actually seemed to listen to our needs before he made suggestions on what he thought we would like. This might seem like a minor point, but for anyone who has worked with creative minds, the creative part likes to create, and sometimes they like to create their own way. In our case though, as the customer, we needed to have it created our way. Mark had a good grasp of this concept, and I offered him a challenge.

We needed a building that had a strong, classic timeless design, but at a low cost. Again, this would give the impression of a more expensive looking building than what it actually was. This was a big challenge to our company, and to Ryan as our developer and Pope as our architect. Even though they all expressed their concern, they also were willing to meet the budget that was set.

Earlier in the process, our facilities engineering Team had concluded we would need a building around 165,000 square feet that would house the entire corporation, and would be our headquarters facility. Not only would the facility include the production of motorcycles, but it would also house all the other functions of a headquarters location.

We established the total project budget at about $10.3 million— with about $8.6 million allocated to the building, and approximately $1.7 million allocated to land acquisition, roadway construction, parking lots, legal and consulting fees (everything else). Factoring all these numbers together meant that the building would have a construction cost of less than $50 per square foot, and fully allocated cost with land and improvements of $60 per square foot. These were some reasonably aggressive numbers if we wanted to construct a quality, well-designed building that included heating and air conditioning in the entire building, including the factory. These costs also included the initial electrical costs for the power requirements of the factory.

Well, Mark, our architect from Pope Associates, didn't want to back away from these numbers, even though many others we had consulted with wanted to. I could see in his eyes he felt challenged by the cause. Mark had been born in Russia and had immigrated to America, so he understood what tough was. He also had a quiet, confident, and studious style. And the buildings he designed seemed to have a flair for the nostalgic and early European influence our country had. With his European upbringing, he was quite familiar with the use of stone, concrete, and wood in designs that would make them unique, yet cost and quality effective.

Through a creative use of these materials, Mark and our Building Team were able to come up with a design that met our style criteria and our budget. Even today, and at the time the building was constructed in 1997, one of the most common comments I heard was that the building looked as if it was overbuilt, meaning too high priced. I still chuckle at that and think our Team must have done a good job. When I told people it cost less per square foot than their home or the local discount mass merchandiser, most were shocked. We had accomplished our goal of designing and constructing a building that was competitive to the marketplace, and cost less than it looked.

Some of it was simple logic and frugal management, and a bit of luck. We were a motorcycle company, and we didn't need any exotic materials and marble floors. Instead, we opted for natural lighting, cement exterior, and rather than marble, a brick floor in the entryway. Not expensive brick, but the kind of brick you can buy at your local lumberyard to use outside since it is rough looking. Well, we used that brick walkway outside, and when you came inside, the very same block guided you to the inside, and with a sand base under the brick. We didn't use any special sealer or grouting on the floor, and just let it look natural, including the sand between the bricks inside the building. It showed character. That is the best way to describe our entire building. We wanted it to look natural and comfortable so that you almost didn't notice it. It has character.

We also decided to leave a lot of the elements of the building exposed. Why cover things up? It looked more functional and natural to leave beams exposed, or steel rafters, as long as the look was integral with the rest of the facility. On the outside of the building, it was mostly the low cost tilt-up pre-cast concrete, along with cement block, and brick. We had the color scheme we desired cast into the concrete and into the cement block, for really no added cost. Basically, it is a flattop pre-cast concrete building, with a creative use of color and materials to give an historic perception.

Obviously, until the building was built, it was all perception and speculation. Oftentimes people asked me what the building would look like. Outwardly I would smile; the town of Belle Plaine is an historic community, and because it was originally built during some pretty isolated and hardy times, it had more than its share of church steeples and bars. And I had been in most every one of them. So I usually answered with a little bit of humor, joking that *"the building would look like a bar with a steeple on it!"* I had to keep my sense of humor somehow.

The building project was progressing well, and on a hurried schedule, like everything else in the company. Time was money, and time was our enemy. Everything had to move fast and accurately. Our Building Team concluded the facility would take about seven months to construct. Mike Bauer, the project manager from Ryan who was coordinating the project from the developer side, informed us they would be ready to break ground in April, and we set a date of Monday, April 14, 1997, for the groundbreaking ceremony.

At Excelsior, we were always foraging for ways to market the company in a grassroots manner and involve them in our milestones. I asked someone with our marketing Team—I don't remember who—to do a little homework on groundbreaking ceremonies. After a few days, I was informed the ceremony usually included a ribbon cutting, and the ceremonial first dig of dirt was with six bald guys and a shovel. I liked that. Hmm, I thought, we can do better than that.

So, as a Team—the new Groundbreaking Team—we were determined to set a world record for a groundbreaking ceremony. You probably realize, as the leader my role was to not know all the details of how things got done, but to help set the strategy and vision, and then motivate and challenge others to accomplish, then get out of their way as they executed the strategy. Oftentimes, I would also be on the executing team, but more as an advisory and consultative team member, because I wanted the leader of the project to feel the ownership of managing the project. We had good people, and it didn't take much to keep them motivated and have them soar to new heights.

Within our company was a group of sales and marketing department people who were designated to our events area. Part of their role was to also recruit additional people to help them, usually gratis, both inside and outside the company. It didn't matter what department you worked in; you could be a recruited volunteer candidate. We planned events and made them happen, and we now set about creating the ceremony.

Well, the Groundbreaking Team set out to establish a Guinness Book of World Records for the world's largest groundbreaking ceremony. And what a ceremony it was. We had over two thousand people in attendance, and most of them brought their own shovels to help with the ceremonial dig. I saw people that were over seventy years old with shovels, and also two-year olds with shovels. It was genuine. It was grassroots. It felt like home.

We had speeches from Mayor Gerry Meyer of Belle Plaine, and from Minnesota Lt. Governor Joanne Benson. Students from the local schools, public and parochial, were in attendance, and we set up bleachers for the high school band to perform. They played great. From my location on the main temporary stage I was able to view the entire crowd, and not only hear the band playing, but to see the red faces from playing so hard. One of the local clergy also blessed the site and the people at the ceremony. This was rural Americana at its best, and during April in Minnesota. The weather was always a challenge. It was cool and windy. A real windy spring day.

So windy that the fireworks set off a fire that the fire department had to come and put out. Most of us in the crowd, including me, thought that was part of the show. Well it was part of the unplanned ceremony. Also, the wind carried off our skydiving team. We had arranged for a skydiving team to form a flying X in the sky before landing on the giant X on the ground. Up high in the sky, we saw the flying Baldwin Boga Brothers jump from the plane and their parachutes open, but we never did see where they landed. Later, I heard humorous rumors that they landed in the next county.

And about the large X on the ground. That was the work of LeRoy Chard, from whom we had bought the thirty acres of land for the factory site. With his tractor, he had someone cultivate into the soil a large X matching our logo that was about 300 feet across.

Well, the ceremony wasn't perfect, but it was real, and played out just as it happened before everyone's eyes. It wasn't scripted out. I never found any of this embarrassing when things didn't go quite right. We tried awful hard, and with limited time and resources.

It was also at this event that I first noticed the families. Not only would Excelsior-Henderson enthusiasts show up, but they also were now starting to bring their families—spouses and children and grandchildren. And I was bringing my family too. My wife Carol and our two children were there. After the ceremony as I was milling about, I spoke to one family that had brought three generations of their family, all of them men. Also, since this was during the workday, most everyone had to take time off from their jobs in order to be there. Real dedication and support. No lip service.

● ● ●

There were only two detail items that weren't acknowledged at the groundbreaking ceremony that preoccupied my mind. We hadn't yet closed on the debt financing, and we hadn't signed a lease with the developer. Imagine starting construction on a $10.3 million building as a new company and not yet having the financing in place, nor a lease signed. But it was close and a calculated risk. Working with the Building Team, I had developed trust in them, and I believed the quality partners we were working with would be true to their word, and letters of intent, and they were.

It also helped that Ryan as the developer was financing about 50% of the building, and they were willing to start construction prior to completing the financing. We were all in some risk together. As Bruce Maus, my hired gun on the building project would put it: "We're all in the soup together." A great incentive to get things worked out. Plus, in evolving the business, we couldn't always do things in a normal sequential manner. Time was too short. The project would take twice as long then, and time was money.

As a company, we were about to embark on something new—debt. We previously didn't have any debt, as we didn't qualify for debt since we were in negative cash flow. The building would be the first significant debt we would establish, and technically the debt wasn't exclusively dependent upon the success of the company for repayment. But the debt was really incurred by Ryan as the developer, and by the City of Belle Plaine in a Tax Increment Financing (TIF) loan package, which is used in Minnesota as an incentive to businesses. The loan basically gets paid off as the property taxes are paid. At Excelsior, we became the tenant and had a 20-year lease on the property, and Ryan and the City were the primary debt holders.

Therefore, in reality the debt was not officially company debt, but we did fully disclose in our financials the arrangements as a capital lease, and carried the building and underlying debts on our Balance Sheet. We always opted for full disclosure; that way there were no questions about the arrangement. Just read all about it in our public documents. Full disclosure made it simple, and was the right way to do it, and then move on.

During May, about a month after the groundbreaking and after commencing construction on the building, Ryan and the City of Belle Plaine, in separate deals, completed the debt financing.

Ryan Companies set up a Limited Liability Corporation (LLC) named Ryan Belle Plaine, and through a real estate investment banking firm, raised the debt. The loan amount was for $5.75 million, with $5 million being used for building construction, and the balance of $750,000 being set aside in a reserve account in the event the tenant—us—had a future problem. Our initial lease term was for twenty years, and basically our lease payments were calculated off of the $5.75 million loan. So even though the total project cost was $10.3 million, plus the $750,000 reserve, bringing the total to just over $11 million, our monthly lease payments were based on the $5.75 million. Running the numbers, this gave us an under market lease rate of $4.29 per square foot, for a brand new building, that some say was a pretty nice building. Now, all this didn't happen by luck; we did have some skill and some talented people on our A-Team. It was a well-executed strategy.

The City of Belle Plaine used the accepted TIF method of financing, and sold bonds through an investment banking firm that amounted to $2.3 million. Like I previously mentioned, this loan would automatically get repaid as the company paid the semi-annual property tax bill. Strategically, a good deal for all parties.

Two questions I was frequently asked were: 1) why didn't we lease a building, and 2) rather than build a building, why didn't we use that money for something else?

The answer to the first question should now be reasonably obvious—we did lease a building, only it was a new one. With the booming economy at the time, there were no vacant buildings of this size, and anything that was remotely suitable required a significant relocation of the company, plus higher lease payments, and high retrofit costs. It would have cost us more money to do something different. We got a better deal to lease a new building. We saved money. I must repeat that since I have had this question asked so many times. We saved money from the first day. Hard for some to believe when they don't have the facts, or listen to rumors. But now you have the numbers.

The answer to the second question may not be so obvious to some, but it is to me. It wasn't our money to spend—so how could we spend it somewhere else? If we hadn't built a building, we wouldn't have had the money; and the money wasn't ours anyway. It was Ryan's and the City of Belle Plaine's, and neither of those parties seemed very interested in giving us their money if there wasn't a building constructed to go along with it. In other words—no building—no money. The two went together. Had we tried to do anything else with the money, it would have simply been fraud. Two reasons that is bad. One, we—and I—operated in full disclosure and with honesty. And two, someone would have figured out that fraud was committed. Every dollar ever raised on the venture went to where it was supposed to go. Bad things happen if you don't do that.

Hopefully this has shed the light on the logic and the actual detailed numbers of what was going on in my head for the strategy, and with the company, regarding building our factory. All in all, it was a good business structure, and one that even seasoned, mature, positive cash flow companies would be envious to have.

• • •

One final thought regarding the groundbreaking ceremony. During the groundbreaking presentations, I was impatiently sitting on the stage when, out of the corner of my eye, I noticed a man sitting in a wheelchair just off my left side and at the bottom of the platform. He had been wheeled through the bumpy field to take part in the ceremony. It was Leo Sullivan, my eighty-year-old neighbor from the farm when I was growing up. I met his gaze, and we both smiled. Big hearty smiles that only come from having known someone so long, and through surviving tough times. He raised his fist high and shook it at me in a wave—a gesture I interpreted as "give 'em hell"—and I gave him the thumbs up. That was the last time I ever saw him before he passed on just a few short months later.

# 20

## Jay Leno Serving Cake

There were also some pretty neat things happening unexpectedly. Jay Leno flew up from Los Angeles to visit us at our small headquarters facility in Burnsville, Minnesota on March 27th. Wow, this was exciting for our small company.

Actually, he was really coming to do a show at the nearby Mystic Lake Casino in Prior Lake, and had called wondering if he and his wife Mavis could stop in and say hi before the show. What could a person really say? This was cool, having Jay Leno stop in and visit us, and he said he would give us free tickets to the show. A bonus.

As you may know, Jay Leno is well known for his skills as an entertainer, and he is also a gearhead. I got a chance to meet him about a year earlier, after being introduced to him by Jed Clampett. Or at least that's what Jay had nicknamed the guy who introduced us. Many years prior to launching Excelsior, I had been reading a local periodical, and there was an article about a father and son team that was in the process of restoring old motorcycles in Minnesota for Jay. I don't know why, but I saved that article for over five years, and after launching Excelsior, one late night at home I was rummaging around the basement looking for the article, and I found it.

After doing a little digging, I realized these guys were hard to find. They were part of the underworld. Not the bad underworld, but the antique motorcycle industry underworld. Everybody they needed to know, they knew, and vice versa. But if you were from outside their network, good luck in finding them. They really didn't want to be found by anyone outside their circle. Being persistent, I tapped some of my contacts in the antique motorcycle community, and they were able to give me an address and phone number.

I first met Bob Chantland and his son Sid by paying them a surprise visit at their aircraft hangar in Anoka, Minnesota. I made the mistake of wearing a suit, and later Bob told me he was alarmed and thought I was from a branch of the government coming to see him. Bob and Sid were familiar with our venture, and over a period of time of getting to know them, I asked if they would someday make an introduction to Jay.

In their inimitable way, they said, "Yeah, maybe someday." But, to me, there was no way to know if that day would ever come. It was a long shot, like a lot of our business. I needed to earn their trust.

About a half-year later, and after several meetings and calls, one day my phone rang. It was Bob Chantland. "Hey Dreamer," he says, "I'm about a block away. Do you want me to call Jay for you?" Bob usually called me Dreamer, and I thought, *Yeah, let's give it a run.* "Yeah Bob," I said, "why don't you stop in and we can call him." *Hmm*, I thought, *let's see how well he's connected.*

Within a few minutes Bob stopped in. Now if you ever meet Bob, Bob is his own man, and basically does what he wants, when he wants, and how he wants to. He's not mean; in fact I find him to be real polite and refreshingly candid. It's just that he's his own man, with his own opinions. He also has a kind heart if he knows and trusts you.

So we go into the conference room, and pull the inexpensive speakerphone to the middle of our old Formica-clad conference table. Bob pulls out a little sheet of paper—that I didn't get to see—and dials a number. He gets Jay's assistant on the phone, and she recognizes his voice. Immediately she transfers him, and next thing I know I hear Jay's voice coming through the speaker phone, saying, "Hey Clampett, how you doing? What's up?"

That's how I had a chance to meet and get to know Jay. Bob and Sid arranged for a meeting with Jay in Los Angeles. One time when I was meeting with Jay, there was a short supply of local hotel rooms, or at least a short supply of affordable rooms, and I bunked out in his shop for the night. Jay was always very accommodating to me, and would enthusiastically show me his antique collection of cars and motorcycles, rattling off specific mechanical details of each one. I was impressed.

One of the things that Bob and Sid told me about before meeting Jay that I will never forget since it aptly applies to people of his presence: Don't ask him to do anything for you, and don't be glamorized by the Hollywood lifestyle. Just be yourself. Stick to what you know, and the reason that you came to see him. Don't be a groupie. If he's interested in what you're doing, he'll ask if he can help. I respected the input. I wasn't looking to get the inside scoop on his life or Hollywood. I took all this advice to heart, for two reasons. First, I believed it was the right and honest way and I can't fake that I'm a groupie or a Hollywood man, and second, I had never met a Hollywood TV star and

I was looking for advice. Bottom line: be yourself. For me that was easy, since that was all I knew how to be.

With Jay being such a gearhead, and well known for his appreciation of quality vehicles, I thought it would be a good idea to get his thoughts on our early styling designs for the Super X motorcycle. Being candid, he found some real misgivings in our early drawings, and challenged us to do better, and more different, and more unique, and had examples of what he meant. I found it real meaningful.

One time when I was visiting with Jay, he was excited about a new car he had just bought. When I say new, I mean, old-new car he bought. I wish I could remember the year, but I think it was a 1930s era Duesenberg, maroon in color. It had just gone through a complete restoration, and it looked elegant; noble really.

Jay was checking out the car as it was being unloaded from the enclosed trailer. After it rolled down, he fired it up. It was quiet and smooth. This was big league. He took a look around at the few guys standing about, including me, and said, "Hey guys, you want to go for a ride?" So a few of us piled in, and away we went for miles, in a million-dollar old car. Like my Dad would tell me later, "You're rubbing elbows with some pretty good company, and in a nice car!" I felt like an old Hollywood star, for a few moments.

One of the constant rumors I heard about our project was that Jay was a big investor in our venture. Now I don't want to get into Jay's business, as that is his business, but this is what I can say about it. On behalf of the company or myself, I never wanted to meet Jay for the chance to try and have him invest. I'm sure he was always being hit on regarding the next best thing, and had probably developed an appropriate sense of callousness toward it. Also, I would approach professional *investors* about investing. Keeping it simple, stick to your knitting. I knew Jay's claim to fame was not his investing skills, but rather his entertainment and media contacts, along with his keen eye for unique vehicle styling.

To the best of my knowledge, Jay was not an investor in the company. I did ask him though, once. As our relationship developed, I got to thinking: I had never asked him if he was interested. Usually early private investors need to be asked, as a certain protocol—they just don't call you up to write you a check—they expect to be asked. So I did get thinking, I didn't want to offend him and never ask. Therefore, one time when I was visiting him in L.A., I did bring it up to him. He took the question and the information all in stride, and said he would have his lawyer, or financial advisor in New York get back to me. Jay wasn't hopeful though. He looked me in the eye and said, "Dan, I know how to make my money in the entertainment business, and I invest it in something I know: old cars and motorcycles." I appreciated the candor, and knew it was true.

About a week later though, I did get a call from his lawyer in New York. Now that was pretty good follow up. He said he had a chance to discuss things with Jay, and that Jay had asked him to call me and explain everything firsthand. Well, I don't impress easily, but I was impressed. Naturally he indicated he was hired to advise Jay on matters, and it was his job to minimize any financial losses and to minimize any potential legal exposure of his client if things didn't work out. Statistically, early stage companies are a risk, and it wouldn't be good advice for him to recommend it. It was the right thing to do, and I was glad that at least as a friend, I had asked Jay the question, and he gave me his response. I never brought it up again.

• • •

Well, when March 27th rolled around, Jay showed up in mid-afternoon with his wife Mavis. I had never met Mavis before—she's a cool woman, and they have been married for years. I had my wife Carol there, along with our kids, and our Road Crew (employees) were invited to bring in their spouses and families. To celebrate his visit— we tried to make it into an event—we had a special cake prepared. This is a little corny maybe, but it was fun. He was a real sport. When he saw the cake, he immediately grabbed a knife, and started slicing up the cake, and personally served everyone there. I observed a good lesson that day, which I never forgot.

Jay also called the local NBC affiliate in Minneapolis, and they stopped out to film him at our facility, and the news channel did a nice feature on the evening news. The local anchorman closed the segment by saying, "Well the company must be doing something right when you have Jay Leno serving cake in your front lobby." It was a good day.

I think Jay liked our venture and the people affiliated with it. At one point, he did ask, "Hey, what can I help you with?" I just paused and let his mind think. He's real fast paced, he never stops, and he rattled off a few things, and would stop himself mid-sentence. Then he hit pay dirt, "How about media? I know media. Do you want me to call some of the media for you?" Great idea—better than I had thought. So he called several editors on our behalf. That was a good lead-in for us.

One time when things were going a little tough, I was talking to Jay and telling him so. He looked at me, and just said, "Hey Dan, just fight the good fight. Fight the good fight." I had read his book, and I knew what he meant.

*Jay helped in more ways than money could have ever helped.*

# 21

## BIGX Goes Up On The Board

Money. There is an old saying among those who have experience raising capital for early stage ventures. If the question comes up on how much money you plan on raising, the answer is: as much as you can. You never have too much money in an early stage venture. If you do have too much, just simply give some of it back. Furthermore, how many companies have failed that had money in the bank? Not many. With money, you can solve problems. Without money, that aggravates any problems. Try raising money in the midst of a problem.

It was time for another round of equity financing. Only this was going to be a little different than any of the previous rounds of equity financing. This was the IPO—Initial Public Offering. Similar to all rounds of financing for a negative cash flow venture, this one already had its nuances.

For one, it really wasn't the *"Initial"* Public Offering; it was a Public Offering. Technically, the offering we had completed a year earlier in 1996 was a public offering, hence that could have been viewed as our first, or initial offering. But since it was a restricted offering to private accredited investors, it was a different structure than a typical public offering. That was the only safe legal harbor we could find after the newspaper had run the article, and had forced our hand into becoming a publicly traded stock earlier than what we at the company would have preferred. But since this next offering would kick off the daily public trading in our stock, it was appropriately deemed our IPO.

Secondly, the market wasn't looking very good. Early 1997 saw a dip in the IPO market, and no one knew how long it would last. Deals were being put off to future dates, or being permanently pulled, or even being significantly repriced lower and for less money in order to get done. All of this is real bad news if you are in negative cash flow since you are not self-sustaining—which is where Excelsior fit in. For companies that were profitable, most could afford to wait until the market improved, and then launch their offering.

Next, we were an early stage venture type of company. They are always hard to finance through a public offering, and incredibly so if you are an early stage manufacturing company based in the United

States. Most early stage companies going public were in the medical, technology, or telecommunication industries, and the institutional investor interest just didn't have an appetite for companies like ours. This was not news to me, this is just the way it was, and had been for some time.

Let me define an institutional investor in case you're not sure what I mean. Publicly held companies have stock that trades, for example, on the New York Stock Exchange or NASDAQ. The stock can be purchased by an individual investor—known as a retail investor; and also by a company that has an investment fund—known as an institutional investor. Over the years, there are significant amounts of dollars that have been invested by individuals and companies into pension funds, retirement funds, mutual funds, and the like. All these funds need to do something with all this money, and they hire staffs of people who determine how and what to invest the money into, with a vast portion of it sometimes going into the stock market, for purchases as an investment. These are called the institutional buyers, and due to their sheer size and volume, they really dominate the stock market over the individual investor.

These institutional fund managers make their living off calculating what the market will do, and investing accordingly. Like any crystal ball forecast of the future, most times it is a little fuzzy. If they are wrong, people get mad about their investment, and it impacts their funds. Accordingly, most fund managers review reports from the stock analysts who are following publicly traded stocks and trying to forecast what the performance of the company and the stock might be. Most stock analysts' jobs rely on making an accurate forecast; therefore they in turn like to research predictable performing companies. An early stage, negative cash flow company is anything but predictable. All sounds fairly logical, and to a great degree, it is that simple, on paper.

The execution of this concept in the marketplace gets complicated real fast. Nevertheless, for us at Excelsior, it was fair to assume that the typical institutional fund would not have interest in investing in our venture. Not only did I surmise this as we planned for our IPO; I knew this firsthand after talking to hundreds of them over the previous several years. But some of our investment bankers thought we would get institutional interest. Privately, I wasn't as hopeful.

By this point in the venture, we were getting a pretty good street reputation of accomplishing our milestones—on budget, and on time. Investors like this. We also had been courting various investment bankers and motorcycle industry stock analysts throughout the country for several years, and continually kept them updated on our progress. Even though for years they indicated we were too early a company, or just simply not the right fit, we would continually stay in touch with them. Being persistent, I believed in the quote by Abraham Lincoln, "I will prepare myself, and someday my time will come." I knew what we had to do to get their interest. We had to hit our milestones and continually move the company forward.

Now it was paying off. Two major investment banking houses that had stock analysts following Harley-Davidson were interested in leading our IPO. This was real good news, but I was also slightly uneasy. Sometimes these big guys leave the little guys when the waters get turbulent. They never tell you that. I just knew that after doing my research on them. And it wasn't just the two firms we were working with; it was an industry standard. The larger firms generally moved together, and could swing or create an industry, as we all saw with the Internet sector two years later.

The other thing about the larger investment banking houses: they all primarily rely on the institutional fund investors, and not the individual investors. It just isn't their market niche. If the institutional investors didn't have an appetite for an individual stock, like ours, the large national investment banking houses wouldn't be able to complete the deal. Only by that time, the train is all the way down the track— the Offering Documents are completed, the road show is done, and you're thinking you're going to get your money. Instead you get a call that the deal can't be done. For some that is mostly embarrassing. For us, embarrassment was the easy part. If we didn't get it done, the company would fail. We needed to be 100%—100% of the time. I was always, *always*, measuring the input. Stressful.

Knowing all this though, it was still an advantage to work with the bigger houses if we could. We were fortunate, and we had a chance to have several of the national players visit us in Minnesota. For the previous several years, we had been visiting them at their location, and now some of them were interested in coming to see us. From New York, Prudential and Oppenheimer sent out their investment bankers and analysts, as did Robertson Stephens from San Francisco, and Dain Bosworth and Piper Jaffray from Minneapolis. We were getting pretty well trained in presenting our story, and had a lot of opportunity to do so.

The best fit and timing was lining up with Dain Bosworth of Minneapolis, and Oppenheimer in New York. They both had analysts already covering the industry, most notably Harley-Davidson. We struck a deal—engagement letter—wherein Dain would be the lead manager on the deal (meaning left side of the document) and Oppenheimer would be the co-manager, on the right side of the final offering prospectus. The IPO would be for $40 million, and on April 3rd we held the customary kick-off meeting, only this time by teleconference since we had national players. We then started the formal face-to-face due diligence drafting sessions on April 15th, my wife's birthday, and just one day after the groundbreaking ceremony. Busy times.

But privately, I was uncomfortable. Yes, it did seem that we were starting to arrive, and we not only had interest from the upper bracket investment banking firms, we had a signed contract to get the deal done. We were marching together down the proverbial "aisle." Only I was still concerned about the downturn in the market, and of being left alone at the altar, with no money, and everyone to answer to on why it didn't get done. If the offering failed, the company would fail, and I knew who would get blamed for the failure—regardless of the market conditions.

This was an opportune time to run a parallel path. We needed to have a back-up plan that could be immediately implemented in the event we needed to promptly shift gears. Our company was a grassroots company, and previously had relied on individual investors to financially support the venture, and they also provided good objective advice. After consulting with various advisors, our new Board of Directors, and figuring out a strategic way to prepare the alternate plan without derailing the primary plan, we laid the alternate plan in place. If the market for institutional deals continued as they were, we as the company would pull the plug on the deal with the big houses, and go with a safer, more predictable route with investment banking firms that specialize in working with individual investors. It was a gamble.

This was also an early challenge for our new Board of Directors. As previously planned, just prior to the IPO we folded the Board of Advisors, and now for the first time established a formal outside Board of Directors. From our Board of Advisors we asked Butch Donahue and Wayne Fortun to continue on and join our new Board of Directors, and also added Dave Pomije, one of our early private investors. Also from our former Board of Advisors, we retained Gale Mellum, our legal counsel, and asked him to be the Corporate Secretary. Fortunately, all of these people were real familiar with our company and they provided solid continuity in strategy and implementation, and were objectively tough, but fair.

I was spending a lot of time plotting strategy with Tom Rootness, our CFO, and Gale Mellum, our lawyer. These were some levelheaded people, and we didn't panic in a storm. Of course the risk was less to them, but still, they were good sounding boards. It reminded me of a few years earlier, when I was closing the deal on my previous company, and there was some last minute posturing by the other parties. As we were riding in the elevator on our way to the meeting, I was a little apprehensive of the outcome, and I asked my lawyer, Moe Sherman, how he could stay so calm. He looked at me and said, "It's not my life I'm trying to save, it's yours." I knew that only too well, and never forgot the perspective on the advice. It was good advice.

We were about 45 days into the drafting of our IPO prospectus, and within a few weeks of completing it, and starting our road show to launch the IPO. But I was increasingly unsettled, and I'm sure I was making those around me uneasy also. The investment market wasn't looking good. There were several articles in the financial newspapers about IPOs just recently being delayed or not getting done. Those that were getting done were being repriced to a lower stock price and raising less money.

As much as I liked our company of Excelsior-Henderson, all the other deals that were being delayed were from companies that were farther along than we were in their business cycle, and some of them even profitable. That didn't bode well for us, as I realistically viewed our firm as a weak candidate for the institutional investment market.

It was time to make a decision. I had been keeping the Board and our advisors informed of my concerns, and we called a quick teleconference Board Meeting on May 15th. We discussed the current state of the investment marketplace, and about the alternate plan, Plan B, that we had developed. The Board was in agreement, and it was time to purposely force the train to jump the track, but onto the parallel track that had been laid: Plan B.

There is a price to switching though. We knew we would lose about thirty days in our offering, and time is money. We had initially planned to launch our IPO in mid-June, and wrap it up just before the holiday of July 4th. Now our best guess was we would have to launch the IPO road show just after the 4th.

Another issue was that no investment banker likes to be informed by a client that it is going to head in a different direction. Especially when it is a small company telling the large national Wall Street investment banking companies, and I was concerned we might burn bridges. I was hopeful that wouldn't happen. But we had to do it. I contacted our lead investment banking firms, Dain and Oppenheimer, and let them know our decision, and fortunately, as professionals, they understood our predicament—I think. I didn't have time to dwell on the issue, and just had to keep moving forward.

Therefore, mid-stream into our IPO, we did switch tracks and engaged two different firms to lead and co-lead our IPO. We contracted with John G. Kinnard as our lead firm, who had completed our previous offering for us, and also with Miller, Johnson & Kuehn of Minneapolis as our co-lead. Both of these firms were significantly less staffed than Dain and Oppenheimer, and were more local and regional in nature. Important to us though, not only did they have institutional investment capability, they also had a large individual investor customer base—known in their trade as "retail;" who are probably the type of customers who would make good investors for our venture. Therefore, one of the factors we were primarily relying on was the retail sector to pull the IPO to success, in spite of the downturn in the institutional market sector.

Another factor was the size of the offering. We were planning on doing a $40 million IPO. That is a large offering amount for these smaller firms; and even harder, and next to impossible in a tough market. We discussed this and mutually agreed to lower the amount of the IPO to $30 million—which was still a stretch given the current market and the relevant size of the firms. So there went $10 million even before we got started. I knew even if we successfully pulled off the IPO, we were now immediately $10 million short in our plan. Even doing a $30 million deal with these investment firms was a big amount, and somewhat risky due to its size. But this was better than being $40 million short and not getting it done. Like the experts say, take the money. It was important to *"Live to Fight Another Day."*

We did have a few factors going for us that I was betting on. One of the investment bankers, Charlie Westling, had just left the Dain Bosworth firm and joined the John G. Kinnard firm, and would be lead managing our IPO. I really liked Charlie and had previously met him at Dain. And he was highly recommended by one of my advisors. I think he was younger than I was, but he had a lot of extra miles of experience on him in financing. And he had an effective style to work with. He was of high integrity, and would deliver bad news in the same manner of good news. He wasn't always trying to sell, but more importantly was trying to get things done, and get them done right. Frankly, I admired him and thought he would do a good job for us.

Also, another guy on the deal team with Kinnard was Jerry Johnson. Several years earlier I had met Jerry, and he also was on the deal team the year before in our offering with Kinnard. So he had experience with us, and us with him. Remember earlier when I mentioned if you ever wondered what happened to those smart guys in high school? Well, Jerry was one of them. Bright, articulate, well educated, young, well-groomed, and a great personality. All of the qualities together that most of us lack in one package. So I was confident of Jerry on our deal team.

Consequently, I did believe we were better off doing an IPO with the smaller regional firms that had retail presence. We finished the drafting sessions on the IPO investment prospectus and filed the registration statement with the SEC on April 29th, and subsequently printed the red herring on June 27, 1997. That was a big day. We had this ready to go ahead of schedule. The Deal Team decided that it wouldn't be best to launch our road show before the Fourth of July, so we planned to kick-off the road show just after the holiday weekend.

• • •

If you are not familiar with a red herring, I'll briefly explain what this document is and how it relates to an IPO. It is the document (prospectus) that gets printed from the information that is submitted to the SEC along with a registration statement, prior to the sale of the stock. The SEC has a time period in which they will respond back to the company with comments on the offering—which they did with us also. During this time period, the company and the investment bankers are on a "road show" telling the story to investment firms throughout the country, and utilizing the red herring as the initial base IPO prospectus that gets provided to prospective IPO investors. Investors review the red herring and basically place orders of interest with their broker on the contemplated upcoming IPO. Upon satisfactorily meeting all of the examiner's questions at the SEC, the registration statement for the securities is declared effective by the SEC. It is at this point that investment bankers tally up their orders of interest, do the final pricing on the offering, the IPO moves to a closing and trading commences. The so-called "bell" is rung on Wall Street for the first day of trading on a new issue stock, and a whole new way of life for a company is commenced.

• • •

We had been fine-tuning our IPO presentation for weeks. In addition to running a business, it is a grueling process. Typically, the CEO and the CFO present the company to the prospective investors, so we were gearing up our presentation skills. We were continually doing dry runs, and getting the presentation materials ready. According to IPO industry protocol, you usually have about 10 to 15 minutes to tell your story, so you had better be good at it. Not only fast, but effective.

If the prospective institutional investor is interested, there might be another 10 to 15 minute question and answer session that evolves. You need to be on your toes. These aren't nice people asking you questions and listening to the presentation. They are professional interrogators, and have heard every story. If they are nice, you certainly don't witness it in these brief meetings. You shake hands before and after the meetings, but they aren't the business friendly handshake. It is more like two boxers before the match, where it is really a ceremonial handshake before the battle begins.

And at the end of the presentation, which was sometimes interactive as questions could be asked during the presentation, I was told that as you are leaving, if the institutional investor wishes you good luck, it is a bad sign. If they say this, the hidden message is they are surely not investing, and you're going to need luck. How nice.

We practiced our presentations with the help of our investment bankers, who continually grilled our CFO and me. Finally, after several weeks it was flowing fairly smooth, and we became walking robots on knowing the script, and we could instantly turn it on and off. Even today, I can still recite most of it as we got to know how to tell the story well in a few short minutes. I learned in the next few weeks that we would be giving these presentations from dawn to dusk.

We had also decided to put together a short video. Our story was best told from a visual perspective, with a tug at passion, and a short video was a good way to capture the story and bring our company to life in front of an audience. The IPO video was about 4 minutes long. I had to go buy a small combination TV/VCR that I would ultimately lug all over the country, and set up just before each meeting kicked off.

Typically, the conference room was unusually silent while the people watched me set up—no one else would volunteer to set it up. They weren't there for small talk, and almost all viewed the set-up time as an unneeded distraction. But after watching the video, it would produce smiles and people liked it.

Our first official day of the road show was Monday, July 7th, and we kicked it off in Minneapolis exactly at high noon. I like that time—it was an appropriate kick-off time. During the next two days, we had about a half dozen meetings in Minneapolis, and across the Mississippi River in Saint Paul. On Wednesday evening, July 9th, we took the show out of town.

Within the next six business days, we would travel to Seattle, Portland, San Francisco, San Diego, Boston, New York, Philadelphia, Baltimore, Chicago, Milwaukee, and back to Minneapolis. I now understood firsthand what a road show was. I have heard some joking banter that the reason for the grueling travel schedule is that if CEOs can survive the trip in good humor and intact, then they should have enough stamina to run a company. They might be right.

We had a lot of fun on our road show; after all, we were a bold new motorcycle company. The investment bankers knew the drill, as they were old pros at orchestrating the road shows. We all flew coach class, but after we arrived at the respective airports, we were greeted by a limousine driver. We were now traveling in style, but with a traveling crew of four to six people, it was an efficient way to ground travel and conduct business at the same time. These road shows are intense since we all knew the consequences—if we weren't successful, the company was doomed. We had to be at our best.

And when traveling during a stressful time, you get to know each other well. It was not a time for indifference, and we all created a sort of camaraderie together. The road show attendees primarily consisted of our CFO and myself from Excelsior, and various investment bankers, analysts, and brokers from the two lead firms of John G. Kinnard, and Miller, Johnson & Kuehn. Most often, we were with Charlie Westling and Jerry Johnson.

During our road show one day in New York, I was wearing a new black suit I had just bought for about $400, just for the road show. After our first meeting that day, I jumped into the limo with the rest of the crew, and as I was sliding across the limo seat, my pants caught on a spring sticking through the seat—New York limos! I tore about a 6 inch, L-shaped hole in the derriere of my pants, and had to make the rest of the meetings that day with a gaping hole and fabric flapping in my back-side. Talk about a little unnerving as we would go to meetings. For the rest of that day, I made sure that the institutional investors we met with never saw my backside. I would back out of the conference room shak-ing hands as we left. It was all part of the story on the road.

Our two lead underwriting firms had been working diligently to have a successful road show and IPO. We had a lot of meetings throughout the country, and with some of the top institutional mutual funds in the country. I met personally with Dick Strong, of Strong Capital Management in Milwaukee, and with the institutional banker for State Street Research in Boston. Throughout the road show, it was an impressive list of invest-ment firms and people with whom we had met.

But at the same time, we were all a little reserved. On the road, most of the meetings were with institutional buyers, and none of us knew if the institutions were buying the story. We were an early stage company—pre-revenue, and certainly a perceived risk to their invest-ment portfolio. Several of them wished us good luck. I knew what they meant, and it didn't bother me. We had an "Ace" backup—the retail market that most IPOs ignore. I believed the institutional players would be more interested the further along we got, and now we had an opportunity to introduce our story to them, and someday the time would come when we would be a good match for each other.

Exactly two weeks after the road show started, we ended it in Minneapolis. The next day, we presented the road show to the rest of the company so they could see firsthand what was going on. The fol-lowing day, Wednesday, July 23rd, 1997, we were declared effective, and our first day of trading began on Thursday morning, July 24th, 1997.

The BIGX stock symbol was on the NASDAQ Board.

We priced our offering at $7.50 per share, and raised the full amount of $30 million, which gave the company a market capitaliza-tion of about $100 million. Total equity raised since inception was now about $45 million—during about a four-year time frame: 48 months, $45 million. About a million dollars a month.

We basically sold to new investors about a third of the company during the offering. Most of the offering was sold to retail buyers, and we had limited institutional interest. No surprise to anyone, and I was just excited we had successfully completed it. The market for IPOs was soft, and for the year, IPO volume was down over 30% from the previ-ous year, so I was just relieved we got it done. Our investment bankers had done an excellent job. They had completed what some others had said couldn't be done. This was a big sized offering for them, and they were successful in accomplishing it.

I always liked, and still do, our new stock symbol, BIGX. Or really, it was an old nickname. I wish I could take credit for thinking of it, but like the late great Sam Walton said in his autobiography, "I never had a new idea, but I heard a lot of them, and implemented a few." We all know he did have new ideas, but he was also good in giving others credit when due.

Big X was a motorcycle nickname from the past lore of the previous Excelsior company. I was always digging up history on the former company, and would marvel at the stories, and would talk and write about it to anyone who would listen. I was on a mission. Over time, the stories seemed to take on modern-day significance. One of the nicknames we adopted from the past was Big X. Big X got the nickname during World War I from the American G.I.s fighting in Europe. Excelsior at the time was one of the suppliers of motorcycles to the military, and had supplied thousands of the drab -colored military Excelsiors, emblazoned with a big X logo on the fuel tank. Hence the soldiers in the battlefield nicknamed the Excelsior bikes "Big X." In our promotional literature and stories, we talked about this and promoted it. It was authentic, and was part of the heritage to our brand and to our story.

Well, apparently this struck a chord with our CFO, Tom. When we were thinking of a stock symbol for the company, he had suggested Big X. I immediately liked it, and it was better than any ideas I had. Sometimes I would look at Tom and say, "Hey, was that my idea?" and he would crack a big smile and say, "Yeah." Then we'd both laugh—we were team players and could humor each other. I remember him looking at me and asking if the symbol seemed right, since it didn't fit the corporate name. For NASDAQ, you are required to have a four letter stock symbol (no more, no less), and most companies use part of their company name to make it easily identifiable to investors. But I liked Big X—the name certainly sounded strong and was memorable, and best of all, it originated from the soldiers out in the field giving their life during WW I. It was appropriate homage to the Excelsior brand, and to American veterans—all of it good enough for me. Therefore, the BIGX stock symbol went proudly up on the NASDAQ Board in New York—and only a limited few knew the significance.

Another milestone checked off. On time, and on budget. We had the chance to *"live to fight another day."*

• • •

While all this stuff was going on at work, it was amazing that I had any type of family life. I was still a young man, just 40 years old, but now with a lot of miles on my frame. I felt compassion for my wife. She was bearing the brunt of all of my absences from the home-life, and she never held it against me. I found out you never really know the strength and character of a person until one's life gets played out, day by day.

Carol was pregnant with our third child, and our new son Hayden Leo was born on Saturday, May 24th, 1997. I thought I knew what love was, but being a new father, again I realized that you really don't feel the intensity of love and passion until you have a child. There is no describing it, and it is life altering. At least for me anyway.

We had just broken ground on the new factory, led our parade in Daytona Beach, launched the public offering, and entertained Jay Leno. All of my children were too young to understand any of this. We now had three children, Hannah, who was five years old; Hunter, who was three years old; and our newborn Hayden. A young growing family that really didn't know me, nor I them. Although I thought I did.

We got some great presents from our friends, but one of them stands out. It seems one of my hired guns had a trick up his sleeve. Several months earlier, Bruce Maus and Jim Stoker, the hired guns on project management, had been working on a surprise. They presented me, on behalf of my newborn son Hayden, with a good-sized rocking horse in the form of a motorcycle, with the Big X Excelsior-Henderson logo on the wooden fuel tank. They had it custom made. I was impressed, and had them autograph the motorcycle rocker for a keepsake. The Excelsior project was so intense, for those that could survive it, we developed a keen sense of camaraderie. Bruce is the type of guy who could smile even as the bullets were flying overhead—cool under pressure. What a nice gift.

Up until this time frame, Carol had been working from our home in her profession, for over fourteen years, as a court reporter in downtown Minneapolis. She was well respected in her profession, and took depositions with a lot of well-known lawyers in the area. As a court reporter, you also see a lot of people at their worst—being deposed—and usually for something that is not good.

We really needed her income in our family since I had decided to not take much money out of the company in salary. That was one of the selling points in raising money. I paid all Vice-Presidents more money than myself, and expected my payday, if I was lucky enough, to someday come from my value in stock. I had a dream.

When we went public, my stock holdings were worth about $13.5 million, so I just kept focusing on keeping the company on track. I hadn't sold my stock, and had now been with the company for over four years. My professional financial advisors were recommending that I should balance out my investment portfolio, and liquidate just a portion of my holdings. Maybe they were right, but I never took the time to seriously consider it, and I knew that our ever-watchful regional print media critics would make a big deal over it if I did. In addition, I held the view that it's "not about the money," but rather to set out and accomplish a difficult goal—building the American dream. I started out owning 100% of the company, and it was always painful raising capital because I knew it was diluting my ownership. After the public offering my holdings in the company were about 14%—if I had more money, I would have bought more stock.

With the birth of our third child, Carol and I decided that it would be best for our family if she gave up her career in order to be the primary person raising our family. It just wasn't working right having three children in daycare, and me never being around. Even when I was around, I really wasn't there. I tried to not bring my problems home, and I do pride myself that my problems stayed at work. I had worked hard over many years, and had trained myself not to bring personal issues to work, and not bring work issues home. It was like I had two separate parts of my life, and I could turn them on and off like a flip of a switch. This may not work for some, but it kept me sane and real focused.

The part that was missing though, is I forgot to bring my mind home. Even when I was at home, I was not involved enough to be part of the family. I was a boarder in my own home, and with my own family, and all caused by my own doing. Only I didn't really realize it at the time, and it took me several years later to figure this out. I didn't become a dad until after the company was shut down. Even today I will get asked about how I feel about losing the company, and I answer, "I gained a family." Now, how bad of a tradeoff is that? At least I didn't lose the most important part.

When my son Hunter entered the first grade, his teacher asked him what he wanted to learn his first year. He answered, "I want to learn more about my dad." My wife never told me that until she knew I could handle it a few years later, when I became a real dad.

# 22

## Throttling Up With Pioneer Dealers

During early 1997 the company also embarked on a new transition—it was time to begin the launch of the dealer network. For years we had been planning this phase, but until the actual time came to implement, the process was only on paper. Our production goal was to launch manufacturing of the new Super X motorcycle in the fourth quarter of 1998, with the anticipation of bringing dealers aboard during the preceding year and a half prior to production.

The initial dealership recruitment goal established back in my 1993 Business Plan was to sign up about 100 dealers prior to production, and as production commenced, then continue to add dealers each year as production increased. By the end of the first production year, we planned to have 125 dealers, and 165 dealers at the end of the second year. This was the initial plan on paper, and until now there was no reason to change it. Over a period of time, however, as we added to the staff of the company and the time came to implement it, the dealership goal did get revisited and adjusted.

From my experience of being in the marketplace, combined with us being a new OEM manufacturer within the motorcycle industry, some spirited debates arose on the number of dealers we needed at product launch—the quick answer was enough to sell our first year production goal, which was 4,000 motorcycles. What was the right number of dealers? Well, there was no crystal ball answer, similar to a lot of issues in creating a brand for a new venture. I was of the mindset we were better off with more dealers at the launch, and increase our goal by about 25%, bringing the goal to about 150 dealers in the first year, and 200 dealers in the second year.

But my thoughts were not in the majority with some other viewpoints, both inside and outside our company. An argument could be made either way. After polling a few prospective dealers, our internal dealer team recommended otherwise, and in fact suggested we reduce the initial number of dealers, since the dealers themselves believed they could sell out our first year of production, and didn't want to have too many other dealers in their area. In theory this may sound okay, and until it gets tested, no one really knows. But I was unsure about this, and eventually learned we should have set up more initial dealers.

Setting up motorcycle dealers for a new product, from a new company, is always a gamble, from the viewpoint of both the dealer and the OEM. What if things don't work out? Also, the motorcycle dealer laws follow the OEM automotive dealer laws in order to streamline the law-making process, and are strictly enforced. Motorcycle dealers are automatically added to the automotive dealer laws, unlike the dealer laws for snowmobiles and all-terrain vehicles. One of the provisions is on geographic territory, and another provision is that once you assign a dealer to a particular area, there is really no way to un-assign it, unless the dealer wants to. In other words, from an OEM perspective, plan for a long marriage, whether you like it or not.

That isn't necessarily bad, but you had better make sure you pick good business partners right off the bat, since it would be impossible to change mid-course. In other words, do your homework upfront, and hope for the best, and continue to modify the plan as you go aggressively forward. This was another time to implement the concept of "working with the A-Team." Our dealers needed to be the A-Team dealers, and that is whom we actively recruited, and for the most part, we succeeded in establishing a dealership with the A-Team dealers in each market we went into.

We did have a lot going in our favor though. With the robust growth in the motorcycle industry, along with dealer associations, we were able to quickly identify the nation's top dealers. We believed the best process was to recruit our dealers from the pool of motorcycle dealers in the nation already in the business of selling new OEM motorcycles.

From a company perspective, we had been tracking all dealer inquiries into our business since the launch of the company, and had a fairly extensive database of several thousand prospective dealers, primarily including two different types of dealer prospects: those who owned existing OEM motorcycle dealerships, and those that wanted to start one. We didn't give too much consideration to starting new dealerships as the cost and time to build that out was unrealistic and impossible. Instead, for many reasons, we elected to focus on the currently established dealer network, and have them add our OEM product line to their existing business.

That was an important part of our strategic plan as it related to the distribution of our motorcycles. No matter how good a product we produced, by dealership law, we were prohibited from selling directly to a consumer, and were required to sell through a dealership channel, and in this case, there was an existing dealer channel. There were over

3,200 dealers of new motorcycles in the United States, with a high percentage of them selling more than one brand of OEM motorcycles. Similar to car dealers selling more than one brand. Some existing OEMs may not like this arrangement because for one thing, it can dilute the brand image, but dealers are independent (legally) and have the right to do this, and many exercise that right—which also was in our favor. No one likes to be dictated to, and we all desire the freedom of choice. By law, dealers had the freedom of choice, as long as they were subsequently approved by the respective OEMs. This worked directly to our benefit. For us, we didn't mind sharing the OEM dealer network with the other brands; in fact we saw it as an advantage. We could learn from what they were already doing. Right and wrong. And, as we found out, dealers have no problem making suggestions on what could be done better by the OEM, so we were an open ear for input.

We needed to recruit, for the first year, about 3.2% of the existing dealers in the United States to add our line of OEM motorcycles to their dealership. Also, with the strong dealer associations and related dealership information, we were able to conduct market research to target the top dealers in the top markets. This was a real distinct advantage of entering the motorcycle industry. The industry, which had been around for over a century, was growing consistently at double-digit growth, and it was state and federally regulated. What this leads to is—a great database of information. We didn't need to invent, nor reinvent, the wheel, in order to implement our distribution. We would simply use the channel of distribution that already existed and was already being used successfully by our competitors.

In addition to the analytical data that was available, with the industry's high profile and longevity, combined with talking to a few customers and industry contacts, it was relatively straightforward to locate the dominant dealers in each marketplace. But at the same time, these A-Team type dealers were not always the easiest to sign up. They are savvy businesspeople, and need to be convinced of the business opportunity, and want to understand the full program before they commit resources. Building out a national OEM dealer network is no simple matter, and it is time consuming and costly, and you really are never done. It must continually be managed, and includes a lot of ongoing communication and training between the OEM and dealer.

We established criteria for our dealers that included the usual items of a strong financial history, a good industry and personal reputation, a nice building and business location, and the ability and desire to add a new product line. Most importantly though was the owner's attitude about bringing on our line of new American OEM motorcycles. For some, this was a psychological barrier. About 30% of the Harley-Davidson dealers chose to carry multiple lines of product, while about 70% of them sold exclusively the Harley brand. For them, our question was: Would they be willing to add another OEM American motorcycle brand, when their allegiance was so strong to Harley? Would they psychologically do this? And, would they take on our product as a defensive measure to prevent others in their market from having the brand?

Regarding the non-Harley dealers selling nondomestic brands (considered U.S. dealers of brands from foreign countries), of which there were about 2,800 in the United States, none were selling an OEM American motorcycle. For them, our question was: Could they psychologically do this? Would they be willing to sell an OEM American motorcycle, going against the almighty—Harley?

One of the ways I would address the passion and allegiance factor was to correlate it to our families and children. Most dealers I know have a strong allegiance to the brands they sell, and rightly so. I have learned you can have more than one allegiance, as long as it is part of the family. Our story was that we were part of the motorcycle family, and if needed to be defined more specifically, part of the American motorcycle family. Just like a parent can have more than one child, and have love and allegiance to all their children, so can a dealer have allegiance to more than one brand, as they are all part of the family. After all, which child of yours do you love the most? I love *each* of mine the *most* and *equally*, and there is no distinction, and in addition I may love certain things about each one that make them uniquely themselves. That's my perception of one part of a family, and I do believe at Excelsior that's how we viewed our dealers, and it's how I think they viewed bringing our brand into their stable.

Either way, there were a lot of questions, most of which would never be fully answered until the bullets were flying in the heat of the battle. Yes, in our due diligence we would ask the questions, listen to the answers, and fill out the required Dealer Applications. In the sterility of our offices, talking about future unknown events, we were all sure it would work. But again, you never know until it gets tested by time.

After studying the industry and the various dealer applications and dealer agreements of the competitors, we put together a comprehensive dealer application and dealer agreement. It was an extensive formal application with goals, timetables, employees and years employed, financial strength, photographs of each respective dealership, and a commitment on the volume of motorcycles they believed they could sell. Some prospective dealers balked at the lengthy application and high effort to become a dealer, but most recognized why we were being so thorough in our selection. Some dealers also had a lot of fun with the thorough application process, and turned in award-winning applications, complete with photos of smiling employees wearing Excelsior-Henderson apparel. Some good forward-thinkers.

This was also the appropriate time for experience, and we recruited an experienced dealer development team to go out and recruit our type of dealers. It was time to tap our industry network for referrals, and one of the people I called was my buddy, investor, and future dealer, Ted Nielsen in Chicago. Ted knew our company well being an early investor and a frequent confidant, and someone I could trust—as we had heated discussions, and yet remained friends. For years, and still at that time, I told Ted that I didn't think he would be a good dealer candidate for us, and why. We would debate and listen to each other's perspective. Several years later he proved me wrong as he became one of our best dealers, but I also think we both learned something from our previous conversations.

One of the prospective sales manager contacts Ted gave me was a guy named Dave Auringer, who coincidentally lived in the vicinity, near where our new factory was being built. One night when I was driving back from the construction site in Belle Plaine—it must have been around 8:00 p.m., I rang Dave up at his home. Dave was a District Manager for Bombardier Corporation out of Canada, and had raced motorcycles in his earlier years. He was a gas and oil type of guy, and had come up through the ranks. He was also cautious, as he had a great career going right where he was.

Over the course of several months we would meet, along with other members of our staff, and finally we were able to have him join us as our first National Sales Manager. He was a great addition to the Team, and he quickly went to work. I do remember one funny early comment though. About his second week with us we were chatting in his office, and he remarked about how nice it was to have the time to get things done without the phone ringing off the hook, and no dealer problems. This wasn't the first time I had heard this type of comment from new people who joined our company. They all had to create their destiny. Nobody was joining and taking over a position on the mountain. They had to create it. I chuckled, and mentioned it would soon change. The cloud on the horizon was an approaching storm, and it would soon be hitting. About a month later, Dave was spinning in his chair, with multiple phones, surviving in the storm he had created.

Ted Nielsen, the Chicago investor who later became one of our ten Pioneer Dealers, also had a surprise for us that showed a lot of class. When he passed the referral on to me about contacting Dave Auringer as our prospective National Sales Manager, Ted mentioned that if we brought him aboard he would send us two bottles of champagne. Sure enough, shortly after Dave joined us, two bottles of champagne arrived. Only it wasn't your ordinary run-of-the-mill champagne—it was two bottles of Dom Perignon. I had heard of Dom Perignon champagne, but prior to then had never tasted any—I wasn't really much of a champagne guy. We gathered all our Team Members around late one afternoon about 5:00, just before darkness sets in during a Minnesota winter, gave a short speech thanking Ted and welcoming Dave, and popped the corks. That was the best champagne I had ever tasted, and I later learned the cost was over $100 per bottle. Good stuff. Ted knew how to do things first class.

After refining and approving the company plan on dealers, Dave quickly went about bringing in some of his contacts to join our venture as Regional Sales Managers, located in their respective home territories. We recruited Dave H. in Michigan, and Mike S. in Colorado, and in less than a year, recruited five more Regional Sales Managers from New York, Tennessee, California, and Wisconsin.

These guys were some of the best salespeople I had ever known. Some of them had worked together in the past during their careers, and if they hadn't worked together, most knew of each other. They had all earned their stripes on the battlefield, and had the various awards for all the achievements they had accomplished as sales managers in the OEM powersports industry. Even though they were all experienced, they were young at heart, and tough. They wore the company colors proudly, and I was proud to have them wear it. They were also very competitive—our A-Team—and had experience in setting up new dealer networks for a new product rollout. It was going to be fun, and they were up to the challenge.

They were also skilled questioners and over their years of experience had heard it all from the folks back at the home office. Field salespeople like home office people, at least from a great distance. But there is a sort of instant disconnect between the two. The home office dreams up all these great things the field gets to implement, only the field people usually aren't included in the idea, until they are told to implement it—and then the home office wonders why there are problems in the field.

Fortunately—and we screened for this in the interviewing process—even though they were skilled questioners, they weren't cynical about it. They were team players—professional war-horses in my opinion—and willing to play hard on the team, as long as they were included on the team. Fair enough.

Most outside salespeople that work far away from the corporate home office will work out of their home, and there can be some disconnect in communication, with them not feeling like part of the team. But we wanted to change this. These guys were our company warriors in the field, and there were no fresh recruits behind them if they stumbled. My belief was to arm them with the best, prepare them for battle, and then let them march off.

Only this time, they marched off in style—or drove off in style. Rather than the typical Ford Taurus for a company vehicle, these guys had brand new, gloss black decked-out trucks—some four-wheel drive turbo-charged diesels—with matching toppers, and new, gloss black trailers, all customized out with full company graphics proudly showing the company colors (logos). These were huge rolling billboards. All of these guys were driving 60-80,000 miles per year. Think about that. That's about a half-million miles of driving by our dealer team in one year, all over America, and in the markets in which we were seeking to establish a market presence.

For years, it was unbelievable the numbers of times I would get a call from someone, from anywhere in the United States, who would say they had seen one of our trucks on the road, and wanted more information on our motorcycles and the company. Our sales guys had great stories about constantly being stopped, and being salesmen, they were more than glad to take the time to educate the questioner. I know, since I got numerous complimentary phone calls from prospective customers.

It was the least expensive advertising we could do throughout the entire country. And there were a lot of side benefits. For one thing, it built great morale for the sales Team, as they weren't familiar with this type of treatment. They were more familiar with the corporate rhetoric of lip service.

There was only one catch for these sales guys though, well really two. One, they had to keep the vehicles UPS (United Parcel Service) clean—and we found out later they took so much pride in their rolling showrooms they were always spotless. Second, in order to keep costs down and get things completed quickly, they had to do the work themselves in setting up the inside of the empty trailers.

These trailers were the symbolic taking-the-company-on-the-road. Only it was more than symbolic. Once the rear door to the trailer was opened, you were immediately transcended in time and place—I wish that was my statement, but I had a prospective customer tell me that was his experience. And I felt the same way.

All of the trailers were generally customized equally inside, except for the unique touches each salesperson added. Each trailer was a rolling mini-company showroom, including a museum of artifacts and photos from both the past and present, along with apparel, videos, and of course, motorcycles. None of this was done glitzy-like, even though it may sound like it. We didn't need an external marketing design group for this. Instead, it was innate and all done in grassroots style, completed in the back parking lot of our offices, over pizza, beer, and some loud music, late into many nights. The later they worked, the more they drank and ate, and the more creative they became. It was genuine, and the trailers reflected that. It was done with quality and a flair for appreciating our prospective customers and dealers. Furthermore, the sales department took great ownership and pride in their rolling company history, and they should have, since they helped create it. It was also a great example of how to integrate the home office with the field.

Another key reason we decided to use these black trucks and matching trailers was because it helped to promote our brand. We were always on the lookout to add value to our brand name, and these sales rigs, along with our salespeople, would be taking the brand on the road, where our prospective dealers, consumers, investors, employees, and vendors might have a point of contact. I was always concerned about every point of contact in communicating and protecting the image of our brand. These sales rigs would not only introduce the brand, but also reinforce it along every point of contact.

On Friday, May 16, 1997, we officially signed up our first dealer; Delano Sport Center in Delano, Minnesota, as Dealer Number 0001. The dealership was owned by Butch and Val Donahue, and Butch was on our Board of Directors. We thought it would be appropriate to have him be our first dealer, and he also had completed a solid application.

We now had our first dealer, who coincidentally was also a Harley-Davidson dealer. With lightening speed, I'm sure this information made it back to Harley. Later, Butch would tell me that Harley was always asking him questions about our venture, and sometimes cold-shouldering him for also working with us.

To commemorate the event of the first signing, we took photographs of the signing, and executed a special certificate memorializing the occasion. We had decided to officially name our first ten dealers as "Pioneer Dealers"; Butch and Val were our first Pioneer Dealer. On our framed special certificate we had boldly printed the word Pioneer, along with the description, *"One who goes before, preparing the way for others to follow."*

We set the date of Tuesday, June 17th as the official date for the signing of our ten Pioneer Dealers. This was a big deal. We invited our new dealers and spouses to visit us in Minnesota, and held a ceremonial signing in a tent set up on the site of our new factory that was being constructed in Belle Plaine. We had cherry picked some of the top dealers in the country, and our Pioneer Dealers were from Illinois, California, Minnesota, Colorado, Wyoming, Michigan, and Indiana. Each of these dealers was well respected in their territory and with the respective OEMs. They represented most of the major OEM motorcycle brands, including Harley-Davidson, Honda, Yamaha, Kawasaki, Triumph and Ducati—and now, Excelsior-Henderson. Establishing our dealer network was another major milestone completed in the company, and considering our early dealers as pioneers was appropriate homage to our brand and venture, and to the future tasks of our Pioneer Dealers. They truly were paving the way for the rest to follow.

The night before our ceremonial signing we had all our Pioneer Dealers meet us at our offices in Burnsville, and together we rode a bus to dinner at the Horse & Hunt Club in Prior Lake. The Horse & Hunt Club, set out in the countryside, was a great place to break the ice and get to know each other, old-fashioned style—and everyone had to leave their guns at home. Earlier in our venture, Allan Hurd, our VP of Manufacturing that we had hired from England, helped enhance a company tradition of *"proposing a toast to the occasion"*—and we would all go round robin until everyone celebrated a toast. We did numerous rounds of toasts, and celebrated well into the evening. All of us actually got pretty good at creating impromptu toasts, and our new dealers displayed they had a lot of character. I remember inadvertently embarrassing Dave Auringer, our new National Sales Manager by comparing him to Neil Diamond. For some reason he reminded me of Neil Diamond, and I expected him to break into song at any moment. Being the good sport that he is, I think he even attempted to sing a few bars from the song "Cracklin' Rosie." In the spirit of the evening, it was all a lot of fun.

At the ceremony, one of our Pioneer Dealers, Lee, from Chicago, looked ill. He had been a Harley dealer since 1966, and unfortunately he did pass away before he ever had a chance to take delivery on a Super X. Every time I looked at the ceremonial Pioneer Dealer photo, I saw Lee proudly standing in the front row, giving the signature Excelsior-Henderson thumbs-up. Lee was a pioneer, and willing to be an early adopter of helping launch our brand. He stepped off the sidelines, and into the game.

I remember these occasions well, as my wife Carol was unable to attend. She was at home caring for our three-week-old son, and it was the day of our wedding anniversary. Another anniversary missed—the third in a row.

# 23

## *Test Riding Through The Road Blocks*

The new Super X prototype motorcycles were undergoing primarily two major projects by our Product Development Team—continual testing and styling changes. By mid-1997 the prototypes had progressed far enough along in testing, and reliability, and the next phase was to start logging on some actual field miles to determine how the motorcycle was performing.

It was time to hire an official factory test rider, and it seemed like everyone wanted that job—in a way I did too, but my skills were better applied in another part of our business. We had people calling and applying for years, but it was not a position to be taken lightly. For one thing, the position was inherently dangerous. The test rider was responsible for basically being the proverbial *"guinea pig."* If something failed on the motorcycle during the field tests, the outcome could be life threatening, and it was the job of the test rider to push the bike to the limit—just like some customers do on a motorcycle. Also, day in and day out, he would have to log nearly 500 miles per day, and feed information back to the Product Development Team.

Another key factor was to have someone who was familiar with American cruiser motorcycles, and understood the characteristics of the ride we were trying to achieve for our future customers. This information, and some of it was certainly subjective, would need to be properly communicated to our Product Development Team, particularly as it relates to the engineering and to the styling. This person would need to be a diplomat, and at the same time be strongly persistent since they were representing the needs of our future customers, and most importantly, the vision of the company that I had established several years earlier, which now pervaded the culture throughout the organization. I didn't have the time to directly supervise this area, nor did I want to micromanage it, but at the same time I needed someone I could implicitly trust who would give me a straight answer, no matter what. And someone who would push the engineering and styling departments vigorously to get a nicely styled, well-engineered product. One we could put our name on and be proud of.

The best person I knew for this job was my brother Terry. He has a twin brother, and is eleven months younger than myself. As brothers we were pretty close, and had remained so even though we chose different career paths. Over the years and in many miles learned the hard way, Terry had developed a genuine way of working with people, and yet standing up for what he believed—he had no pretense. He had ridden motorcycles since his early years on the farm, and had somehow persuaded my father to actually buy a motorcycle for him. That was a first—and last, and I don't think it was a reward for good behavior, but maybe as an incentive for hope of better conduct.

Terry had also been involved with the venture since the first day I launched it, and was really the only person I could trust to fully tell my plans. He had helped me with my previous venture, EverGreen Solutions, and many a late night we would be traveling and working together, and he never wanted any payment. At Excelsior, it was the same. He was my confidant since early 1993 when I launched Hanlon Manufacturing, and he'd helped the business in areas of his skill set. He was skilled in many different trades, and with some of his buddies they had completed all of our commercial buildouts in our leased building. This saved us a lot of money, and kept our landlord happy. During one buildout, they put a big red X logo right in the middle of our museum in the entryway to our facility. Late in the night, they didn't have any patterns for the curves in the big X logo, so they assembled the various sizes of Burger King beverage cups for patterns, and possibly a beer can, and crafted from there. From our early days on the farm, he was familiar with long hours, little to no pay, and left to improvise—*"necessity is the mother of invention."* And the end result looked good.

Terry, or Terrence or T.K., as I customarily call him, had also helped Excelsior by volunteering his time driving our rented or leased trucks, working at the motorcycle rallies, and picking up prototype and antique motorcycles for our growing museum. He would also drive a rented truck all over the country for the many financing presentations we were giving. For years I had made arrangements for us to give presentations at financing conferences, from Indiana, Michigan, Illinois, Ohio, Minnesota, and the east and west coasts, and we needed to take our show on the road. We had motorcycles and the rest of our display, and it was difficult to commercially transport them, and rather expensive. Being frugal, T.K. would volunteer, or we would volunteer him, and he would reliably make it happen.

Oftentimes he would drive alone, or grab a buddy, and drive through the night. I still have memories of him driving the yellow Ryder trucks through the city streets and into alleys as we loaded and unloaded the truck. When I would meet up with him, I would change from my suit to a pair of jeans, and help unload the truck, and minutes later we would all be dressed back up and meeting prospective investors. T.K. was really the first official company volunteer of many more that would follow. He paved the way for the rest of the volunteers, and at Excelsior I never ceased to be amazed at how many people volunteered to help our venture.

Therefore, on June 23rd we officially—meaning he was now being paid—hired my brother T.K. as our factory test rider, and for years he logged the most miles on a prototype Super X. As a brother, I was always concerned about his safety, and obviously our engineering department was as well—he was required to wear full protective gear.

Over thousands of miles, and several months, he did have one mishap that could have been fatal. Just as he was crossing a railroad track, some bolts on the front end came loose, and he dropped the bike and him to the pavement. Fortunately, he wasn't going very fast this time, and he was able to walk away. The R & D lab was called and they sent out a truck to pick him up. A few hours later he was out test riding again.

Through several sources I also learned that T.K. got to know the local constables and highway patrol rather well. It was his job to push the bike to the limit, and we had no formal testing grounds to do that. Most larger, profitable organizations have their own test tracks—also known as proving grounds—or they rent one out. Eventually we would also do that for some of the final intensive testing, but early on we didn't have the financing or the reliability of the product.

On several occasions T.K. got stopped for exceeding the speed limit, but he was generally able to not get ticketed for it. The local enforcers were tolerant of our use of the highways for testing, and they recognized T.K. and our prototype motorcycles. We had a lot of grassroots people helping out, and it was just another form of help along the way, as long as we didn't abuse it, which we didn't.

Even though we were a manufacturer, or prospective manufacturer, we could not use "manufacturer" license plates on our motorcycles. Even though eighty years earlier there were over six motorcycle manufacturers in the State of Minnesota, today there wasn't and the state didn't have a manufacturer's license plate, nor would they allow us to create one. This was a stalemate, which sometimes forced us to pull plates from our regular motorcycles to put on the prototypes. We didn't like doing this, but what else can you do? We weren't about to quit over a technicality.

The state suggested we lobby the legislature to pass a new law, but we really didn't have the time or the money to pursue that issue, nor did we want any reporters to misconstrue our intentions and create a new public relations issue. Instead, it was suggested we apply to the state as a motorcycle dealer since we should qualify, and the state would issue us dealer plates. This wasn't the perfect solution, but it allowed us to legally get our manufacturing prototypes on public roads.

There were some drawbacks to this though. When we traveled to the various motorcycle rallies throughout the country, notably Sturgis, Daytona, and Laconia, it never failed that we would get questioned about our legitimacy as a manufacturer since we always had state dealer license plates, unlike the other legitimate OEMs that were sporting "manufacturer" plates. When you're from out of town, and being an upstart manufacturing company, this didn't help our legitimacy or brand perception one bit. We knew this, but there was little to nothing we could do about it. We just answered the questions, and went about our business.

• • •

It was also around this time that internally the company was starting to lose some engineering momentum. Some of our guys were either getting a little burned out from the long hours, or maybe they weren't sure of the next step, or maybe the transition of moving the product from prototype to manufacturing was just too much. Either way, it was always a fine line trying to figure this out, and determining when to step in, or let the process take its course. We had hired good talented people and it isn't a good leadership concept to over manage them, and yet as a leader, if one delayed action too long, there could be severe consequences for the entire company. We were always just one milestone away from failing—miss a milestone—fail.

That was always the hard part in creating a new company. Ultimately, some of the people that were hired were eventually asked to leave the company. I'm not so sure it was always the right thing to do, but to do things right sometimes you have to. Even though there is objectivity to the decision, I sometimes wonder if some subjectivity creeps into the decision process.

As the company grew and continued to meet milestones, I noticed that some people had a hard time keeping up with the changes. Even myself. Fortunately I thrive on change. Sometimes I felt like I was driving a motorcycle without any mirrors to look back—I just had to keep going forward and keep changing as the landscape changed in front of me. After all, as the leader, I had to be willing to change, and it set a good example for others. I had to quickly adjust to the rapid change, and I witnessed that some had a real hard time with that. Some didn't want to change, or for some reason, couldn't change, and desired the company to remain the same. Also in some cases, the company and the position outgrew the skills the person had been hired for.

Each position would change so rapidly, that in some cases the best that anyone could do was simply carry the torch as far as they were capable, and then ceremoniously pass the torch on to the next person to carry, and so on and so forth. Even though philosophically one can arrive at this concept, I never got used to having to transition people in and out—the reality of executing the concept. People's careers were at stake, and any transition, no matter how it was handled, could have significant impact to a career. There was a lot of passion to our venture, and a lot of passion carrying the torch. Everybody was carrying the torch as best they knew how, for as long as they could.

The company continued to change as milestones were reached and the Team had accomplished what was needed at the time. Maybe it was best to transition people as the company itself was going through a transition, but today I like to think we could have handled this better—but oftentimes I was primarily alone in the company with my opinion on these matters. The company was growing and others internally were weighing in on the decisions, but some of it I do regret.

We were a passionate and intense company, and as the leader, my feet were being held to the fire regarding milestones. I was the point-guy on this issue. From the perspective of the company, I was in charge of ensuring the milestones got reached—without excuses for failure. I wasn't able to perfectly roadmap the future of the company, and sometimes things just unfolded before us as we were building it.

• • •

There was really no one person in the world during current times that had actually taken a completely new proprietary motorcycle from concept into production. The only closely related company was Triumph Motorcycles in England, and they had developed a good strong team of people over a period of time. Even though Triumph was doing okay in their market segment of youth-oriented sport bikes, it was a vastly different product than an American cruiser motorcycle. Other than both products having two wheels, there is very little similarity between them. But from a company launch perspective, there were similarities. We were both new proprietary motorcycle companies that had designed a product from a clean sheet of white paper, and needed to transition from design to production.

We did have one former member of their team—Allan Hurd—as our VP of Manufacturing. Allan was a manufacturing engineer by trade, but also had experience earlier in his career in England in design engineering, and was part of the early engineering group at Triumph. Just before our IPO we promoted Allan to Senior Vice President, and not only in charge of the future production, but now also in charge of R & D and Engineering.

Even though Allan had not led this area before in his career, he had been an observer of the entire process at Triumph, and he quickly went to work. Over the next few months we added additional engineering talent and restructured the R & D and Engineering areas. It was confirmed that under our previous structure, we did lose some time, and we quickly set about getting the project back on an accelerated schedule. We had setbacks before, and had just experienced another one here, but we were now moving forward—fast. We had to finish the testing and the styling on our motorcycles, and transition the product to manufacturing.

# 24

## Our Racehorse Also Had To Plow

From a styling perspective, our new Super X prototypes needed a lot of work before they were market acceptable. But none of that was new or alarming information; it was just part of the natural cycle of product development. It is this evolutionary process that makes product development so challenging and rewarding.

Even though we were really proud of the current generation of prototypes; the market and the motorcycle media were less than forgiving, and correctly so. The prototypes weren't ready for public viewing, and yet that is what we were doing. Not necessarily because we thought it was a good idea, but in a developing company sometimes you have to do things that are a calculated risk. Most product development companies, especially automotive and motorcycle OEMs, never show the non-public prototypes of future models. If they did, competitors would have time to react before the finished product hit the market. In fact, most, if not all, companies guard their product development areas with great secrecy since that is part of the core intellectual property of the company.

In our case, even though our product development was a key intellectual property of the company, we had other parts of the business that would override the secrecy of our future products. In essence, we were opening up our R & D results for all the world to see, including our competitors. And they were watching and learning. They didn't have the same business constraints that we had. They were all internally funded and didn't need to rely on significant outside financing for a business start-up.

Since developing a proprietary new motorcycle requires a significant amount of capital and a long incubation period, even though privately we were hitting our milestones, publicly the industry and the media did not always understand this, and they continually criticized us. Therefore, periodically, we would show our prototypes to the public in order to validate our progress and our serious intentions.

The downside to all this was several-fold. Most of the motorcycle riding public, and the media, were not skilled at looking at EPA- and DOT-regulated factory engineering prototypes. In fact, I would venture to guess that most of them had never seen a factory engineering prototype. I know Ford, GM, and Chrysler never called me to look at one of their prototype automobiles, and in fact, there are scores of media people clamoring to get early spy photos of prototype product.

An important distinction here is the auto industry does show concept vehicles, but these are just as they say. Concept vehicles. They don't work, and are not fully engineered, nor are they fully tested and ready for production, and may never be in production. They are really marketing concept vehicles to gauge consumer interest for the future, and to also show off on what they "could" do. The real stuff that they have already committed to produce in the next year or two is under wraps in secrecy in their product development centers—just like our factory prototypes could have been.

But we had to do things slightly differently. If we had the extra funding and extra talent, we would have taken the traditional separate paths of marketing prototypes versus engineered prototypes. We could have built beautiful looking nonfunctioning marketing-use-only prototypes that the marketing department could use for public events, and at the same time back at our corporate headquarters continue to build engineering mules for the engineers to work on in conjunction with the styling department, all quietly and under wraps. Only that required more money, and a bigger staff, and a duplication of prototypes—none of which we had nor desired. Each generation of prototype alone could cost from $40,000 to $80,000 each, and to build any more than absolutely needed could have been devastating to a tightly controlled budget.

In addition, if we had shown beautiful looking nonfunctioning marketing driven prototypes to the public, we would have been severely criticized. Since we were not a successful, positive cash flowing, existing OEM, it would take an enormous leap of faith to believe a statement from our company that we had the ability to step the prototype to production. In other words, we simply lacked credibility since we were a start-up. And we didn't have any. We hadn't earned that yet. It didn't bother me; that was just the way it was, so deal with it.

The way we dealt with it was to show prototypes that worked to the public and the media, i.e., an engineering prototype. Even though it may not have looked consumer ready styling-wise, at least it worked. I believed it was better that way—at least we wouldn't be criticized for showing the motorcycle consumer something that didn't work. My memory was still too vivid about the Indian motorcycle disaster at the Sturgis Motorcycle Rally in 1993 where they showed a motorcycle that didn't work. But it did look pretty good.

Without getting into too much detail on the differences between our engineering prototypes and the final styled production motorcycles, think of it as almost like building a house. If you were to show someone what your new house looked like before the siding and shingles were installed, and before the interior walls were painted, they might think it didn't look nice, nor did it look finished. That's really what our engineering prototypes were. They just weren't finished yet for the consumer, but the basic structure was there.

Motorcycle consumers, especially ones in our market segment, don't like to be fooled. And they don't mince words if they think you are trying to fool them. Most of the time we were meeting them at the national motorcycle rallies, and the riders had taken time off from their jobs, had done a lot of riding, some partying, and most had enough of life's experiences to warrant having a strong opinion on matters. They were in no mood to be fooled, and we knew it, since we were consumers too. We didn't need to do any focus groups on that issue.

Therefore, most comments we primarily heard were about the fit and finish of our prototypes. The media and the public weren't familiar with seeing product that was not fully styled, and no matter how much we reminded them that these were engineering prototypes, invariably we were questioned continually on the fit and finish. It was almost funny. Some in the motorcycle media would criticize the styling on these engineering mules, when in fact compared to most engineering mules from other OEMs that were never seen, ours were actually nicely painted and chromed since these prototypes were serving a dual purpose. It was a welcome relief when in 1998 we unveiled our production tooled prototypes with the finished styling, and the industry veterans and media gave us accolades on the high quality of the fit and finish. Some even stated it was the best ever on an OEM motorcycle.

We completely dodged the issue of whether our prototypes worked, because we were starting the engines, and riding the motorcycles all over the rallies, in front of all the media and among over a million bikers. It was obvious they worked. We were even doing burn-outs. The prototypes I rode usually smelled of burnt rubber, as I was conducting my own rapid performance testing. It was not unusual for me to be speaking with a prospective customer at a rally, and they would comment on the smell. They instinctively knew what it was, and liked it. If they had to ask what the smell was, that wasn't a good sign.

After a rally in which these prototypes were shown to the public as a highly prized racehorse, they were quickly reduced to plow horse status as the engineers and our test rider went to work. The prototypes would be mercilessly pounded, and sheet metal removed and reworked. By the time the next rally would roll around, we would build new engineering prototypes based on the then-current styling and engineering, and the evolutionary process would start all over again. It was always a little struggle after the rallies. The marketing department needed bikes for recruiting dealers, and the engineers and styling department needed them to advance their work.

Another downside to showing prototypes in advance of production was that it alerted the competition. They weren't napping, nor did we expect them to be. We had one of the most innovative designs in motorcycles and in our engine, and our competitors were taking note. Although they always acted like they weren't. Some of them would identify themselves as they came into our display, and some wouldn't. But we knew most of them—it was our job to know who they were.

It was no wonder that almost all OEM cruiser motorcycle manufacturers came out with a new engine. At the time of our announcement, we had the largest OEM cruiser motorcycle engine. We knew for a fact that, after our announcement, they all went to work, and by the time we hit production, they all had larger engines than we did. But the marketplace knew we were the first, and the first to put all the features together into one motorcycle engine.

Therefore, in spite of any potential downside, the upside was we needed to just carefully manage through any public issues as best we could. The company continued to gain momentum with the prospective consumers, dealers, and the ever-watchful eyes of the industry. This business momentum, along with meeting both our private and public milestones, allowed us to at least have a good story when dealing with the financial side of the business. It all had to work in harmony. Not always perfect, but most of us were singing from the same sheet of music.

Another side benefit to all of the public events and showings we had was that if the public interest waned, it would be a sign of an impending problem that we would need to address. This was another way for us to test the market, and stay close to the prospective customers. With each event, from a grassroots perspective, we were gaining momentum, and instinctively knew we were on the right track.

• • •

Late one warm summer night while I was at my office in Burnsville, I spun my chair around, put my feet up on my old wooden credenza that I had inherited from my previous company, and decided to take a break and flip through the current issue of Cycle World magazine. Since that magazine wasn't necessarily targeted for our audience, I could sometimes flip through it pretty fast. This time though, something caught my eye.

There was a company in Ohio advertising a youth-sized, but real looking, new rechargeable battery-powered cruiser motorcycle for sale. Because I was a gearhead by hobby, and by profession, my kids had a lot of mechanical type toys, and battery-powered jeeps and ATVs that they would ride along with the neighbor kids. I guess I was influencing them. I tore the advertisement out of the magazine and resumed working, with the intent of calling the dealer in the morning.

My son Hunter was just over three years old and, according to my wife, he was already a daredevil—he just liked to test things to the limit. I had to take her word on it, and periodically she would remind me that he might need a male figure in his life—like me, his dad—but I wasn't sure then what she meant. I know I have high expectations of myself and others, and with our children it was no different. Hunter was well past riding a bicycle, and even though he was three years old, he hadn't used training wheels for some time. He was ready for the next big step.

After doing some research on the battery-powered motorcycle, I ordered one and had it delivered to the office—well actually my assistant Jan Crawford did the research and ordered it for me. Her job was to make me look good, including with my family, and she did a wonderful job of it—of course I usually got the credit, but I knew where the real credit belonged. After receiving the motorcycle, I immediately stripped off the brand name and replaced it with Excelsior-Henderson decals. It was a bright yellow motorcycle, and for a young kid, looked and worked like the real thing.

That afternoon, my wife Carol brought the family over to our office/warehouse facility in Burnsville, and pulled up to the rear overhead door where the engineering group was constantly working on our prototypes. They were all family types, and would bring their families in, and today it was my turn. They were going to enjoy this show.

I wheeled the new bright yellow motorcycle out into the parking lot, and Hunter's eyes lit up like a Christmas tree. Since the bike was too heavy for a three-year-old, I reluctantly put the training wheels on. After a short training session on how to use the throttle and the brake, he was off in a blast. There were two speeds, and I tried to keep him in low gear, but he saw where I switched the speeds, and he kept switching to high gear, which I didn't think was a good idea.

After some initial tentative rides, he apparently decided to venture out a little more, and next thing we all knew he was headed off at full throttle. I started yelling, and maybe we all did, and Hunter tried turning around, only to run right smack into the middle of a parked car. That jolted him, and all of us watching feared for the worst. Luckily, he was all right, but I could tell that Carol wasn't so pleased, and I was a little apprehensive about him riding it more, too.

But at home, it didn't take long. Within a few weeks Hunter was safely riding his new motorcycle all over the neighborhood, and without training wheels. He had discovered a new form of two-wheeled freedom. And my five-year-old daughter Hannah couldn't resist all the fun as she also took to riding the motorcycle. Several years later when our youngest, Hayden, turned three, he also learned to ride the battery-powered motorcycle, while the older two children moved up to the larger, internal combustion engine motorcycles.

They will probably never remember learning to ride a motorcycle since they all learned so young. Like a lot of things in life, it is now innate to them.

• • •

It was time for some race action. We were developing a reputation of being an effective grassroots marketing driven company, and we were continually being approached by outside organizations looking for us to do cross-marketing promotions with them, but usually it required a significant fee, or sometimes it was also outside of our target market.

One of our marketing goals was to "own" the state of Minnesota from a motorcycle perspective. When I say "own," I mean from the perspective of the heart. We wanted everyone in the state to know who we were, and more importantly, we wanted most of them to be supportive of our project. We were the start-up grassroots motorcycle company from Minnesota, taking on the established OEM motorcycle manufacturers throughout the world. In people's hearts, we wanted them to feel they "owned" us—and vice-versa. Like a team, we would work together and be a part of each other.

One of the events we decided to sponsor seemed just right. The event was a Grand National Series motorcycle event, sponsored by the

American Motorcyclist Association, and the first race like this in Minnesota since 1959. In the words of the promoter, David Durelle, the Grand National Series is the "Indy cars of motorcycle racing." I guess he would know, since he was a former Grand National Series racer throughout the country.

Because it was a new event in Minnesota, it would give us a chance to be the inaugural sponsor, and would help solidify our presence in the state, especially with motorcyclists in our target market. Also, by being the inaugural race event, we could help to position the event in the marketplace and be involved since its inception.

We struck a deal for a reasonable fee with the race promoter to be the headline sponsor, and the race event was named the "Excelsior-Henderson Minnesota Mile," which was the 19th race event of the year in a series of 22 race events held throughout the country. The race, which we hoped would attract five to six thousand people, was scheduled to be held at the Canterbury Downs horseracing track in Shakopee, on Saturday, September 13th. The featured race was between the national point leaders Scott Parker and Will Davis.

The night of the race, under the bright racetrack lights, several of us had the chance to kick-off the racing events with a ceremonial lap around the dirt track on our prototype Super X motorcycles decked out in parade dress—we had the U.S. flag mounted on one side of the bike, and the Excelsior-Henderson flag on the other. The bikes always looked great in parade dress and I felt proud of our group efforts; as I would gun the engine the drag pipes would bellow, and the flags would fly swiftly in the breeze. With my face in the wind, I could just feel the problems of the moment being swept away—that's another part I like about motorcycle riding. The freedom.

The weather held out, and the race events were a great success. At the attendance gate, we had a 25% greater turnout than what we had anticipated, and the event looked like a "mini Sturgis" motorcycle rally. At the entrance to the race pavilion, we set up our company display, aptly named "The eXperience." The eXperience was our display set-up that we traveled with throughout the country as we brought the company on the road to the motorcycle events. It was a lot of family type fun, and you could hear the roar of the race motorcycles in the background.

The event was such a success that the neighbors were complaining. Shortly after the event, the race promoter was notified through the City Council to not expect to have any more motorcycle races—they were too loud. Imagine that. I never heard a motorcycle that was too loud.

The Hanlon family farm originated during the time of the Civil War, when the land was deeded over to our ancestors by Abraham Lincoln. Early 1980s.

Riding in my dad's lap on a John Deere Model B after planting corn. Spring 1960.

Dressed in our Sunday-finest.
Front row, Susan, Robert; middle row, Thomas, Terrence, Daniel; back row, Sharon, Eileen, David, mom—Mary, and dad—Jerry. February 2, 1966.

My dad harvesting corn with our two-row picker. Nearly every Fall I took
vacation time to assist with the harvesting. Mid-1980s.

Cruis-In Auto Roost—the
former chicken coop—that
we converted into an
automotive shop. I painted
many vehicles in the shop—
cars, boats, motorcycles,
and farm tractors. Late 1970s.

One of the many vehicles I restored in the Cruis-In Auto Roost: a 1970 Dodge
Challenger I bought for $175 during college. It was completely wrecked—nearly
none of the sheet metal is original. My boss at Green Giant didn't believe I
restored and painted it—with flames of course. Late 1970s.

*The second generation of a full-sized foam, and now steel-framed, styling design prototype. Fall 1995.*

*The first officially approved drawing of what would eventually be our new Super X. Drawing J. November 1994.*

*The third generation of full-sized styling design prototypes. The frame was all steel, along with wheels, a Weslake engine mockup, etc. From here, the sketch boards meet the slide rules, and engineering was introduced. Winter 1995-1996.*

Michael Daniels, the proprietor of Weslake Motors in England, putting the finishing touches on one of our prototype Weslake designed engines. Spring 1996.

Rare photo of one of the official first generation of engineered prototypes being built, and includes our first series of running Weslake engines. This actual bike, once completed, was one of the four bikes unveiled to the public in Sturgis, South Dakota, on Monday, August 5th, 1996.

*The external Board of Advisors. Left to right: Jim Morrell, Wayne Fortun, Butch Donahue, Carl Haas, Earl Klein, Gale Mellum, Dan Hanlon, and Ron Sackett.*

*The stock certificate we adopted from the former Excelsior motorcycle company that Ignatz Schwinn owned seventy years earlier. The only significant change was the addition of the red X logo.*

# THE WALL STREET JOURNAL.

*This announcement is neither an offer to sell nor a solicitation of an offer to buy these securities.
The offer is made only by the Prospectus.*

NEW ISSUE

July 24, 1997

## 4,000,000 Shares

MOTORCYCLE COMPANY

Common Stock

Price $7.50 Per Share

*Copies of the Prospectus may be obtained in any State from such dealers as
may lawfully offer these securities in such State.*

| John G. Kinnard and Company, Incorporated | Miller, Johnson & Kuehn, Incorporated |
| --- | --- |

| | |
| --- | --- |
| Advest, Inc. | Cleary Gull Reiland & McDevitt Inc. |
| Cruttenden Roth Incorporated | Hanifen, Imhoff Inc. |
| Kirkpatrick, Pettis, Smith, Polian Inc. | The Seidler Companies Incorporated |
| Van Kaspar & Company | Frederick & Company, Inc. |
| M.H. Meyerson & Co., Inc. | R. J. Steichen & Company |
| Summit Investment Corporation | Traub and Company, Inc. |

## THURSDAY, JULY 31, 1997

*The customary tombstone advertisement we placed in the Wall Street Journal after
completing our $30 million initial public offering.*

*This photo was taken in Jay Leno's shop in Burbank, California as we compared notes. He has an enviable collection of vintage automobiles and motorcycles. He even has a Big X banner hanging on one of his shop walls, which our Road Crew signed and sent to him for his birthday.*

*My son Hunter reaching wide for the handlebars just wishing he could ride one of the Weslake powered prototype Super Xs. My wife was pretty sharp about bringing our children to work, since that was a way to get together. Summer 1996.*

*The banner hanging over main street of Sturgis, South Dakota, that nearly 200,000 motorcyclists would see as they rode through town. The banner proudly proclaims the Excelsior-Henderson Unveiling. Sturgis 1996.*

*On the steps of the State Capitol, Minnesota Governor Arne Carlson and Belle Plaine Mayor Gerry Meyer vigorously discuss which of them would be the first to ride one of the new prototype Super Xs. The Governor won this one. August 21, 1996.*

Dear Dan,

Thank you for coming to visit Belle Plaine. We had an exciting time! It was nice to meet you. We hope you come to Belle Plaine. It was fun giving you the hats, t-shirts, and mugs. We hope you enjoy them.

See you soon,
Mrs. Simones' 2nd Grade

*One of the many examples of some of the unfair tactics the city of Belle Plaine utilized to assist us in making our decision on a factory location—a letter from Mrs. Simones' second grade class. They signed the letter, "See You Soon." I just love that—what a great optimistic attitude.*

*They even sent me all their autographs. If they thought any of this mattered in influencing a decision, they may have been correct—obviously I saved it.*

The first time I saw the golden horses at the top of the Minnesota State Capitol was when my sixth grade class took an all-day field trip. Photo taken a few minutes after Governor Arne Carlson convened a press conference to announce our new factory location. Left to right: brothers Tom and Bob, sister Eileen, myself, my mom and dad, and brother Terry.

Our Guinness Record Book attempt for the largest groundbreaking attendance in the world. We had more than 2,500 people attend, and all helped to break ground on April 14, 1997. I saw several three-generation families—including mine—and they all brought their shovels.

*The new factory headquarters designed and built during 1997—on time and on budget. The Big X sign just outside the building in front of the flags was so large we needed to get a zoning variance.*

*The Excelsior motorcycle factory Ignatz Schwinn built in 1914 on Cortland Avenue in Chicago. At the time, it was billed as the largest motorcycle factory in the world, and included a test track on the roof. After Schwinn shuttered motorcycle production during the Depression in 1931, he converted this factory to bicycle production.*

*The original Henderson motorcycle factory in Detroit, Michigan. It was here Henry Ford ordered his own Henderson motorcycle—factory direct from the Henderson family.*

Our growing Road Crew dealer development team proudly displays their rolling mini-headquarters vehicles. During a one year time frame, these rolling billboards would log nearly a combined half-million miles.

As part of our process of educating our dealers about our brand, and to enhance our relationship, we invited all our dealers in three separate groups to come and visit the factory and experience firsthand the company in action. 1999.

*Our factory test rider, brother T.K., makes the big time with this cover shot on City Cycle Motorcycle Magazine, produced in New York. Not quite like the cover of the Rolling Stone that earlier in his life he was hoping for.*

One of the first motorcycles we had on the farm. My brother T.K. somehow talked my dad into buying this Honda 175 Scrambler for him— note the fashionable bib overalls he wore. We never imagined 25 years later he would be an official OEM motorcycle test rider. Circa 1970.

*The highly automated final assembly line. At the front of this line we assembled the engines, and at the end of the line a finished motorcycle rolled off. Summer 1999.*

*Our new 1999 Super X poses next to the Big X sign just outside the factory headquarters.*

*My three children, Hannah, Hayden, and Hunter, astride serial number one in the factory museum. 1999.*

*An aerial view of our First Annual Shareholders Meeting and Bikers Barbecue. By all accounts, we lived up to the invitation we sent out and did start a rumble. We had over 5,000 people attend, from all walks of life, and from all parts of the country. 1998.*

My wife Carol and I riding into
the tent for our Second Annual
Shareholders Meeting and Bikers
Barbecue. This photo was taken
on my maiden ride after cleaving a
deer on my motorcycle just a few
days earlier. I still had one black
eye, and could barely hold the
motorcycle up. 1999.

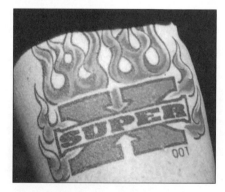

Our first official Excelsior-Henderson
Super X tattoo. Big Al claims the title.
After others started to do the same, he
added the serial number 001—
memorializing him as the first.

*Our growing Road Crew shortly after moving into our new headquarters in Belle Plaine. 1998.*

*Many friends and family volunteered their time to help out at the rallies. Here my mom and dad relax for a quick minute in Sturgis. This was their first return visit to the Black Hills area of South Dakota since their honeymoon in 1949. 1998.*

*The year of 1999 brought along many firsts—one of them being prospective customer demo rides. Our Road Crew provided thousands of demo rides, with as many stories to match. Shoulder-to-shoulder, regardless of rank or expertise, we all worked together.*

*Two of my rally buddies, whom I only saw or met at rallies—Dennis and Tiger—I don't know if Tiger has a real first name. We don't meet to tell the tales of our work careers.*

*The secret handshake with my long time friend, John Stier from Belle Plaine, as we meet in Sturgis.*

*A new motorcycle we introduced for model year 2000—the Deadwood Special. This special edition quickly became a collectible edition, and with factory flames— you know how I feel about flame paint jobs.*

*Kenny Capaul, Road Crew member and chief of our custodial maintenance department, seriously considering riding a Super X out of our eXperience display during one of our many rally events.*

*These Weslake powered prototypes were capable of doing great burnouts. I'm conducting some aggressive testing while doing a fifth-gear burnout during Daytona Beach Bike Week at our rally headquarters, the Peabody Auditorium. Full throttle in fifth gear—the speedometer would read about 120 mph. 1998.*

*Richard and Colleen Selby of Missouri purchased two new Excelsior-Henderson Super Xs, and really got into the Christmas spirit, donning red Santa hats and bows. 1999.*

*Ernie Hartman, a proud WWII veteran, riding his new 1999 Super X. I bought his old one from him—our 1931 Super X.*

*Two famous riders in Excelsior-Henderson lore. Carl Clancy was the first to go around the world on a motorcycle, and Lee Humiston was the first to break the 100 mph barrier—1912. Who was the second? Who knows… Circa 1913.*

*Charles Lindbergh astride his 1920 Excelsior Big X that he bought new from the Engstrom Excelsior dealership in Little Falls, Minnesota. Circa 1920.*

*Ignatz Schwinn purchased the Excelsior motorcycle company of Chicago in 1911, and the Henderson motorcycle company of Detroit in 1917, thereby merging the brands and creating the third largest motorcycle company. Circa 1930.*

*The Excelsior Big X was an excellent choice for competitive hill climbing events. Circa 1917.*

*Motorcycling has always been traditionally a family sport. Circa 1917.*

*The famous Old West cowboy actor, Tom Mix,*
*astride his Henderson motorcycle.*
*Circa 1918.*

*Excelsior and Henderson motorcycles were the popular choice among police*
*forces throughout the world. The Nova Scotia Police force stands proudly*
*alongside their faithful Henderson motorcycles.*
*Circa 1929.*

*The Buenos Aires Mounted Police force astride their Big X twin cylinder engine Excelsior motorcycles. Circa 1918.*

*Three famous racers, Wells Bennett, Bob Perry, and "Blick" Wolters, pictured with factory designer J.A. McNeil. This 1920 factory racing motorcycle bore the new overhead-cam X-twin engine. Sadly, on January 2, 1920, Bob Perry crashed on one of these fast factory racers, and died five hours later. Circa 1920.*

*My family who stood at my side through all my travels of Riding The American Dream. Left to right: Hunter-7 years old, Carol, Hayden-4 years old, myself, and Hannah-9 years old. 2001.*

*My one-year old daughter, Hannah, helping me work on the original Hanlon Manufacturing business plans in the basement office of my home in Burnsville, MN. Summer 1993.*

*Our Super Xs in parade dress at the annual Belle Plaine Bar-B-Q Days celebration. My son Hayden, two-years old, rides along with my wife Carol and I. 1999.*

# 25

## Raising The Flags

It was early November in Minnesota, and the cool weather and snow were beginning to settle in. I've always enjoyed living in a geographical area that truly has a change in the seasons—it definitively marks the passage of time. There was another big season of change on the horizon, not only in the weather, but in our company also. The factory building in Belle Plaine was complete.

We needed to get a variance to install our new corporate sign in front of our building since it was so large. It was our big, bold red "X" Excelsior-Henderson logo mounted to a large concrete block base that matched our building. At night, most signs of this type are lit with interior lights, but we chose to be different. I wanted to create an old nostalgic effect, and one of the ways to do that was to use indirect lighting. We decided to light our sign the old-fashioned way of just pointing ground lights at it. Yes it did create shadows, but it also had an authentic and natural look. It also saved us money.

Being true to our brand heritage and our bold but stately presence, I had the following statements inscribed in large black letters on the cement block base:

BRAND FOUNDED IN 1876

"A PROUD AMERICAN MOTORCYCLE COMPANY"

805 Hanlon Drive

Belle Plaine, Minnesota

The United States of America

The sign was mounted just a few feet off of U.S. Highway 169. Everyone who traveled the road would clearly see the sign and building—thousands of motorists every day. It was now a landmark...by plan.

The move-in date was scheduled for Monday, November 10th. Actually, we planned to move over the weekend so we wouldn't interrupt our work, and Monday morning would be our official first day in the new headquarters building in Belle Plaine. It was just in time, too, as we had outgrown the offices in Burnsville several times over and had people stacked up in hallways working. Temporarily this type of work style was sufficient, but in the long term was not productive.

We met our milestones exactly as we had planned. The building was finished ahead of schedule and on budget. This was no small feat, and many times during the project it seemed like we were going to overshoot the time and the budget. Fortunately, we had the A-Team on the Building Development Team, and we all knew the consequences of not meeting milestones. Periodically, I would have to remind a few people, sometimes not as diplomatically as they might have liked, but in the end everything worked out well. In a few short days the Building Team would be dissolved and we would all move on to new projects.

During the process of constructing the new facility, the issue of flagpoles arose. Normally this could be a fairly minor issue to some companies and people, but it seemed anytime there was an opportunity to correctly position our brand in the public and to our Road Crew, we would carefully scrutinize the imprint of our decisions. I challenged our Team to help me think this through.

A suggestion was made that to show our global presence, we should display the flags of the various countries of our prospective international suppliers and dealers. Personally, I was respectful of this idea, but we were an American company. Yes we did business internationally, and had for some time. I argued the point that when I travel internationally, I like to visit organizations that are proud of their own unique heritage, and I don't feel offended if they take personal pride in their own heritage and fly their nation's flag—and not ours. I want to experience the authenticity of their pride and heritage; through the sharing and respect for one another's heritage we can learn and respect one another. I don't mind the difference. In fact I respect it. While in Germany, do I want to go to a McDonald's restaurant, or do I want to go to a German restaurant to experience their culture? Some choose the former, some choose the latter. In my perspective, neither is right or wrong, just a preference in experience. Anyway, that is what I believe.

The flags would be a symbol for who we were and what we as an organization and culture believed in. When visitors to America desired to visit an American business, we wanted to be on their list of places to stop. Here they could experience firsthand the workings of an American business proudly and respectfully conducting international business. It wasn't lip service.

Therefore, we decided to design a separate flag pavilion right in front of our building in the circular drive. Part of my job was to imprint the culture of our company with our employees and the community, and at my suggestion, we decided as an organization to formally hold a flag raising ceremony the day after we moved into our new headquarters. The next day was Tuesday, November 11th, Veterans Day. Maybe this was coincidental timing, maybe it wasn't.

The Events Planning Team within our marketing department went about planning the ceremony. Almost all of this type of stuff was planned and executed internally, and not through external focus groups or external marketing companies. We had good talent, trusted their instinct and skills as a part of the Team, and kept the focus on being genuine and grassroots. This ceremony was no different.

At the tear-flowing ceremony with all of our employees and families invited, we had the National Anthem sung by LaVonne Moore, a local Belle Plaine resident. We had presentations by the mayor of Belle Plaine—our *"once a Tiger, always a Tiger"* speaker—Mayor Gerald Meyer, the State Senator Claire Robling, State Representative Carol Molnau (who in 2002 was elected Lieutenant Governor of the state), and Gary Fields, the Deputy Commissioner for the state Department of Trade and Economic Development. I don't know why—maybe it was the solemn significance of the ceremony—but each of the presentations was brief, unscripted, and from the heart. I like that. My personal belief and motto is: *"if you can't speak from the heart, you have the worst kind of heart trouble."*

I personally liked the final presentation best. It started at high noon. The presenter choked back his emotion while he was giving it, and it was naturally unscripted and from the heart. The speaker, Maynard Bahrkey, was a war Veteran representing the local Belle Plaine chapter of the Veterans of Foreign Wars. He was senior in age, and presented our company with the American flag and the black U.S. Prisoner of War flag. After his presentation, he helped raise the two flags while LaVonne sang the National Anthem. Some people were struggling to hold back their tears. I was too. We had all been part of something that couldn't be described, but had to be experienced. We then invited all guests to a lunch in our new cafeteria, and a tour of the building.

During my presentation, I had a chance to give one of my personal favorite quotes. I borrowed it from a presentation made on Thursday, November 19, 1863, during the Civil War. It was from the Gettysburg

Address, a short two minute speech delivered by President Abraham Lincoln at the dedication of the Gettysburg National Cemetery, and I quote: "The world will little note, nor long remember what we say here; while it can never forget what they did here." To me, that says it all. I believe in this stuff.

As each of the flags was raised, we played music to commemorate the event. As the State of Minnesota flag was being raised, we played *"America The Beautiful,"* and when the company flag was lofted, we played our traditional song, *"Born To Be Wild."*

There were strong November winds blowing that morning as we hoisted the flags for the first time ever. On the four towering flagpoles we raised five flags. The tallest naturally being the bearer of the United States flag, with the P.O.W. flag mounted just below the U.S. flag. The three remaining flagpoles were exactly equal in height, and just a few feet shorter than the U.S. flagpole. The pole to the east of the U.S. flag bore the State of Minnesota flag—in the direction of our State Capitol, and the pole to the west bore the City of Belle Plaine flag—in the direction of the City of Belle Plaine. The remaining flagpole—centered—bore the company colors: the black and red Excelsior-Henderson flag. With the strong winds blowing, the flags were freely flying overhead at full-mast.

At the base of the four flagpoles, we mounted a permanent ceremonial marker in the center. About a month earlier, late one night, after several drafts, I penned the final wording for the large brass plaque that was permanently mounted to the concrete marker, which was a gift from our developer, Ryan Companies.

The marker reads:

### FLAG DEDICATION MARKER
With great respect, on Veterans Day,

November 11, 1997,

the flags proudly flying overhead

were dedicated at this site.

These flags symbolize

the soul of Excelsior-Henderson,

from the Veterans who have courageously served to

ensure our freedom,

to the Pioneers who have persevered before us.

Located on the prairie, the Borough of Belle Plaine

is home to the Hanlon Family since the 1850s

when they immigrated to America.

The Hanlon Family and
The Excelsior-Henderson Road Crew

For the Road Crew members that would join us after this day, they would never know the company's humble beginnings in the basement of my house, and then moving to the office/warehouse in Burnsville, which we had outgrown. This was now our third location in five years.

I also now had a key for the front door of the building. While the building was being constructed, I took my family out one afternoon for a Sunday drive—Sunday in my family is known as *"Family Day,"* and we plan family activities together to get away from the normal routine of the week, plus generally I never saw my family all week due to my work schedule. When we arrived at the factory the front doors were locked and I wasn't given a key to get in. Previously, the building had not yet been secured, and it was surprising—and embarrassing—for me to not have access.

Well, I wasn't going to let the matter of a locked door deter me. Looking around I noticed an extension ladder on the ground, and I placed it up against the building and extended it to reach the second floor window of my office. Glancing around the premises to ensure the local police wouldn't mistake me for an intruder, I scaled the ladder and was in luck. My office window was unlocked, so I climbed through, and went downstairs to let my family in.

On Monday, I made sure to get a key to the facility.

• • •

Just before the end of the year, and about five weeks after moving into our new factory building, we were finalizing the details on the financing from the State of Minnesota. As an incentive to locate in a rural area and bring in well-paid manufacturing jobs, the state had agreed to provide a loan for our new finishing facility, which was a sep-arate facility located inside our factory.

On Monday, December 22, 1997, we officially closed on the state financing provided by the Minnesota Agricultural and Economic Development Board. The transaction was structured as Revenue Bonds for $7.145 million, in which we would make payments to pay off the loan over a ten-year period. The bonds were sold by the regional investment banking firms of Piper Jaffray and Dougherty Summit Securities to fifteen different investors, primarily in the banking and insurance industry. Like most of our debt financing, in order for us to get the loan, we had to pay into a reserve account the equivalent of about a one-year payment reserve, which in this case was $1.14 million. In essence, by us having to pay a reserve, the net initial loan balance was about $6 million.

As planned, it would take us about eight to ten months to complete the inside of the factory, including the finishing facility. One item we must have inadvertently overlooked though was the timing of the payments, or possibly the state later got cold feet, because it became excruciatingly difficult for us to get all the funds from the loan released to us. We ultimately were required to significantly fund the finishing facility with our own cash, before we were finally able to receive the entire escrow payments on the loan. Talk about a huge unexpected risk.

During late 1998, just before the state agreed to finally release the complete funds on the loan, there was one final, new condition. They also required another outside consultant's opinion on the quality and cost of our finishing facility. There was some outside pressure being put on the state regarding our loan (even though it wasn't yet funded to us), and it was obvious they were seeking to validate we were doing everything correctly, and if not, it appeared they would terminate the loan—and all of this after the facility was already constructed. I don't blame them, and I always felt our company and decisions were an open book for scrutiny—after all, I scrutinized the details also, and if there were any mistakes we wanted to be alerted to them as fast as possible.

The finishing consultant the state hired was from out-of-state, and was intimately familiar with OEM automotive and motorcycle finishing facilities. After a several week review period, we got a clean bill of health. The consultant told us it was one of the most efficient and high quality finishing facilities he had reviewed, and was on a par—except for sheer physical size—with the BMW automotive finishing facility, which is among the best. After the consultant's analysis, the state released the funds to us, and just in time. We had never anticipated providing the interim financing.

Initially, we never planned on constructing our own finishing facility because I didn't believe we would ever get debt financing to construct one until after we were cash flow positive. It is hard to attract loans when the business isn't cash flowing. Therefore, it was not included in the Business Plan during the first several years, and we planned on subcontracting our finishing, which in itself would be a challenge also. There was a market and manufacturing risk to our Business Plan by subcontracting out the final finishing.

Within our target market segment, we weren't intending to compete with the lower priced motorcycles but rather with the upper-end, so our final finish had to be among the best in the industry, and to current automotive standards, which are among the highest final finishing standards. Our customers would be very particular about the appearance of the final product, including the paint and the chrome. Most chrome and paint finishes look nice initially. How about five years later, after being driven fifty thousand miles and subjected to all types of climatic abuse? That is where the true test is, and that is what our finishes were designed to. Does it cost more initial money? Yes. In the long run, is it a better value? Yes.

One of the misnomers about the OEM finishing facility is that it is customarily called a paint booth by observers on the outside. That is old terminology and would be similar to today calling an automobile a horseless carriage. There are paint booths, but they are generally for after-market use and a completely different application. But nevertheless, the layman's language uses the terminology of a paint booth, where in reality, internally we and the OEM industry don't use that term. It is a final finishing facility. Highly automated. Highly regulated for environmental standards. Highly controlled air temperature and humidity, and also highly filtered for dust and dirt contamination. You could not enter our finishing facility without going through an air-bath. If you have ever gone through an automated car wash, and in the end where the air-blowers are—they would be similar to our air-bath.

Anything that was metal and required a final painted finish was completed in our finishing facility. We designed an automated several step cleansing process, followed by an e-coat dipping process to practically eliminate rust—forever. We completely e-coat dipped all our components, including the fenders, fuel tank, and the frame. We were the only motorcycle company in the world doing this at the time.

In addition to any e-coating, we also had powder-coated finishes and baked-on finishes. The final clear-coat was impervious to just about any element. Later, when we launched our production motorcycles, several industry sources hailed the motorcycles as having one of the best OEM motorcycle finishes in the world.

Oftentimes I was asked about how long I wanted our motorcycles to last. I would answer, "One hundred years." Most people wouldn't believe my answer, thought I was joking, and would ask me again. I would give the same answer, and I meant it. It wasn't asking too much. Among my growing car collection, I had a 1940 Packard, a 1931 Model A, and in the company, we had several antique motorcycles, including a 1905 and a 1909 Excelsior. Really old stuff, but if you make a quality product, of metal, that can stand the test of time, it is highly conceivable our motorcycles would last one hundred years. Particularly if you also have a loyal, conscientious consumer who is looking for lasting, timeless quality. Not everyone wants cheap—we were focused on high quality at good value. Anybody who studied our finished motorcycles knew this, and would tell us that.

Constructing the finishing facility was a bit of a gamble. We didn't want to use hardly any of our equity capital to construct it, and would only do so if we received the debt financing, and if we saved money and improved our final product quality. In addition, if we could also lessen risk to the business model, then we would consider it.

The finishing facility was matched to the rest of the scale of the factory of having the ability to produce about 20,000 motorcycles per year, with first year volume projected at about 4,000 units. At our first year projected volume, this yielded an overhead fixed cost per motorcycle of about $285, and at full capacity about $57 per motorcycle. Just the freight cost alone of shipping unpainted components to multiple subcontract vendors for painting would exceed this cost per motorcycle, plus we would have had to factor in any damaged goods from transit and lost time. And our variable costs weren't much more than the fixed costs. In the end, we were able to achieve one of our key goals—control the final finished assembled quality of the motorcycle, and at a cost savings. Also, in studying what other OEMs—automotive and motorcycle—were doing, they all had their own final finishing facilities. Even being rebels, there were some good things we could learn from the current industry.

• • •

It was quite a year, again. In closing out the year we held our Christmas celebration at the OK Corral in Jordan, Minnesota. It's a neat bar and restaurant located in the countryside, just off U.S. Highway 169, and about 5 miles down the road from our new factory. When you walked up to the large double front doors to open them, you could see that the door handles were old handguns. Real ones.

A lot was going through my mind. I had incorporated the company on December 22, 1993, and exactly to the day four years later we announced the closing of the state loan, bringing the total capital raised to $60 million...I need to repeat that—$60 million.

Not for high-tech. Not for the Internet. Not for medical. Not for telecommunications. But for manufacturing—motorcycles—here in America. I had been told so many times that it couldn't be done that I no longer heard it when someone mentioned it to me—I'd become immune to those words a long time ago. I knew it could be done. Motorcycles had been in this country for over one hundred years, and I rode them. So someone was building them, why not us? I just kept pushing forward, one step at a time. I never wanted to look backwards.

On average, we had raised about $1.5 million per month. We had ten different financing transactions over a four-year time period, which meant we averaged a major transaction every five months, with an average transaction size of $6 million. In 1997 alone, we had four major financing transactions that totaled about $45 million. It took nerves of steel to handle this, and I was proud of our Team's accomplishments.

At year-end we had $48 million in assets, of which about $25 million was in cash or equivalents. For the year, our net losses were about $5.9 million—exactly on plan—and the total losses (or investment) since inception was just over $10 million. We were in pretty good shape. For the first time, I realized we were going to get our chance to build new proprietary OEM motorcycles. The first new, independent OEM American motorcycle manufacturer in over a half-century—Excelsior-Henderson motorcycles. The American dream was becoming more real.

# 26

## More Than A Sum Of Its Parts— The Factory

New Years Day in 1998, I drove my family out to our new head-quarters and factory facility. It was a cold and snowy winter day and we were closed for the holiday. These were restless times for me. Our company had progressed a long way, but we still had a long road ahead of us. As my family and I walked through the company museum, and into the factory, it was eerily quiet. Not because everyone had the day off, but because the factory was vacant. Nothing.

Before the end of the year, the factory needed to be full of working equipment, and with the grace of God, we planned to be in production. We developed a theme for the year, and our motto became *"The Road To Glory,"* to commemorate the formidable tasks ahead of us. For the year, our *Road To Glory* would be achieved when we launched the start of production. We were all fixated on this and had a common mission.

A lot of things had to get done: on time, and on budget. I always need to reinforce the *"on time, and on budget."* To me, as the CEO and founder—and just the way I am wired—if things didn't get done on time, and on budget, they may as well not get done at all, because the outcome would be the same—shutdown. We didn't have excess funds or excess time—most start-up companies don't, and we were no differ-ent. How I sometimes longed to be working in a company that was cash flow positive and had at least some history of predictability. Then you at least have oxygen as you execute your options.

A year earlier we had reduced our IPO amount—we were already $10 million short in our future budget. I was fairly confident we had raised enough money to get into production, provided we could adhere strictly to our budgeted costs of equipment and installation. Most of our capital raised was committed to capital equipment projects, and there was no room for overruns.

My concern was now beyond initial production. Even though we had yet to make one production bike, and even though the factory had zero equipment in it, I was already concerned beyond that. I was con-fident of the people we were working with, both on the inside and out-side. The strategy of working with the A-Team, and pushing hard was paying off. But what about staying in production once we reached it? That was my concern. The exact start-up costs were still a bit of a gamble, and we all knew it.

This was going to be the year of focus and transition—focus on the primary tasks of completing the engineering on the Super X while simultaneously preparing and launching the factory for production. This would naturally lead us into a business transition of moving from a developmental stage company into the early stages of an operating, revenue producing company. That part I liked, but I also knew from experience, was that when the transition started to happen, it was like managing your way through a storm. Our best way to handle the future storm was to carefully manage the day-to-day, here and now, so we would be better prepared for the future.

I also instinctively knew that this is where most early stage product development driven firms fail. Most product driven start-up companies need to initially focus on developing the product, and unsuspectingly may not give enough consideration to the next step. You might think that after getting the product developed and tested, the hard work is done. In reality, it is just starting again, but this time in a new direction. The key here is you now need to position the company to make thousands of the product, at a competitive cost structure. And with manufacturing, part of the strategy is volume and consistency. On the surface it appears simple, but applying the principles of manufacturing, along with the costs of setting up production, can overburden an early start-up company. This bothered me, but there was little time to think about it other than to focus on planning and executing.

I cannot overstate the complexities of transitioning from design to production. Designing and making a few prototypes from a clean sheet of paper was problematic enough, but now our next challenge was to make thousands of them—reliably and cost competitively. Some people think that when you have successfully designed and tested a product, you have found the light at the end of the tunnel. Instead, we knew better, and one of our manufacturing engineers would humorously comment that we have now *found* the tunnel, and we are not even *in it* yet. But we did now find it, and we needed to enter it and successfully come out the other side. Which we eventually did, except for a few bad scrapes that, with time, would heal.

In addition, we were now a publicly held company, which handcuffed us slightly because any business issue that arose that could later be deemed material had to be disclosed immediately. And we needed to adhere to that. Fine, if you are a cash flow positive company that has been around for a few years and has significant revenue; the management should be able to at least keep their ship sailing because they have momentum. But for us, we had been taking on water for years; the question was: Could we continue to bail it out fast enough as the ship was being built? We had new issues come up frequently that we had to solve, and in some cases disclose publicly, which could have caused an overreaction in the marketplace. Even though we might have had some of the same issues as our competitors, they didn't need to publicly disclose them because they had resources to solve the problems.

I was no longer concerned about the prototype Super X motorcycles. Our engineering Team and styling group were progressing well, and we had the budgeted funds to move these projects to completion. Again, the A-Team was on top of it. Sure, they had a lot of problems, both present and anticipated, but they had the talent to solve them. It was still a Herculean effort to complete, but I was confident that during the year we would have fully engineered and styled Super X motorcycles ready for production, with production tooling—so that wasn't keeping me awake at nights.

What concerned me was the *"when"* part of getting into manufacturing, and then securing the capital to stay in production. We didn't plan on being profitable from day one, as that would be quite unrealistic. But first things first, and the factory needed to get set up.

• • •

Our strategy for the factory size was to blueprint it for about a five-year time horizon, which yielded a production volume of 20,000 motorcycles per year, with the first year projected at 4,000 bikes, and a reasonably consistent growth curve to the 20,000-unit mark. This was also the smallest sized OEM motorcycle assembly plant that made financial sense—and was projected to be the smallest OEM assembly facility in the world. Any smaller, and you don't need an assembly plant. You may as well not start, since the low volumes will never offset the costs of design and tooling.

This is part of the issue with the barrier to entry in the motorcycle, or automotive, industry. If you truly have your own product, i.e., proprietary, then by definition you have a proprietary design with proprietary tooling with which to create the final product. The method may not be proprietary, but the product is. Once you have invested in the manufacturing tooling, the same tooling will produce one hundred parts, or generally more than 25,000 parts. The only way to ever recoup the significant investment costs of design and tooling is by volume—and lots of it. Yes we could have planned for a lower volume, but we never would have recouped any investment—that would have been a planned failure. I didn't like planning for failure. Instead, we planned for success, and just maybe with the help of many it would happen. That was part of the dream—the American dream.

Once the factory volume was determined, then all the equipment that went into it was sized accordingly to match. No rocket science here. If you have one area oversized, and undersized the next, then an instant bottleneck is created. Therefore, the equipment was sized to eliminate bottlenecks.

Also, a key strategy of our factory was to be well automated, and to control the critical factors of the finished motorcycles. Having an understanding of the industry and manufacturing, I knew there were certain elements of the process we needed to control in order to ensure quality. Certainly, we needed to control our final assembly, and opted to be the final assembler of our motorcycles. By controlling the final assembly, we could control the quality of each component that was going into the motorcycle; hence quality components with a controlled assembly should lead to a quality final finished motorcycle. Which it did for us.

The buildout of the finishing facility was going to take the longest amount of time, so we launched the factory equipment project first. We had a fixed price contract for the finishing system from George Koch Sons of Evansville, Indiana. This firm had expertise in setting up finishing systems, and had worked with both automotive and motorcycle OEMs. They brought up their crew of workers from Indiana, and for the better part of a year they made Belle Plaine their home.

There were also a few other items we needed to control prior to assembly. Most of this is logical when you think about it, which I did, and we studied it. The entire motorcycle is built around a frame, and if the frame is accurate to tolerance, the rest of the assembly goes smoothly and the finished product performs better. Therefore, it was logical to conclude that we needed to build our own frames. It was the foundation to the rest of the entire motorcycle, and again it was customary in the OEM industry to do this.

Regarding our frames, we set up the process to have an outside vendor supply the various tubes and castings, and we controlled the welding of the frames together. We purchased several robotic welding cells from ABB Automation in Fort Collins, Colorado, who again had experience with assisting OEM manufacturers. Using the robotic welders, we were able to control the high quality of the weld, and specific accuracy for close tolerances in frame geometry.

After we were operational, we ran into several manufacturing people from Harley and Honda who asked how we were able to get such exact and smooth welds (no kidding, our frames do look the best). Well, some by luck, but mostly by skill. We designed the frame and the components to be ultimately welded on this exact type of robot—the motorcycle frame was basically robot-friendly. That's one of the advantages of being new. We designed everything as a package together. From design to final production, it was all designed as a packaged unit. We didn't need to retrofit components or a manufacturing process, nor were we hampered by current constraints. We had a clean sheet.

• • •

Another key area was the driveline: the engine and transmission. We had our own engine design, and periodically would discuss with outside vendors the possibility of having our engines assembled by them. One of the parties we had spoken to was Mercury Marine, but they, like all of these types of vendors, found our business to be too much of a risk since we were a start-up and our projected production volumes were way too low for them to consider. Also, we weren't so sure we needed them, but in doing our homework we did meet with several potential engine manufacturers. As expected, we had no takers. They all thought we were dreamers and too great a risk for them to entertain as a new customer. In addition, the economy was so robust they weren't looking for new customers as they could hardly fill the demand of their current customers. The economy was booming, and they were all busy—too busy to take our calls, and treat us seriously.

We had our own designs, and were tooling them up for production. The question was: Who would control the quality of the components, and then the final assembly? Both processes are inherently dependent upon one another. Personally, I had assembled enough automotive, tractor, and motorcycle engines that I understood the process and the quality quite well, but I needed our Production Team to sort this out. This was also a no-brainer. In our R & D area we were already assembling engines by hand, and for most gearheads, the assembly is routine, as long as you know what you are doing and have quality components.

Regarding quality components: that was another critical part of our production process. We needed to have good quality vendors, backed up by a solid quality control department that could inspect the parts as they came in to ensure they were to tolerance. Again, pretty logical stuff, but executing it can get tricky. There are certain things in which the expertise is so specific, that it is best left to the firms that specialize in those areas. Since our Production Team and I were familiar with all this, we had already determined several years earlier what we would do inside versus outside.

Our primary goal was to be a final assembler of our proprietary components manufactured by others, except for our frames—which we built—and except for the final finishing, which we would do. Logically thinking about this, it all made sense. This would allow us to get into consistent production, at a reasonable cost, and at the same time we could control all of the critical factors—at least *"control"* them as well as anyone can, since in reality, how much can you really control? Perfection is a great goal, but I have never reached it.

We didn't plan on doing any casting, machining, chroming, or plating. We weren't going to be making the handlebars, the seat, the tires, rims, spark plugs, mirrors, gauges, electrical components, starters, pistons, camshafts, crankshafts, bolts, fuel injection systems, nor ignition keys. Basically, we didn't *make* any of the 1,000-plus components in our motorcycle—rather we just *assembled* a finished, new, expensive, high quality motorcycle, that as a customer you could observe being built. The misnomer here was the term manufacturer, which is how we customarily referred to ourselves, but really we were an assembler. The cost and time to truly be a full manufacturer would have been astronomical, and with today's technology, it would have been foolish.

The last processes we needed to control were the final assembly and testing. The assembly line was set-up to assemble engines at the front of the line, and by the end of the line, a finished running motorcycle awaited testing. Our plan was to assemble the engines on the same line as the rest of the motorcycle. This is not typical of most OEMs, as they separate the processes, but we were much smaller and had to do it this way. It wasn't bad, as long as you planned for it, which we did.

After the engine was assembled, the next step was to introduce the motorcycle frame. The frames were built about one hundred feet away, and then a few feet away set on conveyors to the automated finishing facility for cleansing, corrosive inhibitor dipping, priming, and painting. After the frame exited the finishing facility, it was moved another seventy-five feet to the assembly line.

Once the frame hit the assembly line, it just kept slowly moving along as components were added. All nonpainted components arrived from our warehouse inventory, which was about one hundred feet away. All painted components—including our fuel tank and fenders—moved directly from our finishing facility to the assembly line.

At the end of the assembly line the bikes would be moved down a small incline, and then up into the rolling road test. The doors would shut, and the next thing you would hear was a roar. We were pretty advanced in having a rolling road test, for all of our production bikes. The bikes were tested for horsepower, torque, shifting, braking, etc., and the test results were integrated into our computer control system.

From there, the bikes were crated and shipped to dealers. Well, before the shipping, our Road Crew workers on the assembly line signed the crates, and they even let me sign a few. It was their own idea to sign the crates. It just came of natural inspiration—we had no focus groups, our whole company was a focus group—since they were so proud of what they had accomplished, they were willing to put their name on it and stand behind it. The *"Road To Glory."* But this is getting a little ahead of the story.

The entire assembly process was highly automated and all tied into our computer control system so that at anytime, a Vehicle Identification Number could be tracked right on the assembly line, to the exact time, components, suppliers, labor, etc. Even our torque wrenches had sensors in them that automatically recorded the torque settings for each motorcycle.

This was all theory at one time, but when we did launch production, the theory was tested, and it worked. And it worked very well.

• • •

Another part of the factory that often gets overlooked is its *working environment.* It was important to me to keep the design of our factory building—both on the interior and exterior—in harmony with our brand and with our corporate culture. I've worked in places that vary from factories to downtown office skyscrapers that overlook a scenic river—and I've forked manure in cattle and hog barns. On long hot summer days I've walked the rows of corn and soybeans, hoeing out the weeds our tractor cultivator couldn't get (or at least that's what my Dad said). But I never understood why the factory environment had to be the way it was. Over the years as my career advanced, along with my education and experiences, I never felt right inside about my new great surroundings when I knew that others just a few feet away in the same building had a working environment substandard to mine.

And I had been there too. Somehow, it was real easy to interpret the message as being less worthy to an organization. I didn't want that to happen with us at Excelsior. Maybe that was supposed to be how it was, but not with me, and not with my company. This was another opportunity to imprint my values by influencing the corporate culture.

First off, I started the company, and I admittedly have an attitude about these sort of things. We may all have different jobs that require different skills to the company and within the marketplace, but we should all be treated equally with respect. Even when I used to shovel manure, I didn't think any less of myself for doing it. It was my job, and my job to do it—and no job lasts forever anyway. Possibly, if I did it well enough, I may even advance to something else. In our new factory, my concept was that generally whatever feature comforts I had in my office for a working environment, I wanted the rest of the company to have too, or I would learn to do without.

I didn't want someone from a poorly lit, hot factory floor to come into my office all upset about something, and immediately notice the difference, that I had windows and air conditioning. From my perspective, there was a simple solution—either take out my windows and AC, or put in windows and air conditioning in the factory—which we opted to do. And bright lighting, with nicely finished floors. We had a nice factory.

The challenge though was to accomplish this smartly. There were certain areas that needed to be very secure, hence no windows, or would need a creative method to obtain natural lighting. Other than in our finishing facility, from nearly every place where a person worked, there was a nice working environment of natural lighting, proper heating and cooling ventilation, and bright lighting. I firmly believe that an enhanced working environment offsets any costs, as long as the reason for doing it is what one really believes inside, and is consistent with the company's corporate culture. If you are just doing it because of complaints, then there are probably more serious management and employee issues—I am talking here about the internal values and motivation that drives a person.

At one point earlier when we were constructing the building, the project was over budget, again, before we could get it back on track. Usually, one of the first things someone on our Building Development Team would suggest is that we could save nearly $200,000 by taking the air-conditioning out of the factory design. Privately, I would fume, and possibly some of it might have showed through. Invariably, the room would fall silent for my reaction. I would ask the person making the suggestion if their office, their home, and their car were air-conditioned. The answer was always yes. I would then ask why, and again, the predictable answer was that it was too hot without it. I would then move in for my point: "If it is too hot for you, it will be too hot for people in the factory. If you need to take out the air conditioning, take it out everywhere in the building, including my office. If you can't do that, then find some other way to get back on budget, and use your creativity." We had a good Team, and with creativity, we would find a way to make it work, *on time, and on budget.* And we did.

# 27

## *Riding In A New Direction*

There were a lot of transitioning projects happening within the company, and one of them also included the Super X prototypes. They were undergoing the final styling and engineering changes, and testing, and then moving to the next phase of production tooling. This was the year of the heavy investment—moving from fully styled and engineered prototypes to production. Not only was it costly to set up the facility for production, it was also a significant investment to now move the product itself to the production mode.

In order to accelerate some of our product testing, we contracted with several firms to assist us. For the static tests, in which the bike was rigid mounted to a shaking device, we were referred to Winnebago Industries, which according to the test equipment supplier MTS Systems, had a testing device we could readily adapt to meet our needs.

Upon contacting Winnebago Industries, our Product Development Team made arrangements to use their testing device. Not only would this save us a substantial amount of money, but also time. The tests primarily consisted of an accelerated simulated road test, in which we found the worst roads we could in Minnesota, and then recorded the readings on an accelerometer as our factory test rider rode one of our prototypes. We then fed these readings into the computer for the test machine, and created a program that would simulate and accelerate the bumpy, potholed road conditions.

After the bike is mounted to the test machine, along with the appropriate weights to simulate a rider and gear, the shaking begins. When conducting tests like this, we were able to log thousands of tough, bumpy miles in short order, and also compare our results with those of our competitors, primarily motorcycles from Harley-Davidson. Cruiser motorcycles are supposed to shake a little, but we didn't want parts falling off. Our simulated road tests confirmed that over time our new Super X motorcycle sustained less damage and part breakage than a Harley-Davidson did. This was real good news to us as they were our benchmark.

Another type of test we contracted out was actual road tests by professional test riders at a testing track. Even though we had our own factory test riders, we also believed that before we did the final sign-off on the motorcycle, we should contract additional testing to organizations that specialize in accelerated testing in an actual road environment. Also, most of these types of guys were former racers, and they just loved putting a motorcycle through its paces, and at high speed. Most of these types of tests that we contracted out were what we called our "high speed testing." These firms and guys were professionals in this area of testing.

The primary firm we worked with on the high-speed tests was Long and Associates, located in southern Texas. They had worked with several OEM motorcycle and automotive companies, and earnestly worked on our tests. In addition to the high speed testing, we were also testing for general durability and evaluating the handling. Periodically, I heard reports back from our Product Development Team that the test riders were falling in love with our prototype Super Xs. I wasn't surprised. It was unique—the type of ride that would grow on you. And it did.

I have to admit: the X was designed as a big cruising motorcycle, designed for good looks and good overall riding, but it was not intended to be a street demon, nor a long-distance touring bike. It was between those parameters, and known in the motorcycle industry as a cruiser—more like a boulevard cruiser—which is the largest and fastest growing segment of the market. You want the bike to look good, and you want to look good on it. And if the bike takes on a somewhat mean stance, and you astride it in that manner, then even better. Certainly, you do want to be noticed. A good cruiser can also take you comfortably around the country, and we wanted to add that feature to our bikes—which we did.

Since the winters were long and cold in Minnesota, and not conducive to testing outdoors, during the winter we set up a company-operated test facility in a small town just outside of Phoenix. My brother T.K., who was our main factory test rider, had contacts near Phoenix who allowed us to set up in their building that specialized in the refurbishment of aircraft parts, mainly propellers. It was perfect. Out in the desert. Quiet. Hot. And very inexpensive. It was practically free. Sometimes it is hard to figure people out. These guys outside of Phoenix didn't have much to give, but they gave all they had. We were real appreciative. I only visited there a few times, and one time with my daughter Hannah, who was seven years old, and son Hunter, who was five.

After landing in Phoenix, we first visited my parents as they were wintering in Mesa. I then drove with my two children out into the desert to the shop, and met the guys, including my brother T.K. It was quiet. No one around knew what we were up to, unless we wanted them to know. The owner, Gary, gave my son Hunter a wooden pistol that shot rubber bands from a clothespin trigger, and he instantly became Hunter's hero. He also gave Hunter a huge bag of rubber bands. A big smile lit up both of their faces. I thanked Gary, as it was an unexpected, and appreciated gift—he paused in his workday to make my son happy. Gary passed-on shortly after we hit production. We still have the rubber-band pistol...

• • •

The tests at Phoenix, Winnebago, and at Long were proving our design concepts. Even though the bike was fairly large as a big displacement cruiser, the tests confirmed what we all already knew. The bike handled superbly. Our engineering staff was doing a great job. With our patented leading link front-end design, it smoothly handled the toughest bumps, and gave very accurate tracking. The anti-dive front braking was unheard of. This feature had never been on a cruiser or touring motorcycle, and it was one of those features that if you never had it, you wouldn't miss it—but once you did have it, you didn't want to do without. It was safe, smooth, and predictable—and it yielded a more fun ride. When most motorcycle riders come to a stop sign, they are fighting with a motorcycle that is bouncing up and down in the front end as the brakes are applied. With our bikes, you could come to a quick stop, and handle it with style that showed you knew how to tame the big motorcycle beast within. You were in control.

We also made some significant changes to the engine. Unlike the standard Harley engine which had an old forked-connecting rod setup, we had a side-by-side connecting rod arrangement which yielded a stronger engine design and a unique style. Our design was more modern and evolutionary, and adapted current automotive and motorcycle engine technology, whereas Harley chose to stay with a design that was created prior to 1915. The former Excelsior company of the time period also used the forked-connecting rod design, as did most all motorcycle companies that manufactured V-twin engines, but we decided not to stay rigid to that concept. Some changes are good.

Even though our engine was a V-twin configuration—which we uniquely trademarked as our "X-Twin" engine—our front and rear cylinder heads were offset by the width of the connecting rods since we had the contemporary side-by-side design. One of the issues we learned about this though was the engine heat. You do get better cooling with this design, but our rear cylinder was placed just a little too close to the inside part of a rider's upper right leg—translating to too hot and possibly uncomfortable. At the last minute, we decided to reverse the offset, and switched the rear cylinder to the inside. This last minute change combined with us seeking to lower the center of gravity of the bike caused us to make significant modifications to our fuel tank.

We were already introducing some new styling characteristics to the market with the design of the entire motorcycle, but the fuel tank was one of the obvious. Where most competitors to Harley were trying to imitate them, I was always conscious that we had to have our own look. Back in the earlier 1900s when functionality would become styling, if an engine needed to fit right into a motorcycle, the former Excelsior company had notched the fuel tank. Today, that was considered gauche by styling standards—since it wasn't smooth and rounded off—and not used anymore.

But we were different. We wanted functionality to show. No smooth rounded plastic covers hiding the real curves below. Instead, our engine and components stood naked to the wind, and we wanted to proudly show them off. The trick was to just make them look good. Since our engine was not only air cooled with closed loop fuel injection, but also dual-overhead cams—the most innovative motorcycle engine of its time—it caused the engine to be slightly taller than most competing cruisers, and our objective was to be low and tough. In order to lower the center of gravity we needed to lower the fuel tank more into the bike. There was no way to do that, unless we notched the fuel tank to practically straddle it over the engine.

I know our Product Development Team had to think about it for a while, but it was a no-brainer for me. They needed to come to their own rationalization, and when they ran it by me for final approval, I quickly gave the thumbs up—they needed no selling. Our earlier prototypes had a notched fuel tank in the right rear quarter section, but now we were adding one to the front on the same side. What a look. None of our competition would dare be so bold and radical. But we were the rebel's rebel. I immediately loved the look of it. Two big bumps for your eyes to visualize. Very distinctive, and something no other motorcycle in the world had. Even as a novice, if all competitor cruiser bikes were painted flat black, brand names blacked out, and lined up, you could pick out our motorcycle's distinctive appearance. We were truly cutting our own path.

I loved it when people asked me what was different about our motorcycles. For one thing, nearly everything—from simple things such as its name, to more complex things like the ride, handling, look, and how one personally felt about it. Yes it did have two tires, one engine, a fuel tank, fenders, spark plugs, etc., similar to all bikes. Just like humans—generally no two people look alike, yet most of us all have eyes, ears, nose, mouth, etc. Beauty is in the eye of the beholder, and it is subjective. That is good—is a brown eye better than a blue eye? Is a black Super X better than a blue Harley Fat Boy?

Depends on your perspective, and that is the magic in marketing. Like Mark Twain once said, "It is the difference of opinion that makes horse races." We were the champions of different opinions, and I viewed this as merely a reflection of one's feeling and their perspective. Who was right and who was wrong? It didn't matter. What mattered, from a marketing perspective, was that we were creating and fostering passion—which wasn't hard to do since we had a bit of that ourselves—and more importantly, it was what the customers thought.

We were challenging the established industry into a new direction, and they didn't always understand or like that. They liked it as it was— and they should, since they created it that way and didn't want it to change. Only, I was thinking from a consumer's perspective.

As a consumer in the motorcycle industry, I had launched Excelsior from a consumer's perspective. Imprinting this into our corporate culture, I believed that if we started with the perspective of the consumer and didn't stray too far away from this concept, we should be alright. Maybe this doesn't sound too innovative or novel a concept, but the *implementation* of it really is. Most organizations I have witnessed pay lip service to this concept—they say it is for the customer but watch the actions and you will find out who it is really for. Themselves—but cloaked in nice words. My preschool-age kids had already figured this out, and it amazed me that some companies still operate that way. And they wonder how to get brand loyalty. Cuts both ways.

The bikes we were designing for production bore little resemblance to the earlier engineering prototypes we had displayed publicly.

Oftentimes in my many presentations, and also in being stopped on the street, I was invariably asked what our production bikes were going to look like. We all knew our engineering prototypes were butt-ugly, somewhat by design. One of my most common responses was: "Imagine an old blanket that cloaked what you thought was an old race horse. And when you lift the old blanket off, suddenly there is this fire-breathing beast just challenging you to tame it." That was my answer to the question on the difference. You won't expect it, and you will be surprised.

# 28

## Starting A Rumble With Shareholders

There are a lot of firsts in a start-up venture. Most everything that needed to get done had never been done by the new venture, including ours. From simple things like ordering stationery, to more complex things like designing a proprietary motorcycle for production. Maybe it was done somewhere else, by another company and other people, at another time, but never done by the present organization with the current people. This is what I mean by a first. And we had a lot of them.

Firsts are fun, yet they are also a challenge. In a mature organization, there are few firsts because most of what is done is tweaking what had been done prior. And if you don't know or remember what was done prior, just read the lengthy company procedure manual. Not so with an early stage venture. You are creating the manual. A pioneer. You get the chance to create from a clean sheet of paper, and then after the first, henceforth it will be tweaked by those that follow, including yourself. My mindset as the founder of a new venture is initially more in line with the creation part versus the tweaking part.

Anytime our organization had a first that was considered significant to the company, I desired to be more or less involved. My primary concern was that if a project was a first for our company on a particular significant task, what culture and experiences would our new Team draw from? I was concerned they would basically imprint the task from their previous company, since our company had never done it before. In theory, this may sound okay, but in rapid succession, you soon have an inconsistent corporate culture and confusion. All of our Road Crew members were *new* to our company.

Also, I don't think the people working on the new project were doing things consciously the old way they had learned, it was almost subconscious and had become instinct to them. My challenge to them, to our new organization, and to myself was, let's create new instincts and step everything we learned up a notch—after all, most of our Road Crew were corporate rebels, and we didn't necessarily like the way we had learned to do things from other companies. Here, we had the freedom to create a new way, our way, the Excelsior-Henderson way. I would challenge them, as it also challenged me, to continue to develop new instincts on better ways to do things. And courteously. No time for grandstanding. We were a Team. Teams win and lose. Not individuals.

My goal was to keep our processes and systems in harmony as they related to accomplishing projects with people. My focus was on the corporate culture, which translated to how our company did things. In my opinion, companies don't do things. People do. So my focus was on the people, which in turn influenced how the company did things. Simple in concept but hard to implement, so I needed to keep trying in order to prevent a culture being created by happenstance. My belief is if you don't tend to your fields, the weeds will soon take over—as a farmer, I had a lot of experience in that area.

As the corporate culture was being developed, more and more of the Road Crew came to understand what the *"Excelsior-Henderson way"* meant. And they should. They helped to create it, and were writing the rulebook on it. As they each learned more about the Excelsior culture, they in turn taught others, and I could actively step back and out of a project as I now knew it was in good hands. As time progressed over the years, it was amazing what could be accomplished. On many occasions, whether at a motorcycle rally or within our company, Road Crew members would come up to me, with obvious pride in their work, and tell me about a project they had managed, or a task they had done, and took ownership in how they had done it in the Excelsior-Henderson way. Yes we were a bold and intense company, but we acted with integrity.

By now you may ask, what is the *"Excelsior-Henderson way?"* Well it is real simple. It is the mission and principles being lived out, one day at a time, one decision at a time, one minute at a time. That is why I took so much time in drafting and believing in the mission and principles. They needed to be timeless and implementable. The Excelsior-Henderson way was really just *following* the principles—no lip service. Ask any Road Crew member about the mission and principles. Most of them, like me, kept a copy in our wallet. After a while, it just became instinct because it was part of our culture.

• • •

We were going to have our first shareholder meeting as a public company. Now if you have ever been to a shareholder meeting of a public company, you know they are fairly dry, and can be quite formal—not necessarily formal in attire, but in structure. They are generally held downtown in a glitzy hotel. You go where you're told to, and sit and behave. Any questions, save them till later. Raise your hand, and if you are lucky, maybe you'll get a response to your question. Though you may not understand the answer, because it will be given to you in rhetoric. Well, maybe not all shareholder meetings are like this, but you get my drift.

Being a long-time Harley-Davidson shareholder and advocate, I had attended several of their annual shareholder meetings. They conducted one of the better ones. You almost genuinely felt welcomed, and I would peg the attendance at about 300 to 400 people. Quite large by shareholder meeting standards. But in my heart, I knew we could do better. I created a Shareholder Meeting Team, and challenged us to think of a creative way to improve the attendance and involvement of shareholders. After all, we were a grassroots company, and our style was inclusive. We didn't shy away from the tough decisions or questions. We welcomed them.

In addition to being a product development driven company, we had a brand and market to build in order to sell our products, and one of the ways to do that was through grassroots events, like motorcycle rallies, and now possibly shareholder events. Logically, who might be some of the staunchest supporters of the company in addition to the Road Crew? Naturally, the shareholders since they own it! Now some might be critical, but that is okay, because most are critical in a constructive manner, just like a parent making suggestions to their children. They simply want to help. Some people may think this is too simplistic, but maybe it isn't. I have given this a lot of thought.

Shareholder meetings can be costly and time consuming, and a distraction to running the business, or they can be designed to be productive. A requirement of all shareholder meetings is that you must send out an annual report and proxy to all shareholders. All shareholders. We had over 12,000 shareholders. That was a lot of shareholders for an early stage company, and a lot of money to spend.

Well, since we were already doing a mailing to everyone, why not step it up a notch, and do something different? We wanted to invite everyone to attend. Not in the usual corporate way, but in a manner in which there was a real invitation to be part of something bigger and better, and maybe special.

After we developed a plan and strategy for the Shareholder Event, and approved a budget for it, it was time to kick-off the implementation. So we created a separate invitation that was mailed along with the standard shareholder information, and the invitation was done in the Excelsior-Henderson way. It was a 4 x 6 folded card, jet-black on the outside, with contrasting white lettering that read:

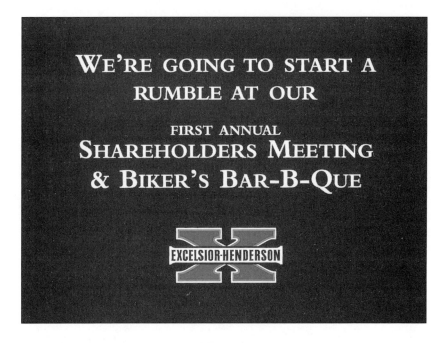

WE'RE GOING TO START A
RUMBLE AT OUR

FIRST ANNUAL
SHAREHOLDERS MEETING
& BIKER'S BAR-B-QUE

EXCELSIOR-HENDERSON

This invitation would immediately let them know that something different was going to happen. Internally, we had just made some new additions to our Marketing Team, one being Krista Heidgerken, our new Events Manager, who was put in charge of managing the Shareholder Event. She had never done one before, but that didn't matter to me. She had managed events before, and was open-minded on most issues, yet firm enough when she needed to be. She was a striking person to work with—once you met her, you didn't forget it. This was one of her first big events for the company, and she stepped things up a few notches. She was the hero of this event.

The Shareholder Event was scheduled to commence at 10:30 a.m. on Saturday, July 25th. We weren't going to rent a fancy hotel downtown during mid-week when people would have to take off work to attend. Instead everyone was invited to the company on a Saturday, and if enough people showed up, we would have the meeting outside in a field, under a tent. We wanted everyone to have the chance to view the company in action—warts and all—and we had nothing to hide. We may not have had much to show yet, but we were all proud of what we did have, and what we were trying to achieve. And maybe, since they were shareholders, they could help us.

One of my concerns was: how do we make plans for the size of the crowd when we had no experience on how many people may show up? It could have been a big "no-show," only we wouldn't have known this until after the event. We decided to try something different and asked the shareholders who planned on attending to call the company in advance. Some of my experienced advisors suggested that the share-holder event and the call-ahead process wasn't going to fly. But I had a premonition for it—call it instinct, and gut feel. But I also *hoped* I was right. Being wrong is not good in a publicly held company.

Shortly after the mailings, our switchboard started to field phone calls—we always had live people answering the phone. I was anxious— you never know. The first few days we received several hundred phone calls. Then a thousand. Then two thousand. Then three thousand. Then four thousand. Then we ordered a larger tent. Time to bring out the heavy artillery.

This was going to be bigger and better than we had planned. Also time to bring out the volunteer militia. We were getting pretty good at this. Krista and her Team put a call to arms for some help in the local community of Belle Plaine. We recruited some high school-age young adults during their summer vacation—including the football players and cheerleaders, and adopted them as temporary Road Crew. We put them through training sessions, and gave them each branded apparel to wear as part of the Team. They were part of our field and detail crew to manage the crowd, and being good-natured young adults, they already had good attitudes.

That was always a stickler for me. When the Team ran the idea by me of getting volunteers from town, again I was an easy sell, as long as they had a plan on how to do it—I also thought that our Team came up with great ideas—better than I could do. But I always stressed atti-tude. Don't take just *anybody*. But take *everybody* with a good attitude. This comes from the gut. Better to take a racehorse and try to slow it down, than to take a donkey and try to speed it up. Just my opinion.

The day finally arrived, and it was beautiful sunny-blue skies. Since I didn't yet have a daily Super X to ride, I drove my 66 GTO convertible—black of course. Even though my family and I arrived early, the show was already set up. At the traffic light on U.S. Highway 169, the Minnesota Highway Patrol was already stationed to direct traffic. Good thinking. Our large semi-trailer with boldly emblazoned Excelsior-Henderson logos was parked on a knoll just as you crested the hill to the factory, and stood out like a huge billboard, which it was. More good thinking.

Maybe the best way to summarize the first annual Shareholder Event is to quote what others had to say about it. We invited several of the media, and here are excerpts from a story:

*Bruce Springsteen's "Born to Run" blared over the loudspeakers outside Excelsior-Henderson's Belle Plaine motorcycle manufacturing plant. The smell of grilled hamburgers and brats mixed with the fumes of hundreds of Harley Fat Boys and Road Kings. Thousands of people crammed into merchandise booths; by the end of the day they would buy more than $65,000 worth of Excelsior-Henderson T-shirts, leather jackets and caps...*

*...The garb worn by attendees seated in the 100-yard-long party tent ranged from bib overalls and seed cap to Tommy Hilfiger golf shirt and crisply pressed khakis to fringed black-leather vest and Mohawk haircut...*

*Welcome to Excelsior-Henderson's first shareholder meeting, a high-octane gathering of investors, stock speculators, bike freaks and smitten townsfolk. The Biker's Barbecue and Annual Meeting, held last Saturday, undoubtedly was one of Minnesota's larger shareholder meetings, with more than 3,000 [my correction—over 4,500] people jamming the grounds. A half-hour after the scheduled start, cars still were backed up for miles down U.S. Hwy. 169...*

*...Moments later, the sound of motorcycle engines roared inside the tent. The Springsteen music died down, replaced by Lee Greenwood singing "God Bless the U.S.A." As the company's bad-boy...brothers Hanlon rumbled down the aisle on shiny black Super X prototypes, the crowd rose to a standing ovation. On stage, another...Hanlon hugged colleagues and gave high-fives, and a camera zoomed in to show Chief Financial Officer Tom Rootness with tears streaming down his face...*

*...Bratwurst and T-shirts. God and country. Nostalgia and sex appeal. Sometimes it's hard to figure out what Excelsior-Henderson is selling...*

*...Typical business types don't understand the Hanlons, nor the Excelsior-Henderson "passion," Dan Hanlon said. "We want to build the*

best bike in America," he said. "Something with heritage and soul. We look at how the bike runs, but we're also interested in how you feel when you throw your leg over an Excelsior-Henderson. This is the kind of industry where macho guys can talk about feelings, and cry," he said, smiling...

...Defending the company's expenditures on brand identification, Hanlon said that "most people think you have to either be a manufacturing-driven company or a marketing-driven company. Why can't we be the best at both? The world is full of great products no one knows about." ...

...Hanlon said too many business people are not "thinking outside the box" and are perplexed because Excelsior is. "We are the new entrants who are coming in and messing it up for everybody else," he said...

...Maybe not all the analysts understand Excelsior-Henderson, but its investors do, Hanlon said. He opened a letter from a fan in Milwaukee; inside, there was an offer for Hanlon to stay at the man's house...

..."Now, how many CEOs can say they get offers of free accommodation from a guy named Tiger?" he said ...

I would say that was a pretty good summary of the event. Along with our current selection of Excelsior-Henderson apparel, we had designed a special T-shirt to commemorate the event, and during the shareholder meeting I announced we would be donating $2.00 to the Scott County Food Shelf located in Belle Plaine for each commemorative T-shirt sold. We sold 3,500 T-shirts, and donated $7,000 to the food shelf. Plus we sold over $65,000 of apparel. To shareholders. Not bad.

Even though our critics would pound us unmercifully regarding us selling T-shirts, I liked the concept. The only criticism we received from people came from those who didn't ride motorcycles—go figure. I didn't view them as our target audience. Our target audience was bikers, and more specifically, those who either did, or desired to, ride American motorcycles. Especially Excelsior-Henderson motorcycles.

And you have to love the concept of selling T-shirts. Almost everyone does wear one—young or old, slender or not so. Especially bikers. And who likes giveaways? Most companies try to do the giveaway thing, but anytime you do that, you run the risk of cheapening the brand, and by definition, giveaways have to be cheap since who can afford to give things away, unless they are cheap? My opinion.

Instead, we always led with quality. Quality first, and quality last. And you had to buy it. Our apparel was designed for our audience, and judging by our sales success, we must have been pretty good at it. At many events, people *bought* our company apparel, and would wear it until it wore out. Buying and wearing our apparel was also a sign of being part of the Team effort in making our American dream happen. For all those who bought and wore the company colors, we were now all together on the same Team—around the world. We all had hope for our dreams, and I hope no one ever takes that away.

We also had our first campers. We had people come from all parts of the country, and a few from outside the country. Planes, trains, automobiles, motorcycles, and even campers. We didn't know where to put the motorhomes, so we let them stay overnight on our premises.

Also, we had invited the family members and friends of the shareholders, and tried to make it a family event. After all, they could be future shareholders, customers, or Road Crew members. I observed and spoke to many families, and had the chance on several occasions to meet three generations from the same family, all attending together. That was cool. The oldest person I met was in their 80s, and the youngest was a baby, including my one-year-old. We welcomed all into our *"house,"* under only one condition, that they respect it.

Even though the main tent was as large as a football field, the tent was overflowing, so we had set up auxiliary tents in advance with monitors for everyone to be a part of the event. We had kids' events to keep the children occupied, and our volunteer militia performed well. We all learned something that day.

But we did have something that stole the show. At around high noon we had a special attraction. We unveiled the unbridled racehorse—the new Super X production intent motorcycle. This was the World's first peek at what the real Super X was going to look like when we hit production in a few months. Cameras were flashing. We had kept the new model under-wraps, and the unveiling brought the crowd to its feet and swarmed the stage. The show was over, and a new phase was beginning.

Our next stop, Sturgis, South Dakota. With over 250,000 motorcyclists. Bikers really. And all there for fun. Time to fire-it-up.

At Sturgis, I was hoping to also meet up with my friend Tiger. Along with his buddy Dennis, he was one of my rally buddies. We only meet at rallies. I don't even know if he has a first and last name, as I never heard anyone use it. Tiger fit him. And he is a genuine biker—which regardless of our status in life, made us all equals.

# 29

## Guggenheim And The Art Of The Motorcycle

Friday morning, July 31st, we were ready to leave for Sturgis. This year the departure would be a little different. In addition to the motorcycles we loaded into our show trailer, we were riding some prototype Super Xs to Sturgis. This would be a good, real-world test, and a lot of fun. Through the grapevine, we spread the word that anybody who wanted to ride with us could join in. We must have had about a hundred riders, and an equal number of spectators who came just to watch, including my folks.

The weather wasn't so keen when we left, but that didn't matter. My brother T.K. did me a great favor, and let me ride our primary Super X engineering mule. It usually had all the latest engineering modifications in it, and was a real guinea pig. Also, since it was the official engineering test bike, there was no styling to it. It looked like it was painted with a spray can, and had wires and gauges hooked up all over to give test readings that were being fed into a computer chip, which could be downloaded later.

The unveiling of our new production intent Super X motorcycles was scheduled for 9:00 a.m. Monday, August 3rd. Early that morning when I awoke in my motel room in Deadwood, South Dakota, and glanced out the window, I noticed it was raining. Not good. We were already pushing our luck by scheduling such an early morning event— most bikers on vacation at a rally don't go to bed too early—but now we had to cope with the weather. I saddled up and rode into Sturgis with a few buddies. In spite of the unseasonably cool and wet weather, we already had a pretty good-sized crowd.

After the customary speeches by various dignitaries, and even myself, we unveiled the new bikes. People cheered, the bikes roared, and the music blared. We were off to a good start. It was exciting, and at the same time somewhat anticlimactic since the bikes' new look had obviously been leaked out by our unveiling at the Shareholders' Event just nine days earlier. Plus I had something else on my mind. I was headed to New York.

Being ever diligent in our business venture, I was not one to pass up an opportunity to tell our story. If we didn't get invited, I would try to invite ourselves. This time we actually were invited by Beth Burnson, a Wall Street All-Star investment analyst at the investment banking firm of ABN/AMRO to present at a finance conference on Wall Street, alongside a dozen other public companies, including Harley-Davidson and Polaris—two of my favorite companies that just happened to be competitors, with pockets so deep that I couldn't even dream of. But I knew we had advantages—we were the underdogs—and we owned the hearts of many. The dreamers, who never give up hope.

Immediately after the unveiling, our CFO and I packed up our bags, and bid farewell to our brethren. We were off to the big city, again, while the show went on in Sturgis. We caught a plane in Rapid City, and flew to New York via a stop in Minneapolis. We landed at LaGuardia, and quickly took a cab to our hotel where the conference was scheduled at the Waldorf-Astoria. This was our second year of interrupting our Sturgis rally by flying to New York to present at this conference, and I was looking forward to it.

The challenge, however, was that the audience was primarily all large institutional investors, and I knew our company just wasn't far enough along in our business cycle for them to have interest. They liked predictable revenues and profits—so did I—but we didn't have any, yet. We were sowing seeds for the future. We planned to someday be positioned as a company in which they would have interest in investing. As I've said before, I really don't believe in the word no—to me it just means, *not today.*

The conference was going great; I had a chance to meet some of my compatriots from our competitors, which was always interesting. Try as they would to ignore me, I just wouldn't let them off that easy. The folks at Harley, though, were always pretty good about saying hi, and asking a few questions, and exchanging small talk. We primarily ran into their CFO, Jim Ziemer at these conferences, and he didn't have an axe to grind with us, nor us with him. In each of our presentations, we would sometimes throw a few jabs at each other, but they were respectful ones. We could banter with each other, and respect the fact that we were all just doing our job.

The best chance meeting I ever had was never a meeting. I tried to meet the guy several times, but he would never lift his head. I wondered how he could see where he was walking. He seemed to walk fine until he got near me, and then instantly his pace would pick up, and his head would lower. It reminded me of our bulls out on the farm before they attacked. I think I would have liked him since I could easily admire his accomplishments based on the things I had learned of his success. But Hall Wendel, Jr., the CEO and Chairman of Polaris and I were never to meet. Ever.

Several years earlier in Minneapolis I had called Hall's office to arrange for a lunch meeting to discuss our motorcycle projects. They had been working on a motorcycle project, but it wasn't publicly announced. In theory, no one was supposed to know about it. The industry dubbed it the worst kept secret in the industry. We all knew about it, but Polaris denied it—go figure. Because I had met so many other industry executives, it just seemed proper to meet someone near our home turf.

At the scheduled lunch meeting, however, I got a surprise. Hall was not there. Instead he sent his President, Ken Larson, and CFO, Jack Grunewald. I hadn't met these guys before, but they seemed like good guys. I admired them based on what I knew of their company and them, but I don't think that was returned to me in kind. They did buy lunch though. The part that perplexed me was that they continued to deny they were involved in any motorcycle project. Nada—I had evidence they weren't speaking the truth—and still they denied it with a straight face. I didn't get it. So much for trying to have an intelligent conversation about our motorcycle projects.

• • •

After our presentation at the Waldorf-Astoria, just before we were leaving, my CFO, Tom, said he had something to tell me, but he didn't want me to do anything radical about what he was going to say. He had found out who Richard Keim was. We both knew the name only too well. He was shorting our stock. He wanted to make money by driving our stock price down, and he was doing everything he could to accomplish this.

Richard was a future buddy that I had not yet had the chance to meet—but I was hoping to someday—and he sure seemed to know a lot about me and Excelsior-Henderson since he had been quoted several times in print media about our venture—as an expert, no less. Invariably, after a few quotes in some article, the quotes would gain momentum and show up in another article. It was all I could do to manage the misinformation he was creating. A guy like him I just had to meet.

He loved to load his verbal machine gun and wildly spray his ora-torical bullets about us all around, which the print media ate right up. He must have felt pretty darned important. I was surprised the print business media didn't challenge him, but I had to admit that his com-ments made for some interesting reading. It probably helped sell news-papers, but that is another story. I wanted to meet this expert, who got his information without having ever contacted me, or anyone at our company. This was a new level of research and expertise and I just had to find out more about it.

Tom pointed Richard out, and I went up to him and introduced myself. His smile disappeared faster than a blink of the eye, and his face went ashen. I knew I would like him right away—he had to look up to me. Now I'm not a very tall guy, but I was to him—as we ensued in a spirited, intelligent conversation. The long and short of the story is, I never heard from him again. That's too bad, since I think we could have been good business friends.

Now that I recognized Richard, I remembered seeing him earlier in the day being real chummy with one of the Harley executives, and hav-ing dinner with one the night before. Maybe a connection, maybe not.

• • •

Tom and I had a plane to catch; we were headed back to Sturgis—in just twenty-four hours we went from Sturgis to New York, and now back to Sturgis. Talk about culture shock. When we got to LaGuardia, we had a few extra minutes but we were still dressed in our suits. I don't mind wearing business suits, but I do that in my own style too, in a mild protest. Unbeknownst to most observers, I always wear a somewhat rad-ical logo T-shirt under my dress shirt—it's a good study in contrasts. We found the nearest men's room, and we changed from our suits into biker clothes right in the restroom stalls. We were probably the only execu-tives of a publicly held company changing into motorcycle clothes in a mensroom at LaGuardia. We went in as business people, and came out as bikers—we were transformed. It was a good conference.

• • •

Two weeks later I was back in New York, and again for a few short hours. Only this time it was for something that was going to be a little more fun. There was a new exhibit at the Guggenheim Museum that was surprising a lot of people—the first surprise being the new exhibit: The Art of the Motorcycle, and the second surprise being the record turnout crowds and interest by attendees. As hoped for, but probably not fully anticipated, was the great interest by a cross-section of attendees. The exhibit attracted not only the traditional museum-goers, but now also motorcyclists, in droves. Even the *New York Times* expressed marvel at the great interest in the new exhibit. Motorcycles as art, at the Guggenheim, no less. I just knew we were in the right industry.

One of our Wall Street research analysts, Steve Eisenberg, on behalf of CIBC Oppenheimer & Company, which was located in the World Financial Center in the financial district of Manhattan, was sponsoring a night at the Guggenheim Museum during the Art of the Motorcycle Exhibit. The event they were creating was titled "History of Motorcycling," and they had asked me to be their featured presenter. Naturally, I was quite honored, and after locating some discounted nonstop airfares, I accepted the invitation. I thought this would be a good opportunity to again have the chance to tell our story, and have a chance to see the exhibit that I had heard so much about.

Flying nonstop from Minneapolis to New York on August 19th was a quick flight. During this time frame there was a lot of travel happening in our venture, with the vast majority of it being incoming to our factory in Belle Plaine, primarily from financial firms and national and international vendors. I wanted us to be easy to get to, and our location was working great. We were only a 45-minute drive to an international airport, and people flying in to see us could usually fly nonstop to Minneapolis, and be at our facility within an hour. Efficient.

I was able to work a few hours at the factory that day, and then departed for LaGuardia where I arrived around 4:00 p.m. After a quick taxi ride into the city, I was dropped off at the Guggenheim, and was presenting by 6:00 p.m. The exhibit was impressive with the vast collection of old motorcycles on display. I recognized many of the old former brand names, and several of the current owners' names. After my presentation, and a tour of the exhibit, I was presented with a nice Guggenheim Museum, Art of the Motorcycle cap—in the right colors of black with red—it matched my suit.

• • •

There was another matter that arose that was unexpected, although not totally. We had a theft. For years I had hoped this would happen. One Saturday evening a few weeks after we got back from Sturgis, our company flag was stolen off our flagpole. According to a review of our security tape, a truck pulled into our facility around midnight, and while the driver waited as the lookout, a passenger hastily jumped out of the truck and lowered the flag to the ground and took it. It all happened in about 10 seconds.

Some might think this was a problem, but we saw this as a good sign. At the rallies and events, and now in front of our building, we were having a lot of thefts. Brand related. Seemed like anything unique with our brand name on it, if we didn't sell it, it was a candidate to be stolen and probably placed in someone's garage for future enjoyment and memories. We constantly had to replace banners, flags, and posters.

On several occasions, at rallies and events, we would catch someone in the act of borrowing these items as souvenirs. At first we would see the look of concern on the person's face as they were caught in the act, but I had instructed our people to just smile, and tell them to have a good time with it.

One night in Sturgis as I was strolling around our tent around 2:00 a.m., I did catch a few guys taking our company banners as souvenirs, but the rally had just started. I asked if they wouldn't mind coming back in a few days. We just chuckled at each other, and a few days later they must have returned, because the banners were now gone. I would always marvel at this. What a great industry. Where people wanted to take our banners and posters. Most companies couldn't give those types of things away. I knew we were now really touching the passion of the grassroots.

# 30

## *Avoiding The Death Spiral*
## *To Live To Fight Another Day*

No year was complete without some form of significant financing, and 1998 was no exception. The transition from product development to manufacturing was costly. We were still tracking to our business plan, which indicated we needed to raise additional funds. At that point in time, as we looked at the horizon, our best prediction was that we would need to raise capital for two purposes: one, to get into production; and two, to stay in production. We didn't need much more capital to accomplish the first goal, but raising the capital to stay in production was my primary concern. We knew we would be losing money at the launch.

But I also knew we had to accomplish this one step at a time. For the moment, I still needed to focus on the task at hand of getting into production, and ensuring we were capitalized well enough for that to happen. Even though our financial strength in the venture was always somewhat precarious, and we were always only one financing transaction away from failure, I did my best to insulate this from the rest of the company. Except for a handful of people that I worked closely with on the financing, most never knew the precarious position we were constantly in. Everyone had their own goals to focus on, and I didn't need more people worrying about the things that I was responsible for.

All of our Road Crew knew the financial status of the venture, and we made no attempt to gloss it over. In fact, during interviews, I told prospective Road Crew recruits that if we didn't raise our next round of financing, we would fail. This really separated the wheat from the chaff, and we wound up recruiting talented people who knew the risk, and knew they could lessen the risk by contributing their efforts to the venture. We were all on a mission together.

Therefore, we all knew the venture would fail if we each didn't do our job. We only asked and knew enough about each other's responsibilities to ensure we were all on track, and to learn if anyone needed help. We held regular meetings within the company bringing everyone up to speed on our financing; we were also now a publicly held company—and all our supporters and critics knew we were losing money. This was unnerving to some, but I took it all in stride. That's just the way it was planned to be. Sometimes, when the print media got hold of our financials, they would belabor the point of how we were losing money. The part they all forgot to print was—we were on plan—we weren't *"losing"* money—we were *"investing"* money in a new venture. As planned. But that story never got out.

• • •

There were three key pieces of financing that came together for us in 1998—we had two debt transactions, one with Finova and the other with the USDA and Dakota Bank, and also an equity offering through Shoreline Pacific.

On the debt side, with the building being readied for production and equipment being installed, we were trying to finance as many hard assets as we could. We didn't want to chew up any more equity than necessary, although we had limited choices in arranging financing, and would nearly have to take any deal that came along. The only bad deal was one that didn't happen. Any deal that did happen was a good deal, for without a deal there was no company.

We were always sourcing contacts for new financing, and we were in conversations with the local branch of Finova, a Phoenix investment company. We had been doing due diligence on each other for several months, and it looked as if we could do a deal together. Due diligence sessions were constantly being conducted on us, and I didn't mind the questions or the scrutiny one bit. We were all just doing our jobs, and if the outside experts found a problem in our business that I didn't know about, then the good part was we knew what issue needed to be solved next. Fortunately, our business model was pretty well thought through and we had a talented staff, and were able to address all the questions.

One of the best methods I had found over the previous several years of raising money for our venture was to get prospective financiers to a motorcycle rally to witness not only the growing motorcycle industry, but also to have a chance to experience our company in action— on the field alongside our competitors and prospective consumers. They would have the opportunity to observe us in action firsthand, rather than just hear a story in the boardroom from our perspective. It was live and unscripted. Plus, most of these financial types were analytical by nature, and had never attended a national motorcycle rally. It would be a good chance for us to get to know them also.

Several of the folks from Finova had traveled to Daytona Beach Bike Week earlier in the spring, and had had quite an opportunity to learn more about the industry and our company. This always helped in the due diligence when explaining some of the nuances of our industry and market positioning. It was that old motorcycle industry saying again: *"If I have to explain, you won't understand."* After a rally, there was usually a little less explaining required regarding some parts of our business. After all, sitting in a sterile boardroom, how do you explain tattoos on adults?

In July, we finalized a debt package with Finova, and through the Economic Development Authority of the City of Belle Plaine, we issued $6.1 million in Taxable Industrial Development Revenue Bonds. In these types of bonds, the city is just a conduit, and has no liability to the transaction. Typical to most of all our debt financing, we had to put $1.1 million of the proceeds into an escrow account in the event we weren't able to make timely payments on the loan, so our real net loan repayment balance was about $5 million. A requirement of this loan was that all proceeds were to be used for factory equipment and for production tooling on our new Super X motorcycle. Just in time.

• • •

Next up was our equity financing. We needed to make up the $10 million shortfall from our IPO a year earlier. The financial market had been improving, but it would never improve enough for a manufacturing start-up—our options in raising equity capital were now limited. It would have been better for us to be a private company, as we had initially planned at this phase, but that option was now gone. Two years earlier that option had been taken away from us by an errant newspaper and reporter hell-bent on a story.

One of the ways to raise equity capital while you are publicly held is through a secondary offering, but our stock price wasn't much higher than when we had gone public a year earlier. In addition we really didn't have any serious investment banking houses willing to do a secondary offering for us. This really would have been our equity financing of choice—if we had choices. Although we did have the usual very small and very new firms indicating they could raise money for us, I didn't have much confidence in them—they had no track record of success—and we were new too. Not a good formula for success.

The only equity financing option that availed itself to us was a convertible preferred stock offering, which by the name itself appeared to be quite innocuous. But it was the fine print in the conversion feature that potentially made the transaction quite lucrative for the investor, which was alright—but in the converse, if the company's stock price was depressed in the future, the conversion had a ratcheting feature that, in effect, could further ratchet downward an already declining stock price. Almost like throwing gasoline on a fire—the financing industry had coined the phrase "death spiral" to describe this type of event if it occurred. Eventually, this would happen to us, which we didn't know at the time, but we all did feel uneasy in our gut.

This was of great concern to us, but we had limited options at the time. We would have to roll the dice and hope our stock price was better a year from now. But that requires a pretty good crystal ball, and I don't know anyone that can predict the market accurately. At least this financing would get us to our next phase in the company, and would allow us to *"live to fight another day."*

But our CFO and I were contemplative about this one. We didn't like it one bit, but we liked the alternatives even less. Essentially, we were like the football team in a prospective jam—we had to drop back five and quick punt, and then take our chances. We were familiar with the features of a convertible preferred offering, and we were scouring the marketplace for the best fit we could find. We decided to enlist the assistance of a broker who was familiar with this method of financing and had a good reputation on both sides of the transaction—their investors and their clients.

Another issue I didn't like about the aspect of this next type of offering was that I knew it was going to take us out of the familiar realm of the retail stock investor, and place us right in the hands of the institutional investors. These types of institutional investors are not the buy and hold type of investor. They have a habit of heading for the door when trouble hits, because they want to get out before anyone else. They won't tell you this, but in doing your homework, which I did, that was just the way it was. If you didn't like it, you didn't take their investment.

If there was trouble on the horizon, they made their money via a hasty exit, rather than holding on and solving the problems. But they were the only ones offering this type of financing, and this was more or less the last stop for most companies seeking financing. If this didn't work, there were usually no other choices. Therefore, in spite of all this, our goal then became to arrange the best deal possible, with the best players we could find.

For several months we had been conversing with a Sausalito, California firm named Shoreline Pacific. They had a real diligent Vice President named Ernie Krauss who was in constant contact with our CFO. After checking out their references and doing additional homework on their firm, we finally agreed to a meeting on May 27th at our facility in Belle Plaine with Ernie and the owner of his firm, Harlan Kleiman.

It quickly became apparent to me we were now moving into a new league. Not necessarily our business, but our potential business partners. Harlan showed up with his staff, and he kept his limousine waiting outside our building in Belle Plaine. Now, if you have ever been to Belle Plaine, this is an unusual sight. But there was good reason for his style. His firm and his talented staff were well regarded, and had successfully accomplished a lot of transactions. Harlan himself had quite a pedigree, and he possessed a certain aura that was both respectful and intense at the same time. Certainly, this had been well cultivated over the years.

True to our form, we invited Harlan and several of his staff to our next national motorcycle rally, which was Sturgis. Even though the rally was about ten weeks away, no matter how fast you try to do a deal, it always takes a lot longer than a person would expect. I was hopeful to have early due diligence conducted on us prior to the rally, and just after the rally try to complete a transaction. We usually had our best company momentum then, and it was advantageous to arrange for a closing while everyone still had current memories of the rally. Investors always get apprehensive, and anytime there is a time lapse, you sometimes have to again plow old ground. I always sought to minimize that.

The pitching was going to be a little faster on this deal, and we needed to proceed with great caution. Since this type of financing was fraught with potential issues, I decided we should do a little double-teaming. This time we were going to engage a different law firm to primarily represent us, and have our corporate counsel at Faegre provide additional review of the documents that our other engaged counsel drafted for us.

It was slightly redundant, but now was not the time to take uncalculated risks. I didn't really like doing this with our lawyers at Faegre and I was hopeful this wouldn't be perceived as lack of faith in their firm. Fortunately, they were real team players, and were willing to work with us in this structure.

Therefore, we engaged the firm of Wilson Sonsini Goodrich & Rosati, based in Palo Alto, California. If you have never heard of this firm, they are considered one of the top in their area of expertise. Plus, they are located in the garden spot of America for the financing of high technology, early stage deals, and they have pretty much worked on every conceivable type of financing imaginable. And they had represented clients on numerous convertible preferred offerings similar to the one we were contemplating. Even though we weren't high technology, we had done a pretty good job of financing the venture thus far.

Shoreline Pacific was busy making introductory phone calls to various prospective institutional investors, and we were conducting numerous phone conferences with them. As I had learned is typical of this process, it began to appear that there was one lead investor in which we were making faster progress and had a mutual interest in working together.

Via Shoreline, we were introduced to Rose Glen Capital located in Bala Cynwyd, Pennsylvania. Our primary contact at Rose Glen was Wayne Bloch, and he and his Research Analyst Tracy flew out to visit us just shortly after we returned from Sturgis. Since we hadn't known them prior to the rally, we didn't have the chance to invite them beforehand and so we had a lot of due diligence to conduct. Fortunately, Wayne and Tracy were fast studies, like all of the finance people I had met. There was some pretty fast pitching, and I enjoyed the process tremendously. So did they. There is an old cliché, *"The Art of the Deal,"* and over the years and the many different types of financing we had conducted, I had grown fond of that concept and empowering a deal to happen. It required a lot of persistence, and tact and diplomacy.

Part of *the art of the deal* to this transaction was that it usually happened reasonably quickly. It was not all that unusual to have a closing within thirty days of the launch of due diligence. By September 3rd, after much mutual arm-twisting, some mutual posturing, and some heated conversations between all of the various constituents to the transaction—all of which can be typical to these high-strung financing transactions—we were set to sign documents and close.

The transaction was for an initial infusion of $10 million of new equity, in the form of a Series B Convertible Preferred Stock. We all believed this amount of financing would see us into production, but according to plan it would not successfully fund us through production to positive cash flow. Therefore, right off the bat we also prearranged an additional $3 million of follow-up financing, provided we and our future stock price met several conditions. Which, fortunately, several months later we did.

Even though the future funding of $3 million was not ever projected to be enough to get us to positive cash flow, at least it was a start. That was how the entire project had to be funded since the beginning early in 1993, and I anticipated that we would continue to be funded in stages, never knowing if there would be a last. Even though I planned for the future, and executed daily for the future, at the end of each transaction, I knew it could be the last. I tried to put that out of my mind, and just move forward, one step at a time.

Shoreline did pretty well on this transaction. Their fees for the first transaction were $500,000. High as this may seem, our general cost of equity was usually about 5% to 10%, payable in cash at closing. Closing. That was the magic word. If we all got to a closing, the cost of capital was inexpensive. If a closing never happened, that was the real expense.

There was a provision in our agreement with Shoreline and with Rose Glen that would come to haunt us later. I was no stranger to this clause. They each demanded the right of first refusal for any future equity financing. For six years I had been fighting that battle with every equity financing, and in my opinion, it was a showstopper. In every previous transaction, I was able to get that language removed from our contract prior to signing, albeit sometimes I had to get rather strong-headed to get this done. Invariably, someone on the Deal Team would say it didn't matter, and my position is if it doesn't matter, then let's take it out—only then I found out it did matter.

My concern was we had a lot of financing to complete—I didn't want to be held hostage and forced to work with someone on consecutive transactions. I just didn't like the smell of it. In the best case, if things worked out, we always had the option to work together in the future—and that method was fine with me; we had proven that we could and would work consecutively with investment firms.

Conversely, if things didn't work out, I didn't want to be forced into a partnership in which our firms didn't work well together. Another concern was that it took away the opportunity to work with new investment firms who knew our previous investment firm could come in at the last minute and execute on their right of first refusal. This basically eliminated any competition. For many reasons, I didn't like the concept, and we had successfully blocked each and every one.

Except this one. This time no matter how hard I negotiated and positioned, there was just no budging. Our CFO and I would alternate between good cop and bad cop. Usually, I wanted him to be the good cop, and it was my role to handle the added stress of being the bad cop. I had gotten pretty good at this, as the transactions oftentimes demanded this. I had to be tough. After several days and rounds of negotiations on just this final point of the first right of refusal, we sensed the end was near—our end that is. There was nothing we could do. We didn't have the leverage to position this contract term, and we very reluctantly agreed to the right of first refusal, granted to Shoreline and Rose Glen. I put away the boxing gloves, smiled and shook hands, and as business friends, we signed the agreements.

The following year, when we went to complete our new rounds of financing, I found out how problematic this clause would be to us. Again, my gut level told me this could handicap our future at the worst time. These types of clauses only hurt you in the tough times—which for this venture had been every day since 1993—and that was when you needed them eliminated the most. It was during the tough times that I wanted to have options, and this clause took away financing options. We were forced into a future relationship.

On the surface, the business and the financing looked good, but I think this is when I started to lose sleep. In spite of all the problems we had over the last six years, I generally felt we were in control of the situation, and that we had options. In my mind I always thought even the best buildings were built with a fire escape, and I always had one handy, and kept this in mind as I negotiated one transaction at a time. They all had to fit together.

But this time, I didn't think we had a fire escape. If we had a fire, there was no way out, except to go through the fire. We potentially had lost control of our destiny. But I didn't know any of this at the time. I just had to keep on playing the cards we were dealt. We were on the eve of production, and we would have to sort out those problems during battle. Besides, at this point, it was all hypothetical. Maybe I was worrying about a prospective future event that wasn't going to happen. That was it: we had to make it not happen.

•••

Before moving on entirely regarding this concept of the status of the company and raising capital during this point in time, there is some clarification I would like to make. It seems there was a misunderstanding among some on whether we had planned on raising additional capital after the just completed transaction on the $10 million with the follow-up $3 million.

Being the CEO and Chairman of the Board, I was certainly responsible for all the actions of the company, whether I knew of them or not. Oftentimes, things would get said and done in the normal course of business that I had no need to know about, which is why you hire people in the first place. It was the opinion of some people that the company, or someone within the company, was making representations that we didn't need to raise any additional capital upon commencement of production.

That was not true. The company and I knew we would need to raise additional funds upon the commencement of production. I believed, and so stated, we had enough capital to get into production, but not enough capital to stay in production. We distinctly knew we would need additional equity capital, albeit at that time, I just didn't know exactly how much, nor how we would raise it.

To further illustrate this point, in the documents related to this current round of financing, and subsequently filed with the SEC, the following statements were included for all to read:

> *Based upon its current estimates, the Company believes that its available cash resources, including the proceeds received from the initial public offering of Common Stock, as well as the proceeds received from the Minnesota Department of Trade and Economic Development and from the Taxable Industrial Development Revenue Bond purchased by FINOVA Public Finance, Inc., a subsidiary of FINOVA Capital Corporation will be sufficient to fund the pre-production operations of the Company. However, the Company may require additional working capital financing prior to commencement of production. Upon commencement of production, the Company will need to obtain substantial additional amounts of fixed asset and working capital financing. However, if sufficient fixed asset and/or working capital financing is not available, the Company will*

*have to look to other means of financing. In addition, if the Company's estimates of the amount of financing needed to commence production of the Super X are incorrect due to unanticipated additional costs of equipping the Company's manufacturing facility, unanticipated problems in the development of the Super X for production, increased labor costs, increased costs of motorcycle parts and raw materials, increased marketing and dealer network development expenses, increased rates of consumption of available cash resources, unanticipated delays in drawing funds held in escrow from the Minnesota Department of Trade and Economic Development or FINOVA financings, the unavailability of inventory and working capital financing, or other unanticipated events, then the Company may need additional equity or debt financing prior to or shortly after commencement of production of the Super X. There can be no assurance that the Company will be able to obtain such financing or that such financing will be available on terms favorable to the Company.*

If that wasn't clear enough, we repeated the same concept—pay close attention—the lawyers do—to the use of the words "may" and "will need"—and I further quote:

*...THE COMPANY MAY REQUIRE ADDITIONAL WORKING CAPITAL FINANCING PRIOR TO COMMENCEMENT OF PRODUCTION; UPON COMMENCEMENT OF PRODUCTION, THE COMPANY WILL NEED TO OBTAIN SUBSTANTIAL ADDITIONAL AMOUNTS OF FIXED ASSET AND WORKING CAPITAL FINANCING—The availability and terms of any fixed asset or working capital financing will depend on a number of credit market factors, including interest rates, liquidity and lending regulations, as well as the business prospects and financial condition of the Company. There can be no assurance that the Company will be able to obtain such financing or that such financing will be available on terms favorable to the Company.*

Finally, in case there still remained any doubt, we added the following language:

*NO PERSON IS AUTHORIZED IN CONNECTION WITH ANY OFFERING MADE BY THIS PROSPECTUS TO GIVE ANY INFORMATION OR TO MAKE ANY*

REPRESENTATIONS NOT CONTAINED IN THIS PROSPECTUS, AND, IF GIVEN OR MADE, SUCH INFORMATION OR REPRESENTATIONS MUST NOT BE RELIED UPON AS HAVING BEEN AUTHORIZED BY THE COMPANY, ANY SELLING SHAREHOLDER OR BY ANY OTHER PERSON.

Not only is this what I believed about the status of the company, this is what we said and what we wrote, and subsequently filed publicly. As a publicly held company, we also were required to file these same documents, of which anyone in the public had the right to view and receive copies. Since our project was being closely followed by both friend and foe, I am sure some people did request copies just as they had in the past.

How this ever got miscommunicated to some, I will never know. No one has come forward to tell me. Or maybe for some it just made for a more interesting story to ignore the facts. Either way, you can now be the judge.

Oftentimes in our venture, I would think of the quote by Mark Twain, "A lie will travel half-way around the world before the truth has time to put its shoes on."

# 31

## Road To Glory

All of us involved in one way or another believed that each year was a make or break year, and this year we had developed a theme to rally around, *"The Road To Glory,"* which signified our common mission of getting into production.

We even created T-shirts with this slogan, and sold them to our Road Crew, shareholders, consumers at rallies, and in our company retail store located in our atrium. This same T-shirt is the commemorative shirt that we had sold at the shareholder meeting, and we just added a shareholder insignia on a sleeve to mark the event (and hold down design costs). We sold just over 3,500 of the Road To Glory T-shirts at the shareholder meeting. Pretty good results I thought.

Communication is always a challenge for organizations of any size, but as companies go, we weren't very large with staff. At the executive level, I had weekly staff meetings with all the Vice Presidents, every other week I included managers, and in monthly meetings I included the supervisors. These were the formal meetings, but most of my meetings were the informal ones. In addition, these people had constant meetings on the various projects they were working on.

Generally, my calendar had anywhere from five to ten meetings planned per day, and my time was at a premium. In spite of all these meetings though, I still couldn't get a definitive answer from anyone on when we would actually start production. That always frustrated me to no end.

A year earlier we had an internal goal of hitting production late in the third quarter—according to our crystal ball—but we announced to the marketplace the fourth quarter. I wanted us to have some margin of error, but we had just used up our margin. The third quarter had passed, and each week our VP of Production would tell me in our meeting that production would soon launch, within the next several weeks. This had been going on now for about six weeks, and my confidence in his answer was getting shaken. But I also didn't want to rattle the ship at this point. I could sense our entire company was pushing hard, and I couldn't ask any more of any of them. I just had to wait, and have faith, or the whole thing could erupt. Therefore, I remained a cheer-leader to the troops.

Privately though, I had to hold our executives' feet to the fire, and it wasn't the first time. If there were problems, let's face up to them and resolve them—*"there's no secrets in the cockpit."* I believed we now had shortcomings in our leadership area, and we needed to address them, even if that included me.

I didn't plan on being the CEO and President until I retired. That was too much to expect after all I had been through, and the skills required of being the founder and CEO of a start-up are different than the skills required of succeeding one, although my plan was to still be involved. I like the challenge of launching—setting sail for an almost unreachable port. Once we had the ship built, launched and sailing, I could hire a better President or CEO to now sail farther and faster. And if they successfully did that, my stock would increase in value. And we would all win. My opinion.

My observation, and that of the Board of Directors, was we were now probably stretched too lean at the upper management levels, and we needed to add talent to back-fill the executive positions, which would also allow us to give more leadership strength to the company. By further training and development of the new layer of management, we could also develop succession and transition plans for the departments.

Therefore we started back-filling in additional management talent, but that is not an overnight thing. We still had to make do with the best we had, and we still had to get to production.

One by one, we were hurdling the obstacles, and I could sense by reading the faces of our Road Crew members in the trenches that we were getting closer. I was still getting the same report from the VP and our CFO, but I could no longer rely on that. And I didn't want to tell them. They were smart, and must have sensed that anyway, plus I didn't want to shake their confidence. They had enough to do and I respected their efforts. They had helped in getting us this far.

On December 7th, Pearl Harbor Remembrance Day, we had a company social gathering at our factory for our Road Crew and their families to celebrate the launch of pre-production. We had a private company meeting in the factory at 3:30 p.m., and at 4:30 p.m. the families joined in. It was a nice get-together, and as usual, it was not uncommon to have three generations of a family attending. That's commitment, and passion. And grassroots. One of our Assembly Team Members, Dawn Hackett, was with her father from Montgomery, and they proceeded to tell me a story about a new foal one of their horses just had. They decided to name him Super X. That was cool. A horse named after our company and bike.

The following Monday evening, December 14th, we had our traditional company holiday party, and once again at the OK Corral in Jordan. Our Excelsior-Henderson Holiday Party Team decided to have a little fun with the planning phases, and had a unique invitation made up by our marketing department. They recruited our Factory Test Rider, my brother Terry, to dress up as Santa Claus, and hitched one of our prototype Super Xs to a sleigh—complete with reins attached to the handlebars and to Santa riding in the sleigh—in front of the OK Corral, and shot a picture. The tag line to the invitation read, "*Santa Rides a Super X!*" That was in the spirit of the company and brand— and for fun they were holding out on me and not letting me know who the Santa was. The night of the party it was cold, but the attendance was good, and we were all pumped to get into production. We could sense that it was getting closer.

A few days later, on Tuesday, December 21st, we announced the closing of additional debt financing, and just in time for our growing production inventory, and just before revenue. It was a $5 million loan package, allowing us to draw funds in the next six months for inventory purchases and accounts receivable—important financing to us on the eve of production. We arranged this with Dakota Bank, in Mendota Heights, Minnesota, and it was a special type of loan from the United States Department of Agriculture (USDA), in which they guaranteed repayment of up to 80% of the loan from the participating bank. This was a special program, not well known at all, that we qualified for by locating in a more rural setting, to bring in jobs, and was part of the Rural Business-Cooperative Service Program.

Finally, on December 30th, in a short commemorative setting at the factory, we rolled our ceremonial first bike off our assembly line— we gave the bike the ceremonial Serial Number 001, but that was more ceremonial than reality. I straddled the bike and hit the start button, and fired it up. I wanted to shift it into gear, and do a massive fifth-gear burnout right there, but something inside held me back.

Long ago I had decided what to do with that first bike. Give it to those that helped me—the Team, which now numbered thousands and thousands of people. Our Road Crew knew exactly what to do with it.

After the traditional ceremony of popping champagne corks—Dom Perignon, now that I had discovered what it was—and the shooting of photographs, we delivered the bike to our Heritage Motorcycle Museum. For our Road Crew and shareholders to view and own. It was theirs, and just a small part of it was mine also.

PART THREE

*FireItUp—Test Our Metal*

# 32

## *It's Okay To Be A Rebel On The Road Crew*

We had a company asset that we were never able to put directly on our balance sheet, and I have always believed it was our most important asset. It was more important than the money we were raising and the product we were designing and manufacturing. It was also more important than the company itself. And yet there was no way to directly account for it. The asset I am talking about here is people. People. Talk about a controversial subject in most businesses and in life, yet probably one of the most mistreated assets I am aware of.

This asset is also probably the pinnacle of lip service—where most organizations today proclaim such pride in how they develop this asset—in regard to both consumers and employees—when in reality it is mostly lip service. I know you can't satisfy 100% of the people, since we do all have unique wants and desires, but that doesn't take away the fact that we could strive to do better, and have our actions be harmonious with our words. Just my opinion.

At Excelsior-Henderson, my vision was to make a different imprint on this concept. I had no brilliant ideas, other than to focus on it as an integral part of our corporate culture. We were building a new company with new people. With all new people I was concerned regarding what culture would be created within our organization and I didn't want it left to happenstance, as I thought the culture would then become chaotic and unclear. I had a clear vision—part of which was simply to treat others as you would want to be treated—with respect. Implementing it was less clear.

To summarize my thoughts on this matter, I didn't know if I was going backward in time, or forward in time. I simply knew I did want a different culture than what I understood about the current business cultures that I had worked in. So to a great degree, my thought was to throw out all conventional thinking, concepts, and even terminology; and rethink and reword everything, and challenge it—and encourage others who joined us to also rethink what they had been trained in this area. I put away all the how-to books on creating a successful organization of people.

Instead, I took my learning from the grassroots people. From whence I had come. It was time to listen. Then implement what I had learned.

My belief is that good people make good companies, not the other way around. I have already mentioned our company Mission and Principles, and how the first Principle was "People Are Our Greatest Asset," and the second one focused on "Working As A Team." To me, this was our key for succeeding in our venture. By attracting the right team of people, this would give us a higher probability of attracting financing, and then achieving our goals—all independent objectives, yet interdependent on each other. Thus was borne the concept of our Road Crew. They became the lifeblood to the heart and soul of the company. We really didn't have employees. We had Team Members, and they were officially bestowed as the Road Crew. And to be part of the Road Crew didn't mean you were a paid Team Member—we had a lot of volunteers, or militia, especially at our numerous consumer rallies and events. What was different about all this? Some of it was as simple as the name, and some was more complex.

And it all centered on attracting good quality people, talented and multi-skilled people capable of being cross-trained, and then empowering them to work as a Team. My hiring strategy was to hire good strong capable people, who were individuals and independent thinkers, yet also Team players—and possibly in some organizations considered a rebel. At Excelsior, being a rebel was okay, as long as you were a respectful Team Rebel, most of the time. And when you weren't, you needed to apologize. Have you ever seen adults in the workplace apologize to each other? Voluntarily? At Excelsior, we did it all the time.

I like to hire people with strong egos. Some people mistake this for a big ego, and there is a fine line between the two. But once you know the line, you can quickly assess through actions on which side of the line someone stands. A strong ego can be an independent, fierce thinker, and yet has a strong enough ego about themselves that they can accept the personal responsibility if something goes wrong, and apologize when they are wrong, and not hold any grudges.

Contrast this to someone with a big ego. A big ego may or may not be an independent, fierce thinker, but will want to take personal credit for success, and will quickly pass blame if things go wrong. And certainly won't take personal responsibility—and never expect an apology, unless it is an insincere one. And then look out for the grudge match, only it might be behind your back, over a long period of time.

I have had to apologize to a lot of people over the years as I admittedly push the envelope hard, and I oftentimes make mistakes. To me that is also part of leadership. If others in the organization either witnessed or experienced me making mistakes and apologizing, it would set a good example for others to follow. Plus, that is simply what I believe, and practice.

Therefore, we admittedly had a lot of strong-ego people on our Road Crew. The key was to foster a culture then of teamwork. Even though we had independent teams of people working on the various projects within the company, they were all interdependent on each other. I have always liked that concept—of being independent, and yet interdependent. Somewhat like the framers to the Constitution of the United States—separate but equal. Each state a separate entity—Independent. Yet depending upon each other in the Union—Interdependent.

When it comes to the concept of teamwork, my concept is it's sometimes best to be blind. Like color-blind. Like age-blind. Like gender-blind. When it comes to the battle of creating a new venture, does any of that matter? Only the skills and results, and the work style in getting things done.

During one interview I had with a candidate, Mike Maxa, for a supervisory position in our factory, I was explaining my concept of the individual and teamwork. I remember Mike politely listening for a while, but I could also see he was restless in his chair. Even though we were similar in age, he had just retired from a career in the military, and had returned with his family to his hometown area. He looked at me and smiled, and said, "Dan, in the military I flew on aircraft, and we had a saying that 'there are no secrets in the cockpit.' We are all together, and regardless of rank, if you have knowledge of a problem, identify it. Otherwise, we are all going down together."

For some reason, we did hire a high percentage of people who had military backgrounds. I like the discipline they bring to their careers, along with a certain level of respect And no bullshit. They were not intimidated and generally had a strong enough ego to bring up an issue, regardless of what rank. I needed those kinds of people in our organization. The united type that could take the hill if they believed in the mission and were so instructed, and knew what to do when they accomplished the mission, and what to do if a retreat was necessary. But generally, with someone of this mindset, a retreat was not necessary.

Therefore, the simple concept was to recruit one person at a time. And I mean recruit. During the 1990s the marketplace was robust, and unemployment was at an all-time low. None of that mattered to us. No matter what was going on in the outside world, I was convinced the good people for our venture needed to be recruited—not necessarily by employment firms—but by us, one at a time, and they in turn would attract others. I was always on the lookout for talent. Twenty-four hours a day, seven days a week, and I encouraged others in our organization to do the same. Whether at the gas station, a motorcycle rally, in church, or a name from a newspaper or magazine article. Always be on the lookout for talent.

In addition to word-of-mouth advertising, and as a supplement to our other efforts, we also did a fair amount of print advertising in specific newspapers. Only we did take a slightly different strategy. Rather than frequently advertise in the very expensive large regional daily newspapers where thousands of help-wanted ads would run, instead we generally—but not exclusively—opted for the independent weekly newspapers that were delivered to the homes in each local community. For a minimal amount of investment we could place large advertisements in these smaller weekly newspapers, and blanket a region within thirty miles of our factory. My perspective on this was we were trying to attract potential candidates from the comfort of their home life and local community. And even those not looking for a new job generally read the local community newspaper. This strategy worked out real well for us.

Very early on we instituted a company policy that *the* final candidate, for *all* jobs had to have a *final* interview with a top executive before an offer was granted. Talk about a time-management issue for our department in charge of hiring. Since I was the person behind this policy, and probably the strongest believer in the concept—at least initially until others adopted it—I had final interviews with about 90% of our Road Crew.

I just loved these final interviews. Only I called them meetings, for that's what they were. By the time I had a chance to meet these candidates, they had already been through a grueling process. We were known as a hard company to get into. Contrary to the job marketplace at that time, we had an abundance of unsolicited applications combined with applications generated from our recruitment process.

I wanted our company to be hard to get into, and in these final meetings almost exclusively every candidate would mention that we had the most thorough and lengthy interviewing process they had ever been part of. And they *had* to meet with the CEO. The process was respectful, but also difficult. We only wanted the best, and we got them. By design, regardless of what position a candidate was applying for, whether executive or entry-level production, we had multiple rounds of interviews, with multiple departments, that occurred over several days, and oftentimes included team interviews. Not everyone agreed with me on this concept, but my thinking was about the home-work. Do the homework upfront, so we can all make better decisions—together—for the candidate about us, and us about the candidate—I was looking for mutual interest, like a marriage. After all, it does cut both ways. Or it should.

We have all been fooled by a first meeting with someone, whether on business or personal, and I was trying to minimize this happening. My thought was you can't fool all of the people all of the time, so pur-posefully our hiring department was instructed to schedule several meetings, with different departments, at different levels of the company, including peers and supervisors, on different days. And we had a form that each interviewer had to fill out and check boxes—quickly, so we didn't burden the process.

We also had formal skill and personality assessments, and reviewed them with the final applicants. We had drug testing and 100% of the time we would check references. At least that is what I expected and was told we were doing. Candidates were also invited to bring their spouses and children in to look around, and have lunch in the cafete-ria if they so desired. Again, my logic on all this is fairly simple. We didn't need a large army. We just needed the best army for our needs. And if we decided to work together as a Team, we were all going to spend a lot of time together, and I wanted to make sure the fit was right both ways. And I was hopeful the fit would be right for their families, and vice-versa.

Therefore, by the time I had a chance to meet the final candidates, they were well primed, and so was I. In these meetings, my role was not to assess the specific skill for the specific position, but rather set the tone for the candidate about the company vision and culture, and assess whether or not I believed the candidate fit in, and again this was vice-versa. This was also a great opportunity for the final candidate to ask any questions, and interview me, which they all did. Some even brought in notepads on which they had written out the questions beforehand. Good talent.

In most of these meetings my time was equally split between listening and talking. Most meetings lasted about an hour, and it gave me time to give my philosophy on the company and our Road Crew. By definition, all of our jobs within the company were different but equally important—we had no unimportant positions in the company. If we had an unimportant position, then again by definition, we didn't need it since it was unimportant. So, all of our jobs were different, and important.

Next, they were all *equally* important. Confusing to some, but I have simple logic on that too. Let's say, take your family and your children as an example. They are all different from one another, but equally important. After mutually discussing our families, I would ask which of their children they liked the best and which was the most important to them. Most people would squirm with this question, including me. So I would quickly ask if they liked them all equally. Then I would also ask if they were all different. Invariably, the answer was "yes" to both of these questions, and by this time a candidate was beginning to grasp what I meant about being different but equal. It all centered around respect and understanding for one's differences, and respecting each other for these differences and treating them equally. Why judge the difference?

For the sports minded, there was also another way to look at this concept. Like a baseball team, there are all different positions. But which is the most important? Is it the pitcher, the catcher, or the first baseman—or any other position? Try to do without any of these positions, and you will quickly find out which is the most important—the position that is absent. My viewpoint on this is that all the positions are different, but equally important to the team.

I would challenge each person that if they were to work for our venture, they would need to act and believe that their job was as important as anyone else's in the company, including mine. And I would directly ask, "Will you be willing to do that? If you can't do that, how can I, and how can others? For this to work we all must be willing to hold each other accountable, otherwise it won't work. Will you do that?" By this time in the meeting, most people were starting to understand the culture and concept, and would readily and confidently answer, "Yes, I will."

Next, another point of confusion arises. If we are all different but equal in our positions, why are we not all paid the same? Even though the positions to the team are equally important, we are all different in our skills, personal attributes, and wants and desires, and the marketplace puts a financial value on these items. In a job, some people think the financial value determines the value of the person. I disagree, and frankly this upsets me. Just because a job pays more or less than another, doesn't necessarily make it better or worse, it just makes it different, for different skill sets. Why put a value judgment on it? Life constantly requires trade-offs, and woe be to the person who determines their self-worth by a financial value.

For example, as the CEO, if I decided to not come to work one day, would the assembly line still run? They wouldn't even miss me. But if an Assembly Team Member decided not to come to work, would that impact the assembly line? It would shut it down until a solution was found. Since we all have different jobs, we have different impacts on the organization, but should have equal self-worth and respect.

I also liked to talk about leadership. I wanted to have everyone in our company be a leader. Sometimes I would get real puzzled looks with that one. And I would challenge people. Leaders don't necessarily need to directly supervise others, but real leaders lead themselves first. As an entry-level assembly line worker you are a leader, at least in my mind— each individual can make a difference. You have to be a leader inside, and by example, lead others, whether they are peers, or people you supervise, or people who are supervising you. Leadership comes from inside, and exudes by what you say and do. Good leaders are harmonious in what they say and do. *"Walk the talk."*

There were also some other interesting things I was learning in these meetings. Generally, the best prepared candidates were those who were applying for our hourly positions, and they usually had the most questions—genuine and tough questions. And they were the most easygoing, whereas for higher paid positions invariably the candidates were a little more formal. Another thing I noticed was when the candidates entered my office, most hourly and entry-level salaried candidates would grab a chair, and pull it up close to my desk, and with enthusiasm put their arms on my desk and we would converse. This contrasted sharply to the managerial and executive candidates, where they would usually push the chair farther away from my desk, sit more formally, and the initial conversation was much more reserved. None of this was surprising, just different.

This was also an opportune time to reinforce the practice we had of an open-door policy. Yes, I know everyone says they have this practice, until you try to use it and you quickly find out it isn't real. Well, it was real with us. Anyone, at anytime, could be questioned about what they were doing or how they treated someone—as long as you did this with respect. It didn't matter if you were the supervisor or not, or the CEO or not—*"no secrets in the cockpit."* Since most everyone had the chance to meet me before they were hired, they heard this straight from the horse's mouth, so to speak. And I did ask a favor of them if we indeed agreed to work together. If they ever experienced or witnessed an abuse of any of these principles or practices, I wanted them to tell me. I wanted them to be a leader, and help correct it. They all promised me they would, and they did.

In these meetings with prospective Road Crew Members it was also imperative for me to address the status of the venture, if they didn't bring it up first. We were never in positive cash flow, which basically meant we were funding the project through equity and debt financing. We were not self-sustaining, and by plan, would not be until during our second year of production—if we executed to the plan and got enough funding to get that far.

This was where one of my real tests would come in. I needed to assess directly if our candidates were up to the challenge. Most people have never really worked for a company that was basically insolvent. It may not seem like a big issue at first, but day in and day out, year after year, it can begin to weigh heavily on one's shoulders. Financially speaking, we were insolvent since the first day, and unless we successfully reached positive cash flow, it was over. Venture finished. We would all go do something different. I needed to address this directly so there were no false expectations. I believe in the concept of what former President Truman said, "I never said, 'give them hell,' I just told them the truth and they thought it was hell." By and large, that is my philosophy. Don't try to hide the seriousness of our situation, but deliver the message factually and sincerely, and then ask if they are up to the task of helping to carry out our mission. I invited everyone to help, if they so desired. If not, I certainly understood. We only wanted those who were dedicated to accomplishing a difficult task, under intense scrutiny, and I wanted to look intently into each person's eyes to assess if they had the determination and persistence to press our project forward in the heat of the battle.

We had more than our fair share of critical local print media, and most often this would be brought to my attention, and I wanted to address this with them, if they so desired. Frequently someone brought in an article or asked a question about some article they read that was hypercritical, and asked my opinion on the matter. I felt then as I do today. Everyone is entitled to their own opinion, and sometimes a writer or media organization can misconstrue—inadvertently or not—certain facts to present a story. But in the end, I challenged each person to do their own homework on the matter, and form their own decisions and opinions.

Everyone in our company had business cards. And we had them ready for the first day of work (most of the time). For some Team Members, this was the first time they ever had a business card from a company that they worked with. For me, it was a no-brainer, and part of our company culture. Everyone takes pride in their work—especially if a company takes pride in them—and in the high profile start-up that our venture had become, our Road Crew was usually asked about the company outside of work. Again, fairly normal simple logic. Some people say the financial cost is too great. I say the personal cost is too great to ignore things like this. If you are looking for cheap, you will find cheap. If you are looking for value, you may find value.

I encouraged our candidates and current Road Crew, when asked about the company, to confidently and politely pull out their business card and introduce themselves. My belief is we had a lot of ambassadors for the venture—and in most companies you do have them whether you like it or not—so you may as well embrace it and enhance it. After all, who should be the best salespeople? Well, hopefully your team of people. And they were all carrying the brand identity. And they believed in it, because they helped craft it.

And everyone had the same type of business card. We didn't have certain types of cards for certain types of people. And regarding specific formal titles on the business cards, sometimes we didn't use them unless there was a specific business reason to do so. Certainly we had titles and rank within the company, as any well-run organization does, but to the outside world I wasn't so sure they always needed to know that. I wanted the outside world to treat each of our Road Crew with respect, and if you didn't know their exact position, they could be the CFO, CEO, or part of our custodial staff. In general, did it really matter? Only to the specific needs of the position and the Team. Otherwise, for example, for an hourly paid assembly line worker, we would identify the position on the business card as "Manufacturing Department," or "Assembly Department," or "Paint Department."

One time I did encounter a frustrated vendor who was visiting our company, and he said he didn't know the manner in which to address people sometimes since he didn't know their specific position and rank. I mentioned that was by intent, and that if he just treated everyone with respect and equally, he wouldn't offend anyone. And specifically, if he needed to know a person's formal title, just ask. No one would be offended. We just didn't lead with our titles. Rather, my concept was to lead as a person—and let the title follow you. Sometimes a little confusion here is good.

We also had an employee stock option program. Not just for the executives and management of the company, but for everyone. All of the Road Crew Team Members were granted stock options in the company, and at the same value for everyone, including any of the executives. No special deals, except everyone was special. Therefore, everyone who worked for the company had a stake in it—they were all owners, and it didn't matter how much stock you owned. As an owner, everyone was entitled to their viewpoint on matters, and as a shareholder, they were entitled to ask the CEO any question they desired. And I encouraged it. Sometimes I didn't always like the questions in the short-term, but periodically a question would be raised in which there was a legitimate issue that needed to be addressed. This is how we all learn, together.

Probably one of the most visual and fun parts of being a member of the Road Crew was the official company apparel. Being motorcyclists, and our company became an organization of gearheads—both male and female—we were well tuned to the types of apparel our prospective customers, and frankly ourselves, desired. Again, we didn't design the cheapest with the idea of giving it away. It was all high quality, with motorcycle industry specific branded designs, which we then sold. People bought our apparel, and for the Road Crew, we offered company discounts.

And the Road Crew apparel was special. We had a unique design placed boldly on the back of the shirts or jackets that stated: Road Crew. Only official company Road Crew Team Members were issued Road Crew apparel, and no one else could buy it. One time in Sturgis at a motorcycle rally, I was offered $500 to sell the Road Crew shirt off my back. But no deal. These were special, and you had to earn them by being on the inside. We all knew that, and the word would spread, making it even more special—having something that others couldn't get, unless they were part of the inside Team.

Bottom line, it was a good deal for the Road Crew, and a good deal for the company. We all won on this one. Immediately when someone was hired, we issued them official branded company apparel, including a Road Crew Jacket, Road Crew Shirts, T-shirts, caps, and a few miscellaneous other items. As we got better with our systems, we even had this issued before the first day of hire, and frequently our new hires would wear their new apparel to work on their first day. These first items were issued free of charge, as part of a hiring bonus and helping to make the new Road Crew member feel welcome and part of the Team. And none of this apparel was required to be worn. Never. You don't force rebels. They rebel.

Periodically, someone in our company management Team thought so much of the idea of our Team Members wearing company apparel at work that they wanted to create a policy to require it. Again, I would bristle at these types of suggestions. Being a rebel myself, I don't believe in the concept of servitude and forcing, but would rather create and foster the desire for others to lead and do it on their own. That is where the real power comes from—doing it on their own because they want to, rather than because they have to.

In general, nearly every day about 99% of our Road Crew Team wore company apparel to work. Not only would they wear it to work, they also wore the apparel on nights and weekends. Part of the magic of this was the apparel was good quality, and fit into the lifestyle of our Road Crew, and the brand identity was harmonious to their beliefs. This didn't happen by accident, but was part of the long-range strategic vision, and was now unfolding before me by itself, taking on a new life of its own. The Road Crew was taking ownership, and I didn't mind a bit.

Another benefit to all this was that it fostered more open and direct communication, on an equal level. In meetings, or in the cafeteria, or just passing in the hallway, it was indistinguishable as to whether a Road Crew Member worked in the manufacturing area or the finance area, or what their formal position was. We generally all dressed to the same level—in jeans and cotton shirts—branded with the company logos or slogans.

The shoes were an interesting area also. For safety purposes, certain departments needed to ensure certain clothing, footwear, eyewear and headwear were appropriate, and for the factory area, we did require that everyone in that department wear steel-toed shoes. Well, steel-toed shoes go well with jeans and cotton shirts, and we offered a shoe allowance for our factory personnel, and we decided that as a small company to be fair, we would offer it to all the Road Crew. Well imagine: we wound up having the majority of our office staff also buy steel-toed work shoes, and wear them voluntarily to work. Whether a person was making $25,000 a year, or $100,000 a year, they were basically wearing the same apparel, including steel-toed work boots—and whether they were a man or a woman. Since my days of working as a mechanic and on the farm, I never got out of the habit of wearing work boots, and I naturally continued to.

Some of the leadership in our manufacturing area insisted that we require uniforms. Privately, I bristled at this, but listened to the arguments. The suggestion was made to contract with outside vendors to supply uniforms so everyone in manufacturing would look the same, but also look different from our office personnel. I didn't like the smell of that one. There were already too many natural items of friction between production and office, and I wasn't looking to add any more. I always love suggestions like this though. If it was such a great idea, maybe the person suggesting it would like to try it out on themselves for a while.

In short, we decided against factory uniforms from an outside vendor, and instead we really just adopted the company apparel as the voluntary factory apparel to wear—plus we saved money doing it that way. We never required, but just encouraged it by having good quality and fair pricing, and the leaders wore it also.

But we did have official company Road Crew apparel that we all came to understand as the official company clothing. For certain photographs and company functions, we would put out the word that the Official Road Crew outfit was required. This consisted of a white Road Crew shirt, with black pants and boots, and usually dark sunglasses for the finishing attitude touch. And just before the picture was taken, the official company thumbs up sign was given.

For a lot of reasons, and maybe by design of having the right skilled people with the right attitudes, and working with a clear focus on a clear mission, we never really needed many people. We were always tightly staffed. When we publicly unveiled our new Super X prototypes in Sturgis back in 1996 to thousands of people, very few knew that we only had a paid company staff of ten people. Ten people in the entire company. And we had designed a proprietary motorcycle for all the world to see, and judge. This was also at the same time we announced on the steps of the State Capitol our new factory location in Belle Plaine. Ten people. By this time we had already raised over $15 million in capital.

The following year we launched construction of our new factory and completed our public offering, raising a cumulative of about $60 million. We only had 27 people in the company at the time of the public offering. Very few people really knew the company from an inside perspective, yet we were already making international news—via print, radio, and television—and had made significant accomplishments. I was quite proud of the Road Crew Team, and part of my pride centered on the fact that we were a small group of people, but yet able to attain significant achievements.

We didn't start hiring a substantial amount of people until shortly before production. At the end of 1998, our staffing level reached about 125 people, and by this time we had raised just over $80 million in capital. During 1999 while we were in production, our peak staffing level was about 220 people. When we launched production during the spring of 1999, we had some interesting statistics. Seventy-five percent of our people had been with the company less than 15 months. Ninety-five percent of our staff had been with the company less than two years, even though we had been in business for seven years.

These were some challenging times. Think about it. Have you ever been with a company where 75% of the staff is new within the last 15 months? That's why I was so focused on the company culture. We were having such an influx of new people that it took considerable effort to assimilate this all into our culture and immediately foster teamwork. And work hard at it we did.

One of the most common questions I was asked by the general public, by bikers at rallies, media, business people and prospective Road Crew members was: what is my opinion on being a union business? How do you really answer that question? My answer was that it simply depends upon the situation. There is generally a time and place for everything. Being a new venture I believed we already were a union, the Excelsior-Henderson Union, and when you joined the company, you were automatically admitted into the Road Crew, which was my version of our union. We were united together. Maybe not all perfectly in harmony, but united as best we could.

But I know the question meant something else. My philosophy in running Excelsior was that if our Road Crew believed they needed a separate union, then that was okay with me. If they didn't need one, that was okay with me also. I have experienced benefits and detriments to both sides. We hired a lot of union people, and it didn't alter my perspective either way, because even in a union all individuals are entitled to their own thoughts. The one thing I did hold firm on though when asked, I would say, "If we do have a separate union, I'm going to join it." The street-smart people would answer that I couldn't join it since I was part of management. I could easily remedy that I told them, I would just hire myself as a production worker and resign my executive position, then join the union. If we needed a separate union, I wanted to find out firsthand why. Maybe I could learn something useful.

Even though we were a motorcycle company, and a gearhead driven company due to our product line, we did have a good mix of the genders. On average our Road Crew was about 30% women, and they worked in nearly every department within the venture, from finance, to marketing and sales, engineering, and manufacturing. Surprising to me, we had a high concentration of women in our production area, including the paint department and assembly line. In fact, our Welding Supervisor was Christine Horn, and when you met her, you didn't forget it and her Louisiana accent. Also, our Warehouse Supervisor was Barb Young who had just moved from South Dakota. Officially we never tracked our staffing by gender or race since we were blind—by intent—to color or race, age and gender. These are just the facts, and I like to think that is how we operated.

We must have been doing a pretty good job at it. Several years after we shut down, I got a letter from Johann Wallace, who worked on our Assembly Team, and lived in Saint Paul. I'll quote directly from his letter: *"I am forever grateful to the Hanlon family for giving me the opportunity to have been part of the Excelsior-Henderson legacy. I must tell you that as a minority, I have never been treated as well as I had with EH and I have told this to others with great sincerity. The experience I had with Excelsior-Henderson ranks with the highest of the most memorable of my life. Thanks for all. I wish you great success in current and future ventures."* I knew Johann well, and would oftentimes chat with him on the assembly line. When he sent me that mail, I was surprised. I never knew he was a minority. I was blind to that, and I think our entire company was too.

Part of my job was to just wander around the company to see what was happening, and I would stumble into some intriguing things. On one occasion I was meandering through the cafeteria, and I happened to observe a meeting of our Production Maintenance Engineering

Team. These guys were seasoned veterans of manufacturing and company politics, and still fairly new to the company. I liked all these guys whom I'd met before. They had intensity for their jobs and it showed.

They were talking about budgets—a dirty word. Allan Strehlow jumped in and said, "Well it's getting close to the end of the year, so we better spend our budget so we don't lose it." My eyes just about popped out of my head, and smoke must have been coming out of my ears. I never said anything directly, but I also knew we needed to do a better job in training and corporate culture. Invariably, people brought in former habits, and we needed them to learn new habits.

As luck would have it, about three months later while I was making my usual rounds, again I came upon another of their Team meetings in the cafeteria. Only this time it was quite different. Now Allan was saying, "No, we can't do it that way, it will cost too much money. We need to find another way. Maybe we can build it, or just do without it." And the Team agreed in unison—they were on a mission. That was all I needed to hear. Allan had become part of the Excelsior-Henderson Road Crew culture, and he was now preaching and practicing it, with his own conviction. I witnessed this happening often—he was *"walking the talk."*

I witnessed a lot of people taking pride in their work. Granted, not everyone that we hired worked out, but we were operating at less than 5% turnover per year. One of the areas that I noticed a lot of pride in was our custodial department. Oftentimes, this part of a business gets contracted out, and we tried that too. Only, it wasn't working so well. Instead, we hired a professional, Kenny Capaul, to manage and work this area. The typical interviewing process was not a good format for Kenny, but I had known him and his family for over thirty years, since we were in school together at Belle Plaine. Everyone had a chance to get to know Kenny, and appreciate him. He always had a smile on his face, when some in his position seemed to have little to smile about. After his father passed away, he lived on the farm with his mother. It was easy to admire him. Kenny is an example of another one of our everyday heroes. We had a lot of them—they weren't just doing their job, but were part of a mission.

As time progressed, it was not unusual to have husband and wife teams joining us, and parents of Road Crew Members or their children. For the size of our company, we also had an inordinate amount of people we needed to relocate, not just nationally but also internationally. We hired several people from England, and also relocated several nationally. Most of our relocations centered around hiring people with direct motorcycle or automotive development and manufacturing experience. It never ceased to amaze me the way people were willing to uproot their family for a new venture like ours. That was part of the magic of being in the motorcycle industry where there was a lot of passion, and people acted on it.

We didn't have any relocation packages for anyone and handled it on a case-by-case basis. Mostly all we ever paid for was lodging for a short time, along with the actual cost of transport for the household goods. Considering we were in negative cash flow, no candidates held our feet to the fire by requiring a generous relocation package. We just couldn't, and simply wouldn't do it. They were all real good sports about this.

We also didn't believe in having any employment contracts. Not even I had one. But we did have Team Member Agreements, which mutually covered the standard items that are expected from an employee and employer perspective, including the matter of properly handling intellectual property, and the importance of nondisclosure.

An overall important part of developing the culture and fostering a team environment was in the use of our communication. In addition to our Team Handbook, we had frequent meetings that included the entire company, new Team Member orientation meetings, and monthly birthday and anniversary day luncheons. Probably some of the best team building opportunities we had were the many company events we held. We didn't hire outside event planning companies, but rather had our own internal department—primarily one person—who would train and develop our Road Crew militia to work our events. It was not unusual to have 30 or 40 Road Crew members working at an event, along with spouses and other volunteers, and later we would rotate names since it became so popular to attend the motorcycle rallies.

Through my entire experiences with Excelsior-Henderson, I heard thousands of statements and was asked thousands of questions by people from all walks of life, and from around the world. There were three statements or questions I heard the most and that still stand out in my mind, and all at different time periods throughout the venture's lifecycle. The first statement I heard the most during the first three years was: *"You can't do it,"* meaning you can't create a new proprietary motorcycle company. Then indeed once we did build a proprietary motorcycle, immediately the next statement I heard the most frequently was: *"Fire it up,"* meaning let's hear that motor rumble, partic-ularly at motorcycle rallies, and even in hotel lobbies. The third most common phrase I heard during the last several years of the company was: *"You have the nicest people. Where did you get them, and how did you do it?"* I heard this last phrase so many times that I *almost* came to expect it.

That final statement was very important to me as the chief archi-tect of our culture. Good people make good companies. And now I was hearing that back from the people with whom our company interfaced. Even though I am more of an instinct driven person when it comes to marketing, I do like surveys. At rallies we were always surveying prospective consumers, and the first question I had put on the survey was a question asking, *"How were you treated by the staff at Excelsior-Henderson?"* We had thousands of voluntary responses, and 99% of the respondents indicated in their own handwriting they were treated excellent or very well. That says it all. It starts and ends with people.

Frequently when I met with people visiting or who were suppliers to our company, they would comment on our people. Usually I heard, *"How do we get them all to wear company apparel?"* and, *"Your people are so nice,"* and *"Your people seem all alike."* By now, you've figured out this wasn't by happenstance. We worked hard on this aspect. If the timing was appropriate, I would ask the person to expand briefly on this. Invariably, they commented on the positive, can-do attitudes, the bright, energetic demeanor, and the loyalty to the company and mis-sion. Judging from what others were saying, it seemed we were on the right track with our people.

Some people might think our attitude about our company culture was a bit soft and fuzzy. Really, it was the opposite. We were an intense, passionate family, the Road Crew family. And like all families, we had our up and down moments, and great intensity of purpose, and a strong common bond. Since we had mutual respect and trust of each other, we frequently grilled each other and held each other accountable—at any level, it didn't matter. It was an intense work environment, and emotions could and would flare. That was okay. We had committed people. Just apologize if you pushed too hard, or made a mistake. Mistakes were happening. We didn't cover them up, or let the next person handle it. Figure it out. If you couldn't, ask for help—and if you didn't ask for help, you were probably going to get it anyway. Correct it. Move forward. At the end of the battle, shake hands, smile, and keep pushing forward. United together. One step at a time.

# 33

## *Shifting Production From Neutral Into First*

The official culmination of our *Road To Glory* theme occurred on Saturday, January 30th, 1999, when we shipped our first revenue producing motorcycle to a dealer. This bike was shipped to Nielsen Enterprises in Chicago, which was owned by Ted Nielsen, one of our original Pioneer Dealers and early investor. Our Road Crew members were all excited and proud of their accomplishments, and as a symbol of their pride they took to autographing the motorcycle shipping crates. Dozens of signatures symbolizing we all stood behind our work. They just did this all on their own.

We never thought of this at the time, but instantaneously these crates became collector's items. We would get calls from dealers telling us stories of how they had showed their—and now also our—customers the crate their motorcycle had come in. Now how often does this happen? Invariably, the customer would ask if they could have the end to the crate where we had all signed it, next to the big, black, Big X logo and company name. And some would display the end-crate on a wall in their garage. I would get letters and pictures from consumers. Imagine that, a consumer asking to keep a crate for a motorcycle. We couldn't have planned or scripted this out. This was just instinct and grassroots efforts at work. And teamwork. And pride. Genuine.

Production was ramping up slowly, about at the pace we had planned, but we had a later start than planned. The annual Daytona Beach Bike Week was slated to start the first week of March, and we had just over three weeks to get bikes built for the promised inaugural demo rides at the rally. We were restless. What if we didn't have bikes? The big question was when could we get production going at a more stable rate? The entire production during the first three weeks of February went toward building bikes for our demo rides. We were literally producing bikes, and shipping them to Daytona as they came off the line. Providing they were working okay—which they weren't and we had to fix it—fast.

We were having problems with these first few bikes off the line. They all looked great, but when we ran them through our detailed, computer controlled rolling road test, we were blowing up about two out of five engines. This was disaster striking. In all of our testing on our prototype engines, we were never able to blow one up, unless we inadvertently ran it out of oil. We would try to blow them up in order to find the limit, but we were never able to find the limit. But now, they were blowing up brand new coming off the line.

This scared the hell out of me. We had come too far, and somewhat fast, but this was unexpected. If we couldn't fix this matter fast, I knew it would all be over, soon. When problems like this surfaced—this wasn't the first nor the last—we immediately needed to figure out one of two things: 1) is it a design problem, or 2) is it a production problem? If it was a design problem, we would need to go through new designs, which takes a lot of time and money, of which we had neither. If the design wasn't the problem, then the question was whether or not the actual manufacturing process was impacting the final outcome of the product.

We were all tense. Stepping a product from prototype to manufacturing requires cutting all new tooling for a product, and most times involves using additional or new vendors, and most certainly a different component manufacturing process than what was used to make prototype components. So we had a lot to figure out, and backtrack on, and fast. Plus, we had all new people working on the assembly line, with an all-new product. Not a good formula for immediate success.

After several days of around the clock working by our engineers and some production members, one of our lab tests showed an inordinate amount of metal filings in the oil. We didn't know if the fact the engine blew up caused the metal shavings, or if there were metal shavings in the new engines that were causing them to blow up.

After disassembling some brand new motors we had put together, and thoroughly inspecting all passageways, we finally found what we thought might be the culprit. Our engine components parts washers weren't cleansing the components thoroughly. We tried changing and improving the cleansing process, and then tested a few engines. They didn't blow.

We tried a few more engines. They didn't blow either. We tried a few more, and again, they didn't blow. Time to resume production. About a five day delay total. But probably years off of my life.

During February, we produced 42 motorcycles, of which we shipped 15 to our dealers, and we retained 27 of these first bikes, mostly for our demo rides, and some for our sales department, and a few for engineering and production. And come to think of it, I got to periodically ride one too. As I would learn in Daytona, these new production bikes also could easily do fifth-gear burnouts.

I wasn't so sure our new bikes would be capable of doing the burnouts that I so much like to do. One of the major due diligence questions, and a concern to me in our business, was the fact we needed to meet Environmental Protection Agency (EPA) and California Air Resources Board (CARB) standards for emissions. Technically speaking, we couldn't manufacture vehicles that didn't conform to these standards, along with compliance to the Department of Transportation's (DOT) regulations on vehicle equipment.

These standards do cause challenges to all OEM manufacturers, and to us as a new one, I was vitally concerned. What if we didn't meet them? We couldn't be faced with that situation. We just had to plan to meet them, the first pass through. Every factor of designing the bike was to take into consideration the meeting of these standards. That was one of the reasons our engine was designed the way it was—very efficient with dual overhead cams, four valves per cylinder, and with closed-loop fuel injection. About as modern as you could get, and at a par with the most modern automotive engines, and more advanced than any cruiser motorcycle engine.

These final tests took several months to complete, and had to be performed on a finished production-intent motorcycle. This means we had to have our production bike tested before we actually commenced production, which is the way we did this. Therefore, we couldn't afford in time nor money—we were a public company, and had staffed for production—to not meet these tests first pass through. To ensure this, we had de-tuned the motor as a final precaution to meeting these standards, particularly the California tests, which are the most rigid. We were the only manufacturer to meet these tests first pass through, and with no modifications for the California vehicle. Except for the required vapor canister, we made no other modifications to our engines to meet CARB standards, and basically were able to ship the same vehicle to all fifty states.

On January 19th, 1999, we were issued a Certificate of Conformity by the EPA, and on February 22nd, we were issued an Executive Order M-37-1 by CARB certifying our vehicles were in compliance. Just in time for production, and yes we were now in compliance. I was always concerned about doing things legally right.

This was both good news and bad news. The good news, we passed first time through and could safely enter into production. The bad news, our engines were de-tuned more than we needed to, and we later would need to continue the tests to find the uppermost limit. That was fine, and would have to wait for future model years. We sometimes got criticized—even though we were on a par with the industry—that our engines didn't have as much power as some expected, and most people never knew why. But inside the company we knew, and had planned to correct it with time. After all, that is what future model years are for. Enhancements.

As expected, the launch of real production also brought with it many new challenges, all at once. Even though we did our best to plan for this, how do you plan for a severe storm? The storm I am talking about is the business maelstrom that would hit upon commencement of production. We knew the storm was going to hit—it was unavoidable—but none of us knew how well we would do once it hit. My theory was to batten down the hatches just before the storm hit, let it hit, then open the hatches and survey the damages, and fix them.

How did I know a storm was going to hit? Well, all the business barometers were signaling it. For example, in the fifteen months prior to production, we had:

- Hired 75% of New Team Members
- Created 100% of New Supplier Network
- Created 100% of New Dealer Network
- Installed 100% of New Manufacturing Equipment
- Installed a Complete New Computer Operating System
- Manufactured an Entirely New Proprietary Motorcycle
- Needed To Raise Capital In Negative Cash Flow

Any one of these above seven factors was enough to give any seasoned business and executive team headaches, and yet we had to accomplish all seven of them *at the same time*. No small feat. And a great risk. No one, including myself, thought we could get through this part without some level of pain. Hopefully, nothing terminal.

Except for one area, we got through this phase surprisingly well, and better than I had hoped. Even though we got a late start at production, we were accelerating faster than planned. During June we shipped nearly $6 million of motorcycles, and our revenue to date was now about $14 million. None of this was taxing our systems and people, and we were poised to grow faster. But we did have some issues to tend.

Even though most of the company and manufacturing was meeting our budgeted costs, our purchased components costs were over plan. We had forecasted our purchased components to be around $9,000 per bike, and our initial bikes off the line had purchased components costs of $13,996. I remember just after we hit production, our CFO came into my office and I had never seen him so distressed. He said with great intensity, "Dan, we just got our first runs out of the computer, and the system is showing our parts costs are around $15,000 per bike." *Holy shit,* I thought. *How in the hell does that happen?* For months both he and our VP of Production had been telling me in our weekly staff meetings, and in presentations to the Board of Directors that our components costs were on plan—and I had them put this in writing to both the Board and myself. How in the hell can we now be off plan? Which was right?

I calmly looked at him and said, "Well Tom, everything is new, including our computer system, and the people entering data into it. Go back and as fast as you accurately can, have your department determine if the system is in error, or if that is really what our costs are." I knew I wouldn't sleep until he got back to me.

The next day he had a handle on the issue. We now had more problems—but all solvable. One, the computer system was wrong, and they were now correcting it. Good news. The bad news: it was only wrong by $1,000 per bike—meaning our true components cost was about $13,996. *Oh shit,* I thought. I quickly grabbed my calculator, and ran the numbers. We could produce 4,000 motorcycles this year, and now with a bill of material over plan by $5,000 per bike, that was a $20 million problem. Handed to me. On my desk. Just like that. We'd lose less money by not producing any more bikes.

This fazed me for about as long as it took me to write this sentence. This called for some fast thinking and some quick actions. Plus, no time to draw the guns and start firing as we needed everyone to pitch in and solve this issue—but privately I also knew I had to deal with some other issues later.

It really shouldn't have been surprising that the costs of our components were higher than plan, but what was surprising to me was my two top executives that managed these areas had been telling me we were on plan up to the very minute that we launched production. The previous day. What about the verbal and written reports they had given me? What about my credibility, and the credibility of the company? Why didn't they know these things, or did they know? I don't think they knew about the impending cost issue. But it was their job to know that. I was counting on them, as that is what they were hired to do. That was an interesting development.

At that point in time, our biggest issues were components costs and our developing relationships with vendors. We assembled a Cost Reduction Team, of which I was a member. Within six months, we had lowered our components costs by $3,000 per bike, to $11,000, for a 22% reduction in costs, without sacrificing any quality. We were now tracking this problem well, and within the next 12 months we would hit our projected cost level—if we got a chance to live that long.

Most of our cost reductions were time related—versus volume related—meaning using a different method of manufacturing, or a different supplier, or transitioning from soft tooling to permanent tooling to lower costs. All of these components were identified, and it would happen over the next 12 months. In my mind, I had now checked this one off. It was okay.

Had we the time, and if we could turn back the clock, we could have delayed production a year while we worked with our vendors and the cost reduction plan. But the investor marketplace and the media were relentless and we would have had no credibility by delaying further. We just had to grind our way through it. One day at a time.

The year of 1999 was a robust year in the economy, and the Internet companies and technology stocks were really booming. Only we were neither. We were a motorcycle company. A what? A motorcycle company, that's what. In fact, an underfunded, new start-up, motorcycle company.

Try getting the attention of vendors when you say that. We had about 1,000 component parts being furnished to us by about 110 vendors, of which about 21 were internationally based. Depending upon how you classify a component, we either had more or less part numbers—for example, is a rim with spokes and wheel bearings and a tire mounted to it one part number or several? On our finished bill of material, we generally listed about 750 part numbers, but if we were to include subassemblies, the part number count would be geometrically greater.

All of our prospective vendors were very busy with the robust economy, and most weren't looking to aggressively add to their business. Business was already too good, and any new business had to come at a premium price. And then we come along. We weren't even on their radar. Our volumes were so low that some refused to bid on it, and when they did, pricing was at a premium. Not all did this. We had some excellent vendors that would bend over backwards to work correctly with us. Most were very good to us, and they and their staff would work night and day to bring our new motorcycle company to life.

It's just the problem ones that a person remembers daily, since the daily issues could also end up on my desk. One of our machining suppliers was based in Faribault, Minnesota, and was owned by a guy named Tom G. Every day when I met with the head of our production, they filled me in on the status of components for production that day. With several components, we were operating on just-in-time (not by choice, we were forced to)—where literally the component would come in that day and be put on a finished bike. Not good. One of the key areas was engine components, and that was the first process on the assembly line, and would hold up our entire production line until the component came in.

Tom's company was holding us up, and so I decided to call him directly. He took my call, and immediately I discussed my concern with him. His response was, "Dan, I know I'm holding you up, but I don't want to ship you any more parts than necessary. I am concerned that you will run out of money and not pay me." I appreciated his honesty, but not his integrity. Why didn't he tell us that sooner?

"Tom," I responded, "you have been an early investor since when we were still trying to raise our first million dollars, and the critics have been saying we were out of money for six years. Well, we're still here, and we're not giving up the fight. But you are. Every time you are late on a shipment, we have to shut down production. Yesterday when you shorted your shipment to us by 20 pieces, we had to shut down the line. We lost sales of 20 motorcycles, which cost me $280,000 in revenue, just yesterday. That doesn't include what you shorted us last week, nor the week before. All told, it's over a million dollars already."

This didn't persuade him one bit. As I put the telephone down, I glanced out my window. I realized we had someone—another one—crumbling on the front line. This type of thinking and action would exacerbate our issues—we didn't need that. We didn't have many missing the schedules, but only a few could be fatal. We immediately started to ramp up another supplier—but this also takes time. It doesn't happen overnight. One man's trash will become another's treasure.

Maybe this was why the company had developed a bit of a reputation and attitude early on that carried forward into the future. In working with people and organizations that were doing what they said they would do, they viewed us as easy to get along with. No surprise there. But we also had some people and organizations that didn't do what they set out to do. We had a big problem with that, and we would hold their feet to the fire. We were damn tough on that issue. And those that weren't meeting their goals were usually the ones squawking the loudest. No surprise there either.

With so many new vendors we knew we were going to have a problem with a certain percentage of them, we just didn't know which ones—until the issue surfaced. Most all told us that they could do what we needed—*Do what you said you would do, when you said you would do it, for how much you said it would cost*—but when it came to delivering, it was a different story. No surprises, but again timing issues we would solve, in time.

Another expected issue—yet unexpected issue—were our competitors in the motorcycle industry. Most never thought we would get this far, and no thanks to them, we had come a long way. But now a few of them seemed hell-bent on making matters worse. In addition to our growing dealer network, one of the areas they could squeeze us on was our OEM vendors in the motorcycle industry. And squeeze us they did. I thought the Federal Trade Commission (FTC) had a problem with restraint of trade, but some of our competitors must not have read that rulebook.

I have dozens of examples, some well documented and some not. Several I personally handled, and I'll recount one here. I was sitting at my desk one day when a call came in to me. "Hi," he said, "I'm _____." "Yes," I said to him, "I know who you are." Next he said, "Well, I'm with _____." I interrupted him and said, "Yes, I know." He proceeded to say that his *"company makes almost all of the _____ for Harley, and he would like to make ours for us."*

I liked this guy right away. Calling me up personally to offer a hand to help. And help he could. I had followed his private company for years. It was my business to know who Harley's suppliers were, and I knew a lot of them. This guy and his company could be real helpful. Except for one problem. A big problem. I knew Harley wouldn't let him, but he didn't know that. Yet.

The short story is I told him to ask Harley if it was okay if he supplied us. He was taken aback—as most private business owners would be—and said he would be damned if anyone could tell him what to do with his business. I assured him we were very interested, and that I would prefer if he check it out with Harley in order to avoid any potential future issues.

About a week later he called me, and was much more hat-in-hand in our conversation. He told me that he did call them, had a chance to think things over, and that he didn't really think our business was a good fit for him right now. Wasn't the first time I heard this. That's why I had him check it out. I made further notes on our conversation, and placed them in my now growing file labeled—FTC Issues-Vendors. I knew firsthand how some companies behaved in the free marketplace—and I had read the Tucker Automobile story, which we were frequently compared to.

Other than our initially high components costs and normal new vendor issues, we were starting to hum along pretty good. Our robotic welders were doing industry-leading welds on our frames, our paint finishes were immediately setting new standards in the industry, the assembly process was generally as planned, and our Team of people were doing a good job. All of these items could have been a great risk, but went reasonably smoothly. We did have one area that concerned me though when we launched production—the foul smell in the air.

In the early spring one day while driving to work, as I got closer to the factory I noticed this smell. When I got to the factory, some people were talking about it too. Most people strongly disliked the odor, but I kind of liked it. It reminded me of growing up on the farm. Our factory was located next to a farming area, and with the advent of spring, the neighboring farmers were spreading manure on the fields. It would waft for miles.

Good, I thought. If the neighbors can put up with this smell, they certainly won't be able to notice anything coming out of our paint plant.

Actually, Minnesota is so highly regulated for paint emissions, with our new modern factory technology, you could put your face into our exhaust ducts and you would have only fresh clean air to breathe.

# 34

## *The Secret Handshake*

Riding the new Super X motorcycle is like no other ride in the world. My opinion. And a growing opinion. But like all opinions, not everyone shares the same one.

The new Super X was not just a motorcycle though. It was never intended to be just a motorcycle. It was more than that, by design. I never set out to build just a motorcycle—well I did and I didn't—but instead to build a company that in turn would design, build, and sell motorcycles. This may seem like a subtle point, but it is a very significant factor to a business plan.

If the goal was to just build a bike, from the many available catalogs I could have just ordered the various parts and assembled one myself for about twenty grand over a weekend. Bear in mind that all these parts mimic the bolt pattern of the popular Harley-Davidson motorcycles, yet not one part would be from them. Instead, the parts are readily available in the robust enthusiasts aftermarket, with enough parts to assemble a complete motorcycle that would obviously bear a distinct resemblance to a Harley. Then just stamp whatever name you want on it, and voila, there is a bike. Fairly logical. Except for one question.

Where is the brand? There is nothing proprietary.

Therefore, the mission of the company was to design and build a *proprietary* motorcycle, and by designing a proprietary bike this was going to require a significant amount of capital and an infrastructure of people—thus was borne the concept of the company. The culture of the company needed to be in harmony with the products it was designing, and vice versa.

So the Super X was different, yet it was the same as all motorcycles. Same in the perspective that it had the required two wheels, fuel tank, handlebars, engine, transmission, tires, etc.—you get the picture. Different in the perspective that all of these items were designed to be unique to our Super X. If a person were unsure if it was truly different, just try to interchange parts with any other motorcycle. Can't be done.

The overall way to look at the design of the Super X is that it is a *"statement bike."* There is a certain aura of quality and elegance, and yet rugged. A study in contrasts—to provoke a feeling. It made a statement.

I always hesitate to talk about the features, since a product—especially a passionate product like a motorcycle—is really more than the sum of its parts—it is the feeling that goes with those parts—it will take you places even before you fire it up. Somewhat like a romance. Even if a person were to ignore the brand name on our Super X, to anyone that knew anything about motorcycles, they would immediately recognize our many signature items.

On the first 1,000 bikes we built there was a special brass plate that we riveted to the upper triple clamp area next to the handlebars that was inscribed, *Initial Production Series.* After the initial series, we changed the brass badge to a new inscription reading, *Hanlon Quality.* I had this idea six years earlier while launching the company after studying the bikes the former Excelsior company had made while Ignatz Schwinn owned them in the early 1900s. He had a Schwinn Quality badge applied to his motorcycles and bicycles, and it seemed appropriate to continue with the tradition of the badge. Also, this type of branding was unique to the modern-day motorcycle industry.

I also took issue with the standard fare of current owners manuals. If you have recently bought a new car, truck, or motorcycle, the owners manuals have grown to a big-sized volume that is not very useful—some due in part to the multiple languages in one manual that seem in current vogue, and also due to all the disclaimers created by intense litigation prompted by the lawyers. Generally, most manuals today are unreadable, both in content and length. That was one of the things we changed, and it started right with the name. We had a *Riders Handbook,* not an owners manual—and printed in one language, English.

Our motorcycle is made primarily of steel that is chromed and painted. In the hands of a careful owner, it is designed to outlast the owner, and can be passed on from generation to generation. My belief is quality and elegance will stand the test of time, and I fully expect our motorcycles to last for over one hundred years.

The entire motorcycle has an aura of a timeless design and the feel of quality—we have a 50-degree, dual overhead cam, four-valves per cylinder, air and oil cooled motor, with a closed loop fuel-injection system. Muffled—slightly—by a dual staggered chrome exhaust system. A belt drive final drive, with a gear drive primary. Aluminum rims with stainless steel spokes. A leading-link front suspension with built-in anti-dive braking—with front brakes that actually worked. The signature front forks piercing the front fender. A single coil mounted rear monoshock—all hidden from view for a classic hard-tail design look. Teardrop shaped fuel tank, with dual notches that accentuate the vibrating big-bore cylinders. Paint finish—luxurious and industry leading. Throw your leg over the low-slung seat, and grab the handgrips where you will feel something different—they have a subtle "X" embossed on them. Put your feet on the footboards—they have the "X" logo embossed for your feet to rest on. Fire it up, and you not only hear a distinct rumble, you feel it—and you can feel it deep inside. Grab the clutch, and shift it distinctly into gear, and unleash the throttle. The big bike handles so well you become one with the bike. You are now entering a new world, your new world.

Does any of this sound unique? Is it a feeling, or just features of a new motorcycle—or maybe both? Well no other motorcycle has these features put together all on one bike. From a physical perspective, these are some of the features that make the Super X different, and admittedly, its own bike.

But we all know it's not just about the features, but the attitude and the soul that goes with it—the feeling. What does it stand for? In our venture, our motorcycle was a reflection of all that we stood for and for what we were trying to do. A culmination of our efforts of breathing new life into an old resurrected motorcycle brand—we were Reborn To Be Wild.

● ● ●

Daytona Beach Bike Week 1999 was a landmark event for us. This would be the first time in 68 years that a motorcyclist would have a chance to demo ride a Super X. And we were all a little worried. These were our early bikes off the production line, and they had some inherent problems since they were so early. Nothing major was wrong, but each one had little issues that were different from each other. Each bike had its own personality.

One of the issues we didn't expect was in engine vibration. We had gone to great pains in our design to engineer in some vibration for feel, and in our earlier prototypes we had dialed this in fairly well. In fact, we spent an inordinate amount of time just on this characteristic, until we got it just right. Only now, something happened from the transition of prototype to production—not surprising. Some of the bikes had an excessive engine vibration—nothing that would really impact the quality of the bike or its performance—but let's just say it wouldn't give the best first impression. Plus, it wasn't what we had designed it to do (after the rally, we quickly corrected this issue).

I was always careful to monitor what prospective consumers thought about our venture, particularly as it related to our people and our products. This all related to the building of our brand name and reputation. In my perspective, brands are created, built, and enhanced by contact—they can also be destroyed by contact if it is the wrong type of contact. Our brand image was being formed by *every point of contact* between our venture—and our vendors, our Road Crew, shareholders, and now with prospective consumers.

Over the years we had carefully cultivated our company image and brand. That was part of the founding mission of the venture. I started the venture for it to have an attitude—just like the motorcycle industry itself has an attitude. This was to be an out-of-the-box type of venture, for I really knew that everyone with whom we'd work would basically have to think and act outside the box in order to be involved with our project. No one could really turn to their rulebook, and look up how to start and run a motorcycle company—or how to finance it. That rulebook was about a century old. So we had to write a new rulebook. Good. That is what I like to do anyway, and with people who are willing to step outside their box, and help write a new rulebook.

Therefore, we at Excelsior never planned on quietly entering the industry. We were entering it as a change agent. Not so bold as to seek to change an entire industry, but bold enough to change how one interacts in the industry. All of the industry players were international in scope, and most companies over a half-century old. The modern-day barriers to entry are so great that the current players in the field don't even think about the possibility of a new entrant—it hasn't happened in over fifty years, so it probably won't happen in the next year.

So whether anyone liked it or not, we needed to be a change agent. Obviously, some didn't like this, whereas others embraced it with a passion—the same level of passion I had—as a consumer. That is where we would take our message. Take it to the people, in the non-traditional manner.

By design, we were a grassroots company, and marketed that way. By definition, it is nearly impossible to define how to be grassroots—

you just simply are or are not—and some of it is by instinct. We didn't go around frequently saying we were a grassroots company—instead that is what we were, and how we acted, and the type of people we tended to attract—and we were *told* we were a grassroots company. Some were well educated, some not. Some were well employed, some not. Some were young. Some were old. But all had a passion. The passion to help build something that on the surface appeared insurmountable and the chances of success nearly infinitesimal—building the American Dream, from nothing.

Those were the kind of people I liked. And as I've mentioned, there is an old saying in the motorcycle industry among our market segment that is appropriate to describe our venture and its grassroots marketing—*"If I Have To Explain, You Won't Understand."* Think about it. It's true.

In general, our target market segment was an adult rider, generally between the ages of 33 to 75 years old. People don't start life in this segment, nor do most start riding motorcycles in this segment, but some do. Great marketers of the day will often speak of the baby boom generation, and the great demographics it brings to the equation of marketing and purchasing habits. Also, in this age segment, life has become full speed ahead, with a lot of responsibilities, time constraints, and an incessant amount of commercialism—everything in life is moving fast. Whereas this may all be good for the economy and our lifestyles, what does it do to one as a person?

That is where our motorcycles and our brand fit in. Where less is more. Where elegance is understated. Where rugged is okay. Where there is no judgment based on your social status, your gender, or your nationality or race. Where you can check out of your normal life for a short time, and enter a new life—all with the press of a button. The starter button.

Imagine a time when you can let your problems be shed with the wind rushing by your head, and you feel something powerful in your hands, and you are in control of it—an untamed beast. Where people don't judge you on how you look or what you wear. Where there is no judging. Just quiet acceptance. And sometimes not so quiet acceptance. Where there is an instant camaraderie. And where there is also instant individualism. Where you are in a crowd, or by yourself in a crowd. Where you can go there for just ten minutes, or forever. And you don't need anyone's permission.

Does this place exist? Yes it does. I've been there, and so have many others.

This is the world of motorcycling with a big American-made cruiser. And you can do this around the world, or in your own garage. A time and place where you don't need your cell phone—you won't hear it ring anyway. A time and place where there is no computer—no fax machine—no email—no "high technology" to dampen your senses—no hold times on the telephone—nobody telling you what to do. Instead you are in your own world, wherever that is to you. Hard to describe? Yes, sure. But that is what our market segment is all about.

As you may well know, none of these things have to do with the *demographics*, but with the *psychographics*. Just a few short years ago you never heard the term in marketing, but today it is gaining a better understanding. For me, and for us, it was the psychographics that mattered. We were looking for certain personality or lifestyle traits, and then sought to address those traits.

In essence, this is a similar market to the market segment that Harley-Davidson is interested in, but we had an added experience. What if you had the chance to be on the ground floor of Harley a century ago? What if today you'd had enough of Harley? What if you never wanted a Harley, but wanted something different? What if you were looking for an alternative—and found out that there was nothing except for Harley as the only independent American motorcycle manufacturer? What if you wanted to take your desire and passions to the next level? There was nothing—you would have to bury your *"what ifs."*

That was how I felt when I got the urge to start Excelsior. I was ready for that next level, only there was no next level. That meant I had to create one. So, yes, we shared the same prospective market segment with Harley, but in my opinion, we also had something unique that they no longer could have. We were the next level. For whatever that meant to one as a person.

But we couldn't say this directly, nor say it this way. It was a feeling, and we had to nurture and grow that feeling, and impart it onto others. And hope others would join the mission.

Some of this was not logical, and some of it was. The logical part was that Harley-Davidson simply had no competition, and did not have competition since the early 1950s. Hell, can you think of any multibillion-dollar company that has had no competition for fifty years? And then how can this one company fill all the needs of a consumer, especially when these consumers have passionate needs—and spend thousands and thousands of dollars, and take time off work to fill this need? Well, logically, we all know that you can't be all things to all people, no matter how good you are.

In the marketplace, there is the marketing concept of the *law of duality*. In short, it basically means that the marketplace can be enhanced and grow with the addition of a new competitor. For example, look at McDonald's and Burger King—together they create a larger market than each alone could. Another example, how about Ford, Chevy, or Dodge trucks? Which one is better? Depends who you ask, and again, even though they are intense competitors, together they increase the size of the market. Another great example is Coke and Pepsi—together they have created a market, and the market is larger than what it would be if there was only one choice. Being a motorcyclist, and a gearhead at heart, I instinctively knew this also applied to us and Harley. Most who would follow our story, also knew this too.

So we were the next level. We just had to do it right, and not take it for granted.

Getting back to Coke and Pepsi, my two favorites—Which one tastes better? Depends upon whom you ask. They both come in tin cans or plastic bottles. They both contain colored water, with or without caffeine. They both have printing on the can—one is red and white, the other red, white, and blue. They both have 12-ounce cans. So really, there is no difference, is there?

Except for the marketing departments. Like the late Charles Revlon once said, "In the factory we make cosmetics, but in the store we sell hope." Same with our company compared to Harley-Davidson, and the same when Coke is compared to Pepsi. Which is better? The answer often is within the eye of the beholder.

The key ingredient here is to make sure you are among the ones being compared to the industry leader—and I don't mean by sales volume, I mean by psychographic volume—the passionate leaders. Does a Ford truck owner argue with a Nissan truck owner on which is the best? No. Does a Ford truck owner argue with a Chevy truck owner on which is the best? Yes. The important part here is you want to be part of the right market family, and then have your arguments within the family. Some people and companies never quite get this concept. And probably the most important factor of all in this equation: you can't tell the customer to include you in the family. They tell you—the manufacturer—if you are listening.

This was my biggest concern. We wanted to be in the genuine OEM American motorcycle manufacturing family, but we couldn't just join it. The customers had to let us in. That is why I was so damn restless at our public unveiling in Sturgis during August 1996. As a company, we were hopefully endearing our way into the right market segment, but at the end of the day, our vote didn't count. We needed the vote of the biker, and they all vote with their feet. If they don't like what they see, they're out of there. And they tell you. Fortunately, we were allowed into the club.

It is a secret club, and you need to know the secret handshake to get in. Seldom is it spoken, as it doesn't need to be, and it wouldn't pay proper homage either. You just know it, and you hang together. We were allowed in the family, into the club. Now, we could dial it up even more, and we did.

Among our Road Crew, we also had our own special handshake at Excelsior. We had a unique handshake—the Excelsior-Henderson secret handshake—that was reserved for only those that were helping to further our mission—Road Crew, vendors, dealers, shareholders, volunteers, etc. This is true; ask any of the Road Crew. They all know our secret handshake.

Practically everything became a marketing opportunity for us, but it had to be genuine, and oftentimes be spontaneous. It couldn't come off and be the type of marketing that was calculated and boardroom stiff. It had to be genuine. By design, most of our company Road Crew were either grassroots, gearheads, or simply passionate people. We would use our intellect, our experience, and our instinct to guide us. It reminded me of Charles Lindbergh when he was asked in early 1927 what type of navigation system he would use to cross the Atlantic. His answer: "Dead reckoning." Meaning no radio, no sextant, no navigator. Just a compass and the stars. And instinct. Trained instinct. If you didn't reckon right, you were dead. That's why it's called *dead reckoning*. True story.

Over the many years of our venture, one of the most common accolades I heard about our venture had to do with our marketing. I wish I could take credit for it, but the real story is everyone involved can take credit for it. Everyone in our company was a de facto member of our marketing department. We all had a passionate interest, coupled with mutual respect. I had a few good ideas, and a lot of other people had great ideas. Regardless of whose idea it was, we tried to implement the ones that felt like the right ones.

That's how we turned a lot of things into genuine marketing opportunities. Whether with a Shareholders' Reunion, or a groundbreaking ceremony, or a flag raising ceremony, or an announcement on the steps of the State Capitol.

At rallies, our ground troops went to work. All over town we had banners, flyers, billboards, and bandanas. Hell, we looked like we owned the place, but at a fraction of the cost. We all had friends in low places who knew how to make things work outside the boardroom, and we knew how to operate below the radar of our competitors. Until we would spring a surprise at a rally.

We had many great slogans, and most of them made it onto billboards, marketing materials, and company T-shirts that we sold. Slogans like, *It Ain't A One Horse Town Anymore, Get Off The Beaten Path, The Mutha Of All Parades, Today Is Resurrection Day, Your Next Tattoo, The Road To Glory, Test Our Metal, Cloning Is For Sheep, Prepare To Get Off, X Marks The Spot, More Horses-Less Bull, You Can't Fake Soul*, and my two favorites, *FIREITUP*, and *Reborn To Be Wild*.

There are several funny stories regarding these slogans, and two of them I especially like. We first used the slogan, *Your Next Tattoo*, at Daytona Beach Bike Week, and had it mounted on huge billboards and some marketing materials. What were we thinking? We had people coming in to our display frequently asking if we could give them an Excelsior-Henderson tattoo. Not in my wildest dreams did I ever imagine that people would take the billboard literally and want to tattoo our name on their body. I was hopeful they might want to someday. But at the same time, I just simply thought it was too much to hope for. But we were having that happen. We already knew of several people who had tattooed our name on their body, and it was now growing. One of our Road Crew, Big Al, was the first to have an Excelsior-Henderson Super X tattoo. After he saw others doing it, he had to modify his tattoo. It now read, *001*, for being the first. You know you are onto something when people are tattooing your brand on their body, and then putting a serial number on it.

Another great unintended story was the constant barrage of questions we got from bikers at rallies about our company and our bikes. At the end of the workday for each rally, we would have a Road Crew Rally Team meeting to unwind, talk about the events of the day, and then depart for the rally nightlife. In several of these meetings, we'd be discussing over beers how bikers were asking us to constantly start the motorcycles, even though we were indoors—which was illegal. We didn't necessarily mind the illegal part at a rally, but how do you really keep starting bikes every thirty seconds? Well, we couldn't, but we had fun talking about it. The phrase bikers used, and as a self-professed gearhead I have also used it for years, was *fire it up*. Out of one of our informal brainstorming Road Crew marketing sessions at a rally, we turned this into a marketing slogan that we trademarked, and sold the hell out of the T-shirts. On a black T-shirt, with the bold letters in white, saying, *FIREITUP*.

These informal marketing sessions at a rally were real effective. Another idea generated from the rallies was taking a picture of prospective consumers on our Super X motorcycle. Our ever observant Road Crew would watch as bikers sat on our bikes, while one of their buddies, or a spouse, would take a picture; or one of us would quickly volunteer to help. From this the idea surfaced for us to set up an informal area in our eXperience display, and shoot instant pictures of bikers on our bikes, and place the photo in a commemorative branded card. This worked so well, we had to discontinue it due to cost. We must have shot over 40,000 pictures before we just had to slow it down.

Music was another part of our brand identity, and we played it at our rallies, ceremonies and events. It is the appropriate thing to do in the motorcycle industry. We had certain songs that we played at everything as a sort of kick-off to launch the ceremonies, whether it was a groundbreaking, public unveiling, a parade, or flag raising, or simply in our company museum for visitors. These were our company songs, and we treasured them, and over several years and several milestones reached, they became a symbolic part of our Road Crew family tradition, which we would share with others. The two songs are: *"Proud To Be An American,"* and *"Born To Be Wild."* These songs signified our venture well. Many a time when we played these to either launch or close a ceremony—they would bring intense thoughts and memories—there were tears in our eyes. We all knew we were a close knit Team, and paying a price for such a difficult venture. Even today when I hear one of those songs, I instantly get placed back in time.

One of the things I enjoyed the most at the rallies was to get out and ride some of our old bikes. We had a growing museum collection that I took great personal interest in, and had bought each antique bike through my contacts in the Antique Motorcycle Club of America, and at under market prices. I especially liked to fire up the 1931 Super X that I had bought from Ernie Hartman in Ohio, and a 1909 Excelsior belt-drive single that I bought from Joe Gardella in Michigan. As soon as I wheeled one of these bikes out of our eXperience display, a crowd would immediately form—not many people know how to fire up and ride these old ones—and cameras would be clicking. As much as bikers like the new iron, there is a certain amount of respect and homage that go to the old—those that traveled the road before us. At the rallies, I rode these old bikes more than the new ones, and it also paid great homage to our brand and heritage—this was something none of our competition could do. Except for Harley, and they wouldn't do it. They had gotten so large, their old bikes were hands-off only and never hit the road under their own power.

Several times I also fired up our twin-cylinder 1914 Excelsior Boardtrack racer. In its day, this machine was capable of 100 mph, and was very similar to the original Excelsior racer that broke the 100 mph speed barrier on a motorcycle in 1912. This was a real crotch-rocket. I usually said my prayers before and after I got off of this bike.

• • •

The 1999 Daytona Beach rally turned out to be spectacular for us. Our annual parade went smoothly, and we proceeded to take Daytona by storm with our new Super Xs. Our demo rides were slated to start on Monday, March 1st, at 9:00 a.m. By 7:30 there was already a crowd forming. True to the now-growing Excelsior tradition, we were ready. And we didn't want to keep them waiting. We opened early, and the average wait for a ride that week was several hours.

We were busy. Our Road Crew Demo Team was new at all this, but I don't think it showed. We were passionately inspired. To work at these rallies, we recruited from our Road Crew, their spouses and children, our Excelsior-Henderson dealers and parts suppliers, investors, and some official, unofficial, rally volunteers, like Panhead and Holly. I guess Panhead has a real name, but I didn't know it the first year—he never used it. He was a died-in-the-wool genuine biker—tattoos all over, big and burly, mean if you didn't know better, and a full white beard—he looks like Santa Claus. He was also a diehard Harley guy—obviously with a nickname taken from a Harley engine—until he met the X. It didn't take long for him to become a loyal X-Man, and he rode those Xs mercilessly. I have never met someone who rode their bike so hard. Flat out. Full throttle. All the time. And he and Holly bought two Xs.

My parents also worked the rallies, along with several of my brothers and a sister. My folks hadn't been back to the Badlands since 1949 on their honeymoon, and on their several trips out to the Sturgis Motorcycle Rally they were able to relive some memories.

And most everyone would volunteer their time. We didn't pay our dealers or suppliers to work with us. They volunteered. But like I learned on the farm, when you have volunteers helping you, like we did with threshing, make sure you feed them well. Which we did. Food and drink for all, and a good showing of appreciation.

There was some great bonding by the Road Crew at these rallies. We didn't need any "sterile" offsite team building sessions; instead we were breathing it live, there at the rallies—with people from every department working together, regardless of rank. Most times, we had to bunk people up two to four together to a room to save money, and it helped to build camaraderie. Generally, I didn't even get my own room—I would share with my brother T.K., our lead factory test rider. If a person ever wondered what it was like to join a carnival and take a show on the road, this was the next closest thing I know. We would work from dawn to dusk, and then enjoy the festivities of the rally during the evening, and at morning revelry, we were all back at it again.

During the course of 1999, we gave nearly four thousand demo rides at the rallies. From Laughlin, Nevada; to Daytona Beach, Florida; to Sturgis, South Dakota; and to Laconia, New Hampshire—the Laconia demo rides were especially memorable. Their state license plates bear the motto; "Live Free or Die"—hard not to like that boldness. We even had demo rides at our Shareholders' Reunion in Belle Plaine on June 5th. Demo rides at a shareholders' meeting. You just have to love this industry. I do.

Observing the demo rides I witnessed some things that I really never expected. Similar to very few OEM manufacturers, we didn't escort our individual demo riders, but instead they could each at their own pace follow a prescribed course. Most would follow the course, and at a respectable rate of travel. But every day we did also get the hooligans. At least 10% of the riders were there to give the bikes one helluva beating—it was worse than any testing we could have imagined. Our bikes were designed tough—and the harder they were flogged, the more our bikes urged them on. It was great to watch. We didn't really mind. That's how we all learned. But man, some were just unrelenting. And if they sped too far off course, our course cop—Panhead—was there to round them up. Only now he was sporting new tattoos on his well-tattooed body—Excelsior-Henderson tattoos. Which he later added a serial number to.

After each demo ride, we offered a special T-shirt—a demo rider black T-shirt with bold white letters, of course—that said *FIREITUP* or *TEST OUR METAL,* on the front, and on the back it said, *Demo Biker.* We were the first to do something like this, and they instantly became collector's items. We also immediately surveyed each rider. Voluntarily, of course. After each ride, one of our Road Crew would ask the rider if they would be willing to fill out by themselves a Demo Ride Review card. On many occasions I observed demo riders sitting on the grass filling out our cards. We must have struck a chord in how we presented this, as we had about 95% of the demo riders fill out the Review card.

The first question was: *How were you treated by Excelsior-Henderson Road Crew Members at the Demo Site?* The next three questions centered on the bike and its styling, fit and finish, and riding characteristics. During the year we had just over three thousand of these Demo Ride Reviews completed at our rallies and events. The first question was a good barometer for me on the quality of our people and how they interacted with the public. We were running a 99% acceptance rate— 91% rated us as excellent, and an additional 8% rated us as very satisfied. Our homework was paying off.

Regarding the bike, in these field surveys by demo riders we were averaging a 90% to 99% acceptance rate on everything. Better than I could have ever hoped for. All of our demo riders were owners and riders of another brand of motorcycle, and had ridden *their* motorcycle to *our* demo site. And they were rating *our* bike this highly, and they didn't even own one. Frequently, as the demo riders were leaving our demo site, they donned their new demo rider T-shirt, and rode away. I just knew we were on to something. We were now going to have customers. Bikers. Riding our Super X motorcycles. And paying more for them than what a Harley would cost. A new level.

• • •

Customers. It took us nearly seven years before we could say we had motorcycle customers. Over the years we did have thousands of customers who were buying our merchandise in anticipation of production, and we had thousands of shareholders, but now we had a new type of customer, on our new product—a motorcycle customer, or as we frequently referred to, *a biker*. Yes, we now had bikers, and achieved what we had set out to do a long time before.

Motorcycling is a passionate and intense sport, and as motorcyclists and businesspeople, we were also an intense and passionate company. I think many of our earliest customers were also of this mindset, and we received many letters from the bikers that bought our bikes. They were doing some neat things with their bikes, including customizing them, and taking pictures of themselves or their family with the bike in the photo, and then mailing these to us.

Several customers included their new X as part of their family Christmas card photos they mailed out. A couple from Missouri, Richard and Colleen, liked their first X so much, they bought another one, and had holiday pictures taken of themselves, complete with Santa hats and huge red bows astride their new Super Xs. Of course, they both had some pretty big holiday smiles on their faces.

For the first time we now had customers riding their Xs to motorcycle rallies, and we had to adjust our company profile at the rallies to accommodate this. With all bikes, there is maintenance required, and we would set up a temporary shop at the rallies to provide maintenance to our customers—direct from our factory Road Crew. It was a good chance for us to interface directly with our customers.

Anybody who owned an X became an instant celebrity. Since there were not that many Excelsiors in the marketplace, anyone who rode one would get instantly questioned on what they thought of the company and their bike. They were instant ambassadors of the company, and if they were looking to be obscure, it was impossible to do on an X.

I just loved meeting the bikers, our new customers. Of course not all was in perfect harmony, but at least we were getting the information firsthand—direct and unfiltered. One of the first things I began to notice when I spoke with our biking customers was that they would come up to me and introduce themselves, and then recite, "*my X is number 533.*" At first this threw me off slightly, but after I heard it enough, I simply couldn't believe it. Each rider had memorized the last few digits of the serial number of their bike, and if they owned several, which was not uncommon, they knew the serial number of each one.

After this went on a few months, I thought I needed to test it. From that point on, every time I met someone who owned an X, if they didn't immediately mention their serial number, I would ask them if they knew it. Generally, they would look back at me like I was non-sensical—of course they knew their serial number, and would tell me. I have yet to meet one of our bike owners who did not know the serial number, by heart. Now, that is passion.

I also witnessed passion taken to the ultimate level. Branding. Tattooing. On one's body. Voluntarily. At each rally, more and more Excelsior-Henderson tattoos were apparent, and the owners would proudly show me their new works of art.

We did have some customers who were not totally pleased with their new bikes, nor with the service they were getting from our dealers or ourselves. Most times, and rightfully so, these were the ones we heard from the most and the ones we remembered the most also. We did have some higher warranty rates on our early production bikes, which was not surprising—it was somewhat of a tradeoff on the desirability of having a low serial number production bike. Overall, we had projected an industry standard of 3.0% for warranty claims, but we were running an average of 1.5%, or nearly half of what we had projected. We tried to keep this in mind when dealing with our other issues.

Over the years we had received an incalculable amount of mail, and it was a busy job for my assistant Jan to keep track of all this. For historical purposes, we tried to retain most letters, and placed them into large black three-ring binders. One letter I remember receiving was from two teenage boys—Joshua and Opokii—from Ghana, West Africa. They wanted a few T-shirts and caps, which I did have sent, to go along with the new riding club they had started—an Excelsior-Henderson Riding Club. In West Africa. According to their letter, *"We should have used motors but we cannot afford and we are kids. We organised this riding club purposely to entertain ourselves."* Apparently, they had read about our company in a motorcycle magazine, and now had their own Excelsior-Henderson riding club.

# 35

## Buying Ink By The Barrel—
## The Good, The Bad, And The Ugly

For some reason, we received an abundance of media interest over the years, which I never initially expected. At most, I thought we might garner a few articles during the years on our project, and I didn't think it wise to expect to have a lot of media coverage. I didn't think it was that big of a deal what we were seeking to accomplish—we expected to be buying a lot of our media coverage, not responding to it.

Granted, the tasks of building the venture were difficult, but if indeed I had thought it couldn't be done, I would never have set out to give it a try. So initially, my plan anticipated a constant challenge to develop and implement a successful media relations campaign. It proved to be a challenge, but not always the challenge I expected.

For the most part, my initial plan was to go about building the business—raising the capital and accomplishing the milestones—*on time and on budget*—and the story would come years later down the road. I knew I was very interested in the venture, and was successful in attracting a few more to join, but I didn't expect the story to be interesting to others. Why would it be? We were just trying to do our best, in our humble little world, in the market segment of motorcycles.

It would be fair to say I underestimated this one. Over the time period of six years, there were well over two thousand media stories about our venture. Two thousand. We averaged over 6.5 articles a week—more than an article a day. Each day. Every day. Around the world. In multiple languages. For one thousand five hundred sixty business days. In a row.

I don't know if this is good or bad, but it is what it is. We had every type of public relations media that I am aware of: newspaper, magazine, radio, television, video, cable, and even the Internet. From small-town newspapers like the *Belle Plaine Herald*, to national newspapers like *U.S.A. Today*, the *New York Times*, and the *Wall Street Journal*. From local television stations to CNN live in Manhattan, New York.

I am not really aware of many start-up companies that were able to have so much national and international media coverage.

We never paid for a monitoring service that tracks all the media coverage. Some companies do that, but I didn't want to spend the money, and I wasn't sure what we would immediately do with the information anyway. It seemed that when a media story hit, invariably someone who read or heard the story would call or write us, and we were able to track it that way—direct from the audience. We were receiving so many media stories and contacts from the media coverage audience, we weren't really trying to generate more, other than normal business relations. I guess our story was interesting on its own merits.

All the people I talk to seem to agree we had a lot of media coverage, and so do I. I think that point is inarguable. Depending upon whom you ask, some people think we had a lot of unfair media coverage, and some think it was balanced—depending upon where they were located in the world. We had a little bit of all of it. The good, the bad, and the ugly.

I think the vast majority of the worldwide media coverage we received that I am aware of were fair and balanced articles about the company. About 35% of our media coverage was international, and probably 99.5% of the international coverage was the type of story that did no harm to the company—and probably did good—and we were pleased to have it. For the most part, the international press positioned us as the little guy—which we were—going up against the almighty—which they are—Harley-Davidson. Many times we had magazines or newspapers sent to us in foreign languages, whether Spanish, German, Japanese, Chinese, Czechoslovakian, Polish, Russian, Danish, Swedish, Italian, Norwegian, and even Greek. Probably a few more too.

Regarding the national media, again I would say we had a lot of coverage, with the vast majority—maybe 95% to 98%—of the coverage being balanced and of value to the venture. Now, generally in all media coverage, whether international or national, there are some segments within each story that you wish they wouldn't say or write, but what can you do? Most of it is in fun, or facetious, and oftentimes they want at least something said that was overly interesting or controversial. When you are not writing or saying the story yourself, you cannot control the entire message. You can only control your portion of the message. Thereafter, the writer, or the commentator can position the story the way they desire. Most of them wanted to have some fun with the story, and for the most part I understood this, and it was fine. Some of it was over the top, but that was to be expected too, because we were sometimes over the top as well.

The local television, radio, and for the most part, magazine coverage was well balanced and mirrored the national and international coverage in content and tone—so nothing perplexing there. Again, if I were to write the articles or be the news commentator, I would do so differently, but they call that advertising, and you have to pay big money for that. This wasn't advertising. This was better. This was third-party generated. Therefore, we were required to take the good with the bad. Other than managing the process and the message, the rest was out of our control.

The media coverage that was the most perplexing was the coverage from one of the daily regional newspapers—the same newspaper that ran a story that then required us to pull a $10 million offering. For some reason they became frequently dissimilar with the rest of the local coverage—including the competing Saint Paul daily newspaper—and most certainly significantly dissimilar with the national and international media coverage. It seems like we made a great story—and usually the great story meant—at least to a few of the business writers and editors—make it controversial.

Within the same newspaper, most writers who focused on the people or community aspect, or business start-up aspect, covered our company in a fair and balanced perspective, similar to the national and international media. Therefore I found that to be consistent and not perplexing—unlike some articles written by a few other reporters for the same newspaper. As an audience, depending upon from which media coverage you learned of our venture—or which writer—this gave you various unique perspectives about our business, and sometimes, myself.

The source of inconsistency might have been the mole we discovered in our midst. Someone within our own organization was deliberately leaking out information, and misinformation, about the company. A newspaper reporter alerted me to this during 1999 as the heat was being turned up on us. The reporter didn't want to admit this, but they had way too much insider information and I was able to get them to confess. They had continued to call our staff until they got someone to furnish them proprietary inside information. When I learned of this, I thought I should bring it up to our Board, but I was slightly reserved. They might think we were overreacting. But instead, one Board member immediately commented they previously had a similar situation within their own company. That's what I liked about working with experienced people that had fought a lot of battles. You get to experience a lot of things that some just wouldn't believe, even when they are confronted with the evidence.

Then sometimes, our competitors would get these local articles, and fax them throughout the industry, including to our dealers, and give the story greater legs than what it deserved. And a few times, the hometown weekly newspaper, the *Belle Plaine Herald*, would pick up a story, and the *Herald* would run parts of it again—but the information wasn't correct. Each time I would call the publisher of the *Herald*, Ed Townsend, and he would express his regrets. He would quote his source as the other newspaper, and the story would go on. On some days, it was a real challenge to manage this flow of information, especially when some incorrect coverage wasn't in sync with the majority of the coverage.

I do think some articles periodically did harm to our business (especially as I previously mentioned with the SEC solicitation situation). We did not expect this, nor could we figure out a way to lessen it. Many years earlier a local politician, who I felt was very successful in managing his image had instructed me that, "you never get the last word in with someone who buys ink by the barrel. They will always control you, if they desire." How and why we received this type of attention, I don't know. Maybe some of it was self-inflicted by clashes with a few within our company, but it still did seem unbalanced, and not fair.

During 1999 we were averaging an article every eight business days from this newspaper. We had more articles than Arctic Cat, Polaris, and Toro—combined—and were in the league with 3M, the Mayo Clinic, General Mills, Cargill, and Medtronic—all organizations headquartered in Minnesota. Other than Northwest Airlines and Honeywell, which had just been sold to Allied Signal, or Jesse Ventura, who had just become Governor of our state, we were one of the most written about stories. Oftentimes, we were front page or headline stories also, but not the kind you would like to be.

Sometimes these articles were provided to some of the national motorcycle industry magazines, who took the information as gospel since the initial coverage was in our own backyard. In essence, it was given more weight, they would publish it, and again we were left to defend information that was unbalanced.

Even though in the totality of our entire national and international media coverage these were considered just a few local articles, it was unfortunate so many people in the regional coverage area were misinformed. This is another time I frequently thought of the quote by Mark Twain, "A lie will travel half-way around the world before the truth has time to put its shoes on."

We also learned a lot about positioning. Generally when I was being interviewed, the interviewer had a notepad and either a tape recorder or a camera rolling. Most of the questions and the demeanor were very pleasant, and I never had a clue if the ensuing coverage was going to be a benefit or a detriment to the company. These people were professionals, and seldom tip their hand so you could see their cards.

Within the motorcycle industry, again other than for just a few writers, we had balanced and fair coverage, with the qualifier that this was third party coverage that we could not entirely control. Most of the large national motorcycle magazines, like *Easyriders* and *American Iron*, and the smaller national and regional publications gave us balanced and fair coverage within the motorcycle industry press. There were just a few, like *Cycle World*, that again seemed determined to periodically make something a problem, and between them and one of the local daily newspapers, would hire and cross-quote each other—an interesting and challenging situation. But by and large, the industry coverage that was in our target market segment was appropriate for a start-up venture. I was grateful for any and all of the media coverage, as I didn't really expect it.

Since our venture was a visual driven start-up in an intense industry, and since we had become a focus of a great amount of media, our venture, along with myself, had become one of the most recognized. Not only in my home state of Minnesota, but primarily in the motorcycle industry—particularly among bikers. Maybe not as well recognized as Willie G. Davidson or Evel Knievel. But probably more recognized than the CEO of Harley, Honda, or Polaris.

Sometimes this notoriety has its price. I had a phone call and two voice mail messages that disturbed me, at least for a short while since they happened so close to each other. Somebody had been calling and threatening to kill me—a death threat, I guess. Maybe in all my years of living I had been threatened that way before, but I couldn't remember. So this was a first.

I had thought our project was reasonably intense, and invoked a lot of passion, some well-directed and some misdirected, but this one I had to think about.

On the one hand I just thought, *ignore the threat and move on.* Until the next call came shortly thereafter, and the next. Then I thought I should at least tell someone in case it really happened. I contacted our corporate security and ran it by him. Because it was part of his job, he thought we should follow up and file a report and possibly investigate it more. For some reason, about halfway through our conversation, I lost my concentration on the matter and my mind drifted back to the challenges facing our venture.

It was time to move on—I had more important things to worry about.

Possibly there were more reasons, but these are some of the reasons there were different opinions regarding the media coverage for our venture. Depends upon whom you asked, and whether they were getting their information from local, national, or international sources. And frankly, since our venture was intense and had an element of passion, I also think in some cases it was as simple as whether or not someone liked our story, or was jealous about the story. My opinion—calling a spade a spade.

• • •

With so many great media stories around the world regarding our venture, there were a lot of stories within the story. Way too many to ever begin to recount here, but one was so unique it still stands out. We were invited to be a live guest on the CNN "Most Toys" show, scheduled for Thursday evening, December 19th, 1996, starting at 7:30 p.m. EST. We had a Super X prototype, one of the same ones unveiled at the Sturgis Motorcycle Rally, crated and shipped via common carrier to CNN's studio in New York City. Upon arriving just shortly before the show, the bike was still in the crate on the main level, and we had to go up to the seventh floor. Only the crate looked damaged. I asked some of the maintenance guys about this, and they said they didn't have a dock for the truck to unload at, so they sort of had the crate dropped off—like a four-foot drop. *Interesting*, I thought. We had to take the freight elevator, and got the bike up into the studio. I had worn a suit, but rather than a shirt and tie, I wore a black long-sleeved T-shirt, with bright yellow and red flames on it. I wanted to make sure the audience got the brand message. The studio guy was asking me about whether we had gas and oil in the bike, which is forbidden indoors. I assured him it was okay. After the show, as we got the bike back down via the freight elevator, since I already had oil and gas in the bike, I fired it up and drove it out of there, and into the damaged crate. How the crate ever got loaded back on the truck, I'll never know. I slipped the maintenance guys a couple of twenties, wished them luck, and flew back to Minnesota.

# 36

## Smoothing The Bumps In The Road

With the advent of production in 1999, the company was now in a transitioning mode and one of the areas I was real watchful of was the area of leadership. We were generally lightly staffed at the senior management ranks, and it was time to bring in additional talent to our company. We usually had numerous applicants for most of our positions in the company, but at the middle and senior management levels, positions were so specialized that we almost always had to recruit for them.

One of the ways we recruited was through our own network of advisors and investors, whom I loved to frequently tap, and usually this would yield some good candidates, along with references we could trust. Periodically though, we had to move outside our network, and would work with local and national search firms to recruit talent. Using search firms worked well at the middle management areas, but I was less confident at the senior, or vice president level. Most of these people would be coming from a secure company, with a secure job, and a larger company, and we posed a great risk for their career. I didn't necessarily believe this, but this is what we usually heard when recruiting. I already knew this. We just had to find the right candidate, and most times we were doing this on our own. I had worked previously as a recruiter, and I didn't hesitate to pick up the phone and contact someone. The answer "no," never bothered me. Not everyone was looking to join a difficult non-high-tech start-up. Early stage companies traditionally do not offer a stable career path.

Remaining from the senior management Team we recruited during 1996 were our CFO and VP of Manufacturing & Engineering—previously we had to make a few transitions for various reasons in the sales, marketing, and engineering area. Some of our leaders were beginning to show signs of battle fatigue from being on the front lines for so long, and I didn't blame them. It was time for some fresh energy. Even though they were not in perfect harmony with my assessment, I was strongly concerned about a few issues in their departments since neither one had accurately identified our over plan production costs, until it was a problem. Not a good surprise, and I didn't want anymore. The final accountability rested with me, and they had delivered a surprise that didn't make me look very good, and I publicly shouldered the blame for it. I never passed it on.

We had operated quite lean at the middle and senior management ranks, partly because I believe in operating lean, and partly because until just recently we didn't have very many people to lead. It was time to add to our ranks to fill some needed leadership and expertise voids, and to also back-fill some of our senior management areas. In the event of an abrupt departure in some areas, we didn't have backup talent. In a mature organization, there is usually some depth, but in an early stage venture like ours there is usually little depth for replacements.

Earlier, our VP of Manufacturing and Engineering had hired for a brief stint a former colleague of his from England, Neil, as our Director of Engineering and that just wasn't working out. He was unfamiliar with air-cooled V-twin engines, and being unfamiliar with American culture he strongly desired to move his family back to England. This was a misstep, and we had to correct it. Through a search firm, we then brought in Victor Van Dyke, formerly with Kohler Engines in Wisconsin, as our new Director of Engineering, and he moved his family to Minnesota.

On the manufacturing front, we had just added a new Director of Manufacturing, Steve Leverenz, who was previously the head of manufacturing for the largest manufacturing plant of Donaldson Company. He was located in Iowa and moved his family to Minnesota. For the first time, we were now well positioned in the Manufacturing and Engineering areas, and I was hopeful not to have any more surprises. Which I didn't have. That was real good, and these guys were solid corporate headquarters performers to work with.

In the finance area, we had been working with our auditor Arthur Andersen since 1993, and our main staff auditor was Randy Strobel. I knew him well, and he obviously knew our company well, and had a lot of varied experience. We asked him to join us as our new Director of Finance. He became instrumental in helping to structure our accounting department, and again he was someone solid I could rely on.

We also hired a young lawyer, Mark Sides, who joined us to manage our legal, contracts, patents, and trademark areas. Mark joined us from our law firm, Faegre & Benson, and we had worked real closely with him on nearly all our financing for several years, along with our dealer contracts. Because of all the legal mandates of an OEM vehicle manufacturer that we were required to comply with, as well as the dealer contracts and all of the financing, we were usually spending in excess of three hundred thousand dollars a year on legal fees. We hoped that since we already knew Mark, we would reduce our costs, and in addition, free up some of my time. Previously, I had devoted a lot of my time in these areas.

In the sales and marketing areas, we were having a little more shuffling than what we would have liked. Personally, I think some of this could have been avoided. Through a referral, we had brought in Joel Norenberg as our Director of Marketing, and he was capable of managing any storm we seemed to be in. Without me expecting it, he became somewhat of a bellwether for the department. When we had an abrupt resignation from our sales director, we appointed Joel as our interim Director of Sales. We had him overloaded most of the time. Not by design, it just seemed to happen that way. Fortunately, Joel was resilient, as good sales and marketing personalities are—and should be. Joel had just previously co-owned a motorcycle dealership in Michigan, and had previously worked with early stage medical start-ups, so he was well versed in being flexible.

While on the lookout for our VP of Marketing and Sales, I had just read an article about the resignation of a guy from Volkswagen. His name was Steve Wilhite, and he had just been named as Grand Marketer of the Year by *Brandweek Magazine* for his leadership in the marketing campaign on the introduction of the new VW Beetle and its "Drivers Wanted" campaign. He was looking for a change in his career, and so I decided that we should ring him up. We did get him to join our company, but it was for about 45 days. There was a lot of speculation and rumors on what happened, but I am not aware of any mystery.

For the most part, after the Daytona Beach motorcycle rally, I think he decided the motorcycle industry was different than he expected, along with the fact we were a damn small company compared to what he was familiar with, and he wanted to return to California. Steve was offered the position as the head of Marketing for Apple Computer in California, and that must have suited his tastes better. I had met his wife, and I do recall him promising her that he would be returning to California. In spite of the fact that he sent me a Ford motif, dark blue Hawaiian shirt, I still have a lot of respect for him. We both knew it just wasn't going to work. He needed more, and I didn't blame him. After such a long recruitment for this position, and not being able to fill it overnight, this did leave a void in the company for some time.

During this time frame I also had another surprise. I guess it was a surprise and it wasn't a surprise. Our CFO, Tom Rootness, came into my office late one afternoon and said that he wanted to resign. He had indicated this same thing in my office several times over the last few years, and each time we were able to come to an agreement where he would stay. But this time was different. I could see it in him, and I didn't even want to question him. He looked tired, and I was worried about his health. Even one of our investment bankers had recently called me specifically to ask how Tom was doing. We were afraid he was going to have a heart attack. We had stressful times in our venture. It was not for the faint of heart. He had carried the torch far enough.

Probably, it was also the honorable thing to do. We had missed our components costs target without his department alerting anyone in advance. I don't remember any finger pointing on this issue, but no doubt there was a question of lost faith in several directions. They were taking the numbers directly from our VP of Production, and did not do an internal audit on the numbers, and then forwarding them on to me, and I to the Board. He, and several others—and I couldn't find fault in the logic—had also lost some faith on the reliability of information being provided by the production leadership.

But this also was going to create another void in the company. Our CFO desiring to leave just after we had announced that our components costs were out of line, and we had to continue to secure new financing. In the midst of a problem. It would have been better to accomplish this either a half-year earlier, or a half-year later, but not now.

This is not a good formula for raising money, as it generally makes the investment market unpredictable. They like stability, and as a start-up we had to struggle to find it. Internally, I wanted to be prepared for something like this and we were now back-filled in our management and that was less of a concern. The primary concerns were the optics of the departure in the eyes of the investment marketplace, along with my concern in recruiting a new strong CFO in the midst of a company problem. A double wham.

Timing is everything, but you don't always get to pick the time. I could only control our reaction to it—just keep moving forward, one difficult step at a time. And with a smile on my face.

# 37

## More Horses, Less Bull

As a company, we were now achieving what I had set out to accomplish nearly seven years earlier—in production and selling motorcycles—but one item continued to need constant diligence—the art of raising the capital to make it all happen. Over the years of raising capital, and we were now around $80 million raised, there was one thing I had learned. It never got any easier, and each one was a risk that it wouldn't get done, or that there wouldn't be another one. I cannot think of one moment during my entire experience with Excelsior that my mind was not thinking about the financing. Troubling thoughts.

Several times I have mentioned the challenge of funding a negative cash flow company. In addition to the business challenges it creates, it is also a psychological challenge. The daily losing of money for seven years in a row can take a toll—even though it was the plan. To put this in context, in my perspective I look at a company that is in negative cash flow to be in a similar situation to a person that is hemorrhaging blood. If the flow of blood is not stopped, and new blood added, you are a goner. And for how long can you continue this, before there is some intervention that you can't control. In other words, to some more or less degree, I thought we might be on borrowed time—this isn't new news, this is just how I felt privately, all the time. Not because of any overall issue with the company, but rather for too many years we had been pulling the rabbit out of the hat at the last minute. I didn't know how much longer we could statistically ensure this would happen. But we had to continue to do this, until we got to positive cash flow. Then I knew I would have a new thought, and forget about the old one.

I love studying financing and the art of the deal, and in preparation for our upcoming financing as I surveyed the worldwide financial landscape, I saw something new on the horizon. The Internet. Or was it a mirage? At first I didn't believe what I saw and heard, so I looked again. Sure enough, the Internet. I wasn't sure what this was, and I never seemed to get a logical answer from anybody, yet it was all the rage—at least in the financial markets and the media. I didn't want to be too embarrassed, so I thought I would study up on it on my own. I opened the dictionary, and the word was not in there. Hmm, too new a concept for my dictionary.

As I conversed with investment bankers throughout the country, I quickly learned what the perception of the Internet was. It was the second coming of Christ, or so it seemed. And unfortunately for us, we were not an Internet company. All of a sudden a new due diligence question, and the most common question I was asked, was, *"What is your Internet story?"* Hell, I thought, we're the same venture we have always been—a start-up venture designing and now building and selling proprietary motorcycles. A new manufacturing company, here in the United States of America.

It was always difficult to raise money for a *start-up*—for a start-up *manufacturing company*—for a *start-up manufacturing company based in America.* None of these factors are considered the darlings of the Wall Street investment bankers—but maybe should be. Over the years, we had honed a process to accomplish raising capital, and we got pretty good at figuring out ways to get our story heard by prospective investors. I loved that. But now, there was a new variable thrown into our formula that I wasn't yet sure how to figure out.

I immediately loved the Internet. Just like when the pioneers must have loved having the postal service deliver mail. Just like when the first time a phone rang and you could talk to someone. Just like the first time you could flip a switch and have light. Just like the first time you could tune into a radio. Just like the first time a television was turned on. Just like the first time I used a cell phone. Just like the first time I sent a fax. These are all great additions to one's business and life, but not a substitute for it.

And now all of a sudden I was being told our business plan was obsolete, and this new Internet thing was going to replace businesses, especially bricks and mortar business in old-line industries—like us. I don't know. I must be a slow study. I just couldn't figure out how this Internet thing was going to machine parts, assemble them, and ship them to dealers, and then on to customers. And then service them on the road, or at a rally. Or maybe, people were going to quit buying motorcycles.

The long and short is, there was a bubble on the horizon that didn't look good for our business. On the one hand, the actual use of the Internet I believed would be a great communication and information tool that a young developing company like ours could take advantage of in getting out our story. A real coup that I didn't expect—a great tool to use in addition to the telephone, mailings, fax machines, and yes, personal interface.

But on the other hand, I was not so sure. In raising money, one of the key factors is timing. Timing. And right now the timing was for the Internet. I didn't know for sure how this would impact us, or for how long this bubble would be on the horizon, or what would happen when the bubble went away. We just had to keep moving forward.

With the company in full-scale launch, our capital needs were now at the greatest—and if there was ever a time to turn back we had long passed it. There was only one way now. We were well staffed, and production was rolling. Cash was flowing in and flowing out—only more was flowing out. Our bank account was short, and had been for some time. The IPO two years earlier left us $10 million short, and the recent production delay and high components costs, meant to me we were, at minimum, short about $30 million. A lot of money, and one of the many reasons I was always proactive on our financing. We never had anyone calling us to finance our deal. We had to go look for it.

On Friday, January 22nd, we were able to close on the $3 million convertible preferred stock offering that was the follow-up offering to the $10 million deal we had completed the previous year, and with the same institutional investor, Rose Glen. Just after closing on this deal, we were immediately scouring the marketplace for any type of financing we could get. But I had something come to haunt us—the right of first refusal. We were meeting with reluctance from prospective investment firms when they found out they could be undercut by a former suitor.

Not only was the right of first refusal an issue, we were unable to locate any other type of financing other than a convertible preferred stock offering. That wasn't the best type of financing for a company like ours, other than if it was the only type of financing we could get, then it quickly became the best. But, for a moment, I thought we might have an ace up our sleeve.

One of the dealmakers, Larry Goldfarb from our last financing, had left Shoreline Pacific and had started out on his own with a few of his business contacts. Larry was one of those dealmakers who seemed to have it all: a former New York lawyer, fast cars, smart, well-groomed, with dark hair—long and slicked back, who had made a lot of money. Larry had been instrumental in structuring a previous financing—I thought highly of him—and he was well aware of some of the obvious potential pitfalls of our current deals. Through his company, he proposed a different type of financing that he could arrange. After several phone conversations with Larry in San Francisco, where he was based, on April 8th I arranged to meet with several of his partners in Mequon, Wisconsin, a suburb of Milwaukee.

Larry and his group were presenting a different type of financing instrument, up to $20 million, that looked like a better structure for the company if we could get it done. One of the primary better factors was that his investors were more long term driven, and not looking to trade quickly out of the stock. That was a big positive factor, as an institutional investor selling in a hurry, or under a problem time frame, could quickly drive our stock down. But a big concern we had was the issue on the right of first refusal. On several occasions I brought this matter up to our investment banker, Shoreline Pacific in Sausalito, California, and with our investor Rose Glen in Pennsylvania, and they both indicated they would sue. I didn't like that word. That was all we needed. We needed to think about it. It was a roll of the dice.

However, this did put some pressure on Shoreline and Rose Glen to perform, and they went diligently to work getting another deal done for us. The next day, April 9th, Rose Glen came to visit us at our factory in Belle Plaine. The lead guy from Rose Glen, Wayne Bloch, arrived and brought his analyst with him. They were primed for some tough due diligence, and they met with several of our upper managers. Since we were now in production, we also made sure they had a chance to get a ride on our new Super Xs, and Wayne, being a good sport, put in an order for his own new Super X.

They seemed interested in ultimately putting a deal together, and desired to bring in a partner. Personally, I would have preferred numerous partners, and told them so. My reasoning, which I never let on, was that it would dilute their control, and would give us more options in the event of a problem. Obviously, they looked at it the other way, and wanted few to no partners, and desired to control it more. So there were some divergent opinions on this.

Shoreline and Rose Glen introduced the new prospective investor—Societe Generale of France. They had a New York office, and our contact was Guillaume Pollet. Guillaume is French, and on April 21st he arrived, along with his analyst Sylvan Tessier, to visit the factory as part of the due diligence on our venture. I immediately liked Guillaume. He appeared to be a straight shooter, and was thorough without being condescending. He didn't seem to quite be at ease visiting us—I wasn't sure why, and chalked it up to his background and in being in unfamiliar territory. Or maybe it was motorcycles.

On May 3rd, we announced the closing of a new $10 million convertible preferred stock offering. Rose Glen was our lead institutional investor on this offering, and purchased $2.5 million, while Societe Generale purchased $7.5 million. I found this rather interesting. The lead investor took the lesser investment. While we were hammering out the details of the financing structure, as usual there were some vigorous discussions. One of them again was on the right of first refusal. Same argument as before, with the same results.

The other part I was questioning was on some of the onerous terms of the deal. I wasn't sure who was in the driver's seat. During the art of negotiating the deal, I was able to find out Societe planned on taking most of the investment, but were letting Rose Glen drive the details of the deal—since they had the right of first refusal. I had a problem with that, and Societe was leading me to believe they didn't need all the terms that Rose Glen did. Because Rose Glen was the small fish on this deal, I was trying to get them to go along with the terms that Societe would accept. But it didn't happen. Rose Glen was digging in.

In general, Societe Generale was probably more of a longer-term holder of the stock, whereas Rose Glen was driven to more short-term results, and were looking for favorable and early trading status. Societe was more flexible on this issue, which is why we were pushing in this direction. But we couldn't get Rose Glen to agree. This would haunt us later.

While all this was going on, Larry Goldfarb and his firm were also real active, and had provided us with a letter of intent for a different deal. I tried to position it that rather than be a replacement for Shoreline's deal, it could be a supplement since I knew in a few months we would need additional financing. But Larry didn't seem to think that would work out. He wanted to replace Shoreline, his former partner and employer. In the heat of the battle, and with the short time fuses we were working under, we just weren't able to get together on a deal. But in my gut, I still feel there might have been something there. Larry was a solid guy.

This now brought the total capital raised to about $95 million, to the best of my accounting. This total included $68.2 million in equity, and $26.5 million of debt. Up to this point, since our first outside round of financing during 1994, we had closed on 16 different transactions, for an average per transaction of $6 million. Every 3.75 months, for five years, we had been closing an average of $6 million.

That's why I was sometimes so restless and intense. I have yet to meet anyone who has been through this many successful, consecutive financing transactions on a start-up venture.

One of the things to remember in the financing transactions is that not all of the money goes to the venture. There are transaction fees, which go to pay the lawyers, accountants, dealmakers, and investment banking firms. Up until now, of the $95 million, we had paid out about $7 million in transaction fees, which on average was about a half-million dollars per transaction. Some entrepreneurs didn't like writing out these checks. I always wrote them out with a smile—it means we had a successful closing. A cost of doing business. We had the chance to live to fight another day.

• • •

I didn't know this at the time, but that was the last round of financing we would ever close for our venture. In eight months it would be over.

# 38

## *Surviving Road Rash*

Our shareholders' meeting—really, the 2nd Annual Excelsior-Henderson Shareholders' Reunion and Bikers' Barbecue—turned out to be another major event. Since this was now our second year for the Reunion, in essence we were able to learn a lot from the prior year reunion, and retained most of the same strategy and implementation. This is where the seasoning of the Road Crew and the company was becoming more visible to me. For the first shareholders' meeting, I had to be significantly involved since it was the first time our organization was handling this. Now, we had created a precedent, and for the second year, I needed only minimal involvement in the planning. I just had to make sure I was there, and prepared for my part.

We held the Shareholders' Reunion on Saturday, June 5th, and the weather gods were being very cooperative. We had a beautiful, warm, sunny day, with a gentle breeze blowing through the large tents keeping the crowd comfortable. Similar to the year before, we had a crowd of about 5,000 people. That is a large crowd for a shareholders' meeting. We had shareholders attending from all over the United States, and this year they were treated to a few new things. We provided nearly 400 demo rides on our new production Super Xs over a four-hour period, and we also opened up the factory for tours. At the Reunion, we launched the first official factory tours, and we had about 4,000 people go through the factory. It was a busy day, and the militia Road Crew did an excellent job. Whether a person was paid salary or hourly, everyone was a volunteer on this day, and we all worked side by side.

We had a new commemorative shareholder T-shirt, "Reignite The Glory," and we sold about 3,500 of them and were able to donate $7,000 to a local charity. We also had our barbecue lunch catered by the local Hutton's Café, and the Belle Plaine High School football players, dressed in Excelsior-Henderson T-shirts, assisted in directing the parking, along with the local police force and State Patrol.

With the assistance of one of our marketing firms, under the lead direction of Ron Sackett (formerly on our Advisory Board), we put together quite a unique 1998 Shareholder's Handbook. In most companies, they call this the annual report, but true to our characteristic, we were different, and renamed it the Shareholder's Handbook. The cover was done in flat black, with a red pinstripe, similar to one of the paint schemes on our Super X, and we had each handbook printed with its own Serial Number, and an actual motorcycle part—Part Number 6899-0008, the oil filter cover plate—riveted to the cover. The title theme of the year for the handbook was, "More Than The Sum Of Its Parts." Ron later told me that he entered the Handbook in a yearly marketing contest held in Minnesota, and it won a coveted award for best annual report.

We had some pretty unique shareholders and at these shareholder events we had attendees who drove up in their Mercedes and crisp golf shirts, and bikers who rode halfway across the country to attend. And they would all mingle well together. There was a common bond; and titles, and formalities, and the size of one's shareholdings were irrelevant. Everyone was equal in importance, as they were all shareholders, even if they owned one share, which several did.

In total, we had about 16,000 shareholders, and had investors from 16 different countries—from Australia to Germany, from the Czech Republic to the Cayman Islands, and from France to Japan. Here in the United States, we had investors from all fifty states, including the District of Columbia. We were well represented throughout the entire world.

Because we were a Minnesota based company, a significant number of our shareholders did reside in Minnesota. About 36% of our shareholders were from the state, with most of the remaining 64% being from the rest of the United States. When I first reviewed these numbers I was surprised. I didn't really know that we had such a wide investor audience from throughout the entire country.

And we had a broad range of investors, from investments over a million dollars, to investors that bought just one share. Oftentimes when I was meeting or speaking with a shareholder, there was no way I could accurately discern between the varied spectrums. I had learned not to make any judgments, as oftentimes I would be mistakenly surprised.

Whereas most publicly held companies have a disproportionate amount of their stock held by institutional investors, we were the opposite and nearly exclusively held by private individual investors—known as retail investors—with the exception of Rose Glen and Societe Generale, as our primary institutional investors. Like one would mathematically expect, we had some private owners with large holdings, and some private owners with less. Excluding any insider

Hanlon family holdings, of which my holdings were now about 12%, 10% of our investors held 60% of our stock, and 25% of our investors held 77% of our stock. Conversely, what this means is that 75% of our investors held just 23% of the company, and all of these investors held 500 shares or less. Put another way, 75% of our shareholders held 500 shares or less. We had a lot of grassroots investors that probably didn't own any, or many, other stocks.

Our stock price was hovering from around $6.25 to $7.00 per share, just slightly below our IPO price of $7.50 two years earlier. A few months earlier, in early February, right around the time we launched production, our stock hit an all-time high of nearly $11 per share. We weren't sure what to exactly make of the stock price, as it was impossible to control or predict. We just went about our business, and tried to respond to as many rumors as we could. There were always an incessant amount of rumors, and our Yahoo investor chat board was one of the most active. We had several thousand postings, and we never knew how many of them were legitimate. I am sure our competitors and critics were having fun on there, particularly when the postings were anonymous.

• • •

Just before the start of the Shareholders' Reunion, I had driven to the factory with my family in my 1940 Packard. Before the Reunion was ready to launch, we were up in my office overlooking the rapidly growing crowd. I was slightly preoccupied, as I usually was, but this time I had something different on my mind. I was in rough shape. A few days earlier I had two black eyes, and now I was down to one black eye, one bloodshot eye that was slightly yellow, and about a half-dozen stitches just below my left eye. Plus, I could hardly move.

Twelve days earlier, on the evening of May 24th, while riding one of our production Super Xs, I cleaved a deer on my way home. It was a Monday, and we had invited the national media to come and experience our company and our motorcycles; we must have been entertaining over two dozen local, national, and international journalists. Later that day, after we all adjourned from the meetings and the riding, I worked in my office until about 9:00 p.m., and then I thought I needed to get home. It was my youngest son's birthday—Hayden was turning two—and I had already missed his party—bad dad. As I was leaving my office, I noticed a lot of motorcycle apparel on the floor as a result of that day's media rides. I don't like a mess, so I thought, *hell, why don't I just put all this stuff on.* I donned my helmet, several sweaters, my leather jacket, and leather gloves. Normally, I would never wear all this. I had so much stuff on I could hardly move.

I took my usual route home from the factory in Belle Plaine, then northeast to Jordan and on to Prior Lake before making my way through Lakeville and into Burnsville, where I live. I was just passing the McDonald's restaurant in Prior Lake doing about 50 mph when, holy shit, a deer jumped out from the darkness and landed right in front of my motorcycle. I had zero reaction time. But in my mind, I had planned this out a long time ago. I knew the first thing to do, and instinct took over. I said, "Lord save me," as I was going down. I didn't know what my next thought might be, or if I would have one.

The next thing I knew the bike was crashing to the ground, and I instinctively knew to hang on—again I had played this out for years in my mind. My head crashed against the pavement—I later learned I cracked my helmet—and the bike and I skidded down the pavement about 250 feet. I stayed with the bike most of the way, partly on it, and periodically it was on me also. After my head hit the pavement, my face was scraping the pavement, but I remembered to lift my head and let my leather jacket take the scraping. Sparks flew all around me.

In an instant, it was over. The bike was laying on its side. I immediately got up, just to see if I could. I looked down the road, and the deer was dead. Dead. I killed a deer on a motorcycle. Damn thing. *Now I'm going to miss seeing my son on his birthday.* I had skidded from McDonald's to the Dairy Queen. Only now everything seemed different to me. Blood was running into my eyes, and they felt weird. I put my weird-feeling hand up to my weird-feeling face, and felt something else weird. My safety glasses had broken and were embedded in my face. I didn't know what else to do, so I just pulled them out.

I was standing feebly at the roadside next to my bike. It was in the way on the road. Cars weren't stopping. So I tried to move the bike. My arms wouldn't work. Approaching cars would slow down, nearly stop, and then curve slowly around the bike, and me, and then accelerate out of there. I don't know why, but I felt like I was in the twilight zone. Nobody was stopping. Just slowly driving by and looking at me. For a moment, I thought I was having an out-of-body experience. I even tried to flag a few motorists down, but to no avail. Same result. I reached for my cell phone, and it wasn't there. Just my cell phone holder. Later, I found it smashed on the pavement. I needed help.

I looked around, and about 100 yards up the road was a Holiday gas station. I knew that station well. I bought a lot of gas from them. I decided to walk to the station. When I entered the station things seemed fuzzy, and I was bleeding, and in a bit of a trance. The register area was busy, and everybody was ignoring me, so I waited in line. I was about the sixth customer. Finally, when my turn arrived, I stepped in front of the cashier. Without looking at me she said, "Can I help you?"

I wasn't thinking too fast, so my reaction was delayed. When I didn't say anything, she looked up at me and began repeating her question—and then she stopped, and I got scared. She looked like she saw a ghost. Her demeanor immediately changed, and she put her hands up to clasp her face, but all I could think of saying was to call an ambulance. She called the police, and I walked back to my bike. I think.

For what seemed like an eternity, but I later learned was only a few minutes, the police arrived, and subsequently an ambulance. As I was sitting in the ambulance, the young lady attendant took my vitals and asked the standard questions. She recognized my name, and when it came to my middle name, she just said, "I'm not going to ask your middle name, I'll just say it is 'Lucky' instead." I smiled. I did feel lucky.

Fortunately, the hospital they took me to was just a couple of miles from my house. By the time we reached the emergency room, my muscles were already getting stiff. I didn't feel like I had any broken bones. Probably all the protective clothing I was wearing helped. After being stitched up and placed under hospital observation for a few hours, I finally called home to my wife Carol about 2:00 a.m. I didn't like having to wake her up in the middle of the night and tell her the news, but she was pretty good about it. I thought about walking home, but my muscles and joints were too sore. I had taken quite a tumble down the highway, and it was going to take some time for my body to recover.

The next morning, I felt like a hundred-year-old man. But I had a lot to do, and was at the factory by 9:30 in the morning. By then, some of the Road Crew were already headed out to pick up the bike from where it had been trucked. According to our engineers, the bike and frame held up damn well. They said it was a good crash test, and they got busy analyzing the bike. Sometime later, the bike did get repaired and subsequently sold internally—I heard the bike was nicknamed "The Deer Slayer."

• • •

As the Shareholders' Reunion was getting underway, I was still physically in pretty rough shape. I hadn't ridden a motorcycle since the crash—not that I didn't want to, but I couldn't. My left hand and shoulder couldn't pull in the clutch and hold the bike up. But for the Reunion, I was scheduled to ride into the large football field sized tent along with my wife. I wasn't sure if I could do that, and I was afraid I might drop the bike in front of thousands of people, or worse, not be able to control the bike and accidentally head toward the crowd. That wouldn't look very good for a leader of a motorcycle company to do that. I popped a few more aspirin, smiled at Carol, and said let's go. When we got to our bike, I threw my leg over the seat, put on my black felt beret and dark sunglasses, gave the thumbs-up sign to a few of the bystanders, and hit the starter button. The bike roared to life, and so did I. Carol jumped on the back, I shifted it into gear, and the bike leapt forward. The show must go on.

# 39

## *Slow Down, Dangerous Curves Ahead*

At our Board of Directors meeting on Thursday, July 22nd, the overall status of the company was generally upbeat—at least for a start-up venture. We had gotten through our first major hurdles of launching production, and instituting a severe component cost reduction project. Our weekly production rate was continually increasing to a current rate of just over 100 motorcycles a week, translating already to an annual run rate of $85 million in revenue.

As the CEO and Chairman, I was always in charge of preparing for these Board meetings, and presiding as Chairman at the meeting. I had done this since the inception of the venture, and usually these meetings lasted about four to six hours. We were meeting in the Big X boardroom in the factory headquarters. We had named all our conference rooms and cafeteria from company and motorcycle industry lore. We had rooms named *American X, Excelsior, Henderson, Sturgis, Cortland Avenue, Ignatz,* and for our finance department, the *100 mph* room.

One of the items I reviewed with the Board was our weekly flash report. Each day I got a quick report in the morning on the status of our production, and each week, by 8:30 Monday morning, I had the Weekly Flash Report—stamped confidential—on my desk giving an overview of the entire status of the company. It was a one page operating statistics report that summarized the activity of the company on the previous week, the month-to-date, and then year-to-date, with the actual performance compared to the original budget, and also to the current forecast. The main areas of focus on the flash report were our units produced, units shipped, bill of materials, inventory, revenue by product line, and headcount by functional area. We distributed this report to all of the management Team so they would have a grasp of the entire business. During June, we had revenue of nearly $6 million, and we had already reduced components costs by $2647, or 19% per unit, which for the month of June was a million-dollar cost reduction. We were now heading on the right track, and we were all reasonably confident of the future, providing we were able to get our next round of financing, which at this point in time we were projecting we would. Our stock price was relatively stable, and was hovering just above $6.00 per share.

I did have concerns though, and I shared them with the Board. We all knew, and we had announced to the marketplace in a press release, that our manufacturing costs were exceeding our initial expectations. Now since the communication and implementation of that issue was underway, we had to deal with the aftermath. It had cost us money to solve our problems. Most problems in business cost money to get solved, and we were depleting unbudgeted funds. On the one hand, I was glad we had the funds since it allowed us to *live to fight another day*, but on the other hand, it was now nearly gone, and would be as we continued marching forward. We needed replenishment.

Only in our case, our unbudgeted spending also had a multiplier effect. The funds were earmarked for our sales and marketing budget, and new product development budget. This was another one of the tough decisions we had to make earlier. When our leader of production finally had determined the actual launch of production, it was four months later than internally projected, and our components costs came in over plan. By my estimate, these two factors combined had the potential to cost our business between $15 and $20 million and we only had $10 million available to cover this problem—that really I was hoping not to spend—unless we had a problem, which we did.

This caused a rapid and unexpected depletion of cash, and we had to rob our budgets in these other departments. But, we knew this did have long-term consequences. We would need to raise money for these areas of our business, or we would have great risk to our distribution channel of dealers and consumers, and also to our new product development area. We were now getting further and further behind in these areas. This wasn't the first time we had to rob these budgets, and our marketing department was getting familiar with it—they never complained too loudly as we were all on the same Team. Someday soon, we knew the priority would and should be on the marketing and sales budget, but when push comes to shove, until you have a high-quality product the funds must be allocated to the product first. We didn't have enough funding to accomplish both at the same time.

At the end of the day, I knew that if we ever ceased to exist, the stories would go on for years on the "what-ifs" or "what caused" the problems. I didn't want it to be a matter of product quality. I have always believed in putting out a good quality product. I more or less believed that it would take an inordinate amount of time and money to sell a new motorcycle that didn't work well—therefore as a risk-saving measure, we needed to have a solid quality motorcycle. If it wasn't, the bad publicity and negative consumer reaction could be harmful, and probably devastating to a start-up venture. Fortunately, we did have a good quality product, which gave us a good base to launch from, and we hoped we could continue to march forward, and continue to fund the business.

We also discussed the status of our executive searches. We had three separate searches in process, and retained the nationally ranked firm of Russell Reynolds to search for a President, and a CFO. We retained a local firm for the search for a VP of Sales and Marketing. It seems that these searches always took longer than hoped, and previously we didn't need to use search firms at this level. Earlier, we had recruited primarily from our advisory network, but now being publicly held, we were being held to more scrutiny on each particular executive position, and we didn't want to have any perceived false starts. Although candidly, if we weren't publicly held, I believed there was some good local talent for a start-up venture—except they didn't have the national name recognition along with a business pedigree that some place a value on.

The one item concerning me the most was the status of our distribution channel—our dealers. Many times over the last several years, due to budget constraints or staffing constraints, we had to short-change this area. At the time, it didn't matter in the short-term, only the long-term, but now the long-term was starting to arrive. In addition to this, there was ever-increasing pressure being put on our dealers and prospective dealers. Unexpectedly, but maybe expectedly, some OEM manufacturers were putting significant heat on their dealers to not take on our OEM line of motorcycles. We had expected some of this, but the issue was now rising above what we had expected, or should tolerate.

Some of the OEMs were making this issue a little more serious than they should have, most notably Honda, Yamaha, and Harley-Davidson. Periodically, Polaris would have some comments, but our distribution channel was so different from theirs, we had little to no overlap—by design. For some reason, Harley continued to put up the strongest fight on this issue, but it is always hard to prove, particularly if you are the little guy—which we were. Over the years, the vast majority of dealers in the United States that sold Harleys had dropped or not added any other lines of motorcycles. By law, they had the option to sell other brands, but for a couple of reasons they chose not to. Some simply preferred to only sell American motorcycles, and since there were no other independent American OEM motorcycle manufacturers, Harley was the only game in town—or was until we arrived. Now, some of the finest dealers in the country that primarily sold Harleys, were also interested in selling our OEM brand. For many, it was a natural fit.

Back at Harley-Davidson headquarters, however, this was something new to them. Nobody there ever had to compete against another OEM American brand. They had the entire playing field to themselves. They did not have an American OEM threat on their soil for nearly a half-century, and they apparently didn't like having us in the marketplace. Privately, I would think, *Move on, and get used to it. The monopoly is now over.* Instead, it is an oligopoly—either way they still have the major advantage. On several occasions, our field reps encountered strong resistance from our prospective dealer because the dealer had been forewarned by the OEMs, particularly Harley, to not take on our line. Of course, this was seldom said in this exact manner. Usually it was a suggestion, of sorts, that if they wanted to stay in good graces with their current OEM they had better not allow themselves to have any diversions, or distractions—clearly translated to the dealer that it was in their best interest to not work with us.

At one point it got so obvious, that at one of the Harley-Davidson annual dealer meetings, they brought in a guest speaker to specifically talk about us, and reinforce the position of Harley regarding dealers not adding our OEM motorcycle line. They couldn't have found anybody better, and they knew it. They brought in John Wycoff, a long-time motorcycle industry wag. I have never met him, nor spoken to him, nor had he ever stepped one foot into our company, but like some, he knew all about it. He had been one of our most vocal public, and private, critics since he had first learned of our project. Even though several times I had tried to contact him and left messages, he never got back to me. He had been frequently quoted about our project—negatively of course, and all for free as he would volunteer it up as an expert. Only now this time, he dialed it up—he was now a paid expert. After that meeting, I heard from several of our dealers and prospective dealers that were fuming. Not only were they being directed, which was illegal, but it was their business, not somebody else's to tell them what to do. They were, and are, independent dealers, protected by Federal and State automotive and motorcycle franchise law. But alas, we all also knew, how do you fight the 800-pound gorilla? That has a near monopoly? You had better have a good plan, with a lot of money.

After another incident, I decided I had enough. I picked up the phone and dialed direct into the CEO of Harley-Davidson. His assistant recognized my name as we had previously met and conversed, and I asked her to transfer me in, which she did. After a few moments of introductory greetings, I quickly and directly got to my point. I expected him to deny these actions, but instead he didn't. He acknowledged they had a legitimate concern about their vendors and dealers working with us, and instead simply reworded some of the comments I had mentioned to him. I believed they were on a legally slippery slope, and I could tell that he disagreed. He was of the staunch opinion that he believed that a vendor or dealer to Harley would not have ample resources to also work with us, and he needed to protect the interests of his company. This didn't assuage me one bit, and even though we were and always have been cordial to each other, we agreed that we would both disagree on these issues. And I still do. I expected this venture to be tough, and to take a few hits below the belt, but this was too much. I knew I would be ready for this someday.

In addition to the file I was keeping on the impact of Harley to our vendors, I also had my growing file labeled FTC Issues-Dealers. This was another time I operated under the philosophy, *I will prepare myself, and someday my time will come*. I couldn't allow anyone to do this.

•••

Early in the evening, just after we adjourned the Board meeting, I rushed to our production area to get the latest daily report. Production was good, but our shipments were down. Some dealers had called in and asked for us to hold shipments. When I rode my motorcycle home that night, I thought I had better check that out in the morning.

The next day, a few more called. And then it happened. I later learned that while we were in our Board meeting, some dealers started calling and asking to have their shipments delayed. In fact, someone from the dealership of a Board member had called that same day, during the Board meeting, and also had requested to have shipments held. None of this was ever brought up to me during the meeting, until just now. I didn't know what the problem was, but quickly found out.

There is a lot of pressure to perform to the expectations of the marketplace and shareholders when you are a publicly held company, and we had committed to the market that we would sell about 4,500 motorcycles during the calendar year, for about $75 million in revenue. We had made this projection long before we launched production, and now we had started production late. After consulting internally, we decided we did have the ability to make up the shortfall for the later production start, and so we were earnestly ramping up production—it was starting to rumble—and at a greater rate than our distribution channel had expected.

On average, for the first year we had projected to ship about 2 bikes per dealer per month, and just a few months into production we were at over double that rate. And the dealers didn't like it. They hadn't planned to sell them that fast, and most couldn't. In addition, we'd had to rob our sales and marketing budgets earlier, and the impact was being felt. We were behind in adding dealers, and in bringing them up to speed via training and support, and even signage in the dealerships. Most dealers did not have a sign outside their business indicating they were an Excelsior-Henderson dealer. With limited resources, we had been focusing a lot of our company energy on the product and production, and after a welcome reprieve of a month, this next issue was confronting us.

Only now, we didn't have the financial reserve to immediately draw from. We were in the early phases of a financing transaction, and seldom can you close on any financing while in this condition. You either need to raise your capital before you know of any problems, or after you have solved any, but not in the middle of identifying it. This is one of the basic rules of financing, and for the most part we had avoided this issue. But now it was staring me in the face.

Had we been privately held, we would simply go about solving our problems, which is challenging enough. Being publicly held though requires us to tell the world of our problems via a press release, and to not gloss over them. This is where the death spiral can begin if you are not careful, and even if you are, it can still happen as some of the media reaction—or overreaction—is out of your control and the word, like a wildfire, will spread. With little regard for the real truth. This in turn will also drive down the stock price, which can make new equity financing nearly impossible.

As soon as you announce a problem, the critics and competitors pounce on it—and won't let go of it—and immediately strengthen any advantage they already have. We were a company on the ropes, and had been for some time because we were a start-up venture—but we were potentially publicly disclosing too many issues at the same time. By deciding to do the right thing of making a public announcement, we also knew full well this would make solving the problem more difficult, and potentially impossible—a self-fulfilling prophecy. Individually, the problems could have been resolved on their own. Collectively, they could, and would, cause more problems.

Volunteering to make the public disclosures was an easy decision to make since it was the right thing to do, but it was a tough decision as it could be setting our destiny. It would get intensified.

# 40

## *Burning Rubber In Beulah*

Sturgis was looming on the horizon, and for a few days it was going to be a welcome opportunity to check things out and get a pulse reading firsthand out in the marketplace with our dealers and customers. I loved the rallies for this. The chance to talk directly with thousands of people, and to observe hundreds of thousands of bikers reveling in the enjoyment of the motorcycle industry. Most casual observers would never guess that during 1999 the U.S. motorcycle industry was well over a ten billion dollar industry, which grew during 2001 to nineteen billion dollars. A huge industry.

On Friday, August 6th, we had a group ride from our factory and left for Sturgis riding our Xs. We made the traditional overnight stop in Mitchell, South Dakota, on Friday night, and late Saturday afternoon we rolled into Sturgis. Even though the rally had yet to officially start on the following Monday, true to tradition, it was already well underway.

On Monday, August 9th, we unveiled our new model year 2000 Super X at One-Eyed-Jack's Saloon in Sturgis. That same day, in Deadwood, we unveiled another new model, our new Deadwood Special. Throughout the entire week, we were providing demo rides at our site in Sturgis, and we were constantly busy from dawn to dusk. Nearly every day, we opened early and closed late. Another of our growing traditions. Over the course of five and one-half days, it was not unusual for us to have 10,000 visitors to our Excelsior-Henderson eXperience display. I believe in the concept of working harder and longer than the competition, even if it is just two minutes a day. Open one minute earlier, and close one minute later. It shows the right attitude.

Even though we had not focused a lot on newer models, we were able to quickly come up with newer models. That was part of our production design concept of having a platform bike. Once we had a bike in production, in theory and for the most part in practice, we would never need to completely design a 100% new bike. We would always be able to use some parts of the previous model, as that is the beauty of manufacturing, especially if you plan for it from a production platform concept—which we did. From our original Super X, we knew we would be able to get about nine different models from this platform by only changing about 5% to 15% of the bike. And if we offered multiple colors per model, we could have a fairly broad product line pretty fast, which I believed we needed to do. We didn't want to be a one-trick pony.

On Wednesday, August 11th, we were scheduled to do some burnouts in Beulah, Wyoming, just across the border from South Dakota. In Beulah, over the last few years, the tradition in this very small town of about a dozen people was to stage burnouts on the main drag, and thousands of bikers would descend on this small town. But word of this event had spread to the authorities, and they were doing a good job of preventing any of the unauthorized melee. Finally, not to disappoint the crowd, a few of us got permission to do burnouts at the local fuel station. Several of us grabbed our Xs, and rolled them into the station. The crowd was already about 50 rows deep, and we lit them up. Smoke from the burnt rubber of the tires billowed high in the air, until we were lost in the smoke. With the straight pipes on the Xs, they just roared. I stopped before my tire blew so I could take a careful ride back to Sturgis and get a new rear tire put on. I had some tires that didn't last more than a half-day, and our Road Crew Team was always good about replacing them for me. It was a good strong showing for our Xs, as seldom could you do this with a new Harley. It might not reliably survive the brutal beating.

Some guys at the burnouts also grabbed their Harleys and tried to light them up. With stock bikes, they were really struggling, and most times it required someone pouring water—or beer—on the pavement to help them get started. And then look out. The bikes and riders were usually a little unwieldy, and anything could happen.

Thursday, August 12th, we had our now Annual Excelsior-Henderson parade, and we paraded our Xs down Main Street Sturgis. If you have never been down Main Street during the Sturgis Rally, you have missed an opportunity of a lifetime. The crowds are so large you can hardly move, and the street is shut to traffic—except motorcycles. Motorcycles only. Lined up and down the street, as far as the eye can see. For the parade, we would have police escorts, and they would clear a path for us. I fired up our 1931 Super X, and rode that as we led the parade. After we tore up Sturgis, we headed to our annual VIP party in Deadwood. Only our VIP parties weren't the normal VIP type get-together. It was Grassroots-VIP—GVIP. Anybody and everybody that was a loyal EH aficionado was welcome, and we all celebrated together, as EH Aficionado GVIPs. Even my buddy Tiger from Milwaukee, and his buddy Dennis made it.

# 41

## *Turning Around The Wrong Way On A One-Way*

Just before we left for Sturgis, we delayed releasing our second quarter numbers until our return, and our share price was reacting unfavorably. I had conducted via teleconference an analyst conference call on August 5th in which I went through a summary on the status of the company, letting the analysts know we would be releasing our final numbers on August 17th. They didn't treat the delay as good news. When we left for Sturgis, our stock was trading at around $5.00 to $5.50 per share, and by the time we returned and released our second quarter results, the stock price had dropped to an all-time low of $3.50 per share. This was going to make it exceedingly difficult to raise money when our stock price was declining, and no one could forecast when it might bottom out and stabilize.

• • •

Under the depressed conditions of our stock price, and in the middle of arranging further financing, we decided to put a hold on our searches for a President and CFO as our recruiters were indicating it was nearly impossible to recruit under the current situation. Their candidates were coming from more stable companies, and viewed us as too risky. We also put a hold on the search for a VP of Sales and Marketing, and decided to hire someone from the industry that we had known for several years. We brought aboard Gary Johnson, nicknamed "Jet" due to his earlier experience with Kawasaki during the launch of the JetSki. Back in 1994, Ted Nielsen, one of our early investors and now among our best performing dealers, had introduced us to Gary.

During this same time frame, we once again engaged Shoreline Pacific to secure our next round of financing, and had several meetings and phone calls to kick this off. We were all optimistic since there were no specific reasons not to be. We weren't making perfect forward progress, but we were making progress. And their clients had a lot invested, and had an incentive to continue to help or lose their investments.

But I did have an issue with Shoreline, and I communicated this to them. The previous financing round with them didn't go as well as I would have hoped, and our stock price was doubled then from where it was today. They had an exclusive—the first right of refusal—and they refused to budge from this requirement. Personally, I don't like going back to the same well so frequently, as the story can get stale, and I was desirous of some new blood, so to speak. We still had a great story to tell, and I believed we could generate additional investor interest. But again, they and their clients would hear none of this. They would enforce their exclusive, and I personally felt it would be at our expense. They now had us over the proverbial barrel, and could continue to dictate the terms of the financing and the timing. We had no options to consider, short of ignoring our legal agreement. I was tempted to take our chances, and discussed this with our legal counsel. On the positive, it would give us an option, but the negative would be that we could have a lawsuit with current investors, and that doesn't bode well when you are attracting new investors. For the moment, we decided to take our chances and continue on with Shoreline and our current institutional investors. We engaged them for the next round of financing. But I didn't like it.

Since the early launch of the venture, I had always believed that as an independent venture, we had a tough plan to execute, and I was always on the search for a strategic alliance, strategic partnership, or even a sale if it meant allowing the venture to survive. This was one of the reasons our company continued to consistently communicate with leaders from other more established companies. Since we were low on cash, I again contacted several prospective strategic partners to determine if they might have interest in some involvement, or an outright purchase of our company. I reviewed with our Board the conversations we had with Bombardier Corporation of Canada, and Arctic Cat, Polaris, Ducati, and Harley-Davidson. So far, other than Bombardier and Arctic Cat, there didn't seem to be any interest other than curiosity, and for the two firms that expressed early interest, they also let me know they couldn't offer much hope—but some. They just agreed to investigate it some more, and arrange for the next round of meetings. Well, it wasn't a quick no, and there was a ray of hope.

• • •

Our primary issues inside the company were adding new motorcycle models, and improving our distribution channel—every facet of it. From adding more dealers to improving our training and support. We had allowed the channel to be undersized compared to our current production rate, and we needed to both increase our distribution channel capacity, and now decrease our production rate to match our distribution channel sizing. As our product offerings and distribution channel would grow, we could then once again increase our production rate. As logical as this may all seem, oftentimes in the heat of the battle, this was a new, and unanticipated battle plan. This needed to be quickly thought through, and then implemented. Bottom line, we were going to need to adjust the structure of the company.

For years, my analysis determined we should project that each dealer would have the ability to sell about 2.0 bikes per month during the first year, on average. Not everyone agreed with me on this, and instead we were now shipping an average of 4.5 bikes per dealer per month, and the formula was not working. After an intense debate, of which I was real pleased with the end agreement, we decided we would forecast that each dealer going forward would receive an average of 1.5 bikes per month. Their initial average request was 2.0—we had been shipping 4.5—and now we would ship 1.5. In general, this was sound logic, which we all agreed to as a new goal. Given that we had about 110 dealers at the time, this averaged out to about 170 bikes shipped per month—or 40 per week—as a new forecast, and as we increased our model selection and dealer count, we would then increase production.

The bad news in all this: it was about half of our current production run rate. That meant we were overstaffed, and our revenue would now be less than initially projected. Accordingly, we had to deliver some bad news, publicly. Privately, this should not have been a surprise. Our business model was still valid. The industry was growing, and our market acceptance was growing. And we were making forward progress. But since we were publicly held, and we didn't have the fuel to move the army as fast up the hill as we had projected—we needed to publicly disclose this. Then prepare for the repercussions this would bring to the business. When you report a problem, it, in turn, increases the intensity of it. Again, this could cause a death spiral, when in fact it really shouldn't. But the investment market, and periodically some media, report in such a manner that there is an overreaction.

On Thursday, September 2nd, we announced to the marketplace we would reduce our Road Crew staff by 97 people, and retain a staff of 119.

There is no other way to describe this, other than it sucked—sorry about the language. Trading was halted on our stock at 1:45 p.m., and did not resume until the next morning. We also announced two additions, from a consulting company, the Platinum Group. We appointed Jack T. as our President, and Terry A. as our part-time CFO. The company was to some degree put on autopilot—but at a much lower altitude—while the financing was sorted out. Other than continuing to add dealers, we had minimal capital to apply to any other part of our business.

Given the limited time frame in which to communicate and implement these changes to the company, and the fact we had put our searches on hold, I had been desirous of outside input. As an organization, we were in some uncharted waters, and were looking for input to validate what I believed we needed to do.

We quickly consulted with our Board of Directors, several of our investors, advisors, and some of my personal business confidants. We were light on executive talent, which is why we initiated the searches in the first place. Upon posing the question to this group, I was given the names of several consulting firms that we might be able to engage on a short-term basis to assist us. The two primary areas we immediately desired to fill were the President and Chief Financial Officer positions. In addition to being the CEO and Chairman, I was the current CFO—as I had been for most of the lifecycle of the venture, and I was desirous of help.

After a few quick meetings—and I am embarrassed to admit, because of timing constraints, after limited due diligence, which is highly unusual for me—during the month of August we initially engaged the firm of the Platinum Group in Eden Prairie, Minnesota. For a fee of nearly $30,000 per month, plus 428,340 stock options, on an interim independent-contractor arrangement, they would provide a President and a part-time CFO, and some marketing assistance to the company and our new VP of Marketing and Sales. On paper, this should work, except for when you add in the dynamics of the personalities, our venture, and the industry we were in.

We put together the new interim business plan, which basically validated what we already knew. We would reduce our staff by about half, and reduce and stabilize our production rate at about 40 bikes per week going forward. At the same time, the plan was to increase and improve our distribution channel. And we needed to raise additional capital to execute the plan and stay in business. Since all of this was fairly logical, we were all in harmony, and agreed to this arm-in-arm. As we shook hands and agreed to the new plan, I was pleased with the new talent we had added to our Team. I liked how they used the word *"we."* This was what *"we"* had decided to do.

Our new President and new CFO, Jack and Terry, were pretty pumped about our new plan. Real confidant of adding a lot of dealers real quick, and they liked using the words *"turnaround"* and *"restructuring."* I didn't mind the words, but was mostly interested in results—the actions. Even though I would find out later they had no experience in running a start-up venture or publicly held companies, they repeated numerous times to me how much Wall Street loves turnarounds and restructurings. I was skeptical. Maybe for seasoned companies that needed this, but for start-up ventures, they were always in a turnaround and restructuring mode—that is part of the issue of lack of predictability of a start-up—and is a problem. After the announcement, our stock closed down by nearly 30%, to $2.50 per share. They didn't say anything to me about this, nor I to them. I just made notes in my logbook.

On Wednesday, September 8th, I brought Jack and Terry to New York to meet with Guillaume Pollet at Societe Generale. Since we were working together on the next financing deal, I wanted everyone to have a chance to meet one another face to face. From there, they decided to continue on their own to meet with Rose Glen in Pennsylvania—they had asked me to not join them. Upon their return, I also teed-up meetings with any potential strategic alliances, primarily with the executive management of Arctic Cat, Polaris, and Bombardier.

In all of these meetings, I was beginning to notice a pattern. I was in the company of some rather important people. And some egos. From previous numerous interactions, I knew all of the people from the other organizations, and frankly, I had a lot of respect for them. We may not have always agreed, but for the most part I do think we shared mutual respect. We were all busy people, and in these meetings we were focused on the issues at hand—sometimes humorously and sometimes seriously.

However, my new guys from the Platinum Group had a new way of conducting business in these meetings. They always seemed to feel the need to lead and be dominant—not only to me, but to everybody in the room. And then the cell phone issue. They would leave them on. In the middle of a conversation, whether they were speaking or listening. If their cell phone rang, they answered it. I remember one specific meeting with Tom Tiller, the new CEO of Polaris. He was in the middle of a statement to our group—in our Big X boardroom at the factory—when Terry's phone rang. Terry didn't even blink, took the phone call and walked out of the boardroom—they did this all the time. Tom paused mid-speech, and looked at me with a knowing look. I liked Tom, even though on the battlefield we were archenemies and competitors. To some degree, I believed we were cut from the same cloth—other than his goals were to build large corporations larger, and mine were to build nothing corporations into larger corporations. There was something missing from these new players, and we all sensed and witnessed it: respect. Something that wasn't missing—big egos.

This other pattern I noticed was the ego part. I'm comfortable admitting I have one, as most people do. And you already know my distinction about the differences between a big ego and a strong ego. For the most part, in my opinion, nearly everyone we worked with— whether a Road Crew member, a supplier or service provider, or a dealer, or even myself—all have strong egos—a confident self-esteem—not big ones. That was one of the things we looked for. But now, I was beginning to feel we had introduced the other type of ego to the organization, and those we interfaced with. I believed I could handle this—as it wasn't new to me—but I was concerned on the impact to our business and relationships.

I generally believe the best way to make someone feel important is to let them be important. I didn't feel the need to one-up somebody, and instead would praise them for their successes. Maybe I was raised this way or had learned it throughout my years, but either way, as an adult, I had made the decision that this is what I believed in. A core value of respect for one another, and what they believed in and accomplished.

After the meeting with the executive members of the Polaris group, including the CEO Tom Tiller, Jack pulled me aside and said, "I'm better than him." I was taken aback, and asked him what he meant. He repeated the statement, and further clarified it for me. "I'm better than Tiller." *Interesting*, I thought. I couldn't, and didn't answer him—I just smiled. When I got back to my desk, I made another entry in my logbook. This was getting interesting.

It was around this time that I finally figured out what the word *"we"* meant. Every time someone from the Platinum Group would use the word "we," admittedly I naively believed it was meant for the Excelsior Team. But instead, "we" meant their own group, and not us together. In many meetings, the Platinum Group staff would use the phrases "us" and "them," and for a while it did perplex me. Finally, I realized it was a relationship of an "us" and "them" mentality. We weren't in the same cockpit. "We" didn't mean "we." It meant "them." I had thought we were all on the same Team.

Over a period of time, from every one of our prospective strategic partner alliances or financing partners, I heard the same thing. The Platinum Group would have to go—either immediately or as a condition of any relationship. I assured them the agreement we had with Platinum allowed us to disengage, when needed.

# 42

## Passing On A Double-Yellow Line

On October 18th, we issued a press release announcing the signing of a letter of intent for prospective financing of up to $4.5 million. The contemplated financing was a convertible preferred debenture, similar to our most recent rounds of financing. I was disappointed with this. We had been asking for $10 million, as I believed any less would have limited benefit to our business, but our new President and CFO believed this was the best amount. They also believed it was important to issue a press release about the letter of intent. I didn't like it. We had never before issued a press release with a letter of intent. Too much can happen during the continuing due diligence and ensuing implementation phase that could potentially derail or significantly change the letter of intent. This was an unneeded risk to our business, in my opinion. Previously, we had only made announcements after we had closed on a transaction.

To make matters worse, they were so sure of the closing date, they put in the press release the transaction would close before November 1st. Of course, they didn't listen to my advice. The first of November came and went—with no financing. Our stock price continued its decline, and hovered around $1.50 per share. As each day continued to be marked off, there was no closing. Weeks earlier, the Platinum Group had held a special meeting with me—offsite—and asked me to keep out of this financing transaction. This was very unusual to me, and personally and professionally I was surprised. But at the same time, I am a team player, and did believe I would observe from the sidelines, for the moment, for the good of the Team—but I was starting to wonder what the Team was. Maybe I could learn something new.

On Wednesday, November 17th, I received an interesting phone call from New York. It was Guillaume Pollet at Societe Generale, who was one of two parties to our contemplated financing in our letter of intent. I was surprised by his phone call, since I had been informed— by the Platinum Group—that he didn't want to talk to me, and I shouldn't with him—and here he was calling me. For some reason, he chose to bypass them, and contacted me directly. He didn't have to say why, and I didn't need to ask. We both knew why.

Even though these were challenging times, we exchanged the customary cordialities, but I could quickly sense he had an active agenda. He was dancing around the issue about the guys from the Platinum Group. I didn't want to let on about any of my own personal observations—hell, I brought their organization in—and I had decided to let others make their own decision. He was concerned about information that he had been provided regarding Excelsior, and the current status of the company, and also about the current status of our strategic alliances conversations. He was seeking to validate what he had been told by them, and apparently something didn't pass his smell test. He wanted my affirmation.

Even though we discussed several items, there were two main areas he was focusing on. He had concern regarding believing what he had been told about the number of dealers we had added and what our real goal was, and he was also interested on when we would complete a strategic alliance with Bombardier. This was a slippery slope. Platinum had not briefed me on what they were telling our financial suitors. Even though that was poor protocol since I was the CEO, as long as we were all speaking the truth, I didn't need briefings, for the moment. But unfortunately, Guillaume knew, and I now knew, he had some wrong information from Platinum about our company. I could tell he didn't want to corner me extensively on these issues, so instead he asked permission to contact a few people that could verify information for him. He knew my style. In all due diligence, I was always an open book. I never had anything to hide, and didn't mind having my comments validated by third parties.

One of the parties Guillaume indicated Societe Generale desired to contact was Bombardier in Canada. By coincidence, Societe Generale had Bombardier as one of their large banking clients in Canada, and had numerous top-level contacts within their organization. Even though he didn't need my permission, he was asking for it to contact them and validate what the Platinum Group represented on the status of our conversations between Bombardier and Excelsior. However, as the CEO, I did tell Guillaume that he was embarking on a path to learn inside information, and that he would be restricted from selling any shares based upon any knowledge he may learn. He assured me he had no plans to sell, but was only validating in order to buy more, and complete the letter of intent. He asked for my direct line, and said he would get back to me directly in the next few days.

The next morning, Thursday, I had a call from Pierre Beaudoin, the President and COO of the Recreational Products Group of Bombardier, located in Montreal, Quebec. I knew Pierre well, and we had met on several occasions. Earlier I had introduced him to the Platinum Group in a special meeting arranged in Canada. He remembered it quite well—as he had similar experiences to the meeting we had with Polaris—and had given me his opinion on a few matters that I was taking under advisement. Pierre indicated Bombardier had a call from Societe Generale, and per his protocol, didn't want the call returned without discussing this with me beforehand. I assured him it was okay to confirm the status of the discussions—we had executed a Non-Disclosure Agreement between our organizations. Which basically was, there were no further discussions currently. We did have them earlier, but Bombardier had put them on hold. We all knew this, and so did the Platinum Group.

But unfortunately, the Platinum Group representatives communicated a different message to our prospective institutional investors. Either the investors must have been sensing it, or they were conducting normal due diligence. It wasn't too hard to predict what might happen. By conducting due diligence they were going to find inconsistencies. Small wonder the Platinum Group didn't want any of the parties talking to each other. We all had a different story. I made more notes in my logbook.

Finally, on Friday, November 19th, at 3:15 p.m. CST, I got a call. On my private line in my office. It was Guillaume Pollet at Societe Generale. He said he'd received a call from his home office in France, and they had decided not to do the deal. And also that Rose Glen wasn't going to do the deal. They were pulling out on us. And that he would no longer expect an exclusive on our financing. We were now free to look somewhere else. He said to relay this message to the Platinum Group, since he didn't plan on calling any of them.

After we disconnected, I took my bottle of water on my desk and threw it hard against the wall. It was a bottle of Evian water. Made in France. I have never drank bottled water from France since. True story.

The next morning, Saturday, I arranged a phone conference with our investment banker, Shoreline Pacific, in California. It was at 9:00 a.m. our time, which put it at 7:00 a.m. their time. Between the rhetoric of the tap dance and the traditional song and dance, basically they had few suggestions. They also agreed to set us free to search for additional financing, and to set aside our previous contractual agreement requiring an exclusive. How nice. A little late—and maybe too late. I held his feet to the fire, and asked him to get moving on some new financing—which he agreed to do.

Two days later, on Monday, November 22nd, late into the day we issued a press release on our third quarter results, and on the status of our financing, which was basically that we needed to explore new options. The release was carefully worded, and didn't exactly say the institutional investors had backed out—we were hopeful to replace them—but it was fairly clear that was the message. It was also the first time we publicly mentioned we were considering strategic alternatives—a sale or strategic partner—which we were. At this point in time, we weren't seriously considering bankruptcy, but without financing it was inevitable. We had known that for seven years, and communicated it as such. We were always just one financing away from bankruptcy, until we achieved our goal of being cash flow positive. Cash flow positive—our Road Crew all wanted that to happen so bad, that if sheer will could make it happen, it would.

There was great debate about including language in our press release about filing for creditor protection. My position was to not bury that in our third quarter release, particularly since we had not seriously considered this option nor had our Board approved for us to pursue it. It seemed premature at the time, and the mere fact of disclosing creditor protection this early might have caused a panic in the market, and an overreaction, and again possibly create a self-fulfilling prophecy that we then couldn't avoid or get out of. The final decision was to leave the language about creditor protection out, as we all came to the conclusion we hadn't adequately considered that option, and that it would do more harm than good to the status of the company. We would announce it if and when we seriously considered it as an option.

I gave our President the go-ahead on the release. Only he had the wrong press release issued. Great. Damage control time. I made another entry in my logbook.

Tuesday morning, we conducted our quarterly conference call with our stock analysts. Present in our Big X boardroom were myself, our internal lawyer and compliance officer, our Director of Finance, and the Platinum Group guys. As usual, I introduced the meeting, and conducted the vast majority of it, as I had for several years. Prior to the conference call, we had prepared our remarks and reviewed them, so we would all be consistent and accurate. Our President was also going to address our analysts. Only he quickly got off subject and began releasing nonpublic information. I was squirming and so was our lawyer, and so was the CFO. Several times we interrupted him, but he seemed to ignore the hint. After the phone conference, we queried him about this, and found out he had no experience in dealing directly with stock analysts. Nor did he take our guidance. I made more entries in my logbook. This was getting dangerous.

Wednesday morning, November 24th, I was in a meeting in downtown Minneapolis when my cell phone began ringing incessantly. I hadn't yet read any of the morning newspapers. One of the daily newspapers had a headline story—**"Motorcycle maker running on empty"**—about our company, and in the first paragraph stated: *"and considering several options, including a reorganization in bankruptcy court."* This sentence was merely repeating what we had incorrectly issued in our press release, and as expected, the avalanche started, and everyone started heading for the exit at the same time. Our stock trading volume increased four-fold from the average, and we lost another 30% in market value. Our stock was now under a dollar.

When I got back to the factory later in the morning, as I walked into our normally upbeat factory, it seemed things were taken down a few notches. Over the last few months I had noticed the Road Crew was slightly on edge, and something new had been developing. When I took my daily corporate pulse-checking walks, for the first time I had begun to notice that an increasing number of Road Crew members cast their eyes downward when we approached. Some of this I felt was normal, given the circumstances, but I also knew they were brave soldiers and had no problem in the past confronting me directly, to my face. Which I respected. Only something was now different.

What I learned in a way was humorous, but had become more of the same of what I was discovering—big corporate politics had invaded, along with the inefficiencies and insecurities that go with it. The Road Crew had been instructed to not converse with me. That the Platinum Group guys were now running the company—of course, it wasn't said in that exact manner, but that was the message that was being delivered. Whether they were or not, it cut against our culture of having the ability to talk to anyone, at any level. The Road Crew had taken to not signing any more shipping crates. I no longer made notes in my logbook on these matters.

The next day was Thanksgiving. This would be an appropriate opportunity to think about a few things over the next few days.

For a lot of combined reasons, the relationship and effectiveness with the Platinum Group was not productive to the company, and not what we expected. Their bold predictions had not panned out. I had observed too many leadership and tactical errors that were inherently costly and distracting to our business—possibly now fatal. Contrary to what was represented to our company when we engaged them, they were inexperienced in certain areas. We had been working with them about four months, and had paid fees of nearly $150,000, and that was enough time to make a judgment. We were looking for them to join the Team, and jump into the boat and grab an oar and start rowing, only it seemed we were rowing from different boats—so to speak. I decided to once again call the senior principal of the Platinum Group, Dean.

Given a different set of circumstances, possibly things could have gone much better. I have no grudge against them, and actually enjoyed working with them under pressure. Every day when they asked me how I was doing, my answer was, "every day above ground is a good day." And I meant it. How bad can it really be when you wake up on the green side of the sod? Our interim CFO, Terry, always chuckled when I answered him. Every day, he knew what my answer would be, but he nevertheless asked the question. It sort of became a bellwether for both of us. I liked him.

Under our former leadership Team I did have concerns about some procedural operational issues, and the issue of accountability—I did believe we could have been doing a better job on our system of controls, and we did see improvement in those areas. Not necessarily cost reductions, but we now had more organization and some improved processes—just like a new President and CFO should be able to do, and they did.

When I never heard back from Dean, I called him again. And I called him again. And I called him again. No word back. When we were signing the contract to engage, he shook my hand and told me he was available 24/7. Finally, his assistant told me he wasn't going to get back to me—Jack and Terry had authority to speak for him. Initially, I thought this was incredulous. But upon reflection, maybe it wasn't. Maybe it was just more of the same. Lip service. Only I had a company to straighten out, and didn't have time for the games. I needed to get back to ensuring a future for the company. Dean never did call back.

# 43

## Lowering The Flag

The investment market was real hot right around this time, and I was just hopeful to be part of it. But the chances were very slim. Raising capital for a bricks and mortar start-up manufacturing company had not been easy, and now the new buzz was the *"clicks and no-mortar,"*—the virtual business. The Internet. Record Internet IPOs were the rage, with phenomenal valuations, and had raised $25 billion, just this year. But alas, we weren't the Internet, and it looked barren on the landscape for a start-up manufacturer. Even though we were a start-up, in the eyes of the investment marketplace, we were called an "old economy start-up." Just like that. I wasn't so sure I knew what that meant. We went from new to old in a blip of the throttle. The investment bankers were asking me if I could make bikes and ship them through the Internet. Hell, I told them, manufacturing is the lifeblood. Nearly everything is manufactured. Even computers, and their expensive suits, and the telephones we were talking on. Even the money they use to buy dinner. But by then, they had hung up on me.

• • •

There wasn't a whole lot of runway left to decide what to do. We had to make some quick decisions. I knew enough that if we ever did need to file a Chapter 11, you want to make sure you do it with money in the bank, since the company needs to operate. Otherwise, it will immediately flow to a Chapter 7, which is liquidation. We had to act fast while we still had operating funds in the bank.

Under the right set of circumstances, I had some confidence that we could put a deal together; there would be some blood and some pain, but the overall patient—the company—would live. At least that was my multifaceted plan. The goal became to attempt a capitalization restructuring outside of bankruptcy, but it would require a lot of cooperation between all parties. Maybe I was naïve, but I had witnessed and been a party to, a lot of cooperation from people—everyday heroes— to bring this venture from a blank sheet of paper to delivering new motorcycles—that customers were buying and tattooing the name on their body. That is really wearing a brand.

With our stock price hovering under a buck, without some type of debt forgiveness, the reality of any new financing was remote—although it was wise to let Shoreline run their game plan in case it worked. But I wasn't hopeful. We were four months into the last deal when it suddenly went awry. It was time for dual tracking.

Debt forgiveness happens all the time when things don't go well. The multifaceted strategic alternative I believed best would be to get all of our stakeholders to give a little, everyone—including me—and we all give equally. If we all cut from 10% to 50% of our holdings, or more—whether it was equity, debt, or creditor payables—that would be better than we could ever hope for in a Chapter 11 or Chapter 7. It would give us the chance to live to fight another day. And by doing this outside of the bankruptcy court, all stakeholders would have more flexibility. In essence, what a new suitor would have the ability to do would be to step in front of any other stakeholder, and gain majority interest of the company, and under a more manageable capital structure.

This was a gamble. It required that all our current stakeholders agree to a reduction, and it required a suitor. We immediately contacted any potential strategic partners we had conversed with in the past, including Harley-Davidson, Polaris, Bombardier, and Arctic Cat. Within just a few days, we either met with them or had conference calls. We were busy and on a mission. Most had little to no interest, and they all indicated that if they did, they would need the company stakeholders restructured, either in a bankruptcy or outside. But either way all stakeholders would need to be restructured. That was fair knowledge, and validation of what we expected. And it was hope that some might be interested.

We also contacted private investment funds, and private wealthy individuals that over the years had expressed interest in the company. We quickly arranged meetings, phone conferences, and continued to present our story. Again, they all agreed, if they were to have any interest, the stakeholders would need to be restructured. Under the current structure, neither a strategic partner nor an investment firm were willing to take a lead position, but several desired to keep close tabs on our developments.

It was time to take our case to our debt holders, especially those that would be most financially impacted if we couldn't secure new financing. Quickly, I contacted all our debt holders, primarily Dakota Bank, Finova, and the State of Minnesota. They were all real nervous about a bankruptcy, as they had also read the paper, and we were in frequent contact anyway. They knew we were in a difficult situation, and were darn curious what we planned to do about it. I didn't like what we were suggesting, but bottom line, the suggestion was: we would all need to take a haircut. I don't know if they didn't take my conversations seriously, but none of them had any support for forgiving any amount of debt, or pushing out payments. In each case, we indicated that without any forgiveness, there was little else we could do. And if we didn't raise new money, my current offer would be the best they would ever see. Ever—at least in my opinion, since none of us had the perfect crystal ball.

Things could only get worse, unless we were to do something about it now. For whatever reason, I had no volunteers agreeing to be wounded. Maybe that was why. Emotionally, sometimes it is better to be forced into a difficult situation, than willingly agree to it. There was no magic wand. We had no volunteers on this one.

Well, we did have a few. Some of our dealers, Road Crew members, vendors, bikers, and current shareholders—all wanting to help in some way, and willing to put in more money. They knew about our growing acceptance in the motorcycle marketplace. On many occasions, I got calls, letters, and had people stopping me on the street, telling me they were buying more stock to help us out. Under a mistaken belief, none of those funds ever went to us, except at the IPO. Afterwards, all funds went to selling shareholders and brokers. The grassroots people wanted to help, but we didn't have a financial instrument available. Plus, I knew it wasn't enough, and it would be fruitless without some debt forgiveness. For it to work, we all had to give together, as a team.

If we could restructure our debt, and dilute our current shareholders and inject cash, we would avoid a crash and start flying again. We now had just over $30 million in sales in the last ten months.

Complicating matters, we were seeking to conserve cash, and had started to miss some payments. We were behind on our December rent, and the building owner had filed an Eviction Summons and Unlawful Detainer with the local District Court—scheduled to be heard on December 30th. We missed our property tax payment. We missed our Finova payment. We missed our State of Minnesota payment. We missed our Dakota Bank payment. Dakota Bank made a run on our bank, New Market Bank, and tried to seize our remaining cash. Luckily, we had alert bankers, and better lawyers than Dakota Bank had, and we stopped them. And we were getting further behind in our payments to our vendors.

And we began to hear reports from our Road Crew Field Sales Team and our dealers, that they were concerned about an impending bankruptcy. Some didn't want to take more bikes, and prospective customers were hesitant about buying an $18,000 product from a start-up company that might file bankruptcy. It was hard to blame them. I couldn't. We weren't going to show false bravado. They had real feelings of being further impacted. We all knew this venture was a sacrifice when we signed on, and most had already given all just out of sheer will to get this far. There was a growing momentum of expecting something bad to happen. They were just waiting for us to stop—we were out of fuel, with no filling station in sight. The self-fulfilling prophecy continuing. With the help of the newly discovered Internet, word was spreading so fast, it was like a wildfire.

It was now on our shoulders. My shoulders. The wagons were circling—and they were no longer our wagons. I was the first man standing seven years earlier. Now, I would be the last man standing. Time to surrender this battle. But not the war. We were all now going to be restructured, whether we liked it or not. I respectfully lowered the flag, and signed the papers. Chapter 11 papers. December 20th, 1999. 9:00 p.m. Then I went home.

• • •

Recently my wife Carol and I were out visiting my folks on the family farm in Belle Plaine, and on the way back to the city, we drove by the former Excelsior-Henderson factory in Belle Plaine.

"Dad," my son Hunter asked, "why don't you work at the motorcycle factory?"

During the years I had been called a lot of things, but of all the names I had ever been called, *"Dad"* was still the best. And the most important. Only it took me a while to figure that out. I had now figured it out.

The motorcycle factory was in my rearview mirror.

"Hunter," I answered, "it's a long story, and I don't know. I'll have to tell you about it sometime. Maybe I will again—someday."

It was then I finally realized. I had a chance to Ride The American Dream. And I still do.

Dreams never die.

# EPILOGUE

## THE LAST RIDE

# EPILOGUE

## Chapter 11—Turning The Heat On

With the company filing for Chapter 11 Reorganization, we were now moving into some uncharted waters. On the one hand I felt rejuvenated, as we would now be able to restructure the company's past debt, with the goal of attracting new investment. We had come too far in the venture to let everything just go, and in my opinion, we were on the cusp of turning the corner. We were in production, had new motorcycle models in the works, and our dealer base was growing. Properly capitalized and restructured, I really believed we had better days ahead. Certainly, better days ahead than when I had launched the company seven years earlier, and had nothing. Now, we had something, only it was at idle.

Simultaneous with the filing, because we didn't have enough capital to continue ongoing operations, we idled the factory and laid off nearly all of our remaining Road Crew. This has got to be one of the most unpleasant tasks in running a business. We retained about a dozen Road Crew, with key skills to keep the business at idle, and the core group that could be valuable to a future re-launch.

On the other hand, I also had concerns. The heat always gets turned up in situations like this. By this I mean that sometimes people become irrational—and sometimes it is those that you least expect. In fact, in tumultuous situations like this, the one thing to expect is to expect the unexpected. With the advent of our bankruptcy petition, due to the perception of possible conflict of interest issues between creditors and counsel, we needed to form a new deal team. This was the part that concerned me the most. We were introducing new senior advisors who had no experience with our company. Granted, we did tap some new talented people, but we lacked the ever-needed continuity that I liked to have on our teams. In addition to my CEO responsibilities, I assumed the role of the CFO, a position I managed for five of the eight years I was with the company.

Shortly after our filing, with the instability of the company we did have a few unexpected management staff that moved on to more stable career environments—it's not surprising—and frankly I didn't have an issue with it. We needed to bring in a new accounting director, which can be a challenging search and position given the status of our company. I immediately started tapping my referral network since we needed someone on short notice, and I contacted Mike Todd, one of my longtime friends from our former employer Honeywell. He suggested an accountant, Gerry Prescott, whom he had worked with previously. Gerry was the perfect hire for us—he had the years of maturity to remain calm and unflappable, with an appropriate dry sense of humor.

Our goal in Chapter 11 was to restructure our equity and debt investments—which basically means that everyone takes a substantial haircut—in order to induce new investments and keep the company viable. In bankruptcy parlance, a Chapter 11 filing is for reorganization with the goal of emerging relatively intact, whereas a Chapter 7 filing is for a prompt court supervised liquidation of the assets.

Since we had idled our factory and laid off most of our workforce, we were skating on thin ice regarding our ability to remain in Chapter 11. Without ongoing operations and new investment, we could quickly move to a Chapter 7 liquidation—which under certain circumstances may have been appropriate. Like primarily if we could not quickly secure additional capital, and if creditors believed they would be better off with liquidation.

New on our deal team was Charlie Burns assisting us with external financing matters; Mike Meyer, a notable bankruptcy lawyer; and Moe Sherman, a top-gun lawyer I had worked with in the past. We assembled an investment summary presentation, and started making the usual phone calls and setting up meetings with prospective suitors. We were receiving some limited interest, but no real endorsers. Since the company was still primarily a start-up venture—and now idled—it did require a fairly significant amount of capital and work to continue. Even though the OEM motorcycle industry is fairly robust, the barriers to entry and remaining in business are daunting.

In my heart, as difficult as it was, I was beginning to sense the best alternative might be for a liquidation of the business to maximize the creditors' position. The main reason I believed this was the financial timing in the marketplace. We were early into the year of 2000 and the Internet sector was still booming, but there were the very early warning signs of the bust. At the time I wasn't heeding any of this since it was out of my bailiwick, but at the same time the events in the financial marketplace were not conducive to our venture. This is what I felt inside. Even though I remained very confident of our business plan, for the first time I began to sense I could not figure a way to successfully finance our way out of this. And I was beginning to witness some irrational behavior.

There was one tremendous thing I did learn at this time. And it all revolved around people. Several of our creditors were very angry—possibly bitter—and some visibly so. Yes, we all lost money—and I am sorry about that—but I was concerned that irrational decisions could be made out of anger. As the Founder and CEO, I was supposed to be the irrational one. In addition, some of my earliest stalwarts headed for the hills at the first sign of trouble; however, an equal number of others seemed to come out of nowhere and who were willing to don the armor and carry on the battle. I came to understand the meaning of the phrase: *When you are in trouble, you will learn who your friends are.*

On February 3rd, 2000, I had a phone conversation that was to change the course of Excelsior-Henderson—and set a new destiny. During the afternoon I conversed with a prospective investor, George Heaton, located in West Palm Beach, Florida. I learned later that the phone conversation was initiated via a recommendation from a former Excelsior executive who was trying to be helpful to our cause.

Previously I had met George Heaton, along with a business partner of his, in Daytona Beach during one of our Bike Week rallies. He was already considered by some to be a somewhat controversial person in the motorcycle industry as he was seeking to consolidate powersports dealerships. Due to some previous business dealings, there had been a few articles within the industry, and being a student of the industry, I had read the articles. Other than that, I had an open mind.

During our phone conversation, I mentioned to George that a Confidentiality Agreement would need to be executed before we could exchange any information. I never wavered from that policy, even when the heat was on. George signed the agreement, and as I would later learn, that was the only agreement he would sign during our bankruptcy process—his signature would become invisible even though his presence would not. Later, he would have others sign the documents.

The long story here would fill a book, and most people wouldn't believe it anyway. That was another thing I learned. In the heat of the battle, some things are so life altering or unbelievable that only those who have been through it could ever understand.

The short story is, *through the involvement* of George Heaton a term sheet was put together whereby E.H. Partners, a newly formed Florida corporation, would buy Excelsior. Being careful in my statements here, what I mean by *through the involvement* is that George never signed any further agreements and claimed to not be a party to any of the companies he represented, yet almost all negotiations and conversations were between our company and him or his lawyers. Later, as a document would need to be signed, a new name would appear as the signatory on the document.

According to those who have had past business dealings with George—and as a matter of public record—during the past two decades he has had major dealings in restaurants, insurance, banking and condominium conversions. Many of those deals have resulted in lawsuits against him.

A common thread to many of those disputes were claims that companies controlled by Heaton would acquire control of a failing company or property with promissory notes, then liquidate the assets and fail to make payments on the notes or other bills.

The summary is, through the involvement of George, E.H. Partners made a proposal, on paper, that in my opinion was too good to be true—at least for the secured creditors. Regarding all the shareholders, including me, the proposal was for all former equity holders to be wiped out.

In essence, E.H. Partners would contribute, or cause to be contributed, $12.5 million and a line of credit for $5 million, in exchange for all of Excelsior stock—yielding a transaction value of nearly $40 million. The part I questioned, though, was that the proposal didn't require our debt holders to forgive any principal amounts of their loans. Essentially, they could remain whole through a bankruptcy, other than for a timing delay in their payment stream. Certainly, this made me look foolish—I had prepared them for write-downs but now they didn't have to take a write-down, and instead had what they considered a bona-fide offer, which they took. I thought the representatives of E.H. Partners were playing the creditors—and shareholders—like a fiddle. My opinion.

I had several concerns with the proposal, primarily with the ability and validity of E.H. Partners. However, my much larger concern was that the proposal, on paper, was so unusually lenient and favorable to the secured creditors, it would thereby halt any other bona-fide offers that might seek to compete with the current proposal. In my view, inherently, no one would or could entertain a new offer, since that offer would need to be higher, and how could it be higher than full payment of principal? The whole thing was so unusual that I didn't expect anyone to take it. But I greatly misjudged—irrational behavior was evident. In times of trouble some just want to believe the knight riding in on a white horse. Who am I to judge, and just maybe I was wrong.

Following customary Bankruptcy Court procedures, a Plan of Reorganization and Disclosure Statement was presented to the creditors and to the court—the shareholders were not allowed to vote on the Plan—and was subsequently approved, with just a few creditors rejecting the plan. Like the City of Belle Plaine, and several of our motorcycle dealers.

There was one near-fatal twist in the plan that was interesting to observe. Under George's request, I had arranged a meeting with him and the representatives of our landlord, Ryan Belle Plaine, which was held in our Big X conference room. Within just a few short hours of the meeting, Ryan's lawyers had done their due diligence and sent a letter to our lawyer stating, "*We are concerned regarding the involvement of George Heaton in this matter. Because of his involvement, we desire to terminate the Lease with Excelsior-Henderson…As part of terminating the Lease, we would oppose assumption of the Lease and confirmation of the Plan of Reorganization.*"

But E.H. Partners was well prepared, and had their own letter. Their lawyers' letter said, among other things, "*As we have previously discussed, Mr. Heaton's current role with E.H. Partners is simply that of an advisor/consultant. Mr. Heaton is currently neither an officer, director nor shareholder of E.H. Partners and it is not contemplated that Mr. Heaton will…*"

But the best was yet to come. After several delays our final hearing was scheduled with Judge Kressel on August 18th. A few days before the hearing, E.H. Partners had convinced our key creditors that they didn't think Excelsior-Henderson would need the full amount of investment, and they all agreed that just $4 million was needed up front, and the balance of the cash would be infused as needed later after we emerged from bankruptcy. Of course I wasn't consulted on this, but I pushed my way into the discussions anyway. Frankly I was appalled. First, through the reorganization plan the shareholder equity was wiped out 100%, and now secondly, the new ownership group stepped into the shoes of all former shareholders for the reduced amount of $4 million.

I couldn't let this happen, so I suggested that Excelsior-Henderson should then not transfer all of its stock to E.H. Partners, but instead pro-rata the shares as the investments came to fruition. This way—

doing the math—we would transfer 32% ownership, and retain the remaining 68% in a trust to be released upon E.H. Partners executing on their commitments. Hence, E.H. Partners would not gain control of the company until they had met all of their previously agreed obligations, which all creditors had voted on. Needless to say, there were some people displeased with my position, and it did not prevail. I was further out on a limb, and by myself.

During the final hearing on the 18th, one of the customary procedures is for the prevailing CEO, me, to testify in court to the validity of the new plan. I had informed our counsel that I couldn't and wouldn't testify agreeably to that question. When I took the stand that day as the only representative of Excelsior, none of the lawyers present questioned my viewpoint on the new plan.

They didn't need to, as there were ample witnesses willing to testify. Of course Heaton was not in the courtroom, but was waiting nearby. Instead, he had found a new CEO, CFO, and a business partner from Florida to testify on behalf of E.H. Partners and the new plan. It was painful to observe and listen to their testimony.

E.H. Partners had a new management team lined up, John H., Jon C., and Julie R.: a CEO, President, and CFO respectively. Jon was initially slated to be the new CEO, and to his credit, he also refused to testify in court. Therefore, E.H. Partners needed a different CEO, and at the last minute substituted John H., who coincidentally had previously lost his position in a former company when the Platinum Group became involved. An interesting chain of events.

Even though there was a last minute change in the Plan of Reorganization that reduced the cash investment downward to $4 million, without objection by the now silent key creditors, the judge ruled that the Plan would be confirmed without a re-vote to all the creditors—large or small. Upon confirmation, the Plan was declared effective as of September 14th.

As expected, I didn't last 30 days with the new organization. Apparently they didn't need me and asked me to go away, so I did. Besides that, I certainly wasn't in harmony with them, and had continued to observe things that I believed were not in compliance with the court approved Plan. Also, they never asked me any questions about the business—even though none of them had ever worked in the motorcycle industry. So I figured they had everything well in hand and wouldn't miss me.

•••

Since I was no longer involved with the company from this point forward, this is the point at which I will have to depart from being an inside eyewitness to the events of the Excelsior-Henderson company. According to various court records, statements were made that E.H. Partners and Excelsior-Henderson were not following the Plan of Reorganization that was approved by the Bankruptcy Court and the creditors.

Over the next fifteen months, there were allegations of assets being sold, with no repayment to the creditors and no attempt at resuming operations. According to one sworn testimony, apparently the doors to Excelsior-Henderson remained locked 24 hours a day, 7 days a week. After significant legal maneuvering, it appeared the creditors were now prevailing against E.H. Partners, and by approval of court action, had a much-publicized auction scheduled for December 6th, 2001 at the factory—long ago idled—in Belle Plaine, Minnesota.

But there was another interesting twist. On the opposite side of the country, in Bankruptcy Court in Florida, E.H. Partners filed a new Chapter 11 bankruptcy, not only on Excelsior-Henderson, which was a Minnesota company, but also on E.H. Partners itself. Their lawyers persuaded the Florida judge to have jurisdiction over the Minnesota company, and the auction was halted—literally on the hour it was expected to be commenced. There were thousands of people at the much-anticipated auction, which never did happen. I was there too.

By a fortuitous happenstance, I was asked by the Florida court to be a committee member on the unsecured creditors' committee. But there was really little left to do. By now the creditors had figured things out, and the wheels of justice were turning. I have always believed that a robber can rob a bank in a minute, but it may take years to catch and prosecute him—but justice will be served; it just takes time to do things right.

The creditors did prevail in their court actions, and in a private sale during the first quarter of 2002, most remaining hard assets were sold to an Arizona company, for a fraction of their value, and for a fraction of the value we could have gotten two years earlier.

It wasn't too hard to figure out the game plan—except for those who were incredibly naïve, or had a benefit to look the other way.

# APPENDIXES

## *The Story—Folklore & Reality*

In passionate business endeavors, it is not unusual to find stories within the story—the behind-the-scenes-type story—and at Excelsior-Henderson we had a few of those, many of which—to tell the full story—were discussed in the main text of the book. Also with passionate endeavors, correct or incorrect information can be misconstrued, and over a period of time the stories can become part of folklore, whether based in fact or fiction, or some combination thereof. In our case, some stories were created on our own, and some not; either way we received an abundance of media coverage that made for an interesting mix of stories—giving creation to our folklore.

Hanlon Manufacturing was a company that I had founded early in 1993 to develop a new proprietary American motorcycle. After developing the evolving business plan, and the ensuing mission and principles, it became more clear to me that for the motorcycle name itself, I was going to seek to secure a brand-name from the past—rather than create a name or use my own last name. These weren't my initial thoughts, but the more research I conducted, and the more time I had to sleep on the various ideas, I finally settled quite conclusively on resurrecting a former name. The big question—what name?

Again, after thorough research, and thinking it through for several months, on behalf of Hanlon Manufacturing I sought to obtain all the trademark rights, and related marks, of the former Excelsior and Henderson names. Subsequently, nearly all trademark applications were filed during a three-month period commencing in December 1993. This was no small feat, but some luck prevailed. It would take several years to tightly nail down the marks, so Hanlon Manufacturing remained the legal name of the company, until I had it legally changed in the first half of 1996—three years later.

From a marketing perspective, we never really marketed the Hanlon Manufacturing name, but instead utilized a marketing poetic license to market the company as Excelsior-Henderson Motorcycles from early on, even though it wasn't the legal name of the parent corporation until later.

After setting the strategic vision and launching Hanlon Manufacturing, the business focus was primarily the implementation of the vision from that point forward until the end. From the onset, since my family and my wife's family knew we had sold our last business, invariably they were curious about what my next venture was. Most of them knew to some degree what I was up to, and some were naturally skeptical—it was quite a tall task to undertake launching a new OEM motorcycle company. Some, I'm sure, must have thought it was a gearhead's pipe dream—and maybe it was. But as you now know, I play long shots.

During 1994 after exhausting my initial investment, I went to seek the first outside round of financing—and over a period of time—nearly every one of my seven siblings invested cash into the company. And so did my wife's family. They were early adopters and investors into the company, and to the best of my knowledge, I am not aware if they ever sold their stock. I never asked any, and they didn't volunteer the information. I know most had the occasion to sell, and over the course of six years would have made well in excess of ten times their money, but we never talked about those matters. There was a quiet faith, and in a few instances where money was lost, also a quiet lack of faith—normal I would guess.

Over a period of time, there were five additional family—or extended family—members directly employed by the company. During the first half of 1994, my brother Dave was hired to join me at Hanlon Manufacturing. The previous year he had abruptly lost his position as a district sales manager—he had pursued a career in field sales—and was in search of a new job, and I had suggested he could join my company. On several occasions we conversed via the phone—the Internet wasn't mainstream yet—since he was located in Michigan with his family, and I was in Minnesota. Initially Dave was not receptive to my new venture, and told me many times that he didn't think anyone could compete against Harley-Davidson. He was certainly more enamored with them than I was. He also told me he would never work for me—I'm still not sure what that meant. I just took all this with a grain of salt.

But none of this was new to me. I had a lot of naysayers—some right from the start and some developed over a period of time. What was interesting though, as I further explained the business plan and the approach—and as I continued undaunted to make progress—invariably some people became convinced that, yes, by God, it could be done. Difficult maybe. But possible.

During this same timeframe I decided to give some of my founder's stock to three of my four brothers—the fourth brother, Bob, already had his own business doing well, and frankly I just didn't think of giving him any, but I should have. Anyway, I issued some of my founder's stock to my brothers Dave, Tom, and Terry—all at my previous cost, which is basically nearly zero—a benefit to starting companies by yourself.

Tom and Terry were appreciative and thanked me. Dave expected more stock since he was going to work at the company, so I simply decided to give him 20%—thinking I was being reasonably generous and we could move on. Well, that didn't go over very well, and as a team player in the end I gave my older brother 45% of the stock of Hanlon Manufacturing, and I retained 55% (net of what I gave to my brothers Tom and Terry). I wasn't so sure it really mattered, since if the company succeeded, we would all do well, and if it failed, it didn't matter how much each person owned.

Along with the stock, Dave sought a role as President. Since I was the CEO and President of Hanlon Manufacturing, the parent corporation, I established a division and appointed Dave as the divisional President, reporting to the parent corporation.

Shortly thereafter, even though it wasn't correct, Dave wanted to create a story through which he could tell the media he was a founder of the company. He suggested this would create a good media story of two brothers that started a motorcycle company, similar to Harley-Davidson. Though it wasn't correct—which made me uncomfortable—I went along with it for marketing purposes and for the benefit of the relationship.

Within six months after my brother joined the company, he also asked if he could hire his wife to work for the company in administrative positions—and later their son and daughter. What do you really say? I like and respect my family. And I learned something about myself—I can be fairly objective and down-right tough when dealing in business matters, but I am not always in the best business mind when it comes to family.

Hanlon Manufacturing was never intended by me to be a private family-employed company—I knew we had millions of dollars to continue raising over a long period of time, would take on thousands of investors as a public company, and had shareholders to answer to—and I didn't want any potential conflicts of interest, or conflicts for that matter. Over the course of time, there were a few instances in which I had to mitigate some questionable business behavior.

But at the same time, the company was fairly small during the first few years, and I didn't really know if any of this mattered, yet. But, as time progressed and the company matured and evolved into different departments, the family structure became increasingly less effective as sometimes there wasn't a good transition between the skills of a person and the changing needs of an evolving position. When these types of potential misalignments happened in business, I could usually be objective about what to do, but with family involved it can be more difficult—especially if family is in management positions.

During mid-1997 just before the public offering, with the division legally folded into the parent corporation, this created a void in title for Dave, so I appointed him as Co-CEO, without really giving it enough thought. I intended to bring in a President for the parent corporation—or promote someone from within—but I came to find out there wasn't perfect harmony on this issue. Other than myself, Dave was the only family member that was in a management position with the company.

Just after the IPO, and shortly after Dave's appointment to his new position, he asked to meet with me about a new marketing idea he had. He told me his thoughts about how there would be a distinct marketing advantage to having his wife now be marketed also as a company founder—thereby being the only OEM motorcycle company that had a female as a founder. There were several issues I had with this; one, it wasn't true, and now by two accounts; and two, the company was already into its fifth year of business, and there were numerous articles that didn't support this. Who would believe it? I didn't want to cultivate family issues, and even though I was uncomfortable about it, I went along—even though it further perpetuated a myth. It was marketed this way for the next two and a half years, until the company was shut down.

In conclusion of company employed family members, as I previously mentioned, my brother Terry officially joined the company as our factory test rider in 1997. Unofficially, he had been involved in one form or another since very near the beginning in 1993—other than my wife Carol, I think he was the first person I told about launching the venture. You have to know my brother Terry to understand.

Most of my extended family had contributed to the company, in some form or another. From being an investor or service provider, to volunteering at the Sturgis Motorcycle Rally, and to being good moral supporters—not to mention knowing when to sometimes not get involved.

# Doing It Again—The Second Time Around

Q. Would I do it again?
A. *In a New York second.*

Q. Do I really think it can be accomplished?
A. *Yes—but indeed difficult. With great barriers to entry.*

Q. What did I learn most?
A. *Probably about people. Great things can be accomplished. Watch out for some people.*

Q. What would you do differently?
A. *Nothing can be generally done the same way twice.*

Q. What would you do the same?
A. *Always do your homework. Listen to your gut. Work with the A-team. Say thank-you.*

Q. Do I have any regrets?
A. *Yes—but not many—I thought we would make it.*

Q. What about all the people who helped?
A. *They are battle-scarred veterans of the war, just like me. They are my heroes and should be proud. The bikes and company are etched in history, for generations to come.*

Q. Some people are mad.
A. *It's a free country. We all tried our honest best—it was a pretty tough venture.*

Q. Could it be done again?
A. *A lot depends on timing—things need to line up. The industry continues to be robust.*

Q Any final comments?
A. *It was a helluva ride. Always pursue your dreams. I do.*

# Mission & Principles

## MISSION

To Design, Manufacture And Sell Profitably Throughout The World Premium Quality American Made Motorcycles That Are Reminiscent Of The Legendary Unequaled Lifestyle Experiences Of The Earlier Years Of Motorcycling

## PRINCIPLES

1. People Are Our Greatest Asset.

2. We Will Maximize Our Enterprise Value By Working As A Team.

3. Our Products Will Be Proudly Made In The United States Of America.

4. We Will Build The Best Heavyweight Motorcycles In The World.

5. We Exist To Serve Our Dealers & Customers. They Are Part Of Our Team & We Need To Always Understand Their Value.

6. We Will Have Fun... Our Team, Families, Dealers, Customers, & Shareholders.

7. We Will Make Our Products Available Throughout The World.

8. Integrity, Honesty, Persistence, & Knowledge Will Be Expected, Fostered, & Rewarded.

9. We Must Profit In Order To Provide A Livelihood For Our Team, Families, Dealers, Customers, & Shareholders.

# Road Crew Listing

Lynn D Ackerson

Richard J Adams

Richard N Ambrookian

Kirk H Anderson

Randolph G Anderson

Keith M Artmann

Dave L Auringer

Mark A Baadsgaard

Shawn P Bailey

Brad W Banister

John A Bastian

Leigh A Bauman

Steven M Beane

David W Becker

Julie G Becker

Cecil J Becker Jr

Duane A Bendorf

Shannon R Beneke

Alan D Benz

Coy J Berg

Gerry L Berger

Jamie J Berger

Mary J Beussman

Kathleen A Bienapfl

Karla M Biersdorf

Jason D Bladow

Gerald A Blomquist

Anna M Boegeman

Randy S Bolinger

Karen M Boril

Mark A Bouska

Heath T Bowden

David L Bowman

Scott B Brossard

Bonnie M Buesgens

Joan M Bullard

David A Burger

Greg J Busch

Kenneth Capaul

Terry B Carlson

Colette F Cauwels

John J Cermak

Randy G Chambers

Marysia A Chaves

Chad Christensen

David W Christensen

Amy K Clifton

Steve R Corey

Tim J Courant

Jan K Crawford

Richard L Cronk

Paul R Crum

Susan L Dahlke

Glen M Dahn

David J Danielson

David A Danson

Derren J DeGonda

Dana A Derhaag

Nancy J Deziel

Mathew W Dhaene

Victoria S Dolney

Jill M Drees

Diane M Dulany

Susan L Dvorak

Matthew P Egan

Charlette M Enfield

Grant M Erickson

Julie A Erickson

Pamela A Erickson

Julie J Erlandson

Rick W Evenson

Jeffrey S Feldman

Sean M Feltmann

Rae L Fimon

Ronald L Fischer

Joel T Fisher

Edward Fonnier

Karen C Freer

Daniel L Friesner

Ricky A Galewski

Roland J Gerken

Diane L Gerres

Jennifer L Goettl

Keith A Goetz

John C Goodman

Bobby L Gorden

Connie J Gorden

Brenda M Gratz

Rebecca M Grimm

Emily K Gruetzmacher

Jeni L Grunseth

Gary A Grunst

Dawn D Hackett

Steven H Hagen

Sean P Halloran

Steven J Hammes

Martin P Handberg

Kristen E Hank

Daniel L Hanlon

David P Hanlon

Jenny L Hanlon

Terrance K Hanlon

Scott A Hanna

Robert T Harrison

Larry P Hartnett

Paul M Hartwig

Karl R Havran

Krista Heidgerken

Andrea J Heitzman

Paul G Hewitt

Randy J Hilgers

Dorothy D Hinderscheit

David A Hoffman

Scott T Hoffman

Marvin A Holbrook

James A Holroyd

Christine A Horn

David A Hrejsa

Michael T Hubbard

Allan C Hurd

Edward J Jannusch

Brian L Jensen

Gary H Johnson

Randy G Johnson

Bruce D Jones

John P Jones

Lisa A Jones

Loren E Karnes

Gary A Kechely

Jamie J Kechely

Troy J Kelley

Connie L Kelly

Eddie L Kendall

Vance J Kesler

Karl P Keup

Dale E Kinney

Frederick A Klitzke

Wendy S Koepp

William J Kohlhagen

Bonnie K Krant

Stephen C Krengel

Frederick C Krueger

Craig A Krusniak

Michael D Larsen

Lori A Latzke

Jennifer R Lau

John J Lavoie

Timothy J Leary

Patrick P Lebens

Kermit A Lee

Karen J Lenzen

Steven J Leverenz

Randy Levine

Richard L Link

Peter J Loomis

John A Lubbers

Barbara J Lyons

Nancy E Lyons

Scott E Maas

Lynn M Mackenthun

Daniel T Malinowski

Bonita K Malz

Kimberly N Maresch

Thomas M Marron

Richard R Martland

Bradley V Maus

Michael J Maxa

Steven F May

Brian K McDonald

Steven A McLean

David A Mecredy

Troy A Menth

Randall J Miller

Sherry L Miller

Matthew P Minnichsoffer

James R Montgomery

Ivar D Natins

Robert G Neborak

Diane M Nerison

Jay M Nerison

Angela M Nordhausen

Joel S Norenberg

Theresa M Norman

Steven T O'Brien

Nichole M Oelfke

Chet M Olson

Randy B Olson

Robbin H Oxendale

Michael S Paar

Holly R Palma

Robert W Panning

Katherine A Pass

Kenneth G Pautsch

Alan L Pederson

Leroy J Petrick

Tony N Pink

Steven C Pittman

Steven W Potter

Frederick E Powers

Gerald J Prescott

Wendy L Rademacher

Allen K Rech

Anna M Renne

Jerome M Rief

Thomas R Robinson

Thomas M Rootness

Jodell K Rowland

Barbara J Sames

Jeff J Sasse

Cory G Schaak

Janice L Schallow

Paula P Scheffler

Derrick T Schmidt

Jennifer M Schmidt

Kenny L Schmitt

James R Schmutz

Diana M Schoenbauer

Ricky T Sellner

Mike D Shell

Mary K Shotliff

Mark A Sides

ValRee K Simek

Sheri A Simmonds

Gary R Simons

Eric E Sly

Patrick C Sogge

John W Splinter

Garr S Spriggs

Judy A St. John

Jean M Steffl

Robert C Steger

Terry M Stier

Laurel J Strand

Allan T Strehlow

Randy W Strobel

Robert P Strobel

Kristen K Swanson

Steven M Swanson

Stephanie K Testa

Geoffery J Thomas

Kathleen A Thomas

Walt J Timmerman

Orville W Tischer Sr.

Dean Toensing

Dianne Traxler

Chad R Trost

Nickolas L Trumbo

James L Tryon

Paul G Turner

Robert W Utech

Anna M Valeri

Michael A Van Brunt

Paul A Van Brunt

Victor Van-Dyke

Kenneth M Wagner

Johann D Wallace

Suzanne L Walsh

Rick L Waltz

Michael J Walz

Annette L Weber

Jon M Weibel

Bill O Weiss

Allen N Werthauser

Jason E West

Thomas J Wheeler

Linda Whetzel

Steven F Wilhite

Michael A Willger

Randall S Williams

Betty H Wolf

Steven T Wolfbauer

Neil A Wright

Barbara J Young

Thomas A Zolen

# Dealer Listing

| No. | Dealership Name | City | State |
|---|---|---|---|
| 57 | A & B Cycle | Mobile | AL |
| 160 | A Tech Cycle Service | Sioux Falls | SD |
| 93 | Action Motorsports | Idaho Falls | ID |
| n/a | Alaska Cycle Center | Anchorage | AK |
| 91 | American Classic Cycles | Cherry Hill | NJ |
| 34 | American Speed, Inc. | Houston | TX |
| 87 | America's Motorsports | Nashville | TN |
| 88 | America's Motorsports | Madison | TN |
| 55 | Anderson Sales & Service, Inc. | Bloomfield Hill | MI |
| 40 | Atlanta Excelsior-Henderson | Marietta | GA |
| 36 | Barnett Excelsior-Henderson | El Paso | TX |
| 102 | Beaudry Motorsports | Post Falls | ID |
| 95 | Beaverton Excelsior-Henderson | Tigard | OR |
| 52 | Beechmont Motorsports | Cincinnati | OH |
| 141 | Bend Recreation, Inc. | Bend | OR |
| 4 | Bert's Motorcycle Mall | Azusa | CA |
| 101 | Big # One Excelsior-Henderson | Homewood | AL |
| 7 | Bob's Excelsior-Henderson | Fond du Lac | WI |
| 123 | Branchville Motors | Ridgefield | CT |
| 70 | Brenny's Motorcycle Clinic | Bettendorf | IA |
| 24 | Bryan Excelsior-Henderson | Moore | OK |
| 77 | Budke Motors, Inc. | North Platte | NE |
| 47 | Bumpus Excelsior-Henderson of Memphis | Memphis | TN |
| 65 | Capitol Cycle Company, Inc. | Macon | GA |
| 81 | Capodice Power Products | Bloomington | IL |
| 51 | Carolina Excelsior-Henderson | Columbia | SC |
| 138 | Cedar Creek Motorsports | Cedarburg | WI |
| 153 | Celli's Cycle Center | Scottsbluff | NE |
| 105 | Champion Motorcycles | Costa Mesa | CA |
| 64 | Clawson Motorsports | Fresno | CA |
| 39 | Cleveland Motorcycle Company | Mentor | OH |
| 152 | Coleman Powersports-Falls Church | Falls Church | VA |
| 151 | Coleman Powersports-Woodbridge | Woodbridge | VA |
| 150 | Con's Sport Center | Palm Bay | FL |

| No. | Dealership Name | City | State |
| --- | --- | --- | --- |
| 85 | Cycle Rider's, Inc. | Orlando | FL |
| 86 | Cycle Rider's, Inc. | Longwood | FL |
| 18 | Cycle Stop | Rochester | NY |
| 1 | Delano Sport Center | Delano | MN |
| 27 | Desert Motorsports | Scottsdale | AZ |
| 103 | Destination Excelsior-Henderson | Tacoma | WA |
| 96 | Dick Lane Powersports | Broken Arrow | OK |
| 84 | Donahue Excelsior-Henderson | Sauk Rapids | MN |
| 30 | Downtown Excelsior-Henderson | Seattle | WA |
| 66 | Durham Excelsior-Henderson | Durham | NC |
| 90 | Engelhart Center | Madison | WI |
| 130 | Excelsior-Henderson Country | Beaumont | TX |
| 58 | Excelsior-Henderson Cycle Center, Inc. | Waterloo | IA |
| 20 | Excelsior-Henderson of Dallas | Garland | TX |
| 125 | Excelsior-Henderson of Edmonds | Edmonds | WA |
| 21 | Excelsior-Henderson of Essex | Bloomfield | NJ |
| 72 | Excelsior-Henderson of Green River | Green River | WY |
| 82 | Excelsior-Henderson of Jackson | Jackson | MS |
| 120 | Excelsior-Henderson of Redlands | Redlands | CA |
| 37 | Excelsior-Henderson of St. Petersburg | St. Petersburg | FL |
| 60 | Excelsior-Henderson Sales | Columbus | NE |
| 62 | Fairfield Cycle Center, Inc. | Fairfield | CA |
| 106 | Fort Collins Motorsports | Fort Collins | CO |
| 135 | Gatto Cycle Shop | Tarentum | PA |
| 115 | Gold Coast Motorsports | New Hyde Park | NY |
| 63 | Golden Gate Cycles | San Francisco | CA |
| 11 | Great Lakes Motorsports | Burton | MI |
| 111 | Great Lakes Motorsports | Burton | MI |
| 133 | Hahm Motorsports-Anaheim | Anaheim | CA |
| 132 | Hahm Motorsports-Marina | Marina del Rey | CA |
| 100 | Hansen Motorcycles | Manitowoc | WI |
| 140 | Hinshaws Motorcycle Store | Auburn | WA |
| 44 | Howell's Fine Motorcycles | New Kingstone | PA |
| 155 | Ithaca Recreation Sports | Newfield | NY |
| 73 | Jim & Jim's of Ukiah | Ukiah | CA |
| 41 | Joe Harrison Motorsports | San Antonio | TX |

| No. | Dealership Name | City | State |
|-----|-----------------|------|-------|
| 3 | Kersting's Cycle Center | Winamac | IN |
| 69 | Killeen Powersports | Killeen | TX |
| 107 | Koogler Sales and Service | Fishersville | VA |
| 156 | Lake Country Motorsports | Waukesha | WI |
| 121 | Leo's South | Lakeville | MN |
| 124 | Libby's Sales & Service | New Haven | CT |
| 149 | Link Cycle | Cooperstown | PA |
| 13 | Louisville Excelsior-Henderson | Louisville | KY |
| 142 | Lubbock Sports Center | Lubbock | TX |
| 12 | Maverick Cycles | Cheyenne | WY |
| 26 | Metro Motorcycles, Inc. | Glendale | AZ |
| 46 | Michael's Reno Excelsior-Henderson | Reno | NV |
| 14 | Mid-Continent Excelsior-Henderson | Wichita | KS |
| 139 | Moto Marine | McAllen | TX |
| 116 | Nault's Excelsior-Henderson | Manchester | NH |
| 117 | Nault's Windham Excelsior-Henderson | Windham | NH |
| 2 | Nielsen Enterprises | Lake Villa | IL |
| 38 | North End Cycle | Elkhart | IN |
| 136 | North End Repair | Plattsburgh | NY |
| 98 | North Star Excelsior-Henderson | Albert Lea | MN |
| 154 | Northstar Sports | Isanti | MN |
| 109 | Owen Excelsior-Henderson | Charleston | IL |
| 92 | Paducah Excelsior-Henderson | Paducah | KY |
| 108 | Palm Beach Excelsior-Henderson | Boynton Beach | FL |
| 129 | Penton Excelsior-Henderson | Amherst | OH |
| 75 | Performance Excelsior-Henderson of Charlotte | Pineville | NC |
| 6 | Pikes Peak Excelsior-Henderson | Colorado Springs | CO |
| 54 | Plaza Cycle | Salt Lake City | UT |
| 42 | Powersports of Cutler Ridge | Miami | FL |
| 43 | Powersports of Ft. Lauderdale | Ft. Lauderdale | FL |
| 119 | Powersports of Ft. Myers | Ft. Myers | FL |
| 114 | Powersports of Naples | Naples | FL |
| 89 | R & S Cycle | Albuquerque | NM |
| 45 | R Excelsior-Henderson | Rice Lake | WI |
| 118 | Ragsdale Superstore | Shrewsbury | MA |
| 157 | Ramer Motors | Omaha | NE |

| No. | Dealership Name | City | State |
|-----|-----------------|------|-------|
| 74 | Redding Excelsior-Henderson | Redding | CA |
| 71 | Regency Excelsior-Henderson | Jacksonville | FL |
| 146 | Rice Excelsior-Henderson | Rapid City | SD |
| 50 | Riders Excelsior-Henderson | Birmingham | AL |
| 122 | Rider's World | Shavertown | PA |
| 79 | RJ Sport & Cycle | Duluth | MN |
| 144 | Roadside Marine | Williston | VT |
| 147 | Rosenau Powersports | Dearborn Heights | MI |
| 148 | Saginaw Powersports Center | Saginaw | MI |
| 97 | San Diego's House of Motorcycles | San Diego | CA |
| 110 | San Luis Motorsports | San Luis Obispo | CA |
| 8 | Santa Cruz Excelsior-Henderson | Santa Cruz | CA |
| 99 | Shawnee Cycle Plaza | Shawnee | KS |
| 67 | Shelton's Exelsior-Henderson | Goldsboro | NC |
| 68 | Shreffler's Land of Lincoln | Manteno | IL |
| 158 | Sky Powersports | Lake Wales | FL |
| 137 | South Coast Excelsior-Henderson | Chula Vista | CA |
| 19 | Spitzies' Motorcycle Center | Albany | NY |
| 80 | St. Louis Powersports | Valley Park | MO |
| 59 | Star City Motorsports, Inc. | Lincoln | NE |
| 131 | Staz's Excelsior-Henderson | Henderson | NV |
| 22 | Steel Excelsior-Henderson | Chattanooga | TN |
| 112 | Stephen Wade Powersports | St. George | UT |
| 113 | Street, Track 'n' Trail | Conneaut Lake | PA |
| 15 | Suburban Excelsior-Henderson | Thiensville | WI |
| 10 | Sun Enterprises, Inc. | Denver | CO |
| 5 | Team Butch | Grand Rapids | MI |
| 53 | Toledo Excelsior-Henderson | Sylvania | OH |
| 25 | Town & Country Motorsports | Chandler | AZ |
| 17 | Town & Country Sports Center | Cement City | MI |
| 28 | Tucson Motorsports | Tucson | AZ |
| 61 | Valley Forge Excelsior-Henderson | Norristown | PA |
| n/a | Washington Motorsports | Washington | NC |
| 35 | Woods Fun Center | Austin | TX |
| 16 | Yellowstone Sports Center | Belgrade | MT |

# *Investment Summary*

| Use of Funds | In Millions |
|---|---|
| Product Research & Development | $24.0 |
| Marketing, Sales, & Branding | 10.5 |
| Motorcycle Tooling Costs | 8.0 |
| Building Costs | 11.0 |
| Factory Equipment | 12.0 |
| Parts Inventory | 5.0 |
| Excessive Components Costs | 7.5 |
| General Operations, Including G & A | 6.5 |
| Computer Equipment, Systems, etc. | 3.5 |
| Investment Banking & Transaction Fees | 7.5 |
| Total Investment | $95.5 |

# Customer Letters

Asample of the many thousands of letters we received—overwhelmingly positive, and very few were not.

---

To the folks at Excelsior-Henderson:

I recently read of your financial struggles. I wanted to send you a note of encouragement.

There are a lot of people who want to see your company be successful. Please keep trying.

I really hope things work out for you.

Wishing you success,
A non-employee, non-stockholder friend

---

Mr Dan,

a quick note to remind you of how many people are out here wishing and praying for your success. We are so proud to say Excelsior Henderson Motorcycles are made in Minnesota ∞

Recall "things are always worst before the storm : dont give up 5 minutes before the miracle" ∞

Happy Thanksgiving

D K. Schmidt

Hello,

I just purchased a 1999 Excelsior-Henderson, "I could have bought a Harley-Davidson" but the Excelsior offered a lot more.

I would like to know if the founder of the "New" Excelsior-Henderson Company would ~~will~~ personally sign a large poster of the bike for me. I hope I'm not asking for too much. Thanks a lot. [Jeff

Dear Dan;

My name is Artie Cioe, Jr. I am the very proud owner of 1999 Super X # 766, and I want you to know it's THE best bike I've ever owned.

Keep up the good work, hang in there, and if there's something I can do to help, just give a call. 312-▮▮▮-▮▮▮▮ ANYTIME.

Sincerely

Artie Cioe J.

P.S. Thanks again for an exceptional motorcycle.

---

EXCELSIOR-HENDERSON,
  I PURCHASED SUPER X #831 AND I AM VERY HAPPY WITH MY BIKE. I SOLD MY HARLEY-DAVIDSON AND I DON'T REGRET IT. I'M REQUESTING A BROCHURE FOR MY COLLECTION. I WOULD ALSO LIKE A CATALOG OF ACCESSORIES AND MERCHANDISE. IS THERE A CURRENT NEWSLETTER OR MAGAZINE THAT FEATURES MONTHLY ARTICLES OF THE SUPER X? IF THERE IS CAN YOU PLEASE SEND ME ALL THE INFORMATION YOU HAVE.
                          THANK YOU
                          DAVE LOPEZ

Dave Lopez
▮▮▮▮▮, CA 93▮▮

# Winston Churchill—Writing a Book

Writing a book is an adventure. To begin with, it is a toy and an amusement. Then it becomes a mistress, then it becomes a master, then it becomes a tyrant. The last phase is that just as you are about to be reconciled to your servitude, you kill the monster and fling him to the public.

*—Winston Churchill*